MP GRAPHIC NOVEL

Yu-Gi-Oh!
•DUELIST•

Vol. 5

BLUE-EYES
ULTIMATE DRAGON

STORY AND ART BY

KAZUKI TAKAHASHI

《MAIN CAST》

YUGI MUTOU/YU-GI-OH
武藤遊戯

Using the power of his Millennium Eye, Pegasus stole the soul of Yugi's grandpa, and forced Yugi to enter a "Duel Monsters" tournament on his private island, Duelist Kingdom. Little did Yugi realize that the tournament was all part of a plot by Pegasus to beat Yugi and gain control of Kaiba Corporation! Kaiba rushed to the island to defend his fortune and rescue his little brother Mokuba from Pegasus. But despite their common enemy, Kaiba is still no friend of Yugi's. While Kaiba went to Pegasus's castle to confront the mastermind, Yugi and his friends found themselves trapped in an underground maze…facing the deadly Meikyû Brothers in a special "Duel Monsters" two-on-two match!

高橋 和希

SO, MY READERS, DID YOU GET THE *YU-GI-OH!* CARDASS
TRADING CARDS SET? (ONLY AVAILABLE IN JAPAN...SORRY!)
OF COURSE I HAVE THEM MYSELF! WHEN I WENT BACK HOME
FOR THE NEW YEAR, I THOUGHT I'D SHOW THEM TO EVERY-
BODY IN MY FAMILY, BUT TO MY SHOCK, MY FATHER HAD THE
CARDS ALREADY! "I GOT 'EM OUT OF THIS DISPENSER
MACHINE...THE TRICK IS TO SPIN THE KNOB TO THE RIGHT..."
OF COURSE, EVERYONE DOES THAT! TURNS OUT HE TOOK THE
BUS TO THE NEXT TOWN JUST TO BUY THEM! UM...DAD...
PLEASE DON'T BUY CARDASS CARDS AT YOUR AGE...!

A ... to
th ... n
u ...
Shonen Jump magazine in 1996. **Yu-Gi-Oh!**'s themes
of friendship and fighting, together with Takahashi's
weird and wonderful art, soon became enormously
successful, spawning a real-world card game, video
games, and two anime series. A lifelong gamer,
Takahashi enjoys Shogi (Japanese chess), Mahjong,
card games, and tabletop RPGs, among other games.

Yu-Gi-Oh! DUELIST

Vol. 5

CONTENTS

Duel 38: The Final Card

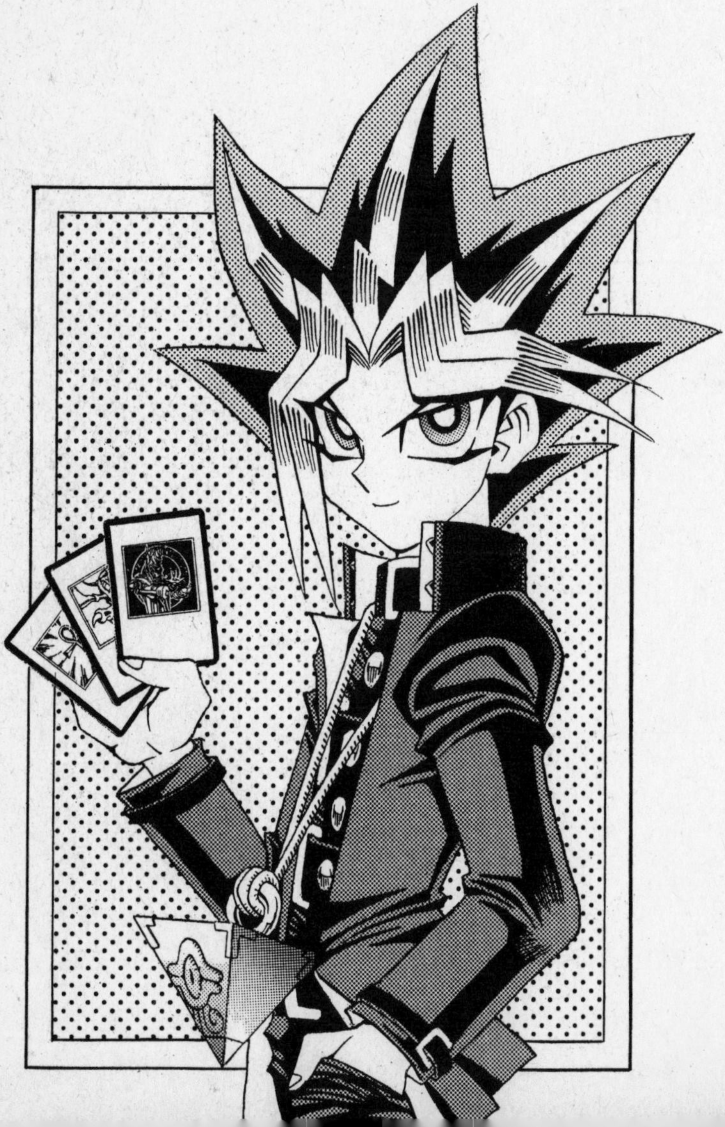

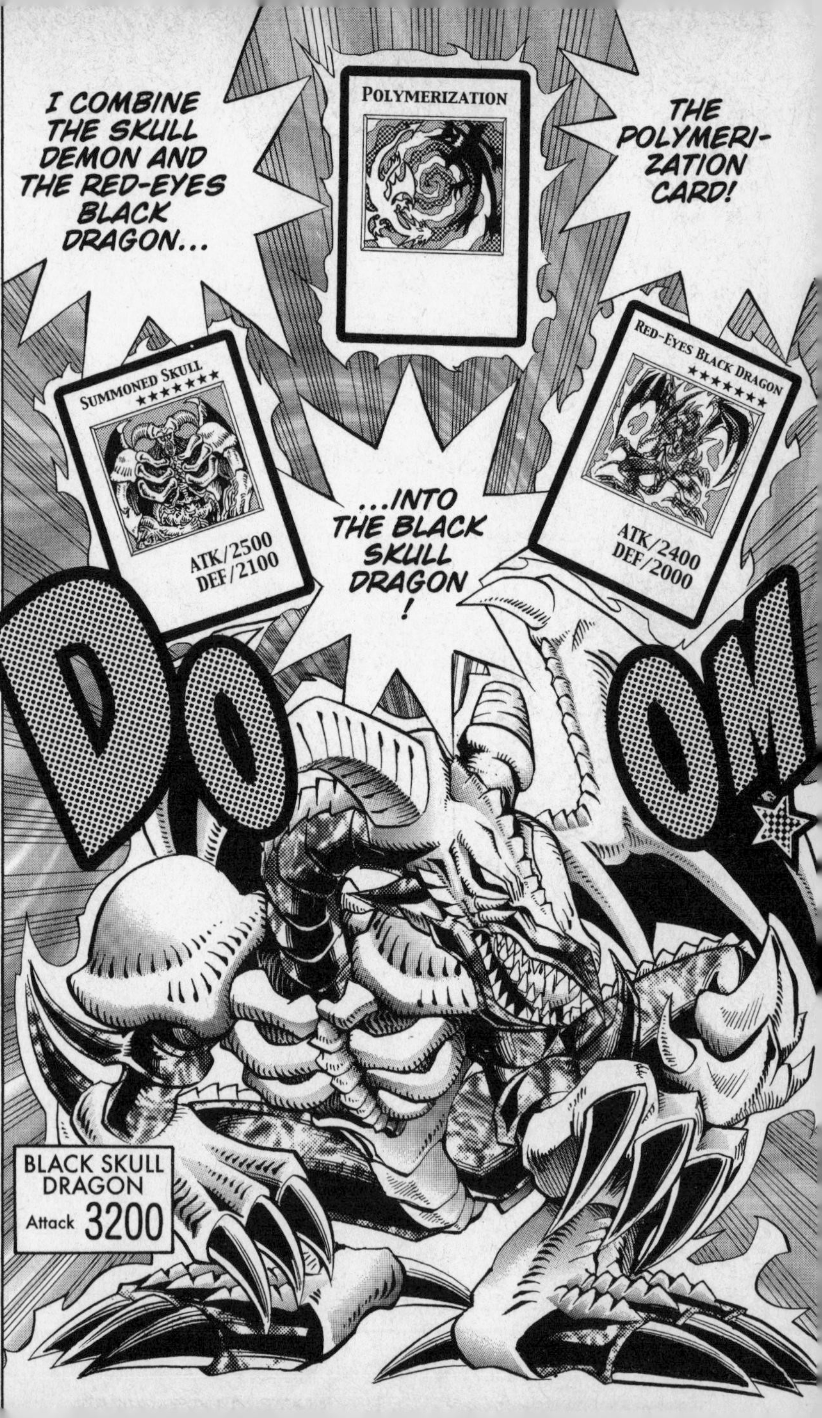
THE POLYMERI-ZATION CARD!
POLYMERIZATION
I COMBINE THE SKULL DEMON AND THE RED-EYES BLACK DRAGON...
RED-EYES BLACK DRAGON
ATK/2400
DEF/2000
SUMMONED SKULL
ATK/2500
DEF/2100
...INTO THE BLACK SKULL DRAGON!
DOOM
BLACK SKULL DRAGON
Attack 3200

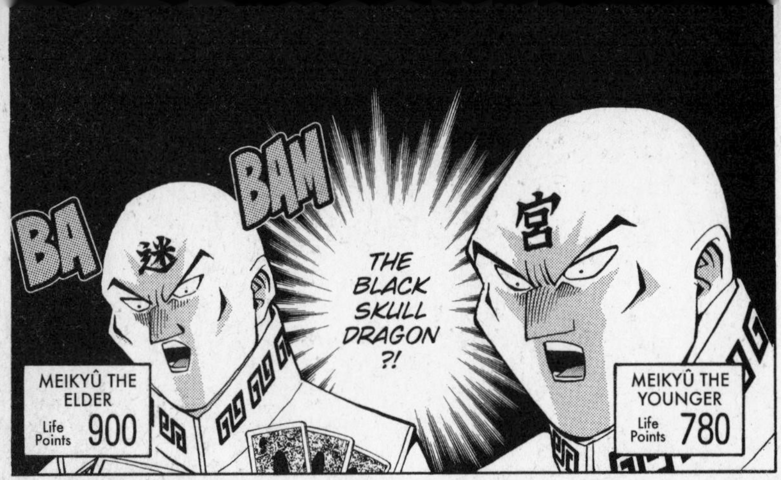
BA BAM
THE BLACK SKULL DRAGON?!
MEIKYÛ THE YOUNGER Life Points 780
MEIKYÛ THE ELDER Life Points 900

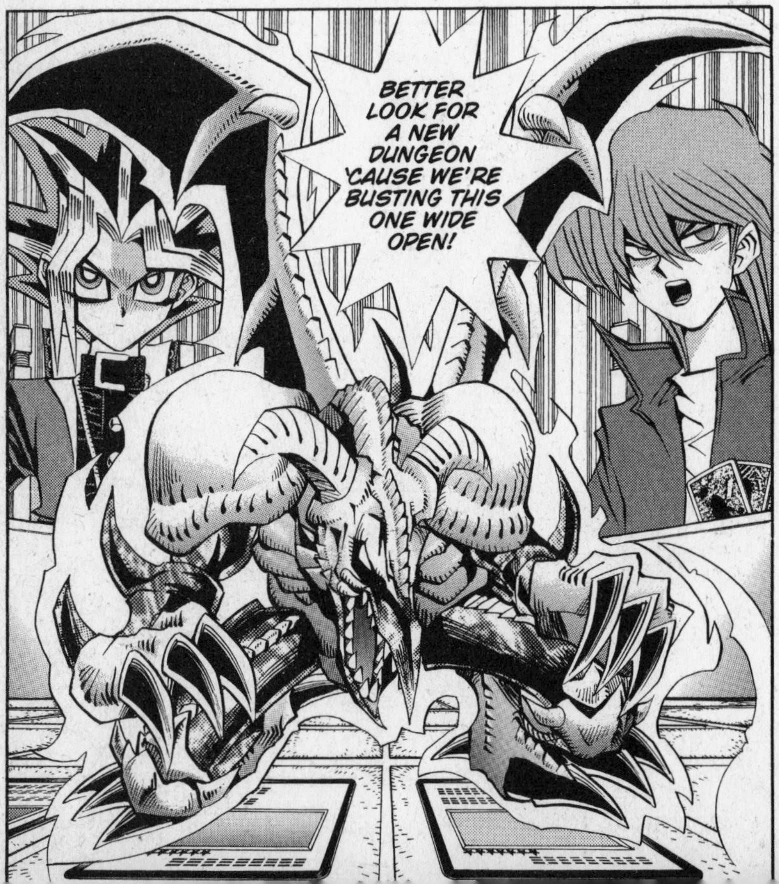
BETTER LOOK FOR A NEW DUNGEON 'CAUSE WE'RE BUSTING THIS ONE WIDE OPEN!

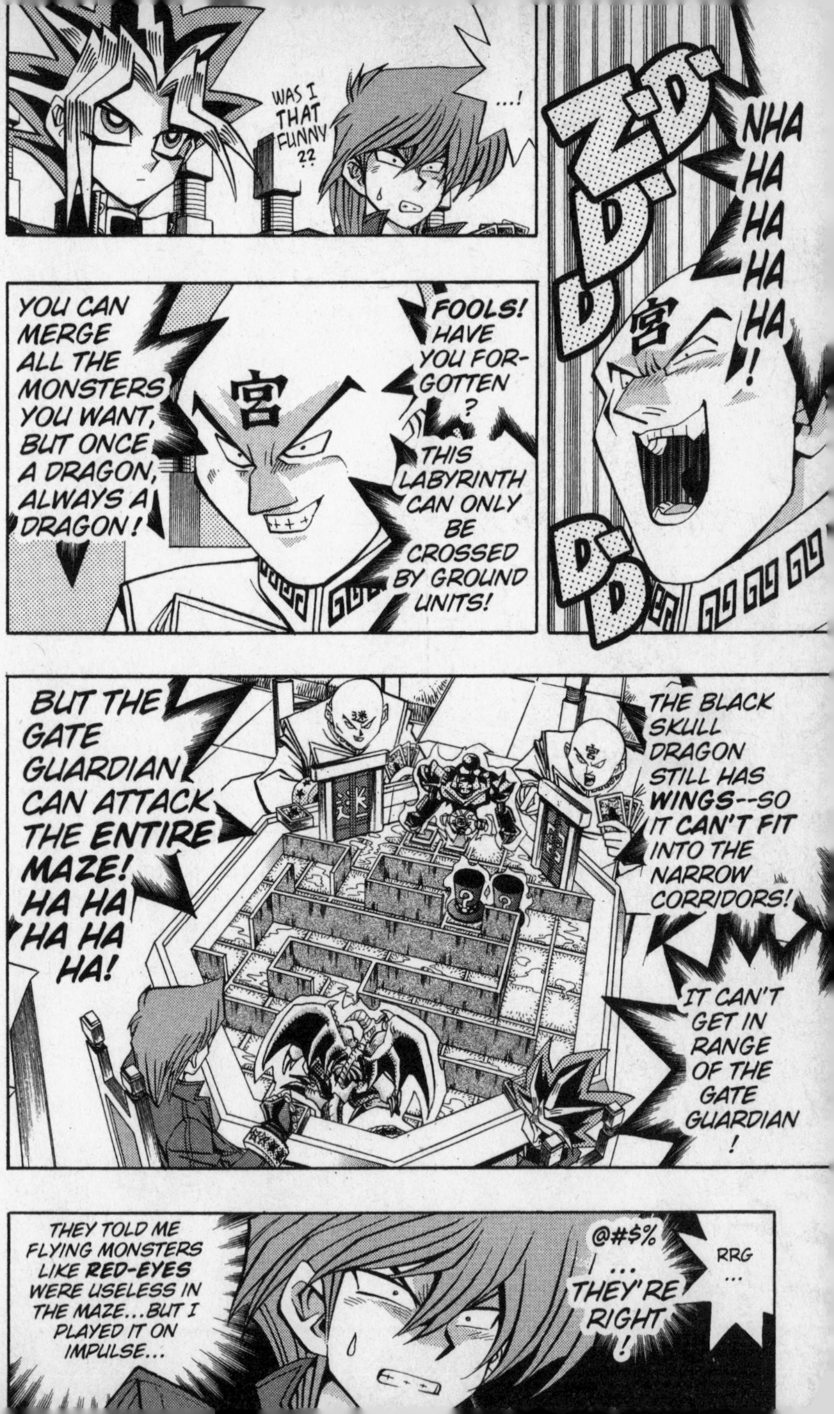
ZDDD
NHA HA HA HA HA HA!
DDD
...!
WAS I THAT FUNNY ??
FOOLS! HAVE YOU FORGOTTEN ?
THIS LABYRINTH CAN ONLY BE CROSSED BY GROUND UNITS!
YOU CAN MERGE ALL THE MONSTERS YOU WANT, BUT ONCE A DRAGON, ALWAYS A DRAGON!
THE BLACK SKULL DRAGON STILL HAS WINGS--SO IT CAN'T FIT INTO THE NARROW CORRIDORS!
IT CAN'T GET IN RANGE OF THE GATE GUARDIAN !
BUT THE GATE GUARDIAN CAN ATTACK THE ENTIRE MAZE! HA HA HA HA HA!
RRG ...
@#$% ... THEY'RE RIGHT !
THEY TOLD ME FLYING MONSTERS LIKE RED-EYES WERE USELESS IN THE MAZE...BUT I PLAYED IT ON IMPULSE...

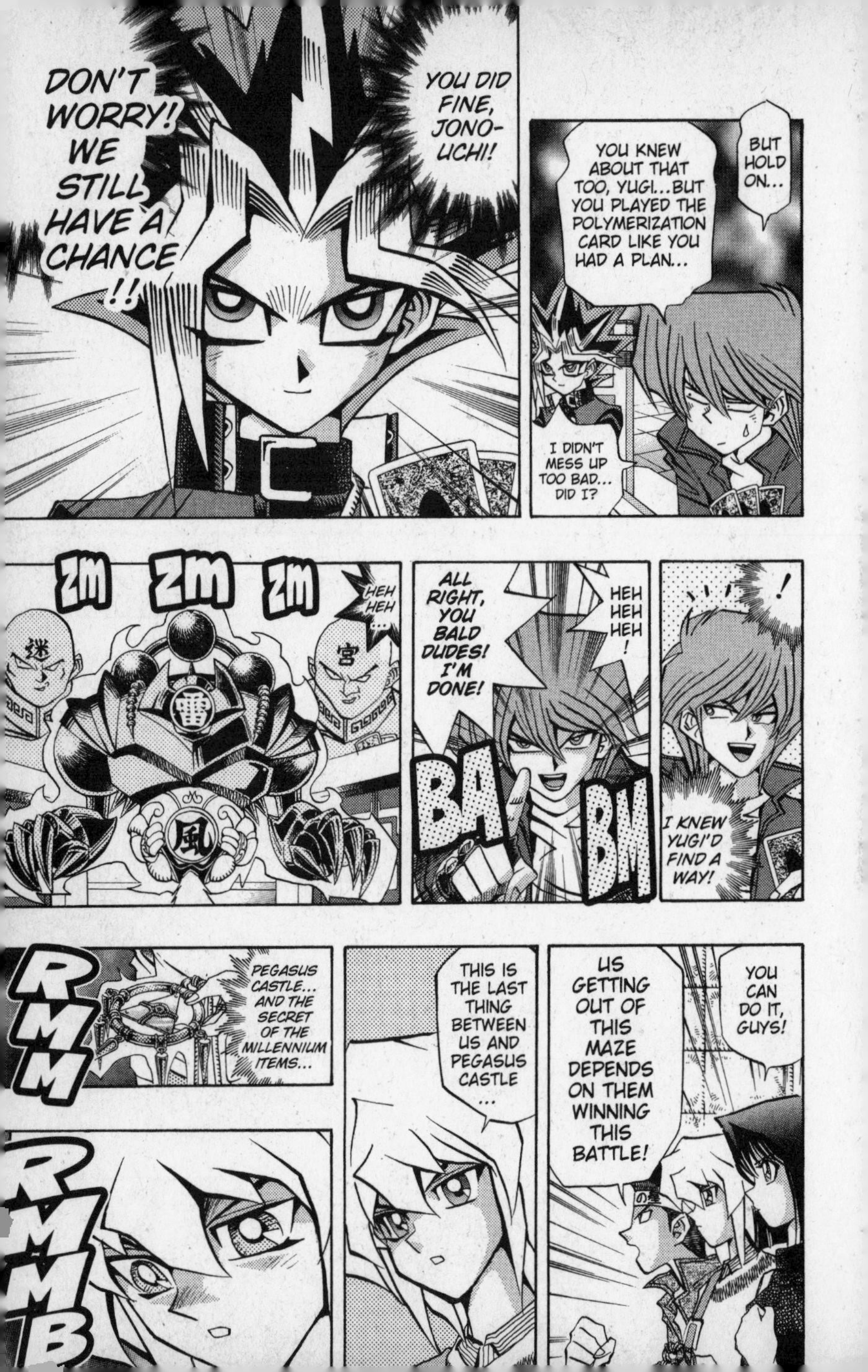
BUT HOLD ON...
YOU KNEW ABOUT THAT TOO, YUGI...BUT YOU PLAYED THE POLYMERIZATION CARD LIKE YOU HAD A PLAN...
I DIDN'T MESS UP TOO BAD... DID I?
YOU DID FINE, JONOUCHI!
DON'T WORRY! WE STILL HAVE A CHANCE!!
!
I KNEW YUGI'D FIND A WAY!
HEH HEH HEH!
ALL RIGHT, YOU BALD DUDES! I'M DONE!
BA BM
HEH HEH...
ZM ZM ZM
YOU CAN DO IT, GUYS!
US GETTING OUT OF THIS MAZE DEPENDS ON THEM WINNING THIS BATTLE!
THIS IS THE LAST THING BETWEEN US AND PEGASUS CASTLE...
RMM
PEGASUS CASTLE... AND THE SECRET OF THE MILLENNIUM ITEMS...
RMMB

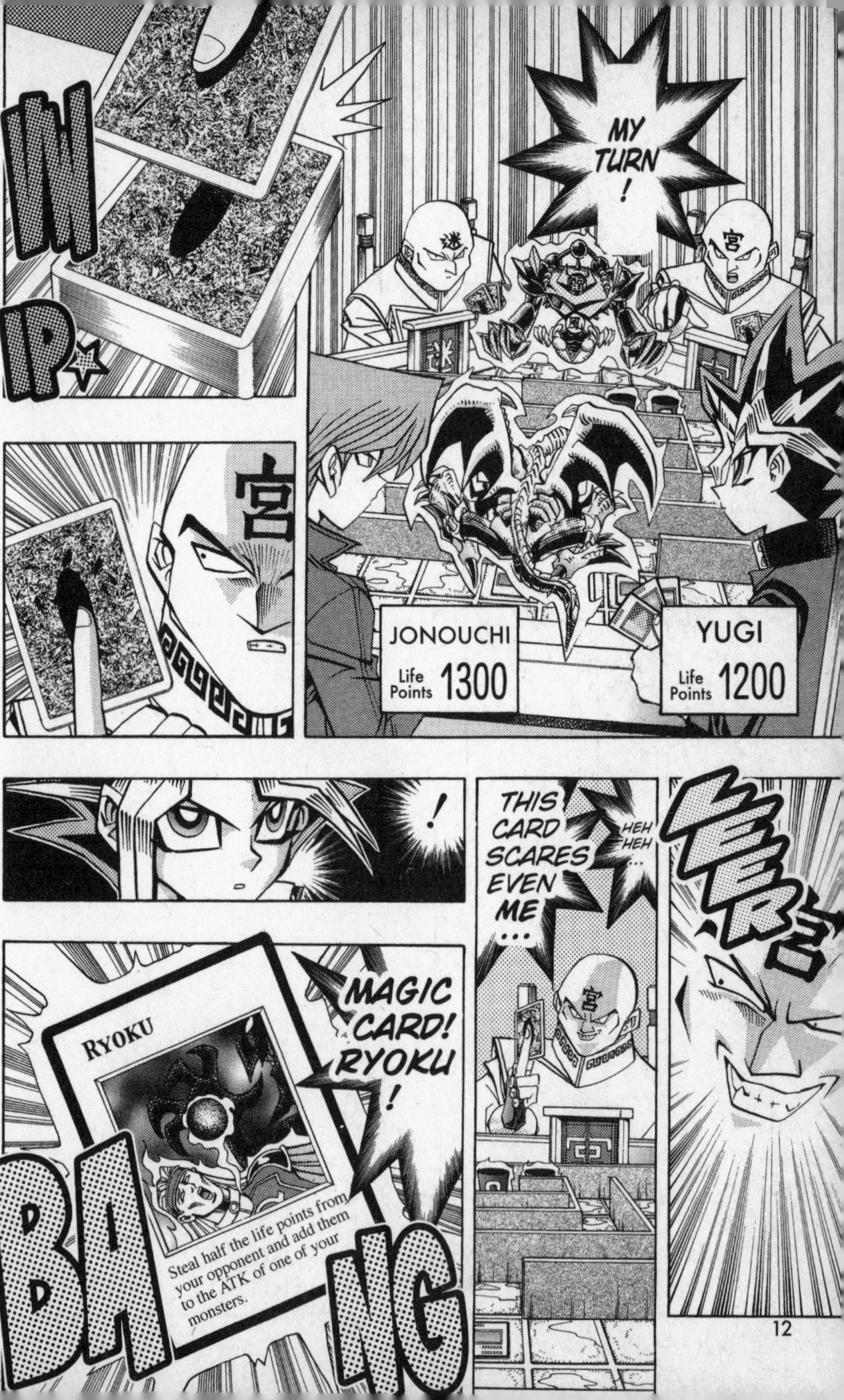
MY TURN !
JONOUCHI
Life Points 1300
YUGI
Life Points 1200
THIS CARD SCARES EVEN ME ...
HEH HEH ...
!
MAGIC CARD! RYOKU !
RYOKU
Steal half the life points from your opponent and add them to the ATK of one of your monsters.
BANG

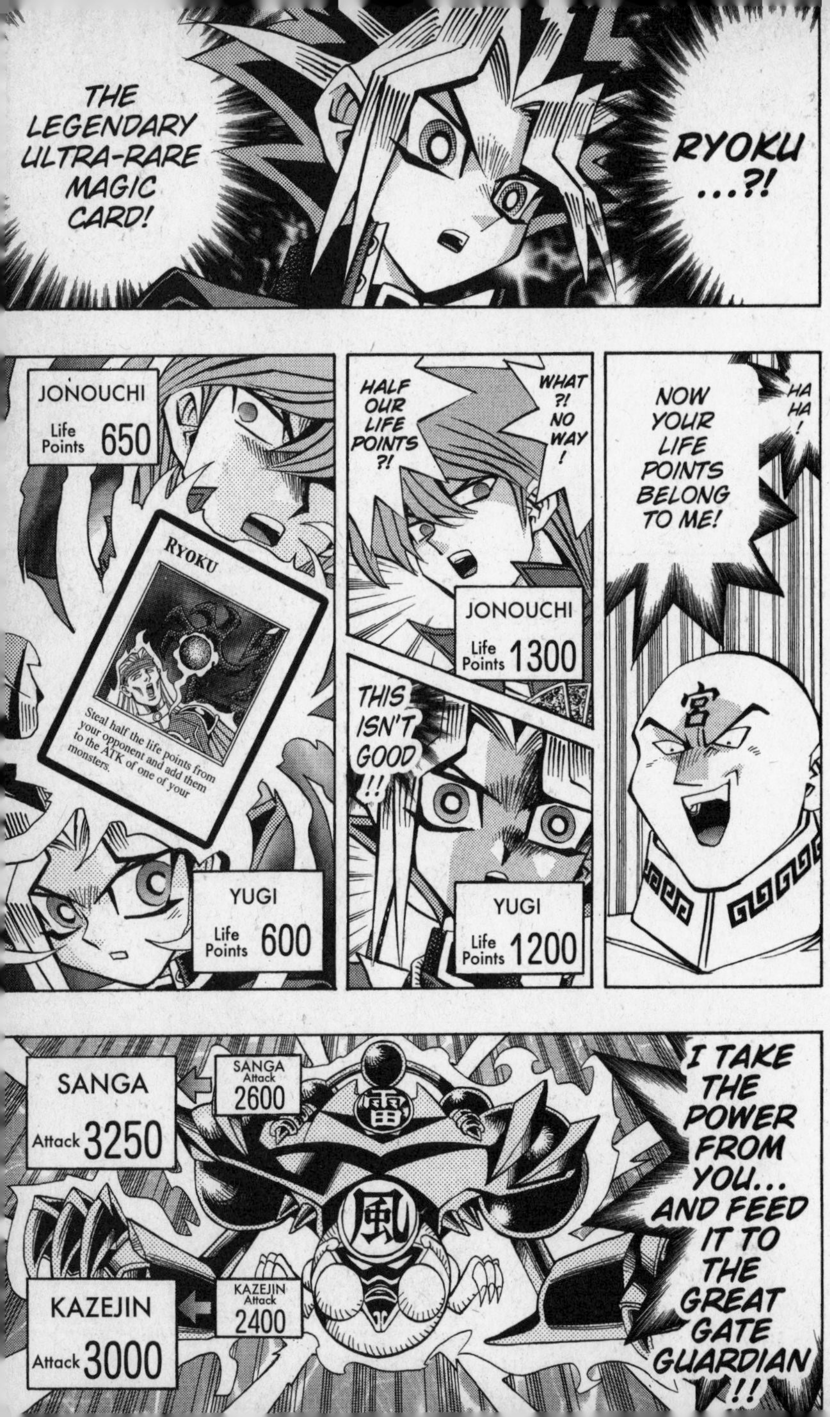
RYOKU ...?!
THE LEGENDARY ULTRA-RARE MAGIC CARD!
HA HA!
NOW YOUR LIFE POINTS BELONG TO ME!
WHAT?! NO WAY!
HALF OUR LIFE POINTS?!
JONOUCHI Life Points 1300
THIS ISN'T GOOD!!
YUGI Life Points 1200
JONOUCHI Life Points 650
RYOKU
Steal half the life points from your opponent and add them to the ATK of one of your monsters.
YUGI Life Points 600
I TAKE THE POWER FROM YOU... AND FEED IT TO THE GREAT GATE GUARDIAN!!
SANGA Attack 2600
SANGA Attack 3250
KAZEJIN Attack 2400
KAZEJIN Attack 3000

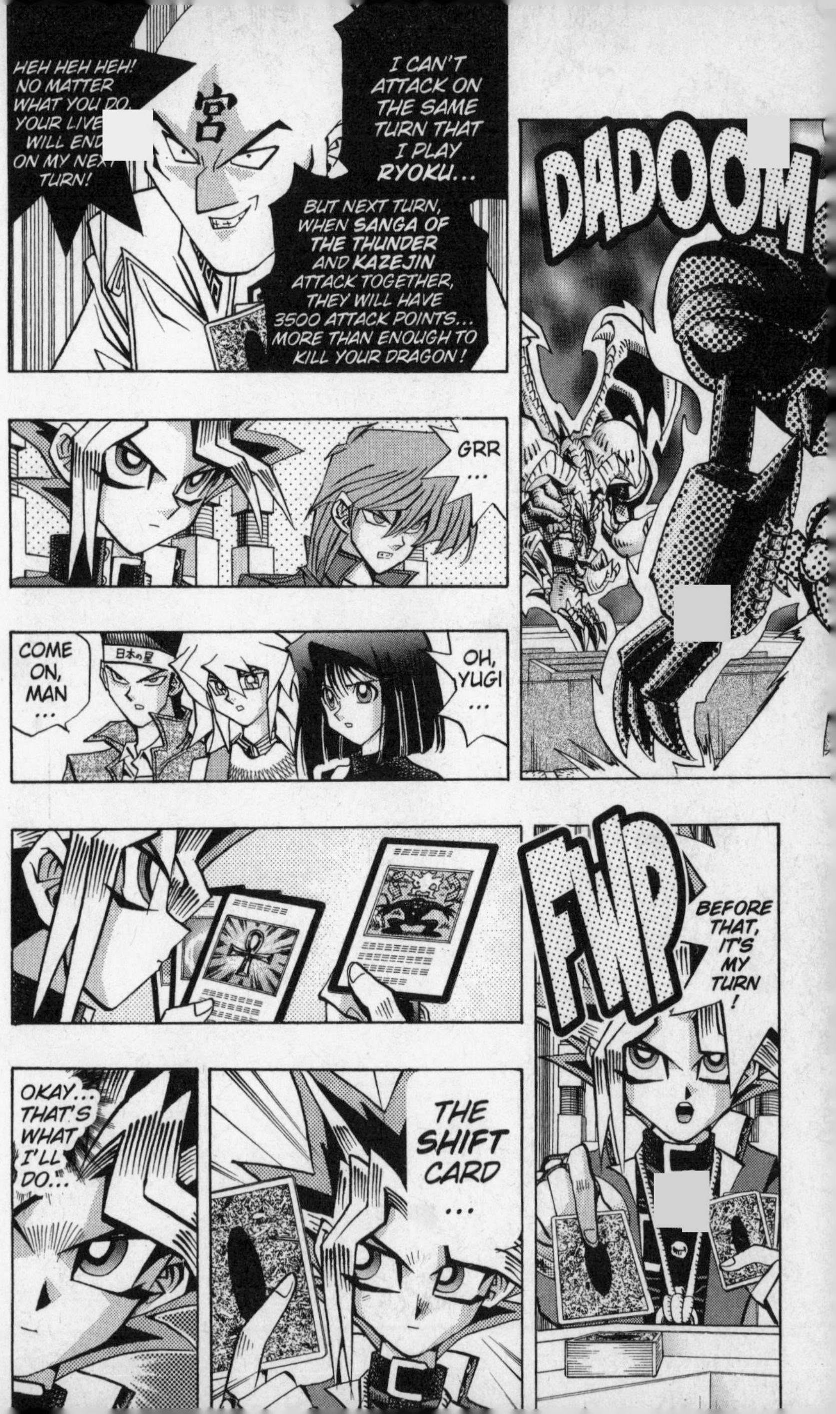
DADOOM
I CAN'T ATTACK ON THE SAME TURN THAT I PLAY RYOKU...
BUT NEXT TURN, WHEN SANGA OF THE THUNDER AND KAZEJIN ATTACK TOGETHER, THEY WILL HAVE 3500 ATTACK POINTS... MORE THAN ENOUGH TO KILL YOUR DRAGON!
HEH HEH HEH! NO MATTER WHAT YOU DO YOUR LIVE WILL END ON MY NEXT TURN!
宮
GRR ...
OH, YUGI ...
日本の星
COME ON, MAN ...
FWP
BEFORE THAT, IT'S MY TURN!
THE SHIFT CARD ...
OKAY... THAT'S WHAT I'LL DO...

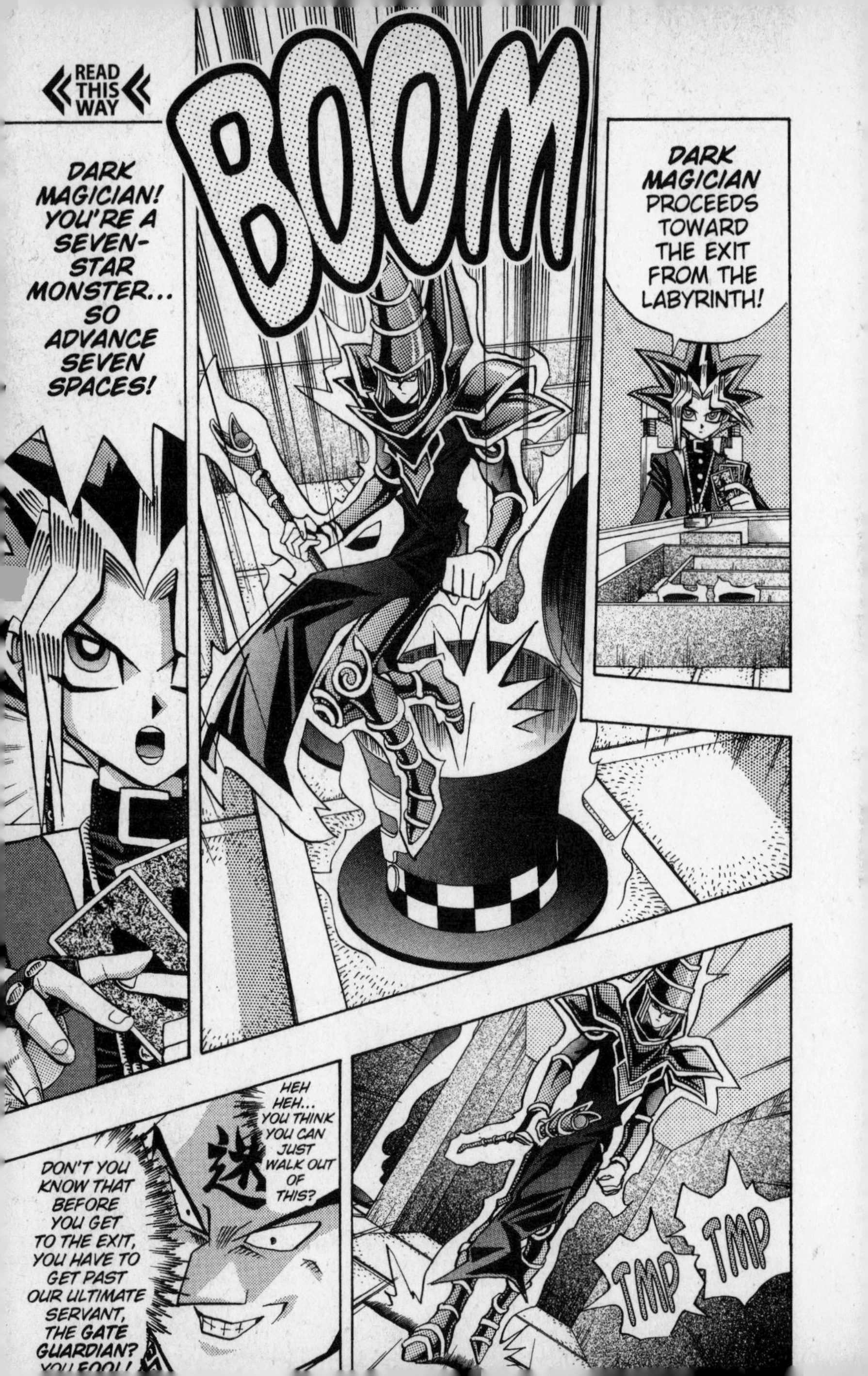
READ THIS WAY
DARK MAGICIAN PROCEEDS TOWARD THE EXIT FROM THE LABYRINTH!
BOOM
DARK MAGICIAN! YOU'RE A SEVEN-STAR MONSTER... SO ADVANCE SEVEN SPACES!
TMP TMP
HEH HEH... YOU THINK YOU CAN JUST WALK OUT OF THIS?
迷
DON'T YOU KNOW THAT BEFORE YOU GET TO THE EXIT, YOU HAVE TO GET PAST OUR ULTIMATE SERVANT, THE GATE GUARDIAN? YOU FOOL!

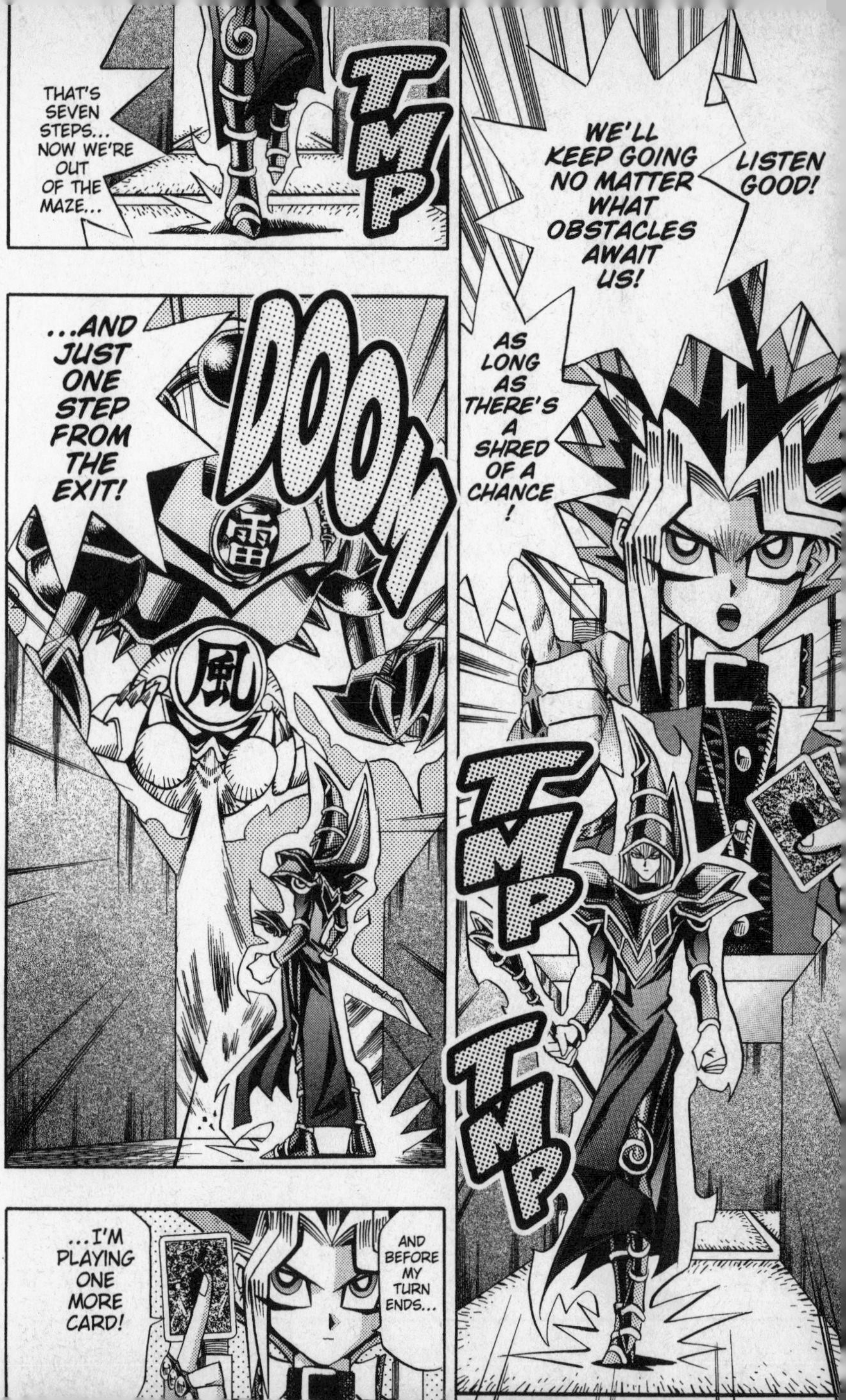
LISTEN GOOD!
WE'LL KEEP GOING NO MATTER WHAT OBSTACLES AWAIT US!
AS LONG AS THERE'S A SHRED OF A CHANCE!
TMP
TMP
TMP
THAT'S SEVEN STEPS... NOW WE'RE OUT OF THE MAZE...
DOOM
...AND JUST ONE STEP FROM THE EXIT!
AND BEFORE MY TURN ENDS...
...I'M PLAYING ONE MORE CARD!

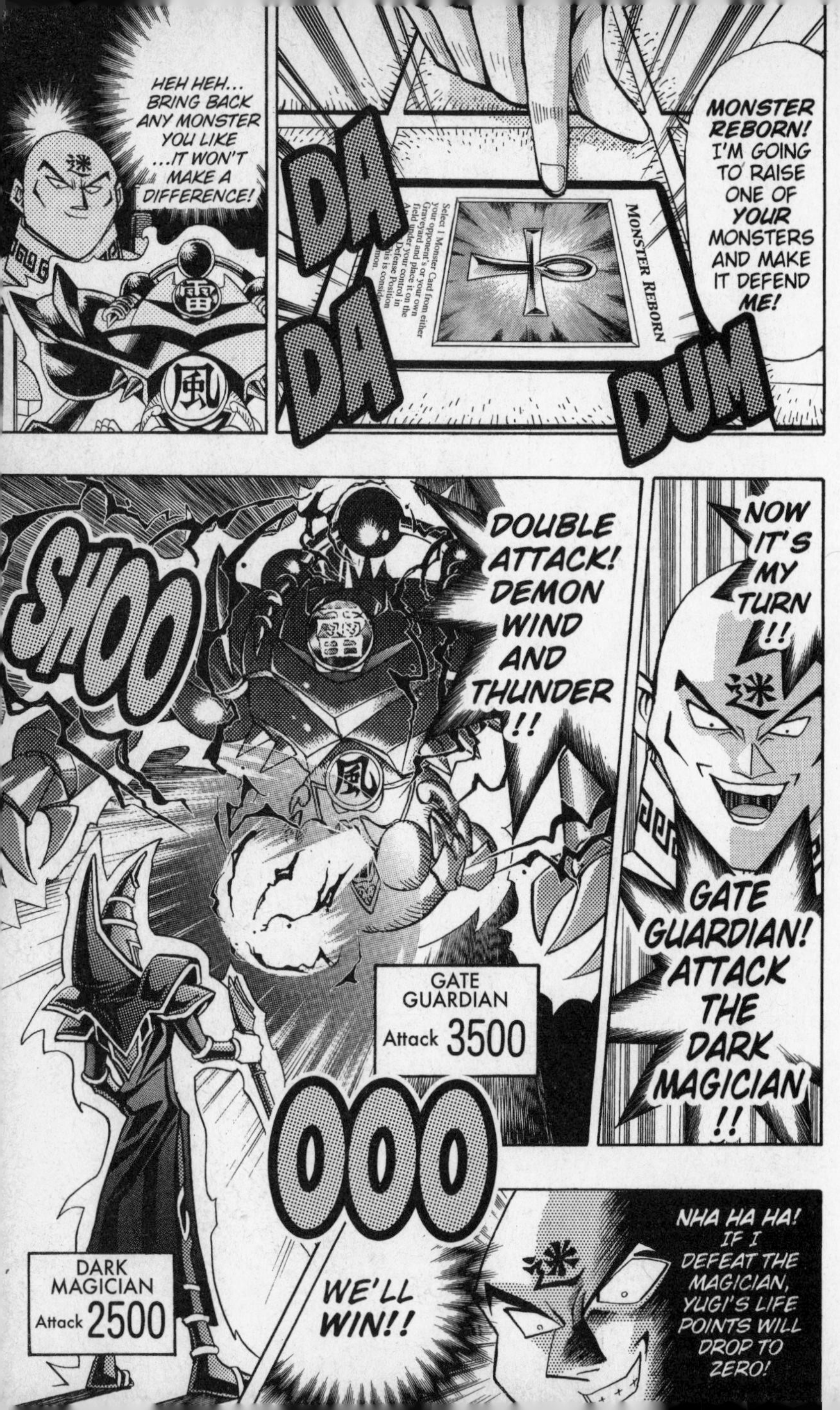
MONSTER REBORN! I'M GOING TO RAISE ONE OF YOUR MONSTERS AND MAKE IT DEFEND ME!
MONSTER REBORN
DA DA DUM
HEH HEH... BRING BACK ANY MONSTER YOU LIKE ...IT WON'T MAKE A DIFFERENCE!
NOW IT'S MY TURN!!
GATE GUARDIAN! ATTACK THE DARK MAGICIAN!!
DOUBLE ATTACK! DEMON WIND AND THUNDER!!
SHOO
GATE GUARDIAN Attack 3500
OOO
DARK MAGICIAN Attack 2500
NHA HA HA! IF I DEFEAT THE MAGICIAN, YUGI'S LIFE POINTS WILL DROP TO ZERO!
WE'LL WIN!!

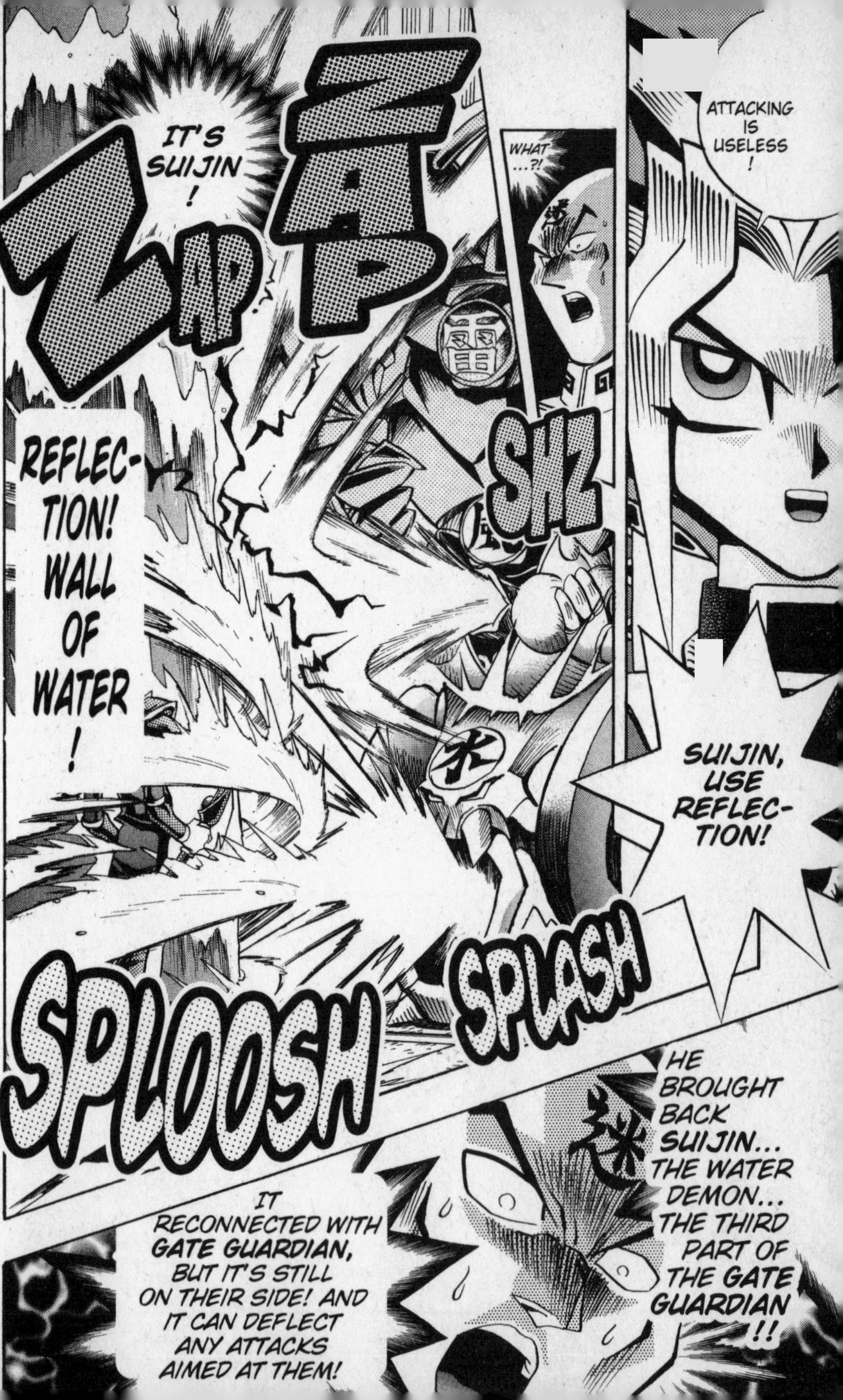
ATTACKING IS USELESS!
SUIJIN, USE REFLECTION!
WHAT ...?!
SHZ
ZAP
ZAP
IT'S SUIJIN!
REFLECTION! WALL OF WATER!
SPLASH
SPLOOSH
HE BROUGHT BACK SUIJIN... THE WATER DEMON... THE THIRD PART OF THE GATE GUARDIAN!!
IT RECONNECTED WITH GATE GUARDIAN, BUT IT'S STILL ON THEIR SIDE! AND IT CAN DEFLECT ANY ATTACKS AIMED AT THEM!

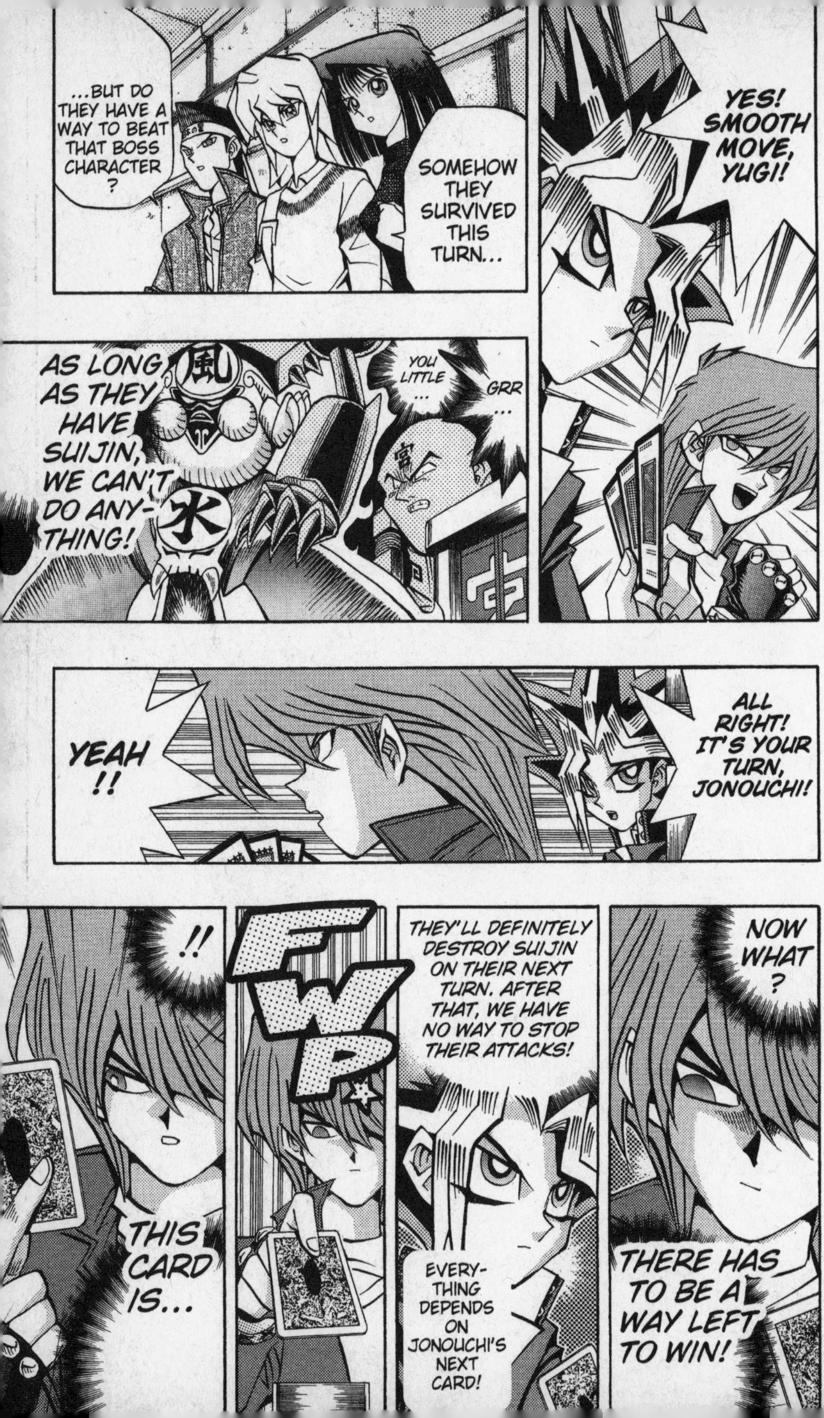
YES! SMOOTH MOVE, YUGI!
SOMEHOW THEY SURVIVED THIS TURN...
...BUT DO THEY HAVE A WAY TO BEAT THAT BOSS CHARACTER ?
GRR ...
YOU LITTLE ...
AS LONG AS THEY HAVE SUIJIN, WE CAN'T DO ANY-THING!
ALL RIGHT! IT'S YOUR TURN, JONOUCHI!
YEAH !!
NOW WHAT ?
THERE HAS TO BE A WAY LEFT TO WIN!
THEY'LL DEFINITELY DESTROY SUIJIN ON THEIR NEXT TURN. AFTER THAT, WE HAVE NO WAY TO STOP THEIR ATTACKS!
EVERY-THING DEPENDS ON JONOUCHI'S NEXT CARD!
FWP
!!
THIS CARD IS...

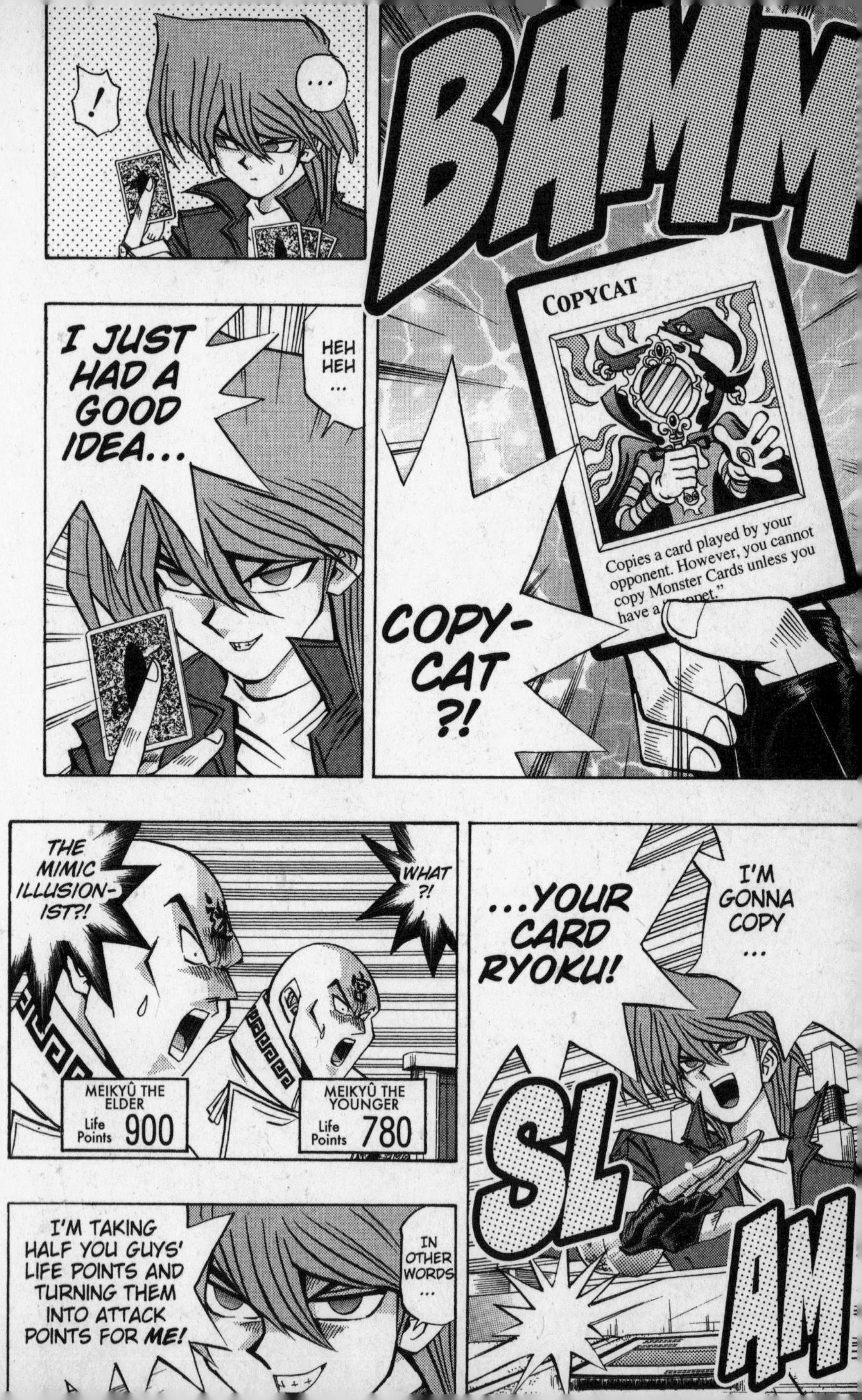
BAMM
COPYCAT
Copies a card played by your opponent. However, you cannot copy Monster Cards unless you have a
COPY-CAT?!
!
...
HEH HEH ...
I JUST HAD A GOOD IDEA...
I'M GONNA COPY ...
...YOUR CARD RYOKU!
SLAM
WHAT?!
THE MIMIC ILLUSIONIST?!
MEIKYÛ THE YOUNGER Life Points 780
MEIKYÛ THE ELDER Life Points 900
IN OTHER WORDS ...
I'M TAKING HALF YOU GUYS' LIFE POINTS AND TURNING THEM INTO ATTACK POINTS FOR ME!

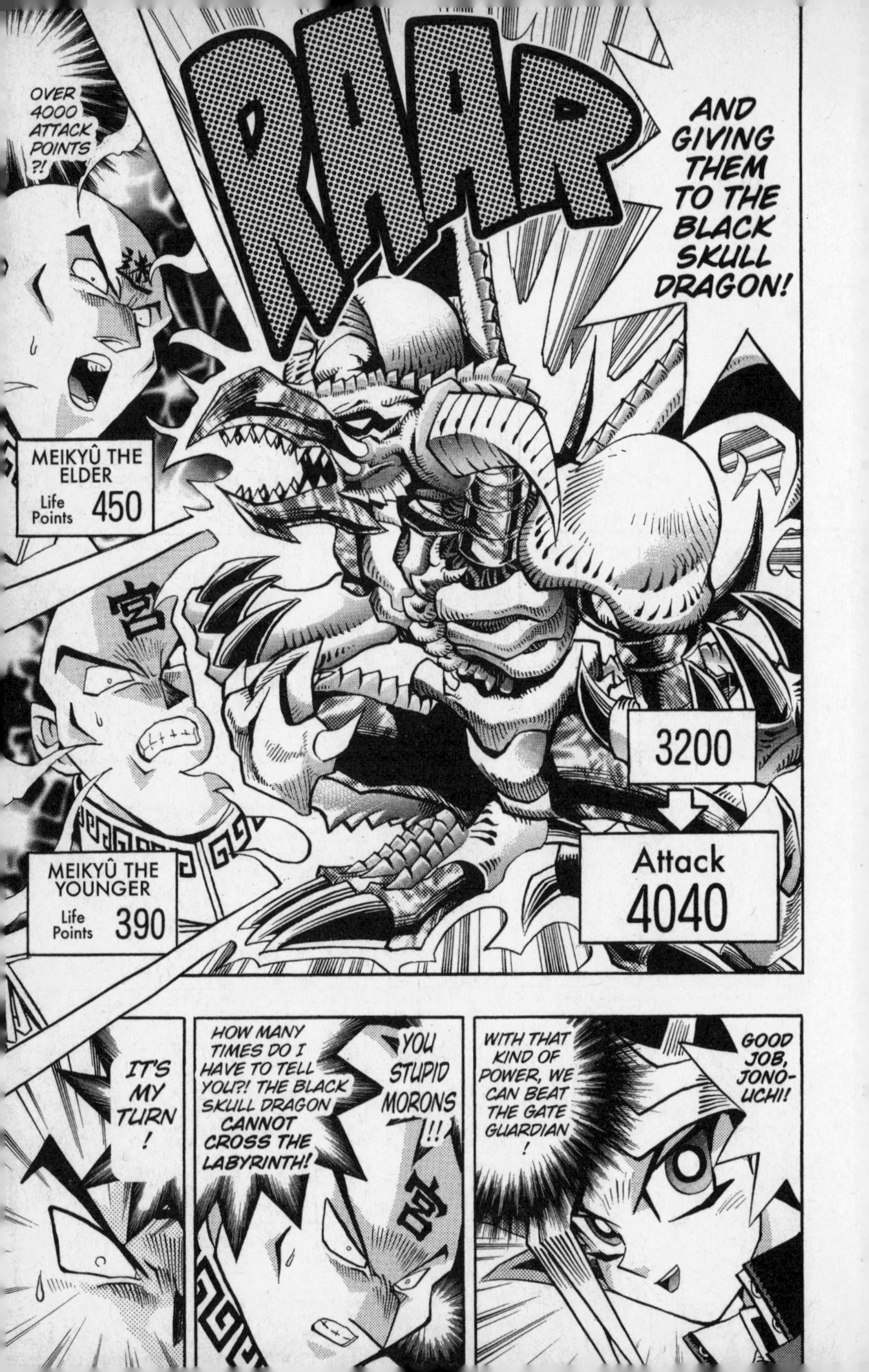
AND GIVING THEM TO THE BLACK SKULL DRAGON!
RWAR
OVER 4000 ATTACK POINTS ?!
MEIKYÛ THE ELDER Life Points 450
3200
Attack 4040
MEIKYÛ THE YOUNGER Life Points 390
GOOD JOB, JONO-UCHI!
WITH THAT KIND OF POWER, WE CAN BEAT THE GATE GUARDIAN!
YOU STUPID MORONS!!
HOW MANY TIMES DO I HAVE TO TELL YOU?! THE BLACK SKULL DRAGON CANNOT CROSS THE LABYRINTH!
IT'S MY TURN!

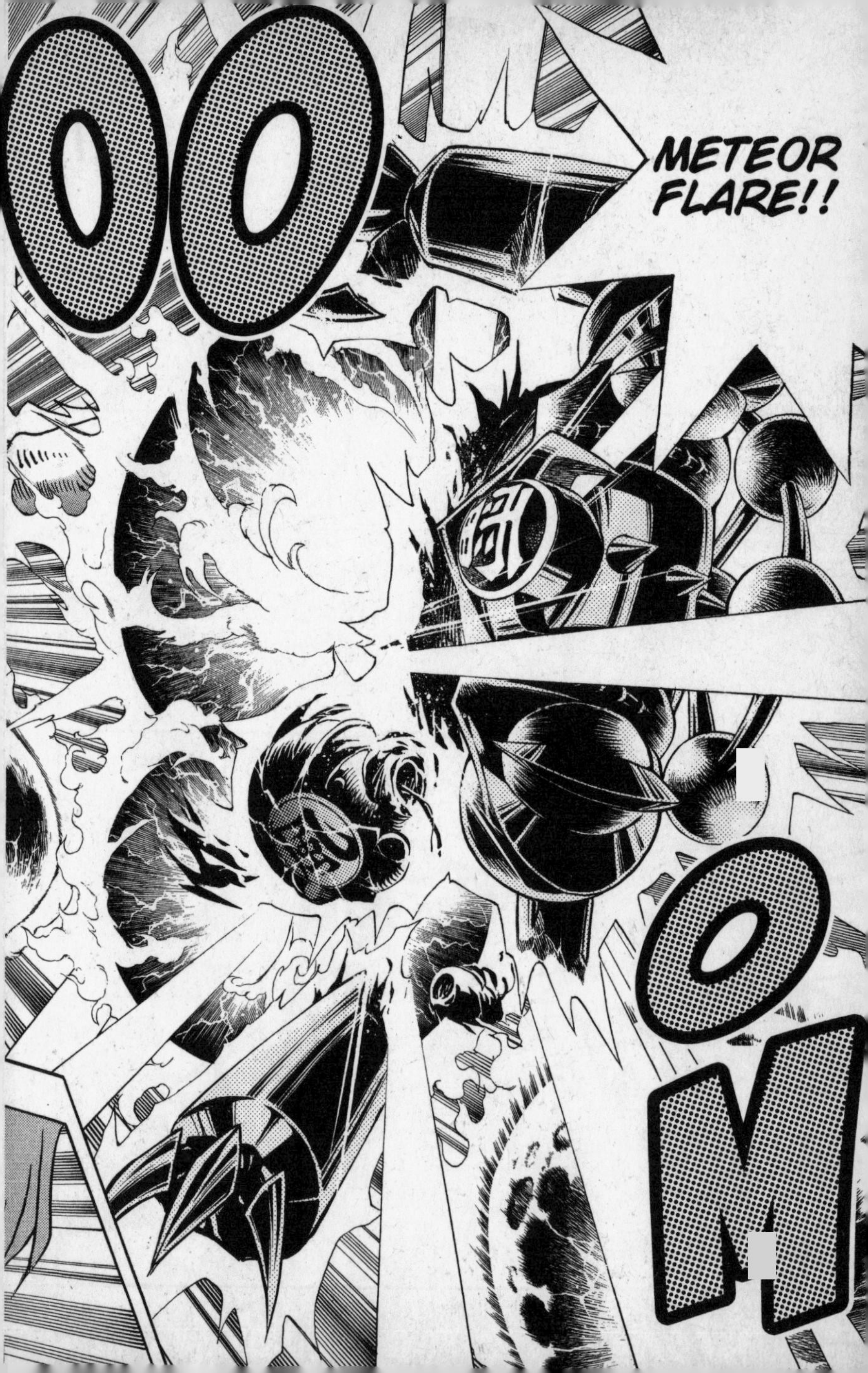
METEOR
FLARE!!
OO
OM

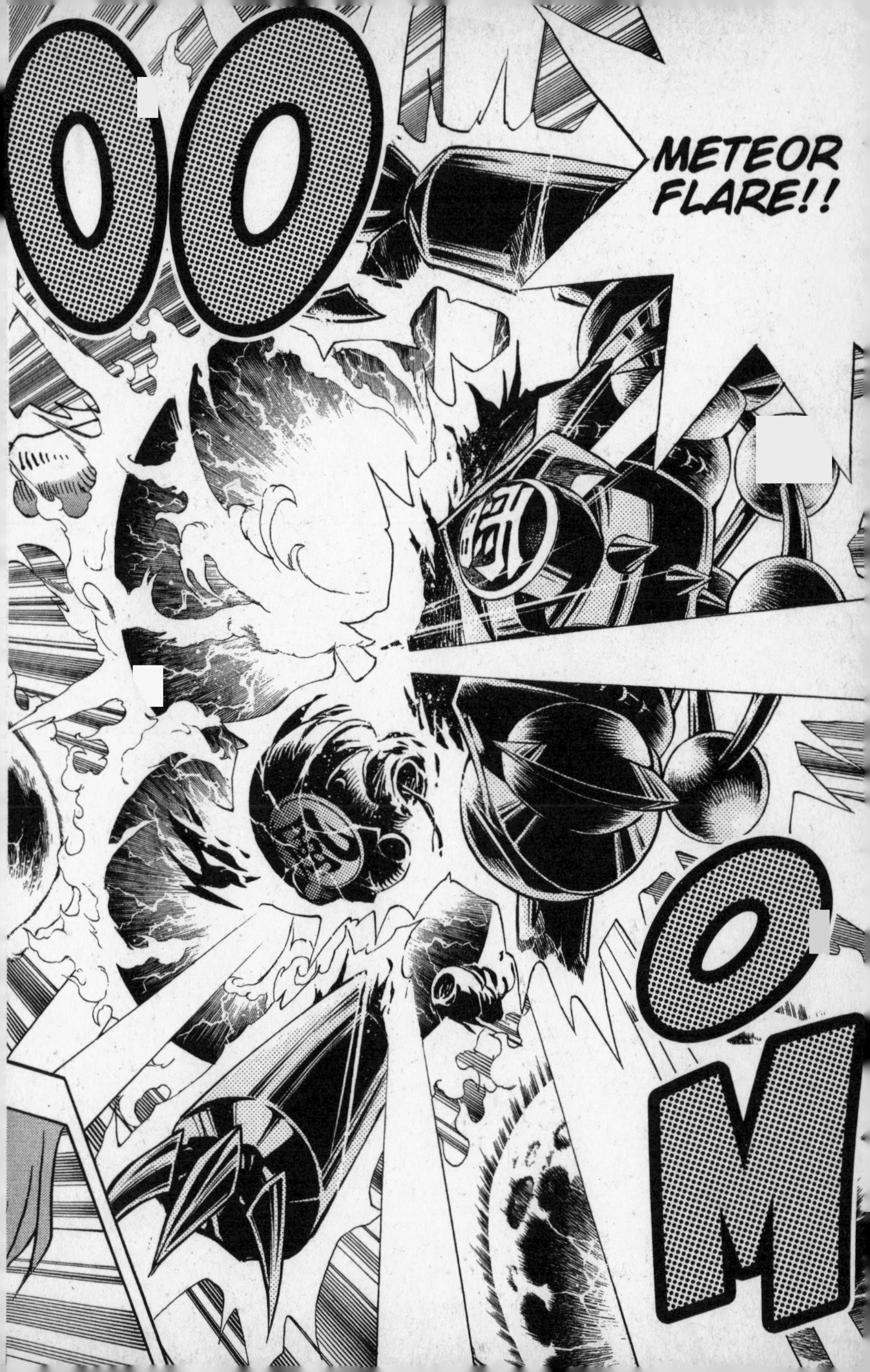
METEOR FLARE!!
OO
OM

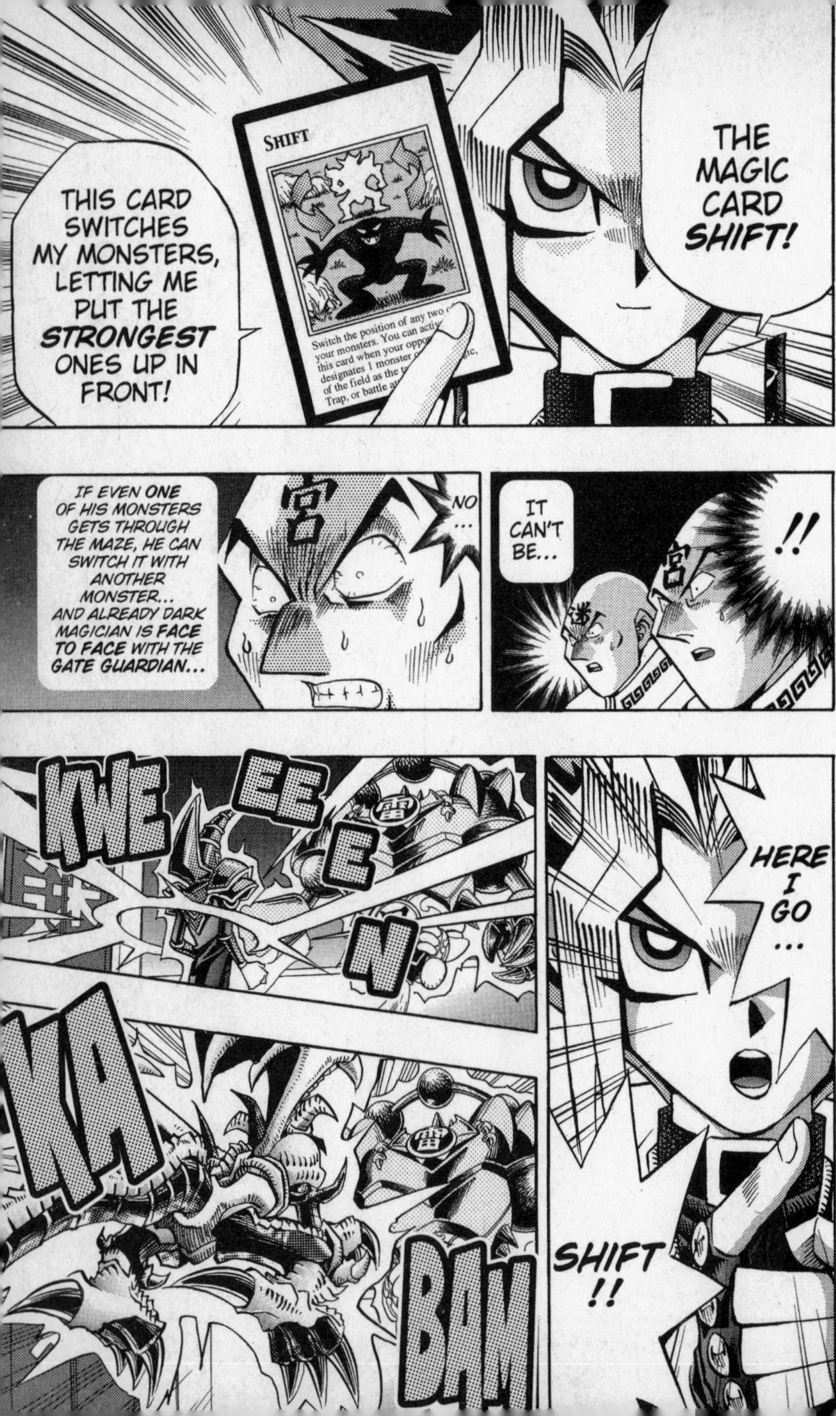
THE MAGIC CARD SHIFT!
SHIFT
THIS CARD SWITCHES MY MONSTERS, LETTING ME PUT THE STRONGEST ONES UP IN FRONT!
!!
IT CAN'T BE...
NO ...
IF EVEN ONE OF HIS MONSTERS GETS THROUGH THE MAZE, HE CAN SWITCH IT WITH ANOTHER MONSTER... AND ALREADY DARK MAGICIAN IS FACE TO FACE WITH THE GATE GUARDIAN...
HERE I GO ...
SHIFT !!
KWEEEN
KA
BAM

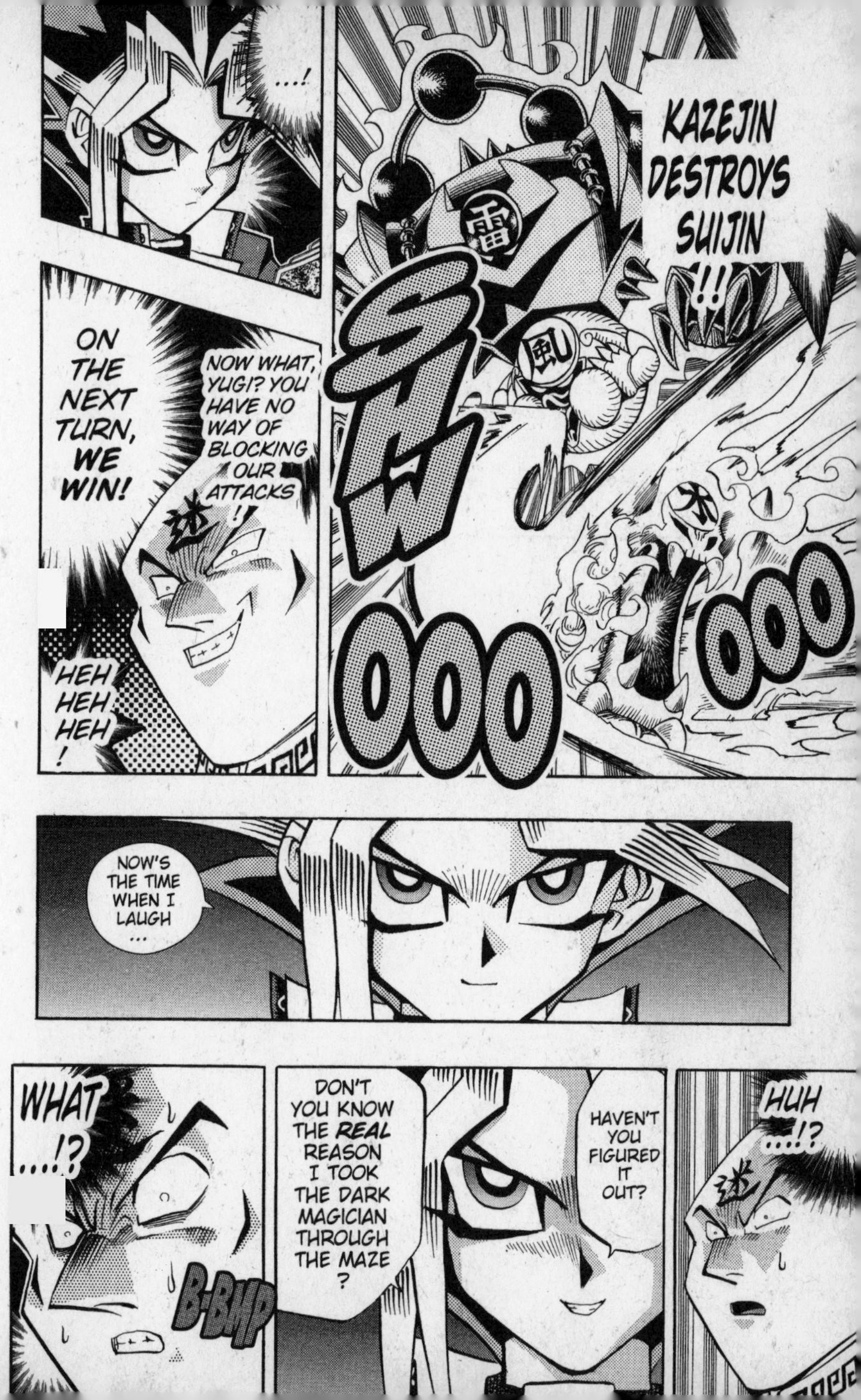
KAZEJIN DESTROYS SUIJIN!!
SHWOOOOOO
...!
NOW WHAT, YUGI? YOU HAVE NO WAY OF BLOCKING OUR ATTACKS!
ON THE NEXT TURN, WE WIN!
HEH HEH HEH!
NOW'S THE TIME WHEN I LAUGH ...
HUH ...!?
HAVEN'T YOU FIGURED IT OUT?
DON'T YOU KNOW THE REAL REASON I TOOK THE DARK MAGICIAN THROUGH THE MAZE?
WHAT ...!?
B-BMP

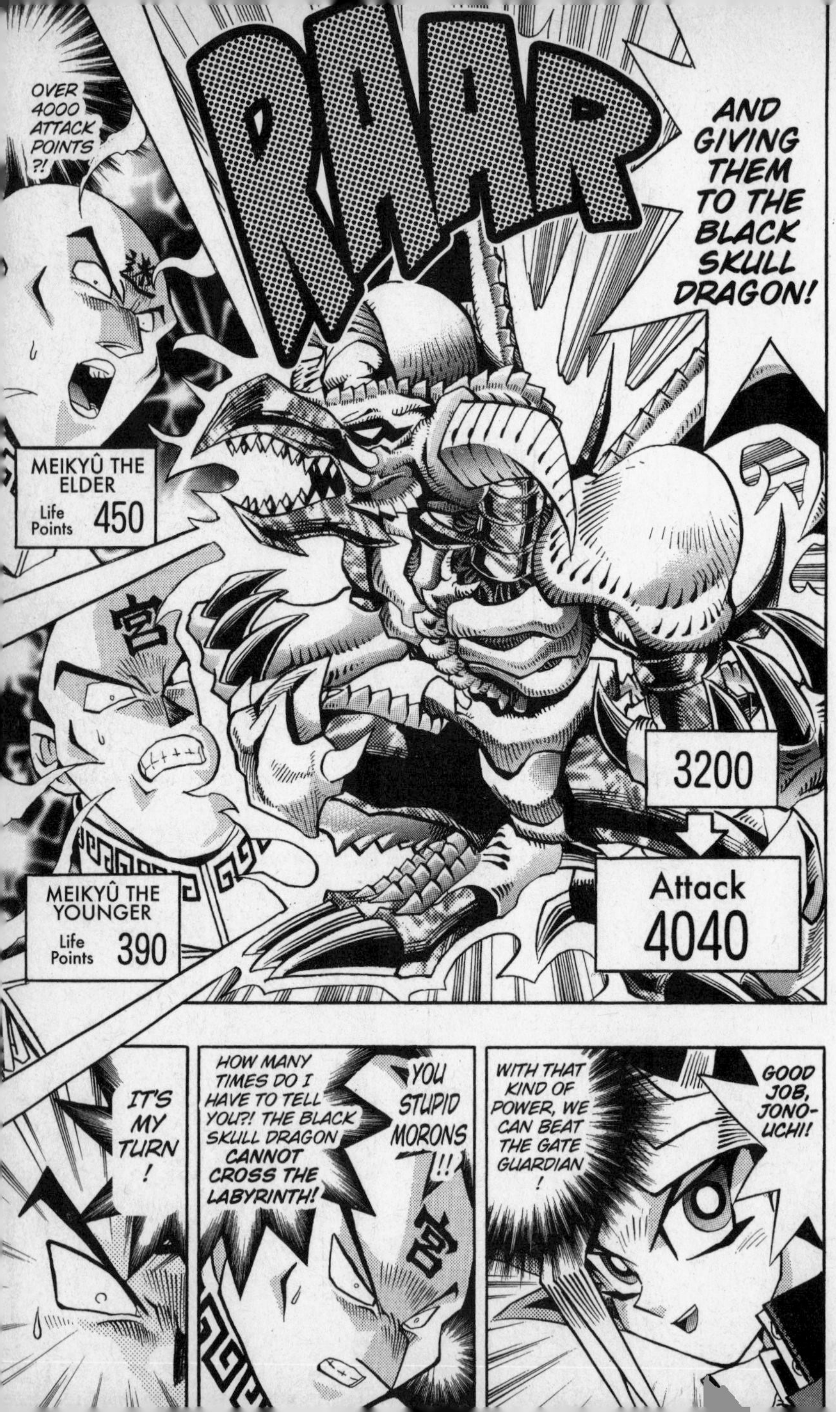
AND GIVING THEM TO THE BLACK SKULL DRAGON!
RAWR
OVER 4000 ATTACK POINTS ?!
MEIKYÛ THE ELDER Life Points 450
3200
Attack 4040
MEIKYÛ THE YOUNGER Life Points 390
GOOD JOB, JONO-UCHI!
WITH THAT KIND OF POWER, WE CAN BEAT THE GATE GUARDIAN!
YOU STUPID MORONS!!
HOW MANY TIMES DO I HAVE TO TELL YOU?! THE BLACK SKULL DRAGON CANNOT CROSS THE LABYRINTH!
IT'S MY TURN!

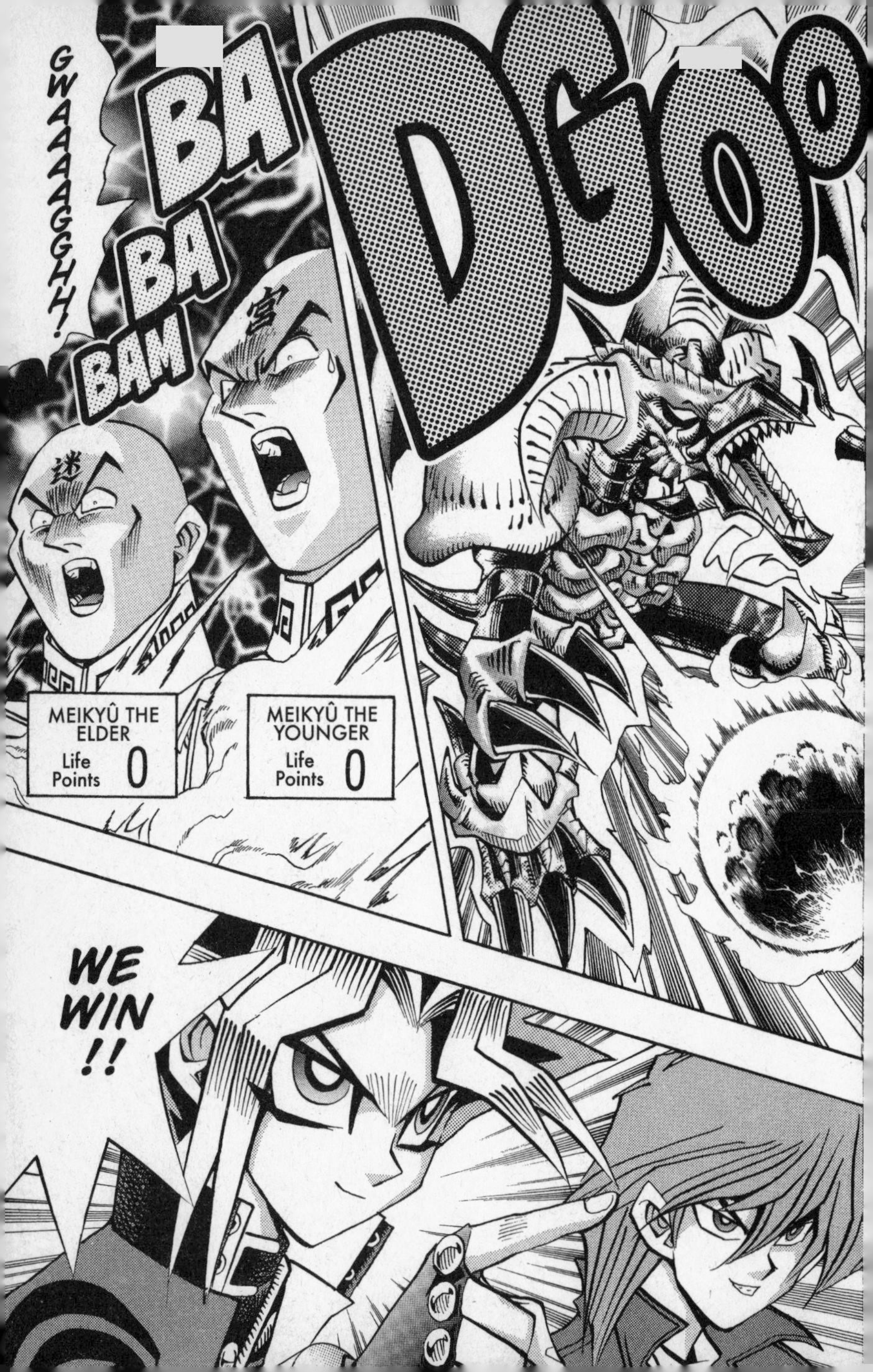
DOOO
GWAAAAAGGHH!
BA BA BAM
MEIKYÛ THE YOUNGER
Life Points 0
MEIKYÛ THE ELDER
Life Points 0
WE WIN !!

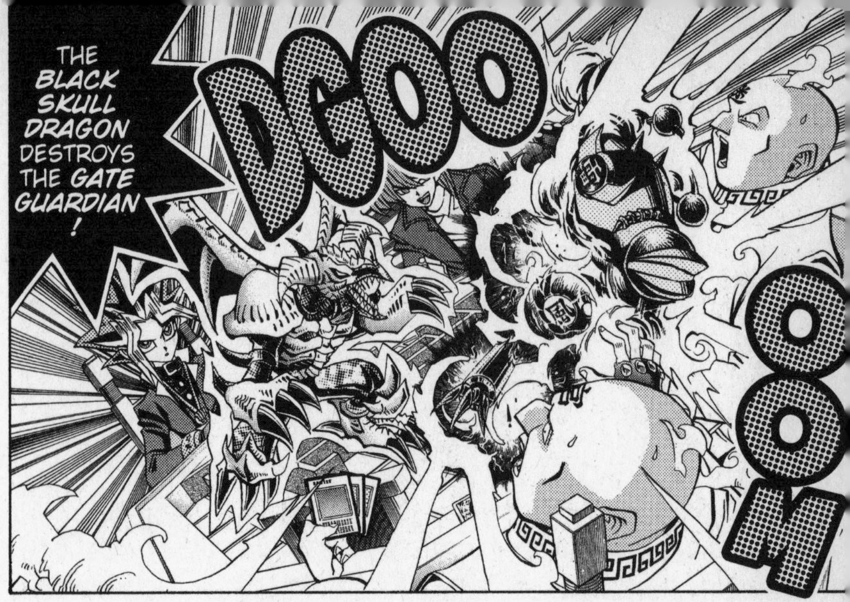
DGOO
OOM
THE BLACK SKULL DRAGON DESTROYS THE GATE GUARDIAN!

Duel 39: Choose Wisely!

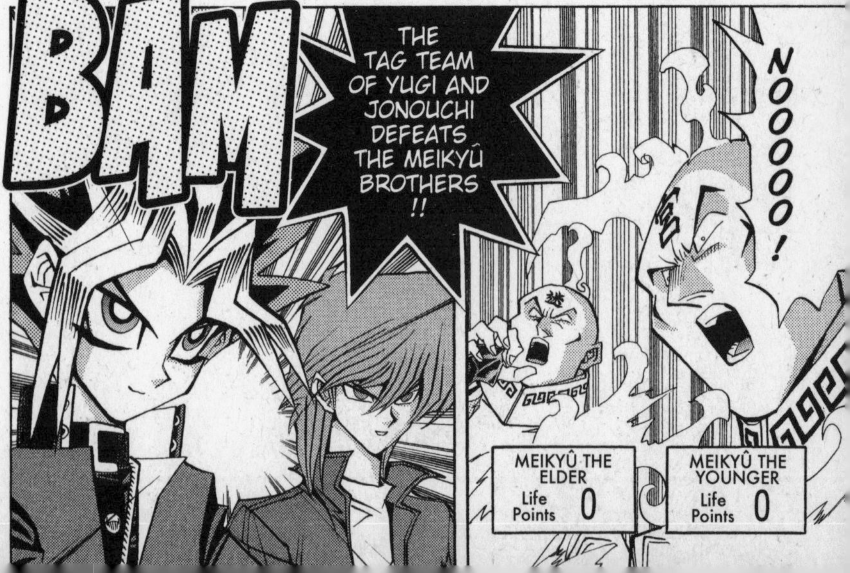
NOOOOOO!
THE TAG TEAM OF YUGI AND JONOUCHI DEFEATS THE MEIKYÛ BROTHERS!!
BAM
MEIKYÛ THE YOUNGER Life Points 0
MEIKYÛ THE ELDER Life Points 0

READ THIS WAY

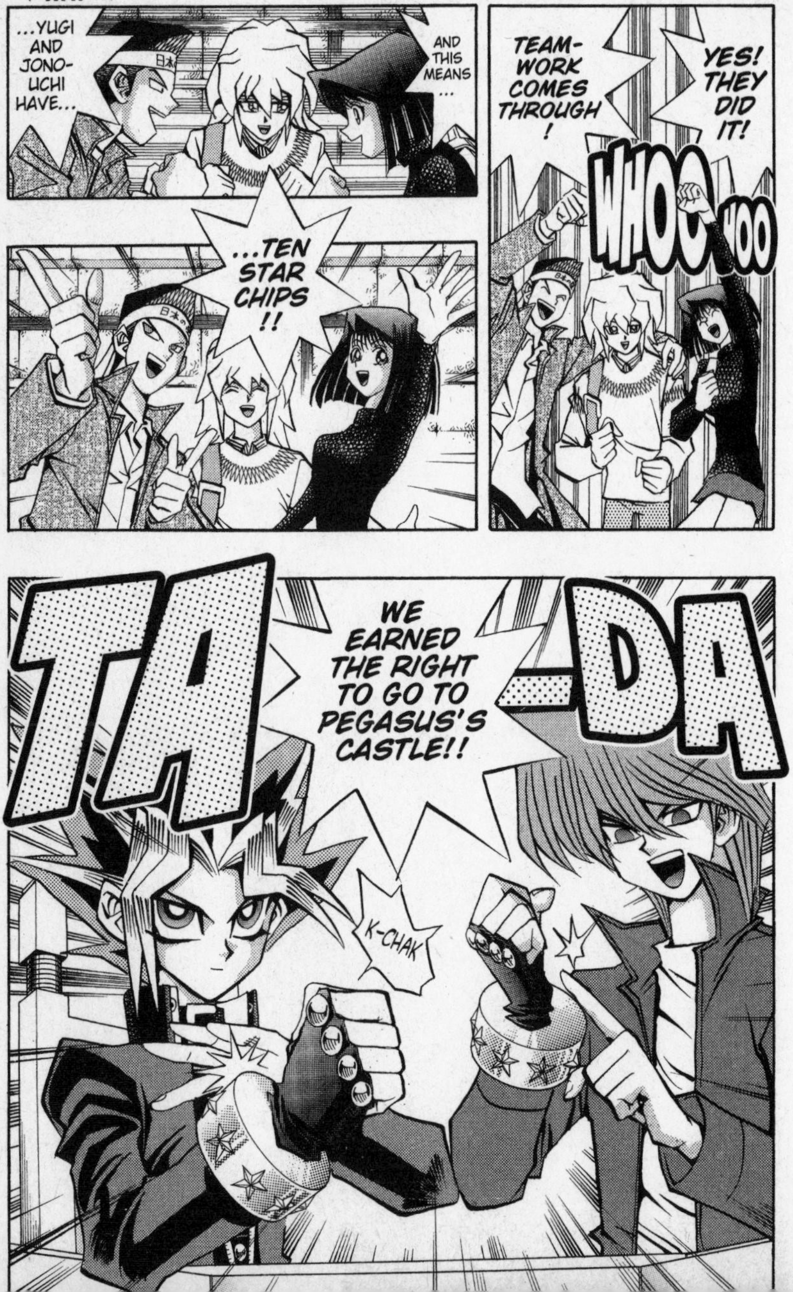
YES! THEY DID IT!
TEAM-WORK COMES THROUGH!
WHOO HOO
AND THIS MEANS ...
...YUGI AND JONO-UCHI HAVE...
...TEN STAR CHIPS!!
TA-DA
WE EARNED THE RIGHT TO GO TO PEGASUS'S CASTLE!!
K-CHAK

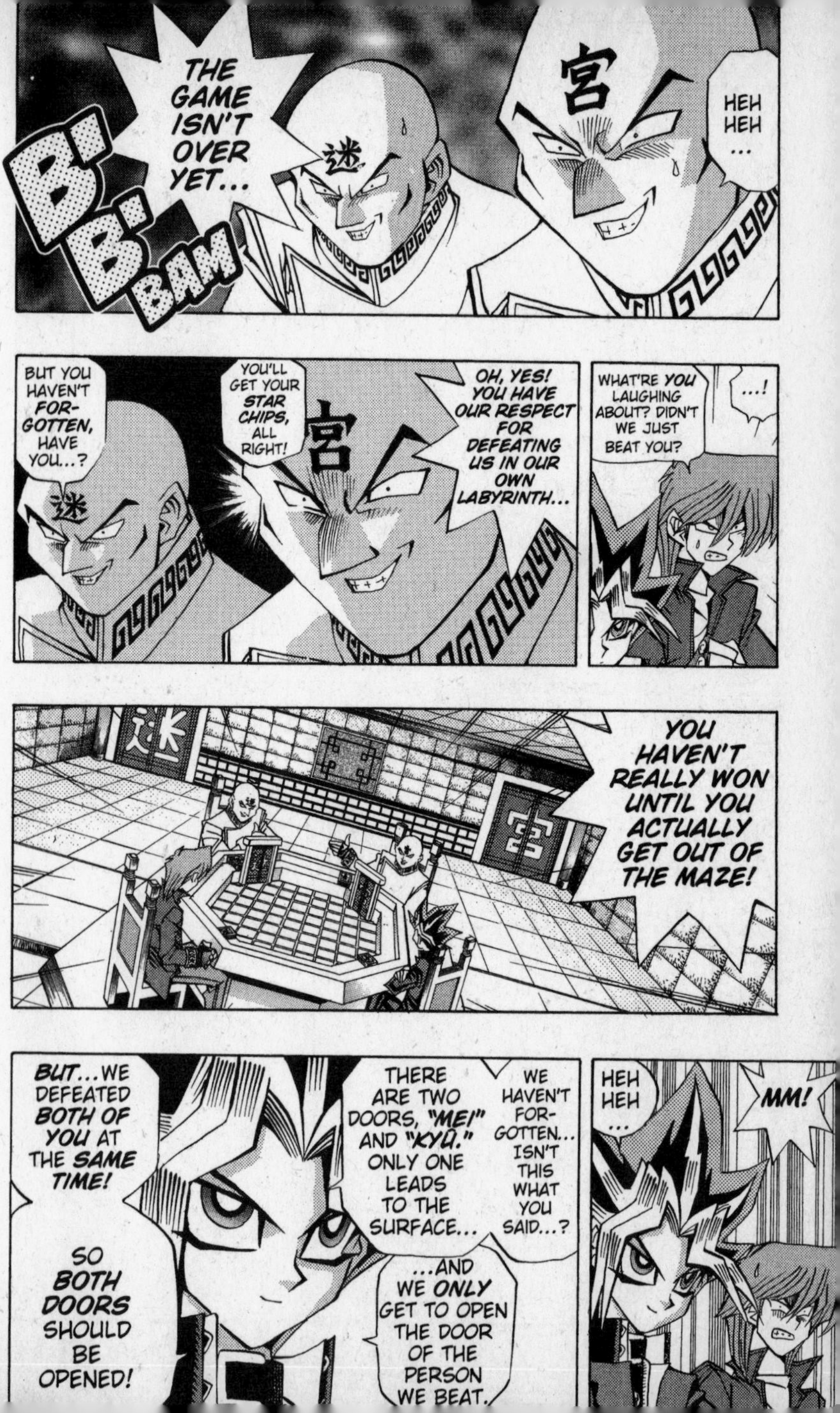
HEH HEH ...
THE GAME ISN'T OVER YET...
B'B'BAM
...!
WHAT'RE YOU LAUGHING ABOUT? DIDN'T WE JUST BEAT YOU?
OH, YES! YOU HAVE OUR RESPECT FOR DEFEATING US IN OUR OWN LABYRINTH...
YOU'LL GET YOUR STAR CHIPS, ALL RIGHT!
BUT YOU HAVEN'T FOR-GOTTEN, HAVE YOU...?
YOU HAVEN'T REALLY WON UNTIL YOU ACTUALLY GET OUT OF THE MAZE!
MM!
HEH HEH ...
WE HAVEN'T FOR-GOTTEN... ISN'T THIS WHAT YOU SAID...?
THERE ARE TWO DOORS, "MEI" AND "KYŪ." ONLY ONE LEADS TO THE SURFACE...
...AND WE ONLY GET TO OPEN THE DOOR OF THE PERSON WE BEAT.
BUT...WE DEFEATED BOTH OF YOU AT THE SAME TIME!
SO BOTH DOORS SHOULD BE OPENED!

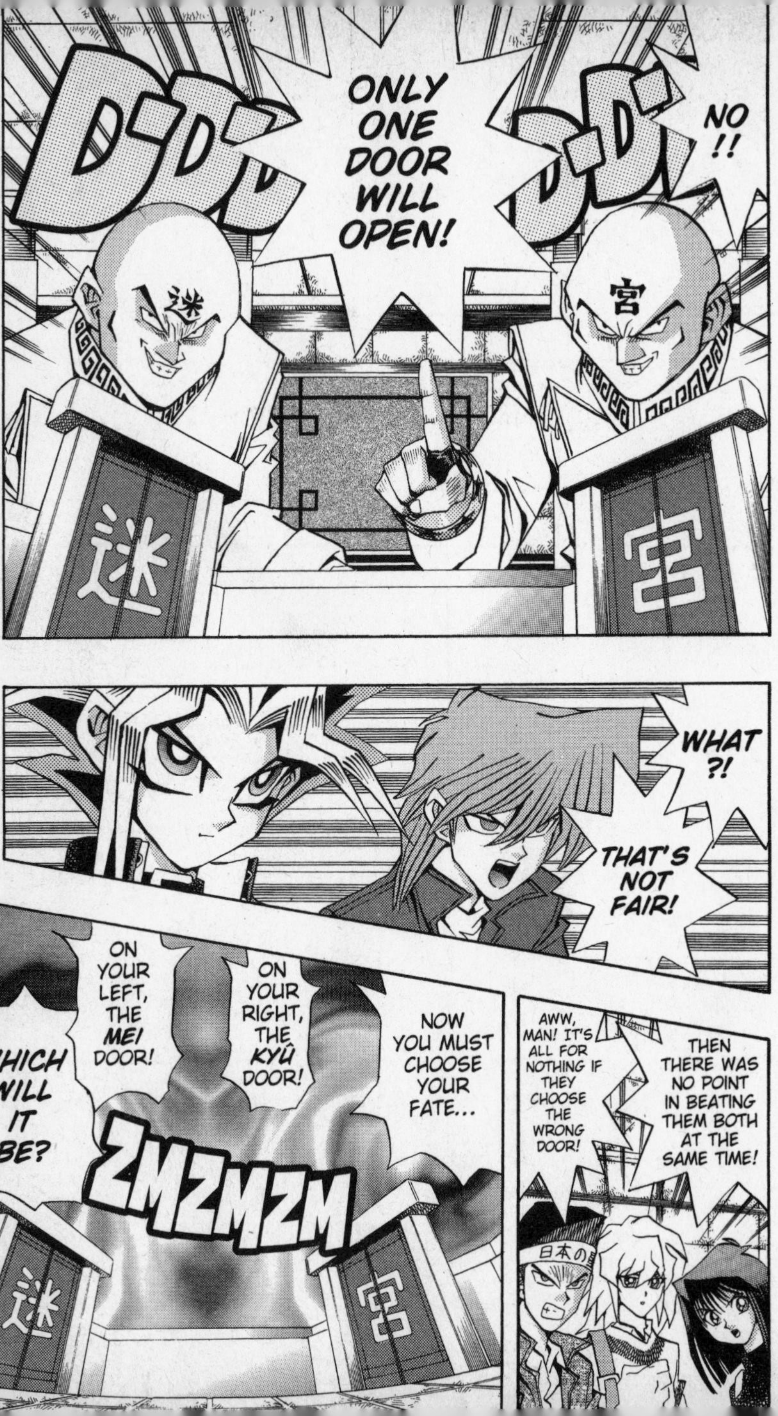
D-D-D
NO !!
ONLY ONE DOOR WILL OPEN!
D-D-D
宮
迷
WHAT ?!
THAT'S NOT FAIR!
THEN THERE WAS NO POINT IN BEATING THEM BOTH AT THE SAME TIME!
AWW, MAN! IT'S ALL FOR NOTHING IF THEY CHOOSE THE WRONG DOOR!
NOW YOU MUST CHOOSE YOUR FATE...
ON YOUR RIGHT, THE *KYŪ* DOOR!
ON YOUR LEFT, THE *MEI* DOOR!
WHICH WILL IT BE?
ZMZMZM

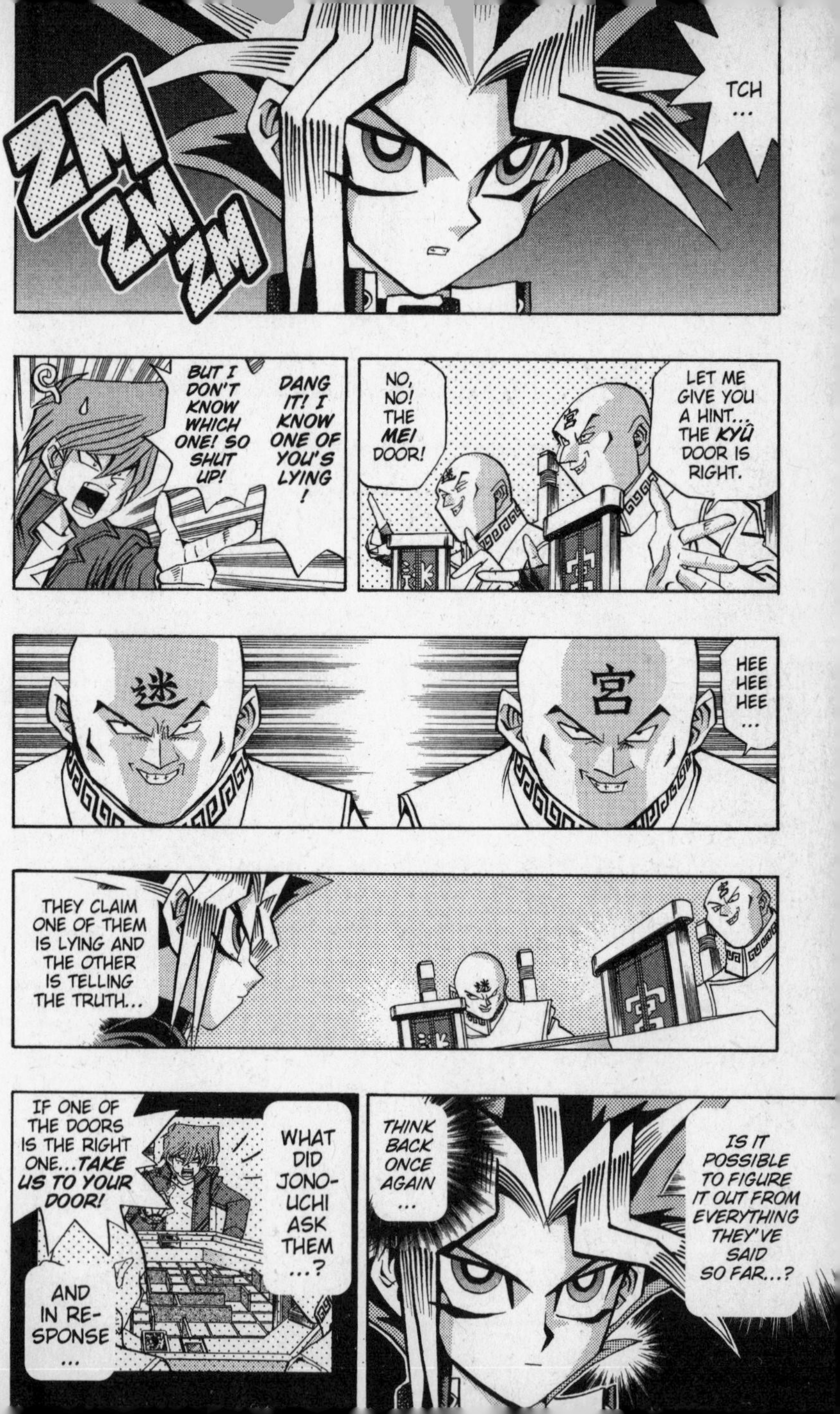
TCH ...
ZM ZM ZM
LET ME GIVE YOU A HINT... THE KYŪ DOOR IS RIGHT.
NO, NO! THE MEI DOOR!
DANG IT! I KNOW ONE OF YOU'S LYING!
BUT I DON'T KNOW WHICH ONE! SO SHUT UP!
宮
迷
HEE HEE HEE ...
THEY CLAIM ONE OF THEM IS LYING AND THE OTHER IS TELLING THE TRUTH...
IS IT POSSIBLE TO FIGURE IT OUT FROM EVERYTHING THEY'VE SAID SO FAR...?
THINK BACK ONCE AGAIN ...
WHAT DID JONOUCHI ASK THEM ...?
IF ONE OF THE DOORS IS THE RIGHT ONE...TAKE US TO YOUR DOOR!
AND IN RESPONSE ...

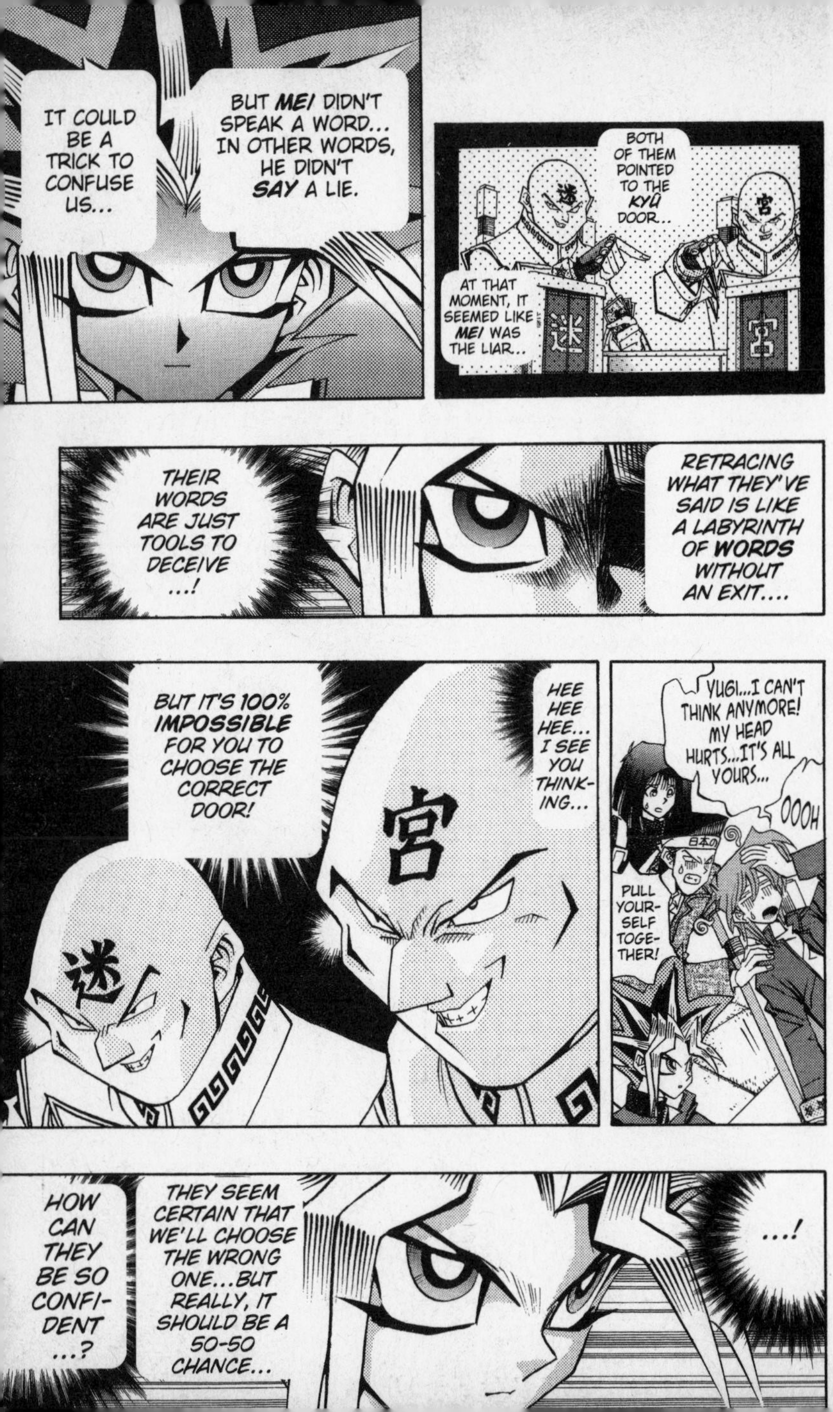
BOTH OF THEM POINTED TO THE KYŪ DOOR...
AT THAT MOMENT, IT SEEMED LIKE MEI WAS THE LIAR...
迷
宮
BUT MEI DIDN'T SPEAK A WORD... IN OTHER WORDS, HE DIDN'T SAY A LIE.
IT COULD BE A TRICK TO CONFUSE US...
RETRACING WHAT THEY'VE SAID IS LIKE A LABYRINTH OF WORDS WITHOUT AN EXIT....
THEIR WORDS ARE JUST TOOLS TO DECEIVE ...!
YUGI...I CAN'T THINK ANYMORE! MY HEAD HURTS...IT'S ALL YOURS...
OOOH
PULL YOURSELF TOGETHER!
HEE HEE HEE... I SEE YOU THINKING...
BUT IT'S 100% IMPOSSIBLE FOR YOU TO CHOOSE THE CORRECT DOOR!
宮
迷
...!
THEY SEEM CERTAIN THAT WE'LL CHOOSE THE WRONG ONE...BUT REALLY, IT SHOULD BE A 50-50 CHANCE...
HOW CAN THEY BE SO CONFIDENT ...?

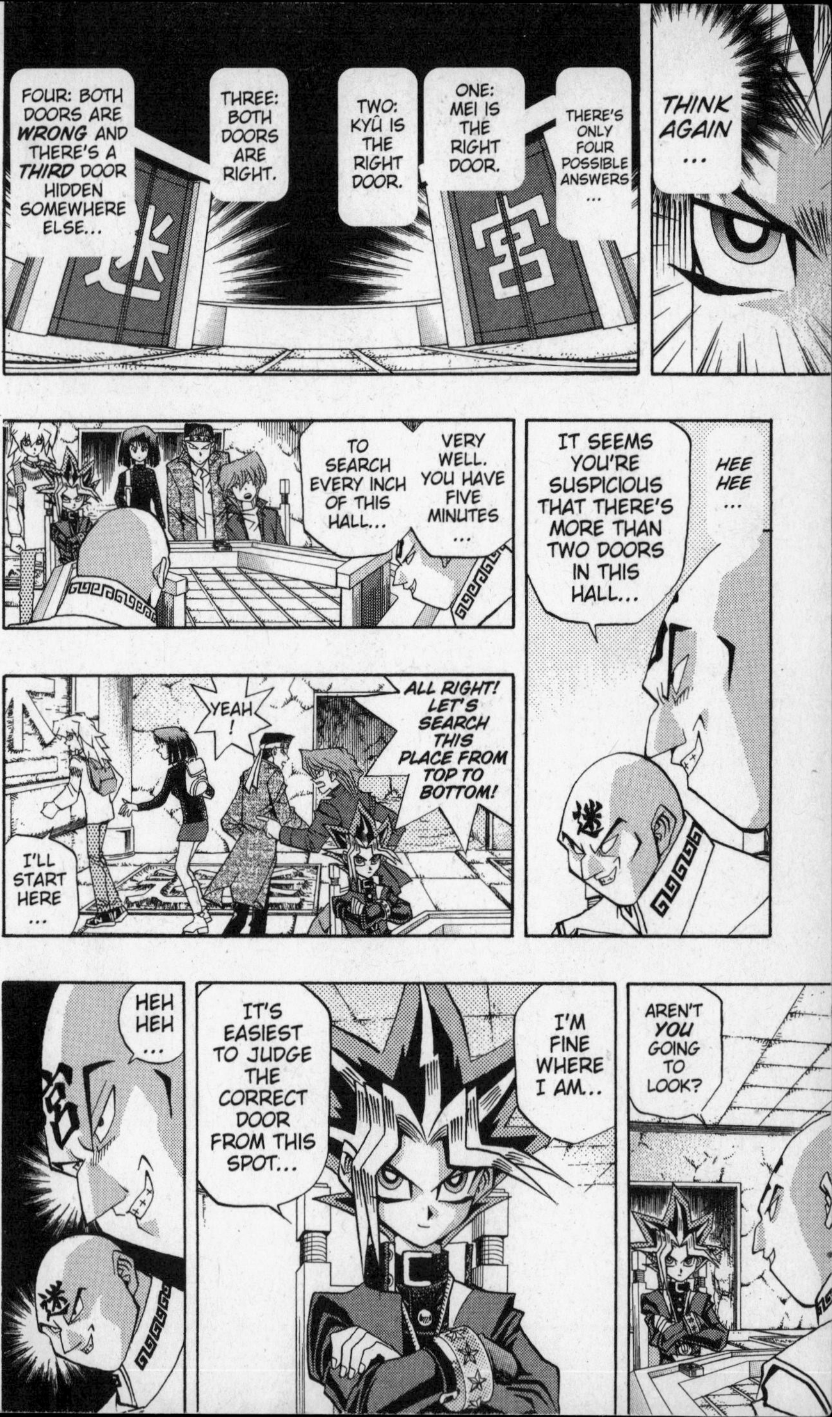
THINK AGAIN ...
THERE'S ONLY FOUR POSSIBLE ANSWERS ...
ONE: MEI IS THE RIGHT DOOR.
TWO: KYŪ IS THE RIGHT DOOR.
THREE: BOTH DOORS ARE RIGHT.
FOUR: BOTH DOORS ARE WRONG AND THERE'S A THIRD DOOR HIDDEN SOMEWHERE ELSE...
HEE HEE ...
IT SEEMS YOU'RE SUSPICIOUS THAT THERE'S MORE THAN TWO DOORS IN THIS HALL...
VERY WELL. YOU HAVE FIVE MINUTES ...
TO SEARCH EVERY INCH OF THIS HALL...
ALL RIGHT! LET'S SEARCH THIS PLACE FROM TOP TO BOTTOM!
YEAH!
I'LL START HERE ...
AREN'T YOU GOING TO LOOK?
I'M FINE WHERE I AM..
IT'S EASIEST TO JUDGE THE CORRECT DOOR FROM THIS SPOT...
HEH HEH ...

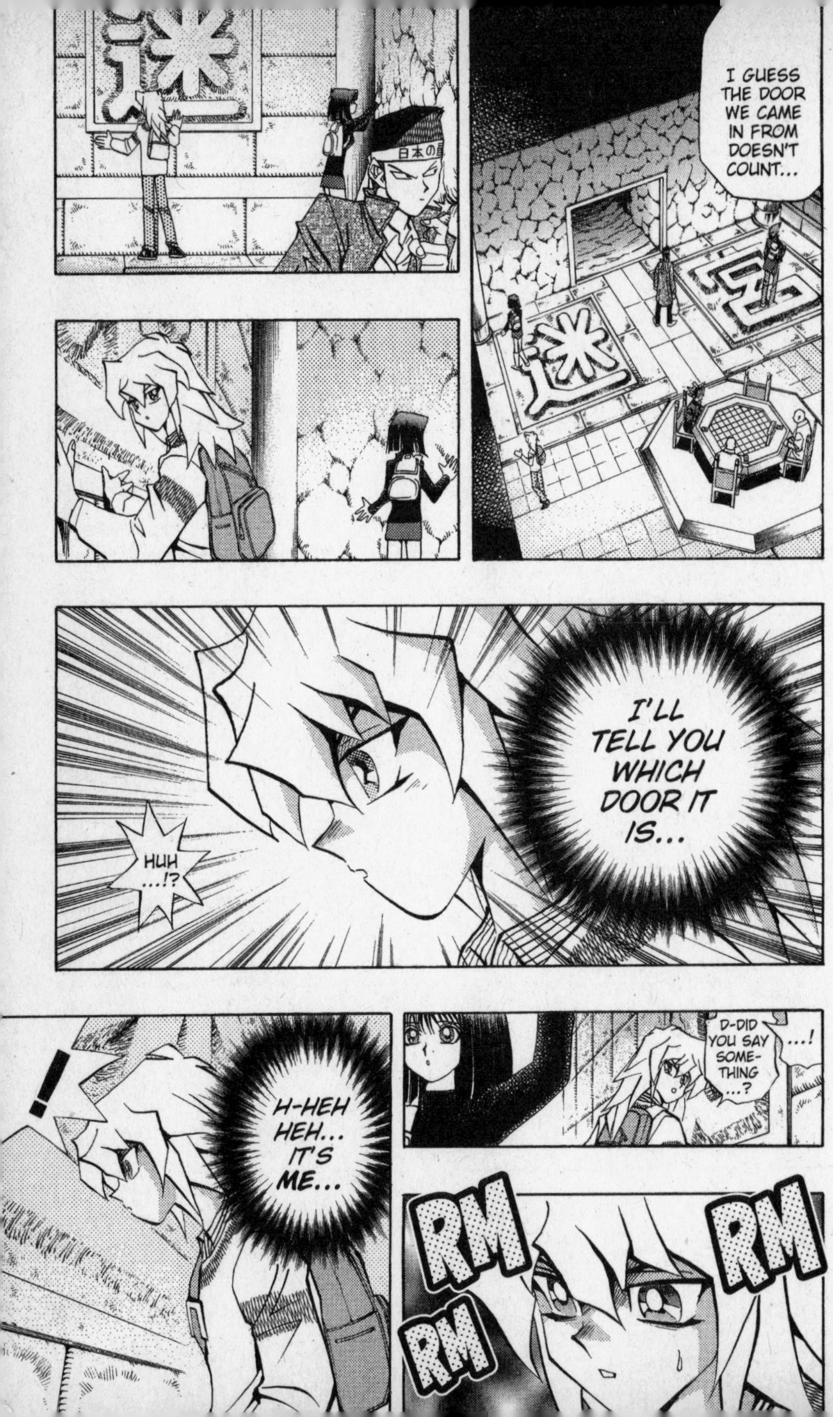
I GUESS THE DOOR WE CAME IN FROM DOESN'T COUNT...
I'LL TELL YOU WHICH DOOR IT IS...
HUH ...!?
...!
D-DID YOU SAY SOME-THING ...?
RM RM RM
!
H-HEH HEH... IT'S ME...

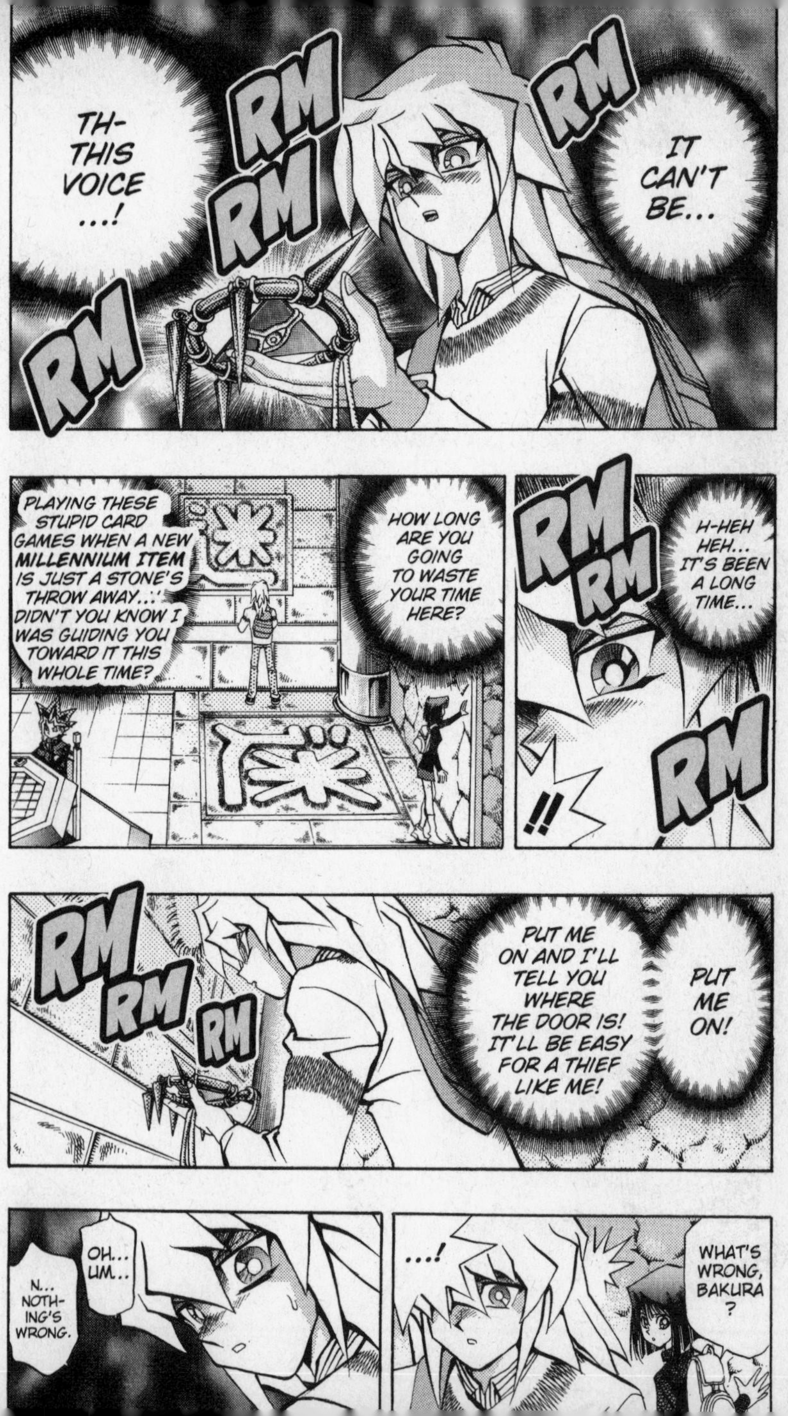
IT CAN'T BE...
RM
RM
RM
TH-THIS VOICE ...!
RM
RM
H-HEH HEH... IT'S BEEN A LONG TIME...
RM
!!
HOW LONG ARE YOU GOING TO WASTE YOUR TIME HERE?
PLAYING THESE STUPID CARD GAMES WHEN A NEW **MILLENNIUM ITEM** IS JUST A STONE'S THROW AWAY...! DIDN'T YOU KNOW I WAS GUIDING YOU TOWARD IT THIS WHOLE TIME?
PUT ME ON!
PUT ME ON AND I'LL TELL YOU WHERE THE DOOR IS! IT'LL BE EASY FOR A THIEF LIKE ME!
RM
RM
RM
WHAT'S WRONG, BAKURA?
...!
OH... UM...
N... NOTHING'S WRONG.

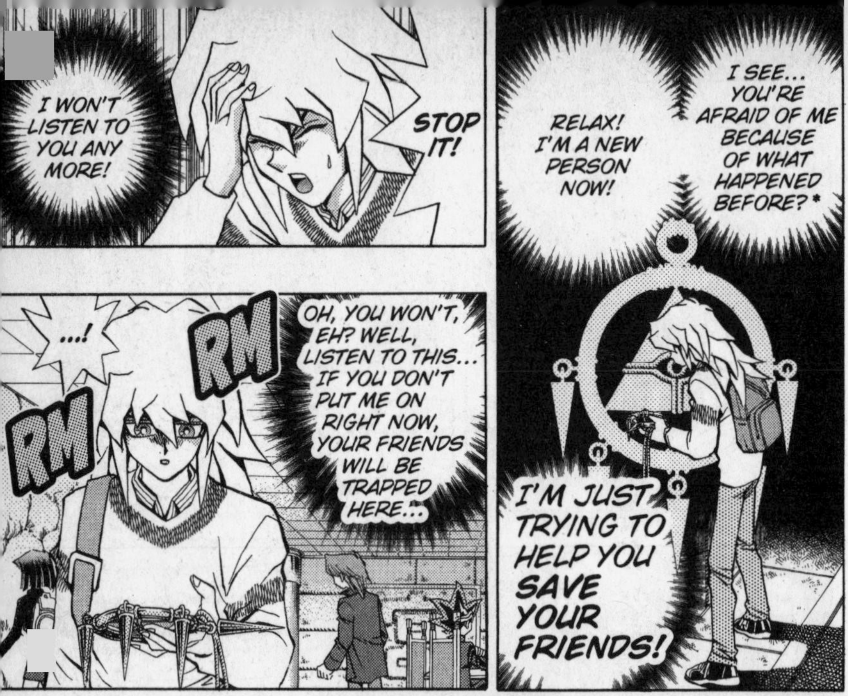
I SEE... YOU'RE AFRAID OF ME BECAUSE OF WHAT HAPPENED BEFORE?*
RELAX! I'M A NEW PERSON NOW!
I'M JUST TRYING TO HELP YOU SAVE YOUR FRIENDS!
STOP IT!
I WON'T LISTEN TO YOU ANY MORE!
OH, YOU WON'T, EH? WELL, LISTEN TO THIS... IF YOU DON'T PUT ME ON RIGHT NOW, YOUR FRIENDS WILL BE TRAPPED HERE...
RM
RM
...!

* SEE THE ORIGINAL *YU-GI-OH!* VOLS. 6 AND 7 FOR DETAILS!

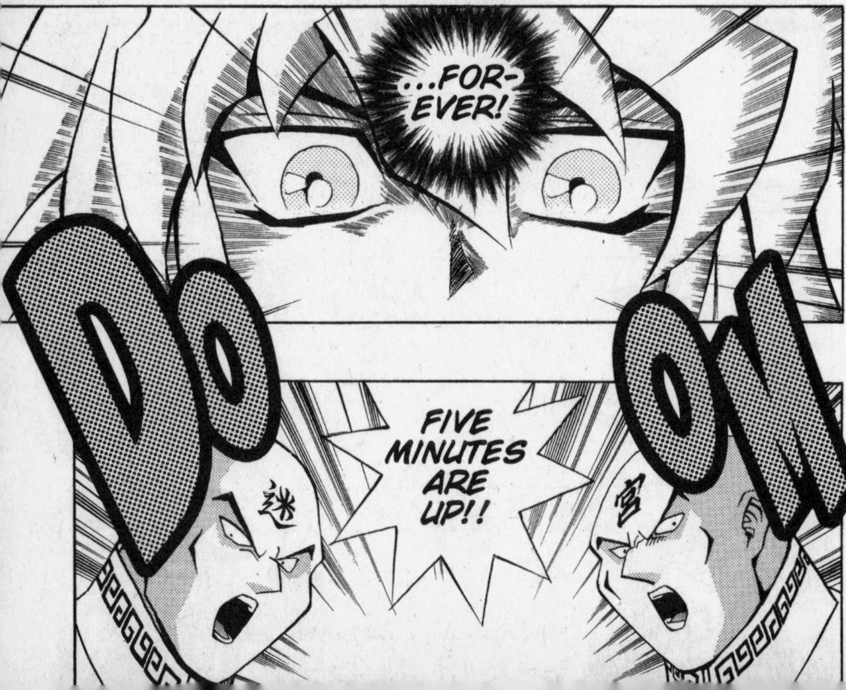
...FOR-EVER!
DOOM
FIVE MINUTES ARE UP!!

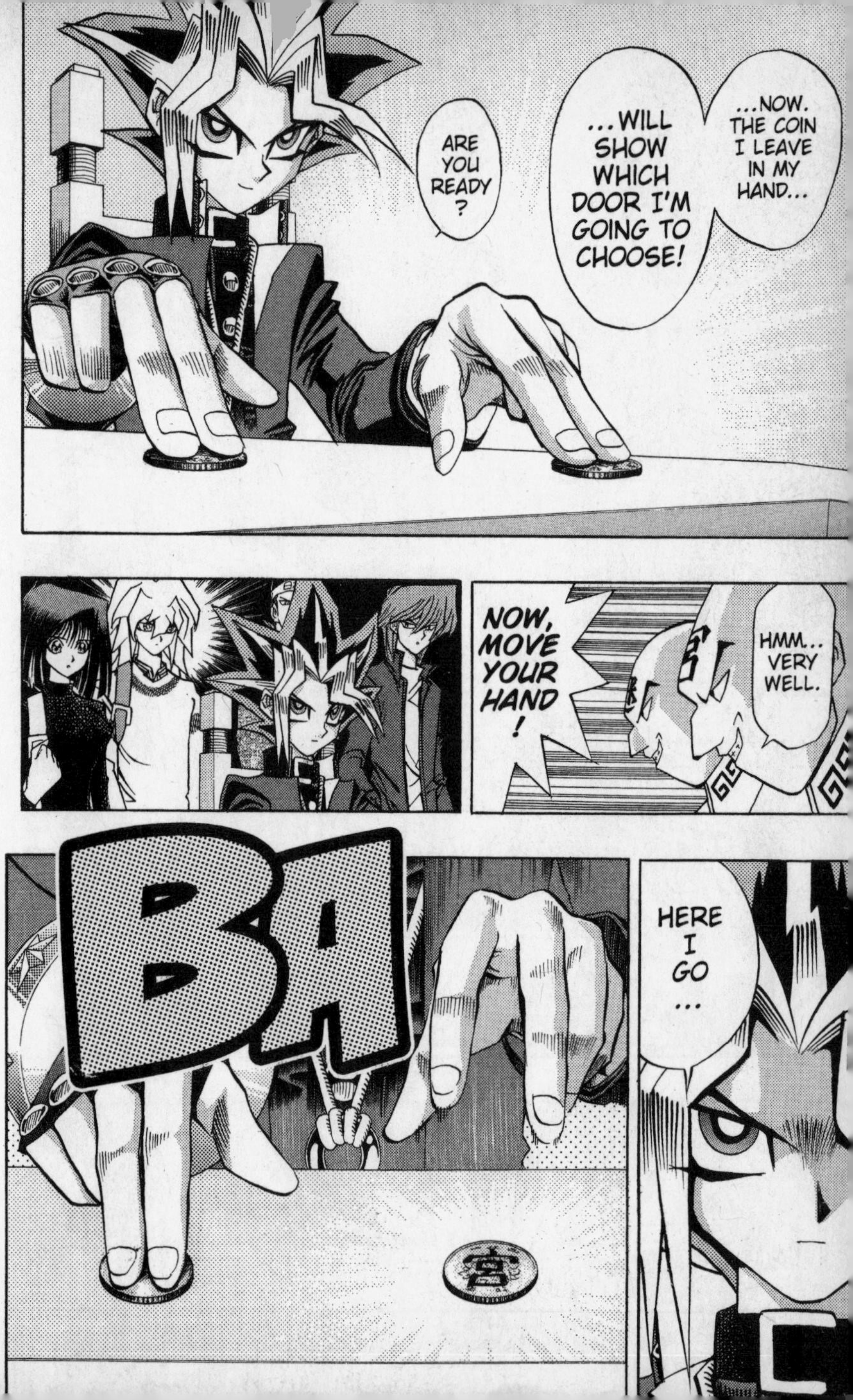
...NOW. THE COIN I LEAVE IN MY HAND...
...WILL SHOW WHICH DOOR I'M GOING TO CHOOSE!
ARE YOU READY?
HMM... VERY WELL.
NOW, MOVE YOUR HAND!
HERE I GO ...
BA

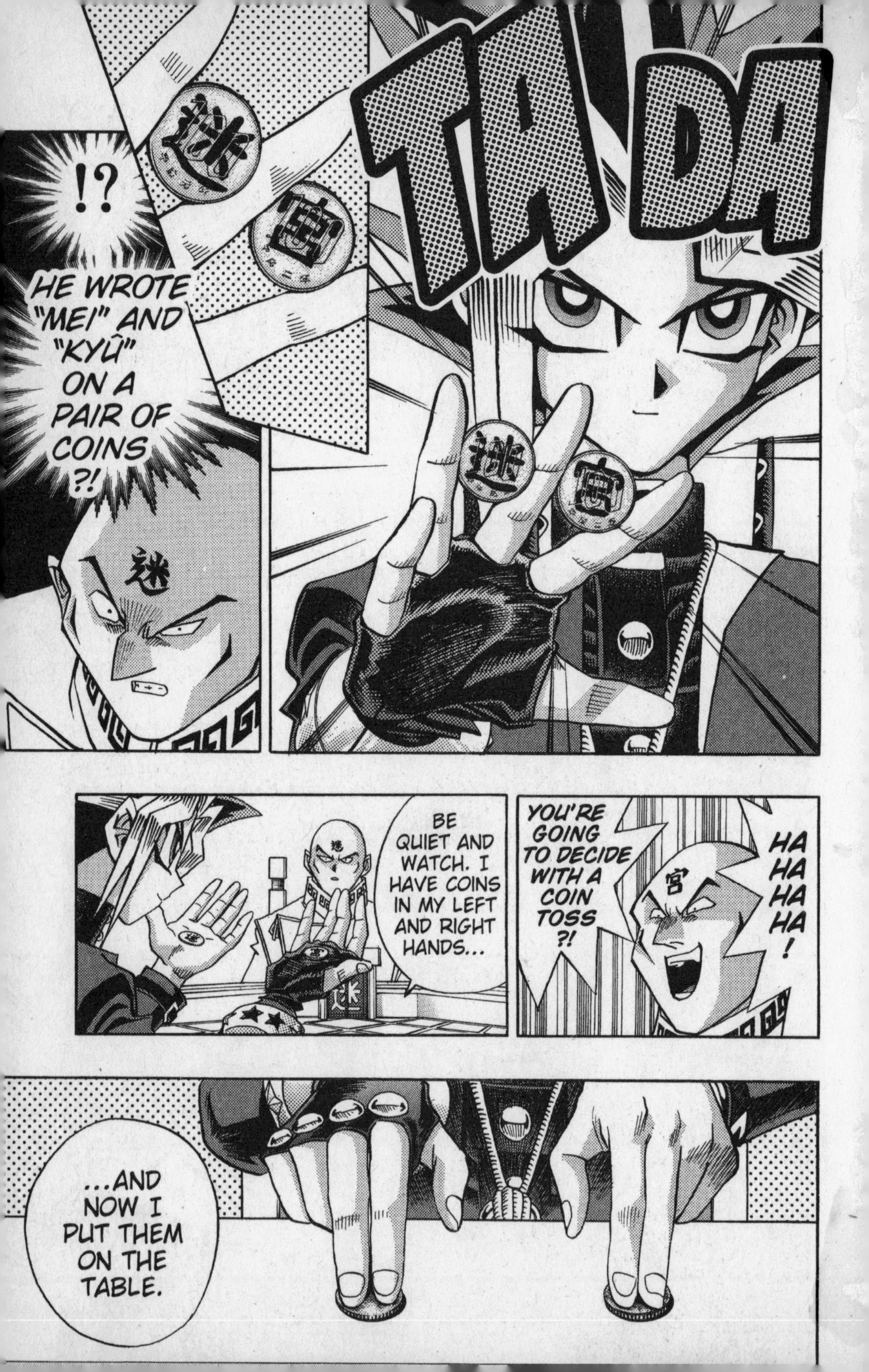
TA DA
迷
宮
!?
HE WROTE "MEI" AND "KYŪ" ON A PAIR OF COINS ?!
YOU'RE GOING TO DECIDE WITH A COIN TOSS ?!
HA HA HA HA!
BE QUIET AND WATCH. I HAVE COINS IN MY LEFT AND RIGHT HANDS...
...AND NOW I PUT THEM ON THE TABLE.

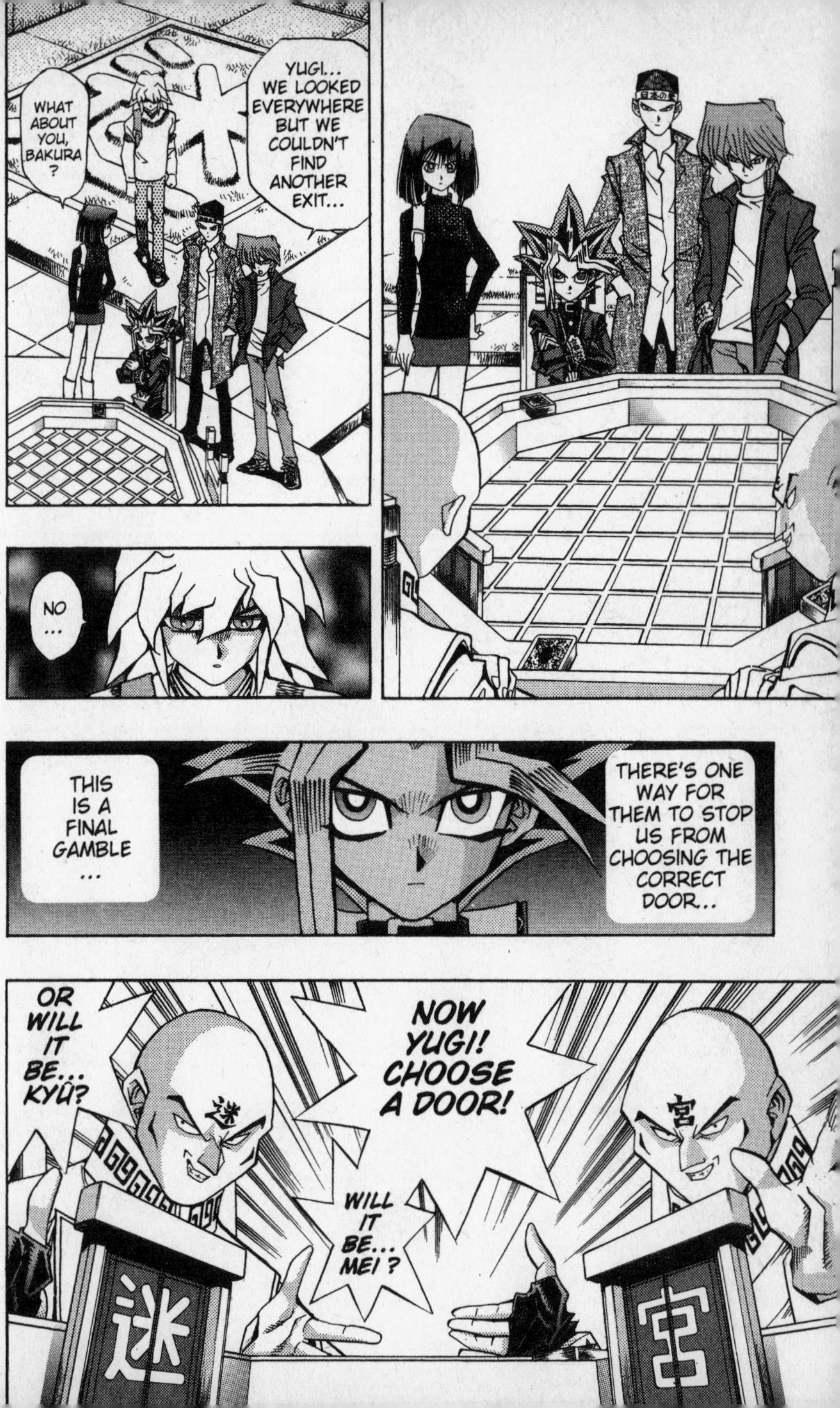
YUGI... WE LOOKED EVERYWHERE BUT WE COULDN'T FIND ANOTHER EXIT...
WHAT ABOUT YOU, BAKURA?
NO...
THERE'S ONE WAY FOR THEM TO STOP US FROM CHOOSING THE CORRECT DOOR...
THIS IS A FINAL GAMBLE...
NOW YUGI! CHOOSE A DOOR!
WILL IT BE... MEI?
OR WILL IT BE... KYŪ?
迷
宮

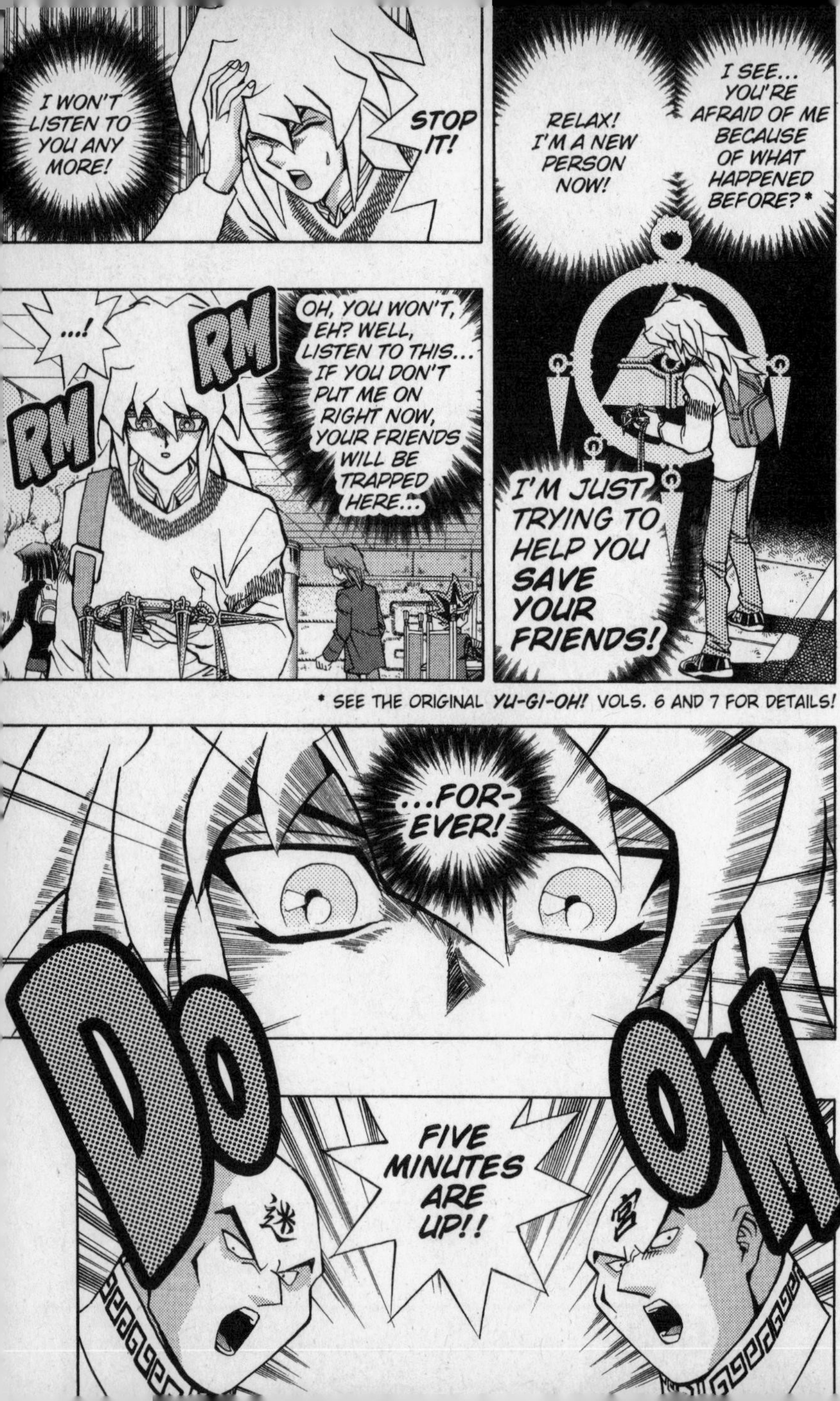
I SEE... YOU'RE AFRAID OF ME BECAUSE OF WHAT HAPPENED BEFORE?*
RELAX! I'M A NEW PERSON NOW!
I'M JUST TRYING TO HELP YOU SAVE YOUR FRIENDS!
STOP IT!
I WON'T LISTEN TO YOU ANY MORE!
OH, YOU WON'T, EH? WELL, LISTEN TO THIS... IF YOU DON'T PUT ME ON RIGHT NOW, YOUR FRIENDS WILL BE TRAPPED HERE...
RM
RM
...!
...FOR-EVER!
DOOM
FIVE MINUTES ARE UP!!

* SEE THE ORIGINAL *YU-GI-OH!* VOLS. 6 AND 7 FOR DETAILS!

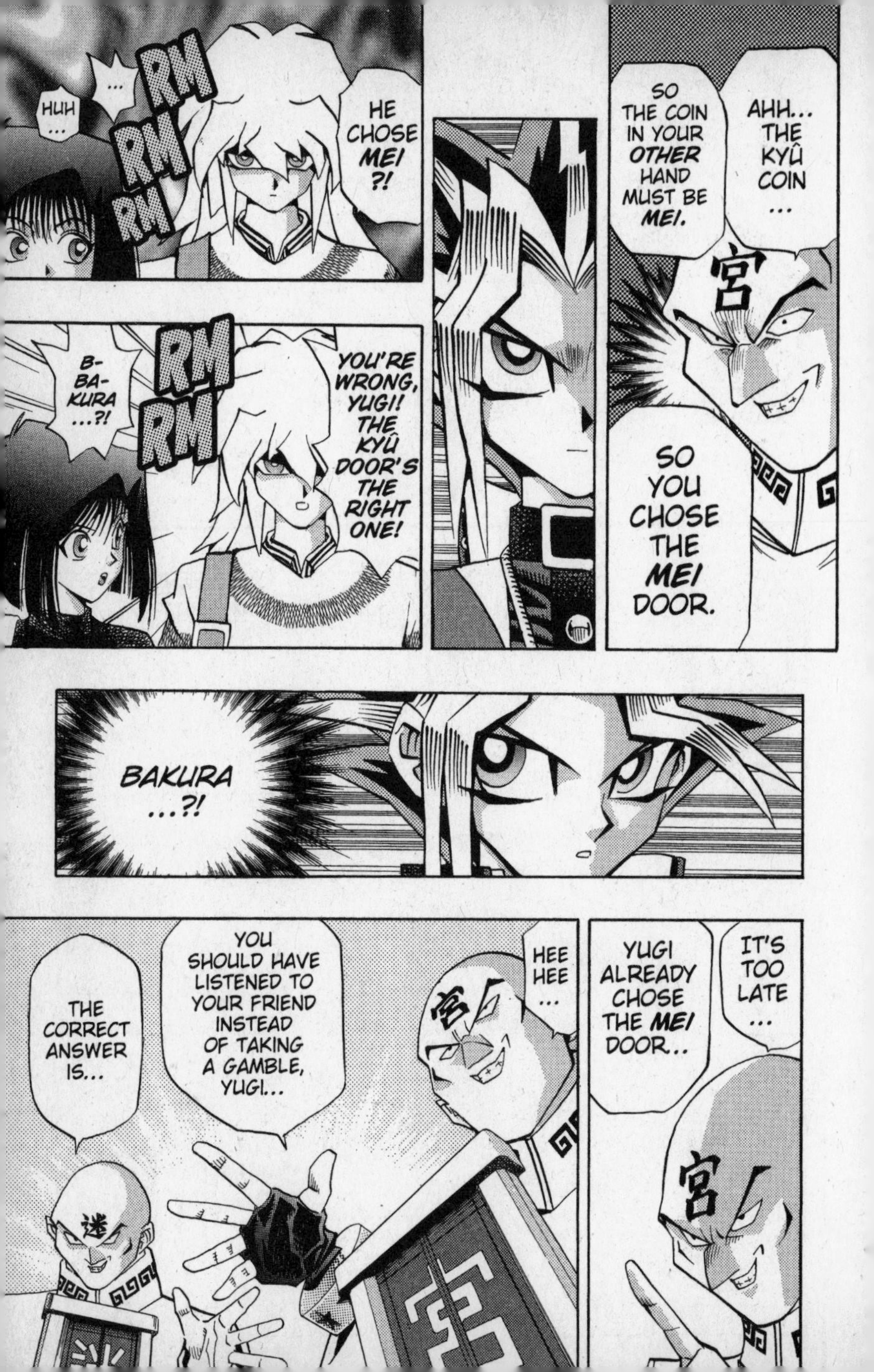

AHH... THE KYÛ COIN...
SO THE COIN IN YOUR OTHER HAND MUST BE MEI.
SO YOU CHOSE THE MEI DOOR.
HE CHOSE MEI?!
RM RM RM
...
HUH...
YOU'RE WRONG, YUGI! THE KYÛ DOOR'S THE RIGHT ONE!
RM RM
B-BAKURA...?!
BAKURA...?!
IT'S TOO LATE...
YUGI ALREADY CHOSE THE MEI DOOR...
HEE HEE...
YOU SHOULD HAVE LISTENED TO YOUR FRIEND INSTEAD OF TAKING A GAMBLE, YUGI...
THE CORRECT ANSWER IS...

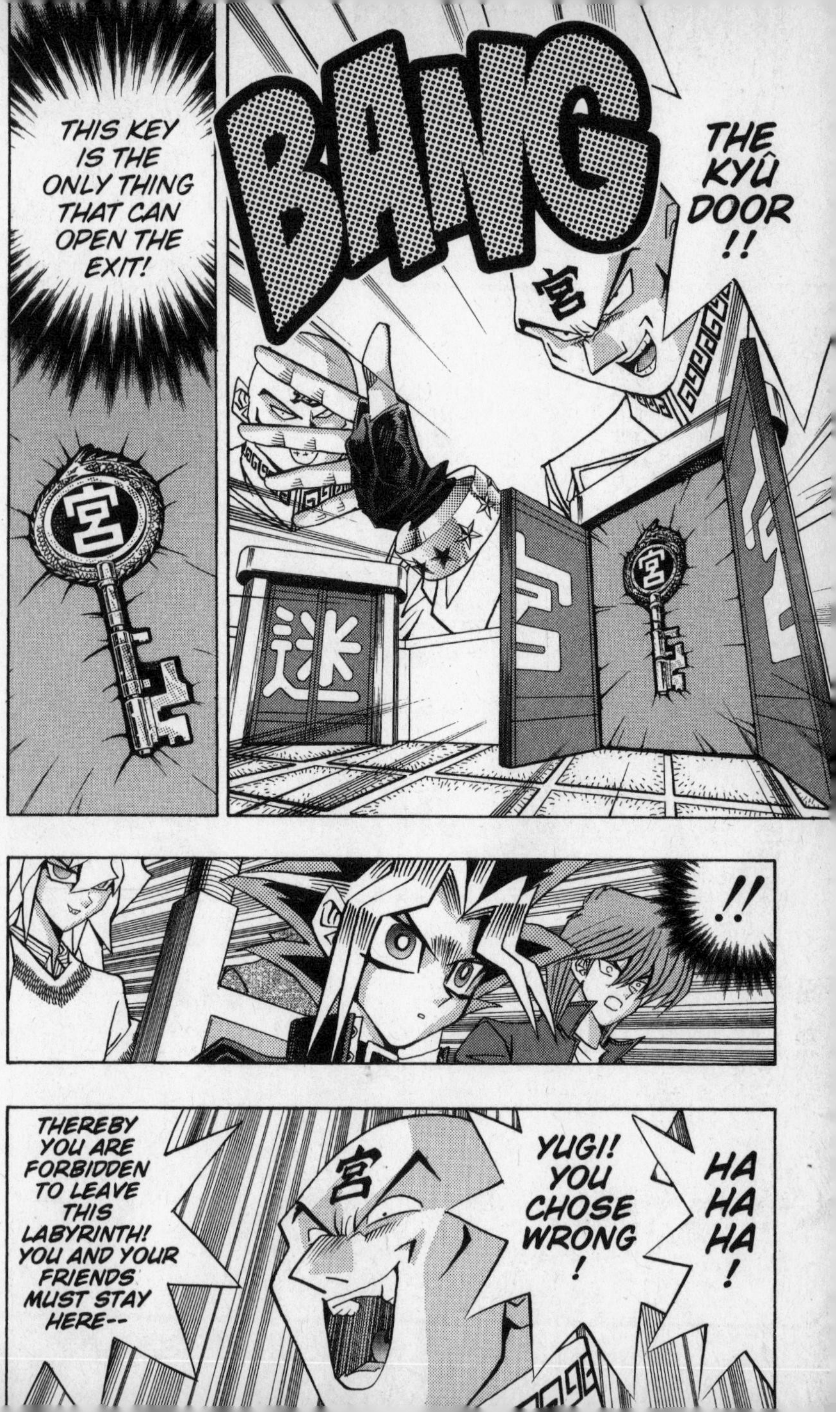
BANG
THE KYÛ DOOR !!
THIS KEY IS THE ONLY THING THAT CAN OPEN THE EXIT!
!!
HA HA HA!
YUGI! YOU CHOSE WRONG!
THEREBY YOU ARE FORBIDDEN TO LEAVE THIS LABYRINTH! YOU AND YOUR FRIENDS MUST STAY HERE--

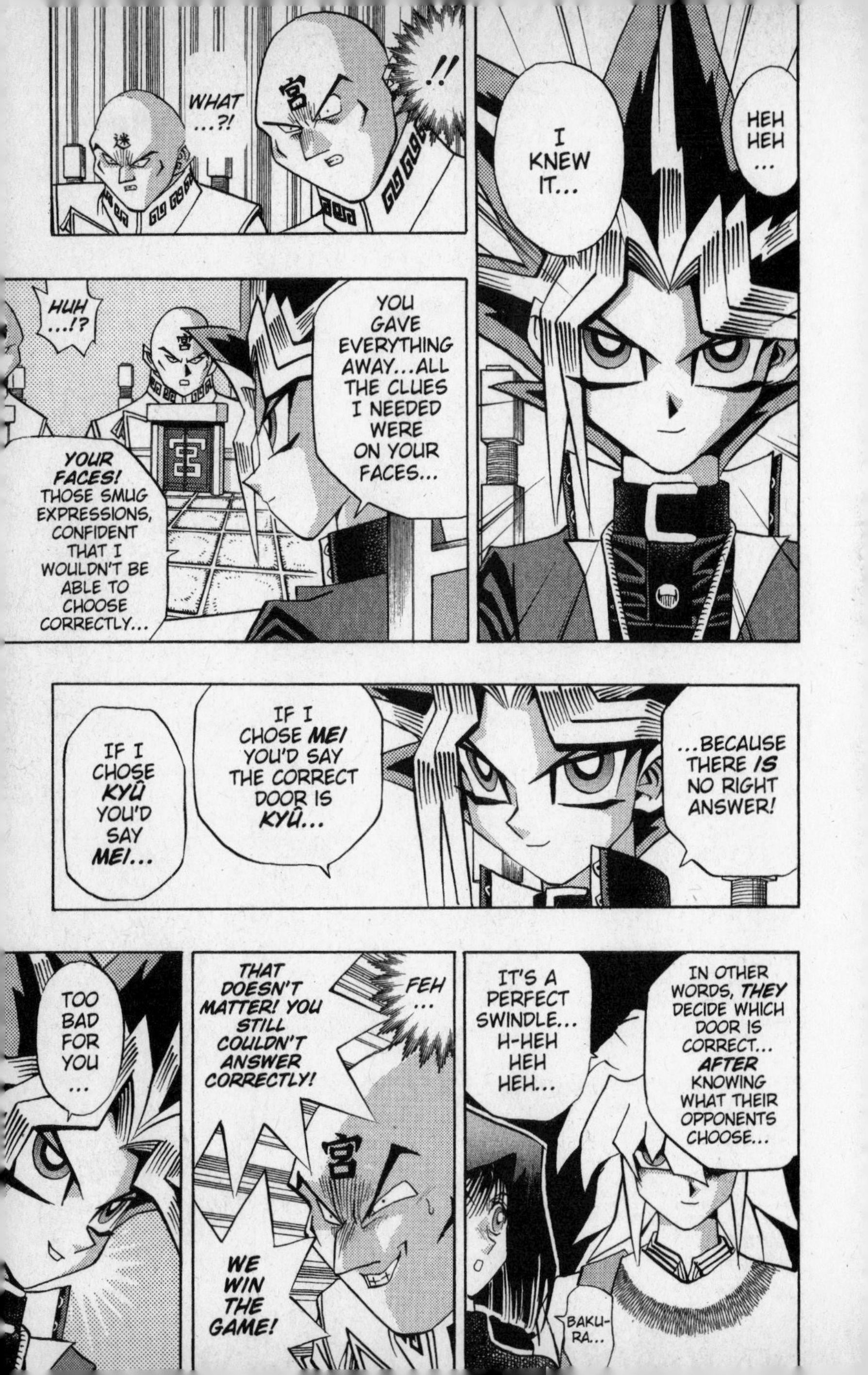
HEH HEH ...
I KNEW IT...
!!
WHAT ...?!
YOU GAVE EVERYTHING AWAY...ALL THE CLUES I NEEDED WERE ON YOUR FACES...
HUH ...!?
YOUR FACES! THOSE SMUG EXPRESSIONS, CONFIDENT THAT I WOULDN'T BE ABLE TO CHOOSE CORRECTLY...
...BECAUSE THERE IS NO RIGHT ANSWER!
IF I CHOSE MEI YOU'D SAY THE CORRECT DOOR IS KYŪ...
IF I CHOSE KYŪ YOU'D SAY MEI...
IN OTHER WORDS, THEY DECIDE WHICH DOOR IS CORRECT... AFTER KNOWING WHAT THEIR OPPONENTS CHOOSE...
IT'S A PERFECT SWINDLE... H-HEH HEH HEH...
BAKU-RA...
FEH ...
THAT DOESN'T MATTER! YOU STILL COULDN'T ANSWER CORRECTLY!
WE WIN THE GAME!
TOO BAD FOR YOU ...

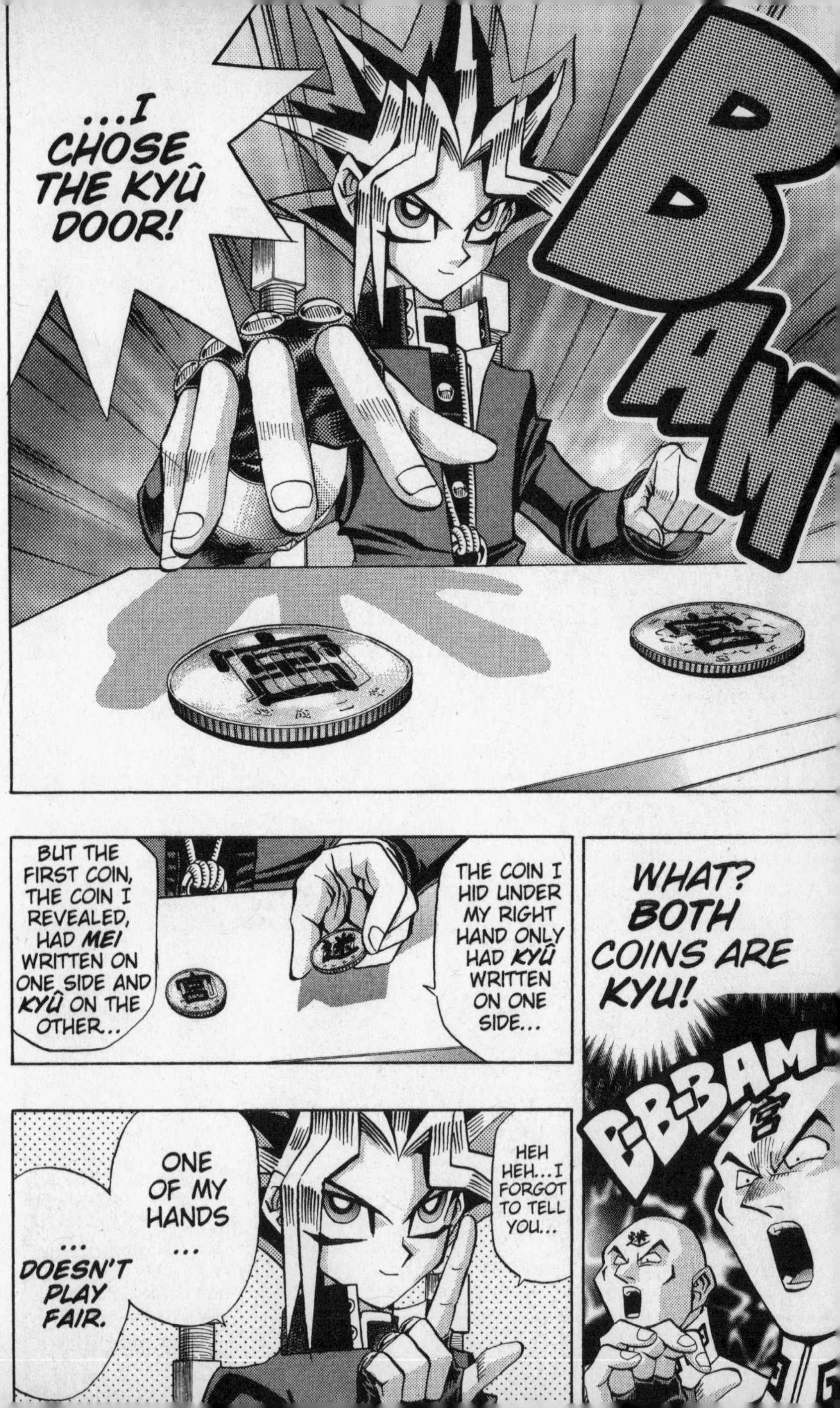
BAM
...I CHOSE THE KYÛ DOOR!
WHAT? BOTH COINS ARE KYU!
B-B-BAM
THE COIN I HID UNDER MY RIGHT HAND ONLY HAD *KYÛ* WRITTEN ON ONE SIDE...
BUT THE FIRST COIN, THE COIN I REVEALED, HAD *MEI* WRITTEN ON ONE SIDE AND *KYÛ* ON THE OTHER...
HEH HEH...I FORGOT TO TELL YOU...
ONE OF MY HANDS ...
... DOESN'T PLAY FAIR.

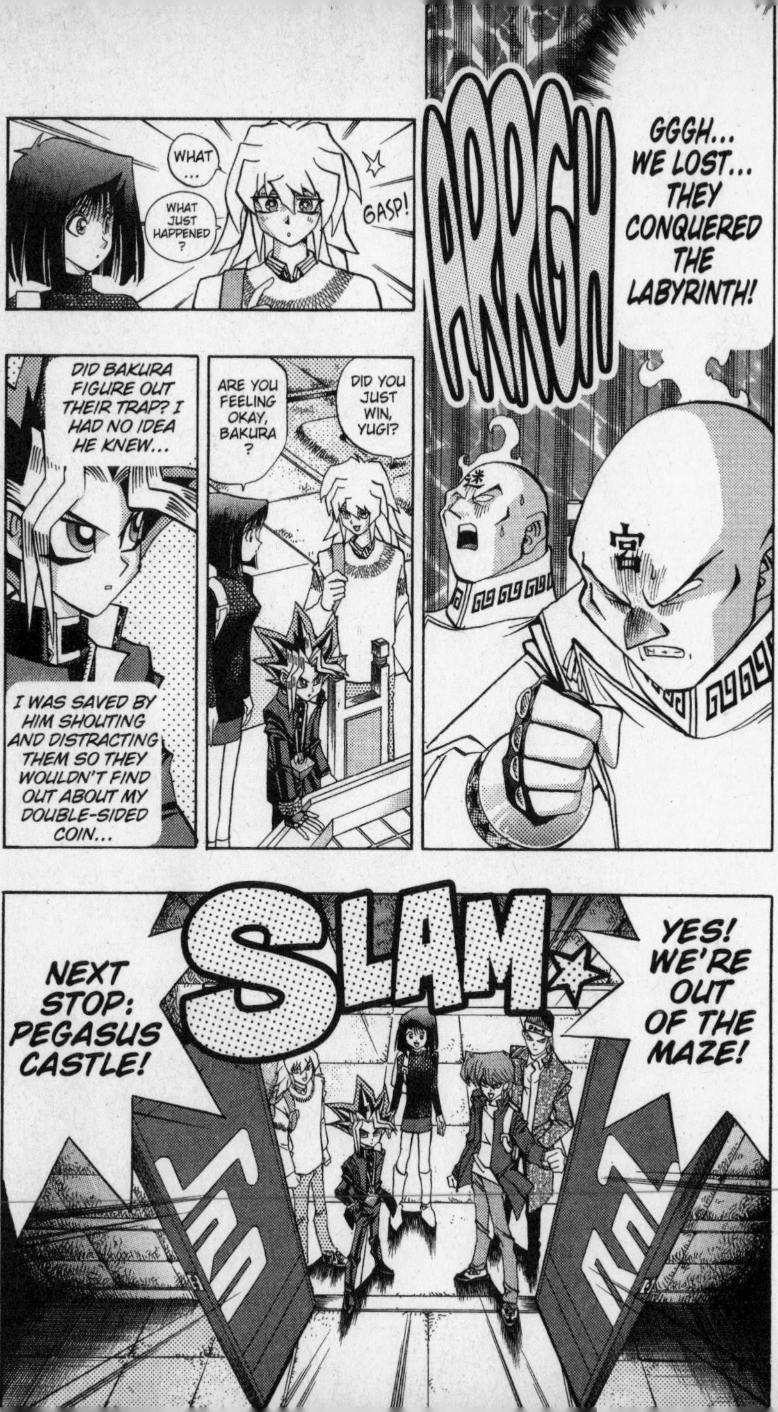
ARRGH
GGGH... WE LOST... THEY CONQUERED THE LABYRINTH!
WHAT...
WHAT JUST HAPPENED?
GASP!
DID YOU JUST WIN, YUGI?
ARE YOU FEELING OKAY, BAKURA?
DID BAKURA FIGURE OUT THEIR TRAP? I HAD NO IDEA HE KNEW...
I WAS SAVED BY HIM SHOUTING AND DISTRACTING THEM SO THEY WOULDN'T FIND OUT ABOUT MY DOUBLE-SIDED COIN...
SLAM
YES! WE'RE OUT OF THE MAZE!
NEXT STOP: PEGASUS CASTLE!

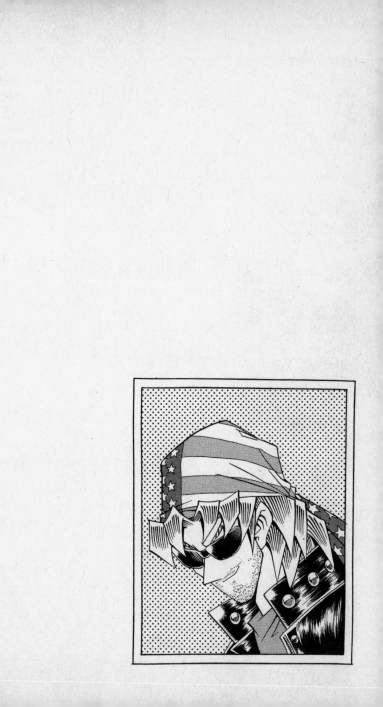

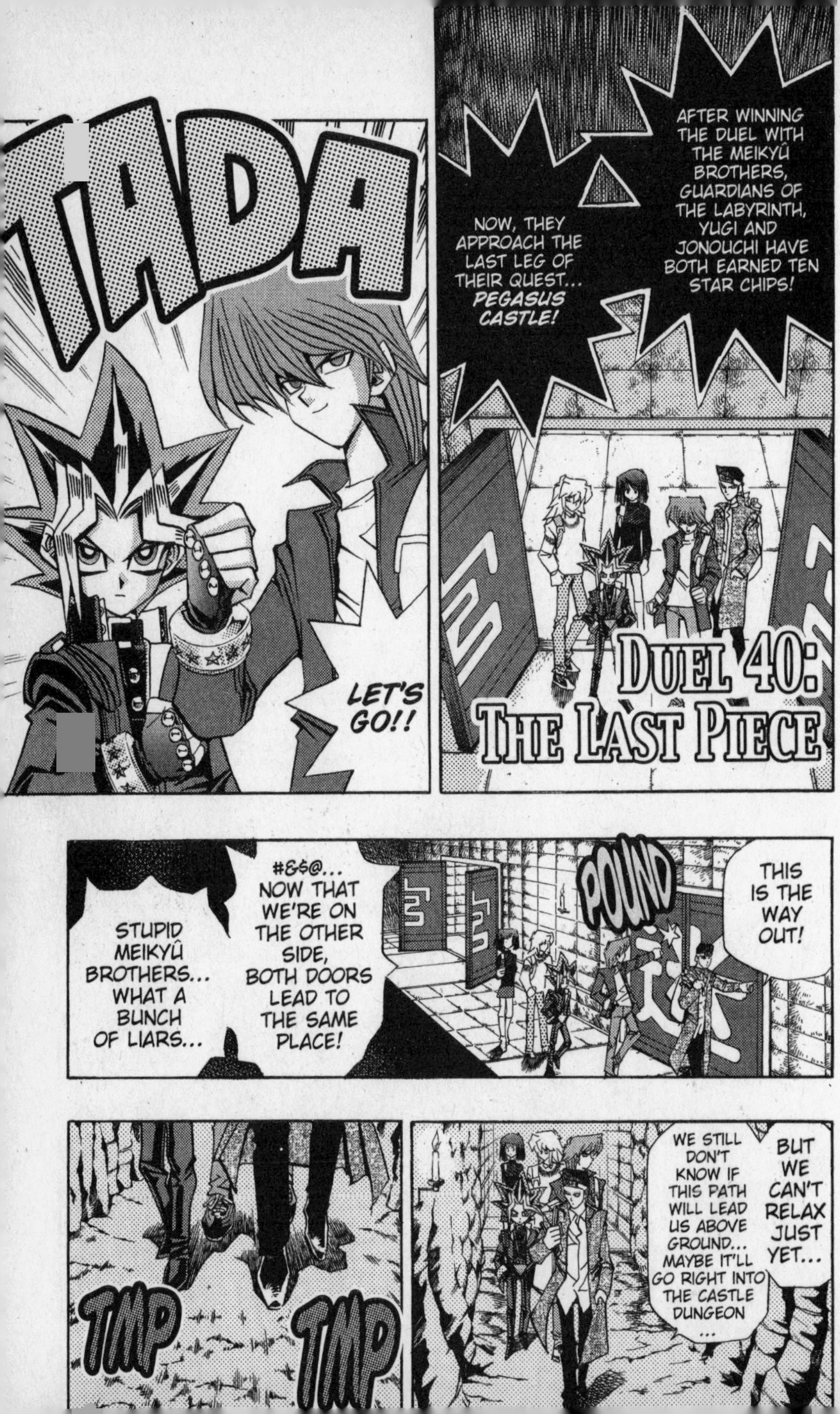
AFTER WINNING THE DUEL WITH THE MEIKYÛ BROTHERS, GUARDIANS OF THE LABYRINTH, YUGI AND JONOUCHI HAVE BOTH EARNED TEN STAR CHIPS!
NOW, THEY APPROACH THE LAST LEG OF THEIR QUEST... *PEGASUS CASTLE!*
DUEL 40: THE LAST PIECE
TADA
LET'S GO!!
THIS IS THE WAY OUT!
POUND
#&$@... NOW THAT WE'RE ON THE OTHER SIDE, BOTH DOORS LEAD TO THE SAME PLACE!
STUPID MEIKYÛ BROTHERS... WHAT A BUNCH OF LIARS...
BUT WE CAN'T RELAX JUST YET...
WE STILL DON'T KNOW IF THIS PATH WILL LEAD US ABOVE GROUND... MAYBE IT'LL GO RIGHT INTO THE CASTLE DUNGEON ...
TMP
TMP

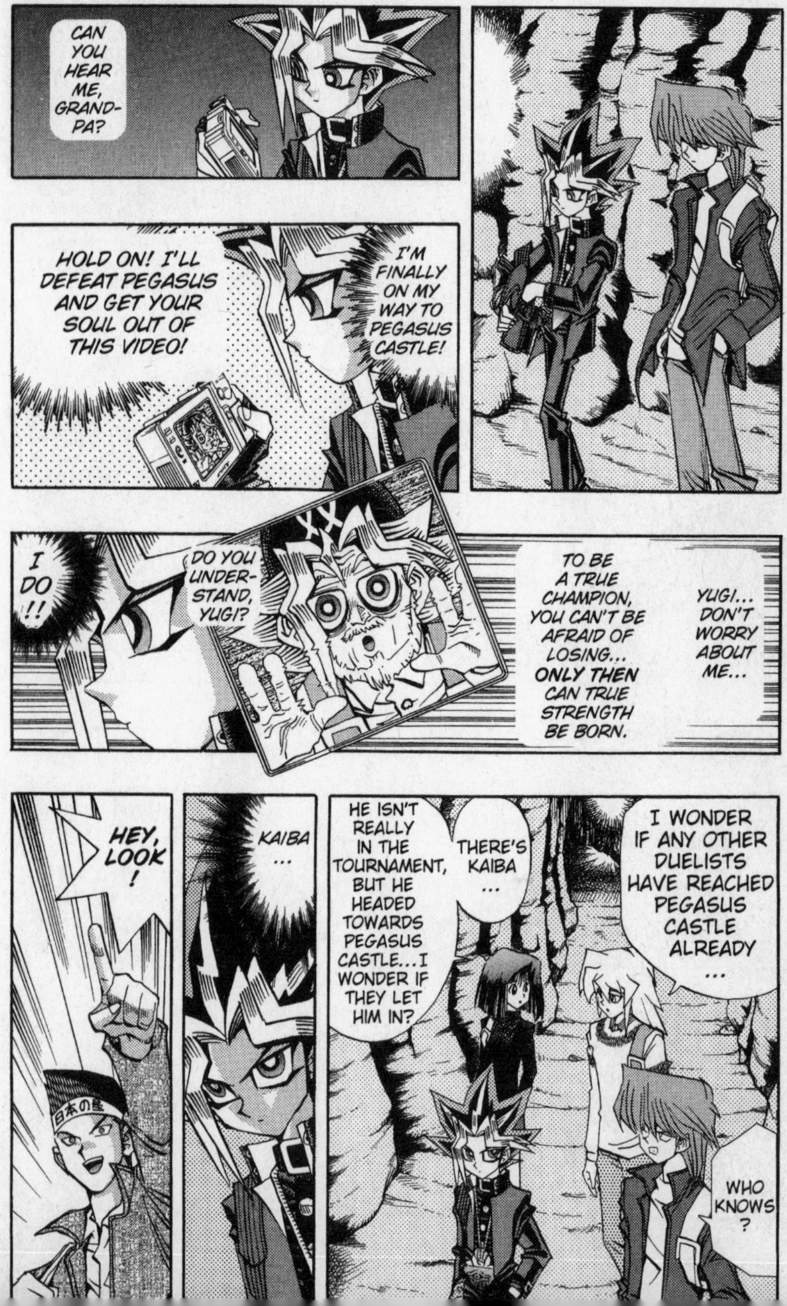
CAN YOU HEAR ME, GRANDPA?
I'M FINALLY ON MY WAY TO PEGASUS CASTLE!
HOLD ON! I'LL DEFEAT PEGASUS AND GET YOUR SOUL OUT OF THIS VIDEO!
YUGI... DON'T WORRY ABOUT ME...
TO BE A TRUE CHAMPION, YOU CAN'T BE AFRAID OF LOSING... ONLY THEN CAN TRUE STRENGTH BE BORN.
DO YOU UNDERSTAND, YUGI?
I DO!!
I WONDER IF ANY OTHER DUELISTS HAVE REACHED PEGASUS CASTLE ALREADY...
WHO KNOWS?
THERE'S KAIBA...
HE ISN'T REALLY IN THE TOURNAMENT, BUT HE HEADED TOWARDS PEGASUS CASTLE...I WONDER IF THEY LET HIM IN?
KAIBA...
HEY, LOOK!
日本の星

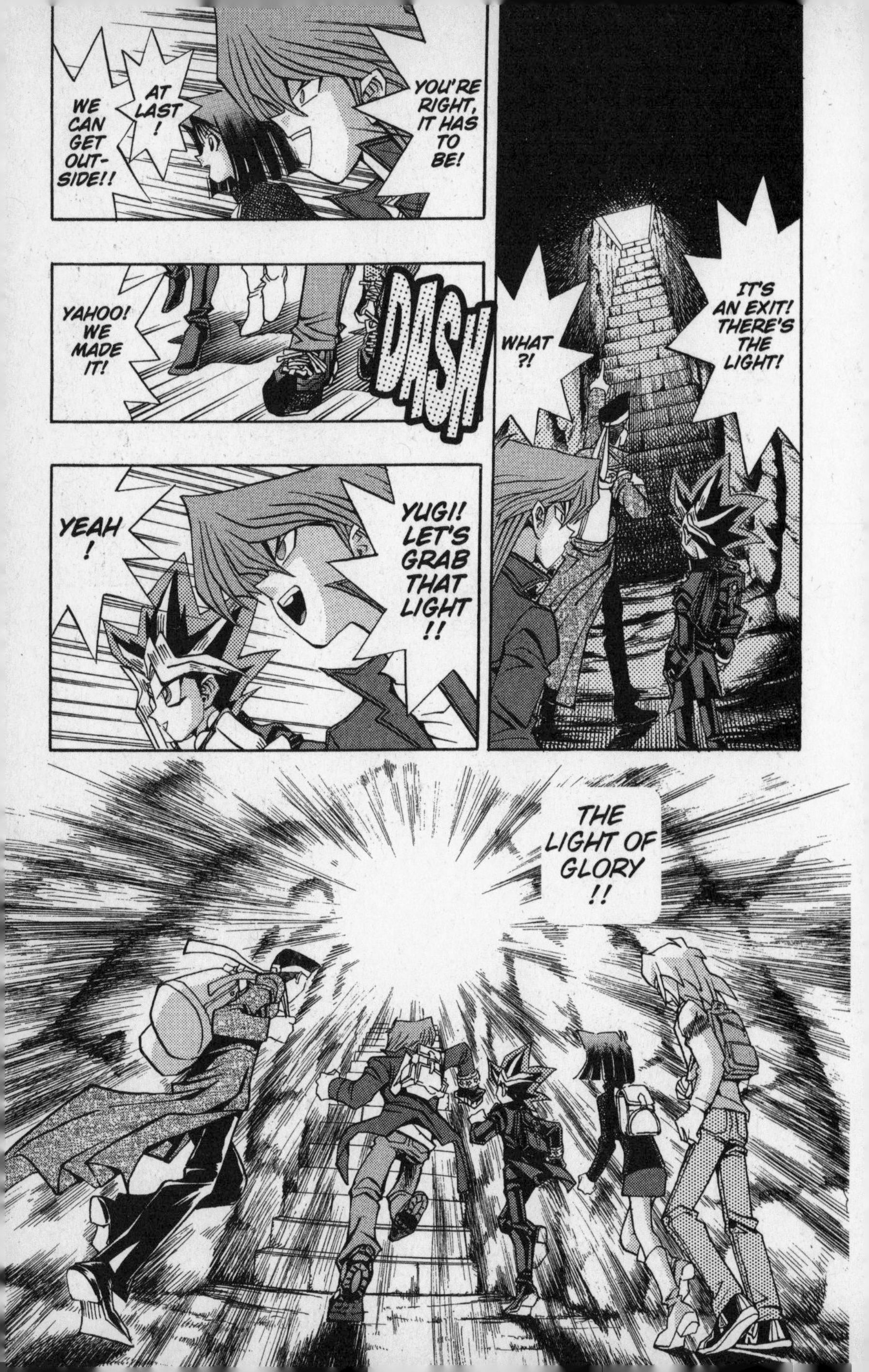
IT'S AN EXIT! THERE'S THE LIGHT!
WHAT ?!
YOU'RE RIGHT, IT HAS TO BE!
AT LAST !
WE CAN GET OUT-SIDE!!
DASH
YAHOO! WE MADE IT!
YUGI! LET'S GRAB THAT LIGHT !!
YEAH !
THE LIGHT OF GLORY !!

DUEL 40: THE LAST PIECE

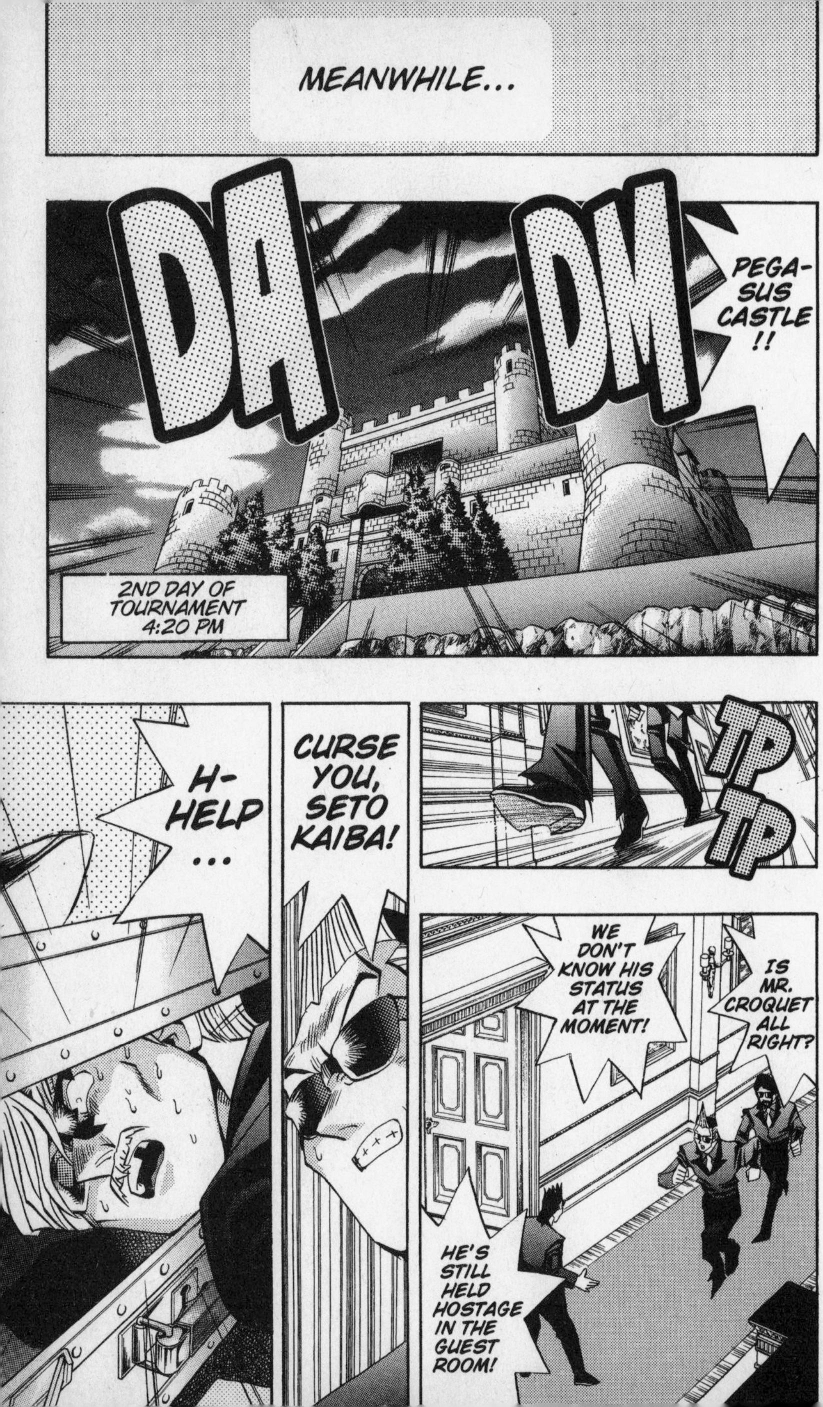
MEANWHILE...
DA DM
PEGA-SUS CASTLE!!
2ND DAY OF TOURNAMENT 4:20 PM
TP TP
IS MR. CROQUET ALL RIGHT?
WE DON'T KNOW HIS STATUS AT THE MOMENT!
HE'S STILL HELD HOSTAGE IN THE GUEST ROOM!
CURSE YOU, SETO KAIBA!
H-HELP...

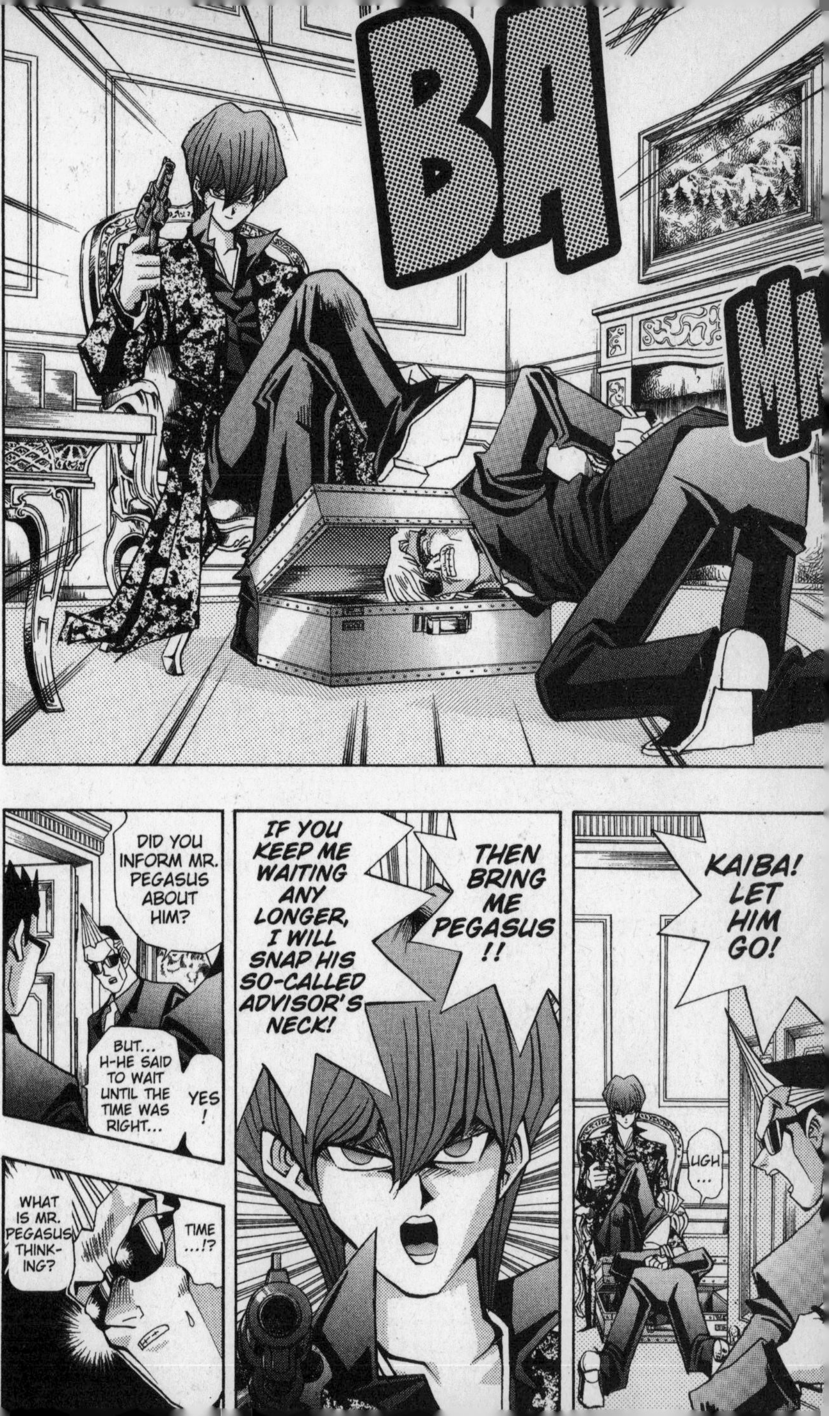
BA
M
KAIBA! LET HIM GO!
UGH...
THEN BRING ME PEGASUS!!
IF YOU KEEP ME WAITING ANY LONGER, I WILL SNAP HIS SO-CALLED ADVISOR'S NECK!
DID YOU INFORM MR. PEGASUS ABOUT HIM?
YES!
BUT... H-HE SAID TO WAIT UNTIL THE TIME WAS RIGHT...
TIME...!?
WHAT IS MR. PEGASUS THINKING?

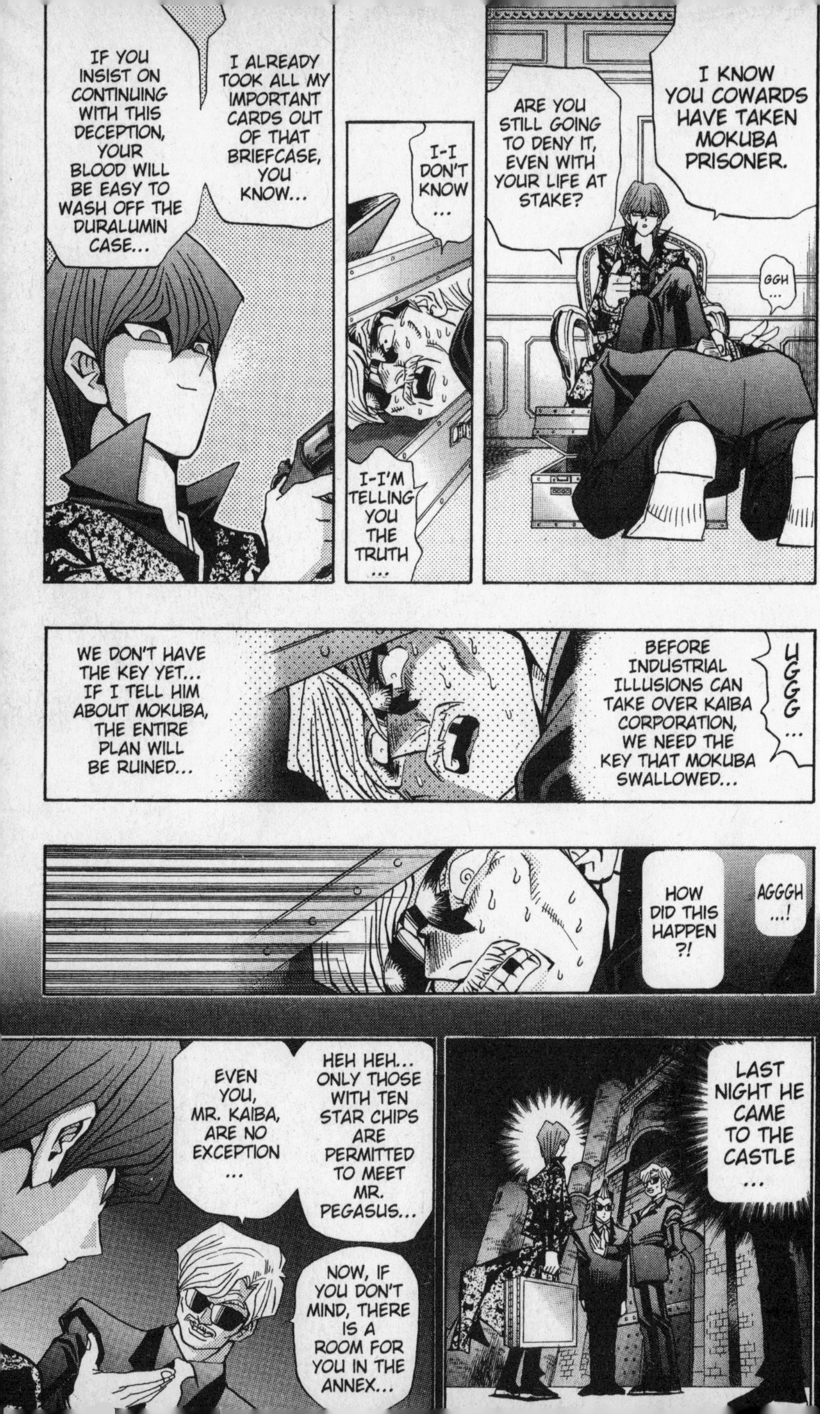
I KNOW YOU COWARDS HAVE TAKEN MOKUBA PRISONER.
ARE YOU STILL GOING TO DENY IT, EVEN WITH YOUR LIFE AT STAKE?
GGH...
I-I DON'T KNOW...
I-I'M TELLING YOU THE TRUTH...
I ALREADY TOOK ALL MY IMPORTANT CARDS OUT OF THAT BRIEFCASE, YOU KNOW...
IF YOU INSIST ON CONTINUING WITH THIS DECEPTION, YOUR BLOOD WILL BE EASY TO WASH OFF THE DURALUMIN CASE...
UGGG...
BEFORE INDUSTRIAL ILLUSIONS CAN TAKE OVER KAIBA CORPORATION, WE NEED THE KEY THAT MOKUBA SWALLOWED...
WE DON'T HAVE THE KEY YET... IF I TELL HIM ABOUT MOKUBA, THE ENTIRE PLAN WILL BE RUINED...
AGGGH...!
HOW DID THIS HAPPEN?!
LAST NIGHT HE CAME TO THE CASTLE...
HEH HEH... ONLY THOSE WITH TEN STAR CHIPS ARE PERMITTED TO MEET MR. PEGASUS...
EVEN YOU, MR. KAIBA, ARE NO EXCEPTION...
NOW, IF YOU DON'T MIND, THERE IS A ROOM FOR YOU IN THE ANNEX...

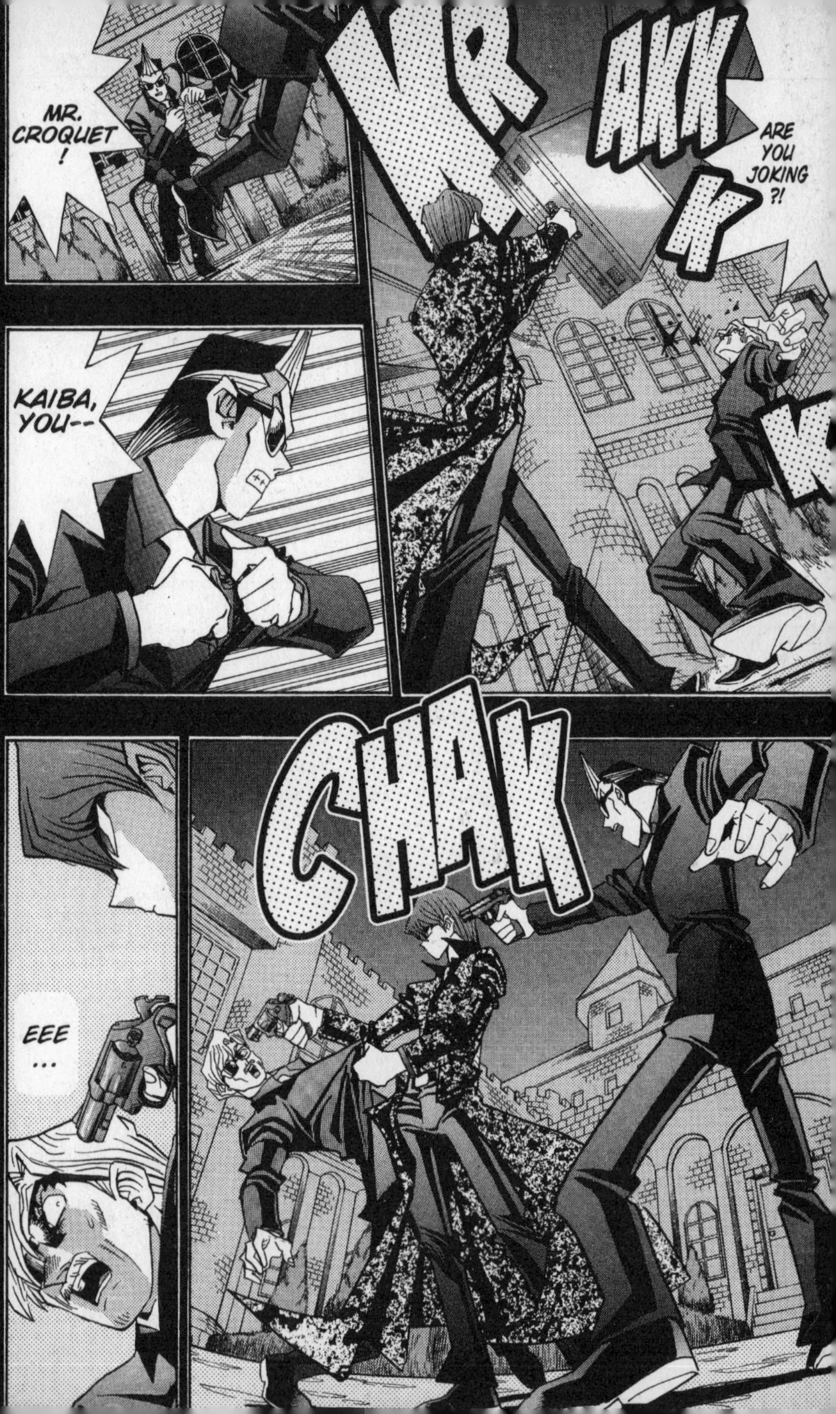
WR
AKK
K
ARE YOU JOKING?!
MR. CROQUET!
KAIBA, YOU--
CHAK
EEE ...

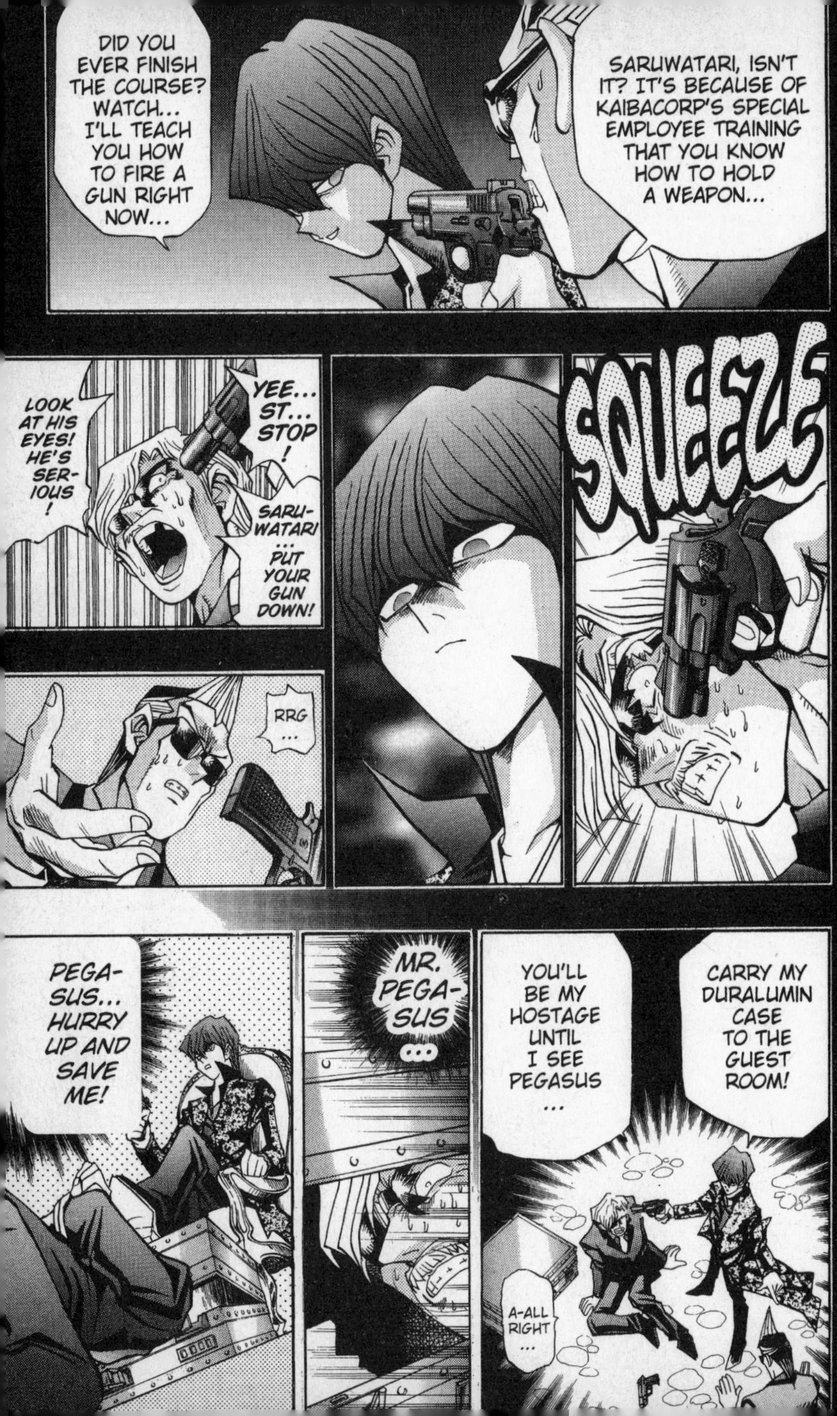
SARUWATARI, ISN'T IT? IT'S BECAUSE OF KAIBACORP'S SPECIAL EMPLOYEE TRAINING THAT YOU KNOW HOW TO HOLD A WEAPON...
DID YOU EVER FINISH THE COURSE? WATCH... I'LL TEACH YOU HOW TO FIRE A GUN RIGHT NOW...
SQUEEZE
YEE... ST... STOP!
SARUWATARI... PUT YOUR GUN DOWN!
LOOK AT HIS EYES! HE'S SERIOUS!
RRG...
CARRY MY DURALUMIN CASE TO THE GUEST ROOM!
YOU'LL BE MY HOSTAGE UNTIL I SEE PEGASUS...
A-ALL RIGHT...
MR. PEGASUS...
PEGASUS... HURRY UP AND SAVE ME!

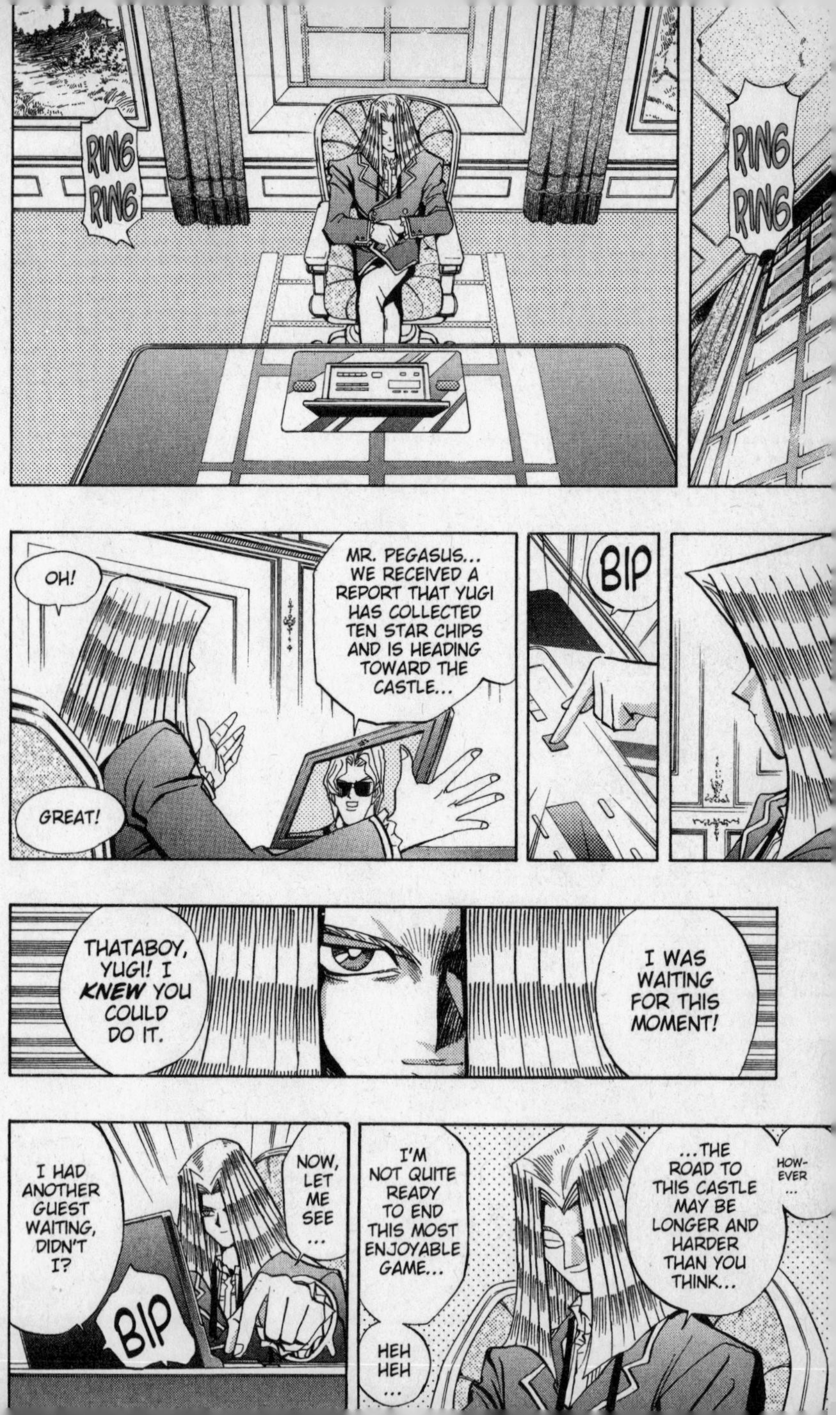
RING RING
RING RING
BIP
MR. PEGASUS... WE RECEIVED A REPORT THAT YUGI HAS COLLECTED TEN STAR CHIPS AND IS HEADING TOWARD THE CASTLE...
OH!
GREAT!
I WAS WAITING FOR THIS MOMENT!
THATABOY, YUGI! I *KNEW* YOU COULD DO IT.
HOW-EVER...
...THE ROAD TO THIS CASTLE MAY BE LONGER AND HARDER THAN YOU THINK...
I'M NOT QUITE READY TO END THIS MOST ENJOYABLE GAME...
HEH HEH...
NOW, LET ME SEE...
I HAD ANOTHER GUEST WAITING, DIDN'T I?
BIP

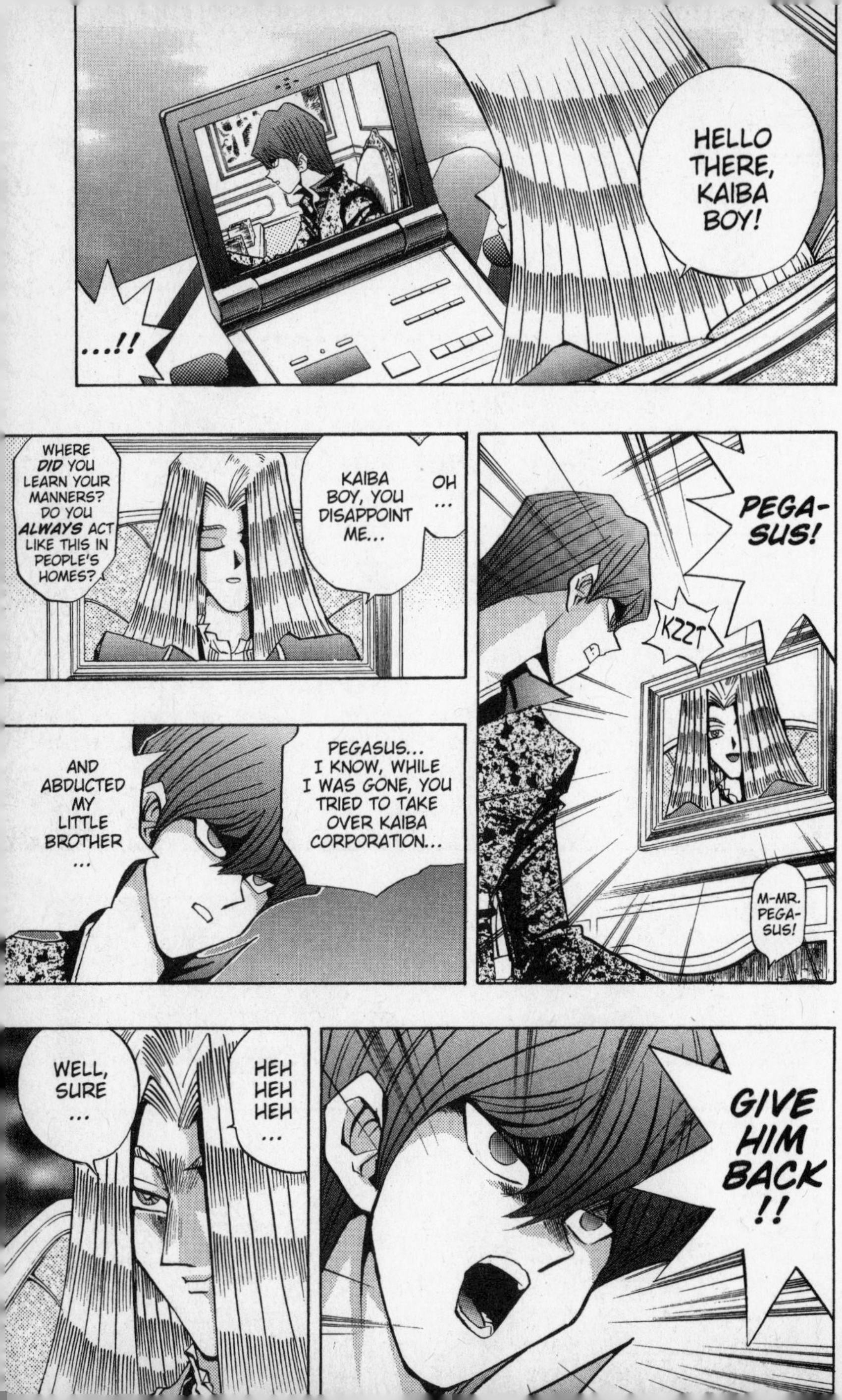
HELLO THERE, KAIBA BOY!
...!!
PEGA-SUS!
KZZT
M-MR. PEGA-SUS!
OH ...
KAIBA BOY, YOU DISAPPOINT ME...
WHERE *DID* YOU LEARN YOUR MANNERS? DO YOU *ALWAYS* ACT LIKE THIS IN PEOPLE'S HOMES?
PEGASUS... I KNOW, WHILE I WAS GONE, YOU TRIED TO TAKE OVER KAIBA CORPORATION...
AND ABDUCTED MY LITTLE BROTHER ...
GIVE HIM BACK !!
HEH HEH HEH ...
WELL, SURE ...

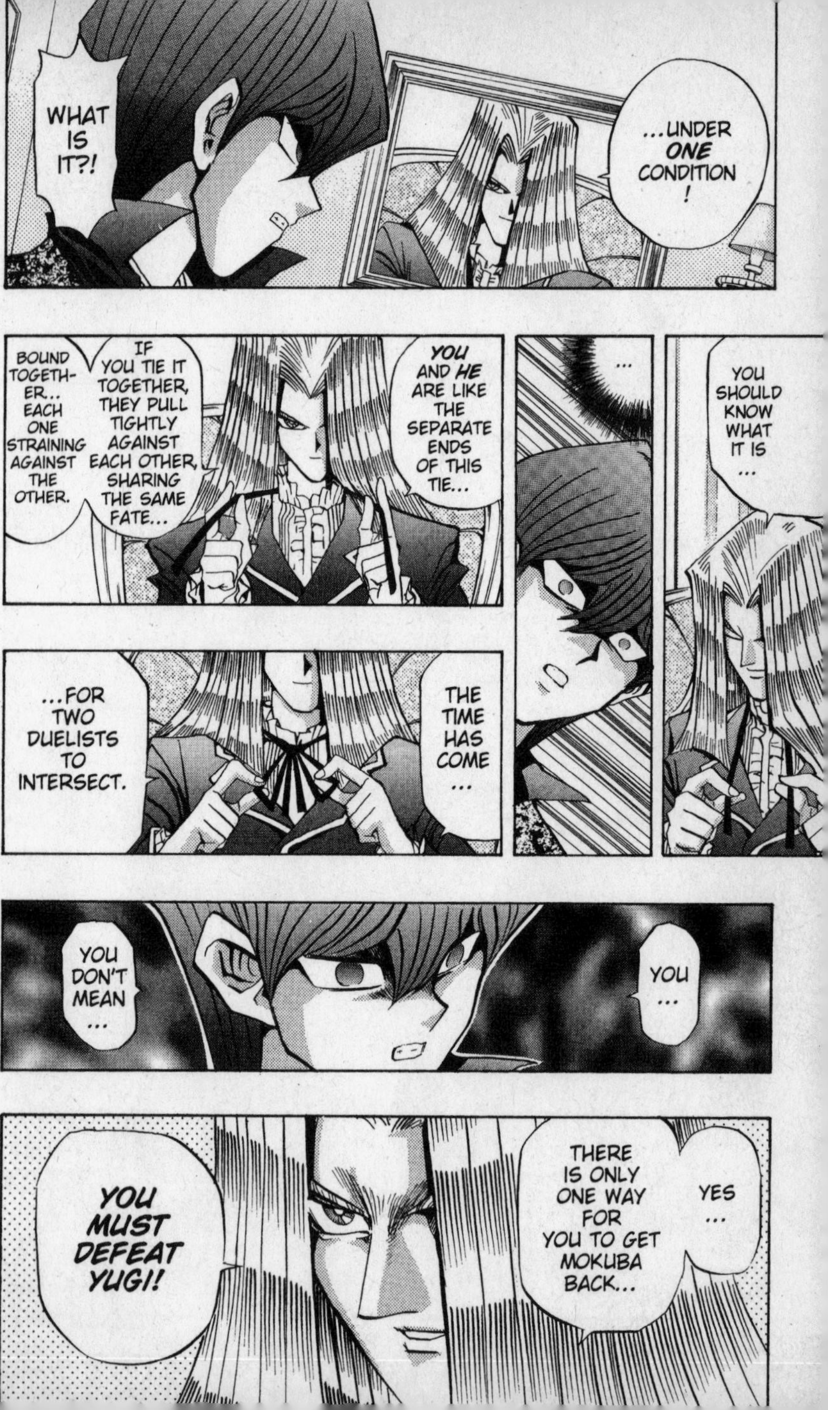
...UNDER *ONE* CONDITION!
WHAT IS IT?!
YOU SHOULD KNOW WHAT IT IS...
...
YOU AND *HE* ARE LIKE THE SEPARATE ENDS OF THIS TIE...
IF YOU TIE IT TOGETHER, THEY PULL TIGHTLY AGAINST EACH OTHER, SHARING THE SAME FATE...
BOUND TOGETHER... EACH ONE STRAINING AGAINST THE OTHER.
THE TIME HAS COME...
...FOR TWO DUELISTS TO INTERSECT.
YOU...
YOU DON'T MEAN...
YES...
THERE IS ONLY ONE WAY FOR YOU TO GET MOKUBA BACK...
YOU MUST DEFEAT YUGI!

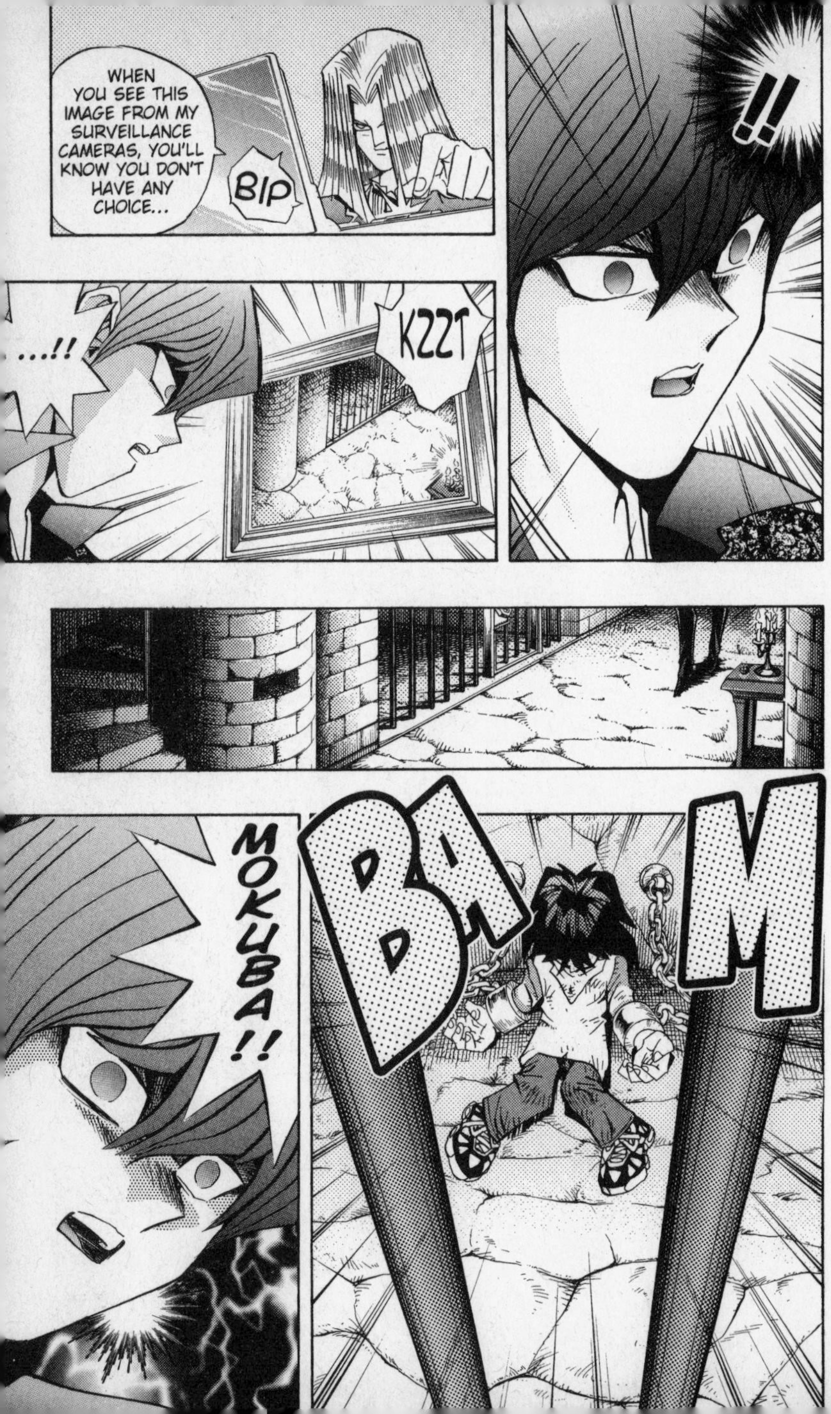
!!
WHEN YOU SEE THIS IMAGE FROM MY SURVEILLANCE CAMERAS, YOU'LL KNOW YOU DON'T HAVE ANY CHOICE...
BIP
KZZT
...!!
BAM
MOKUBA!!

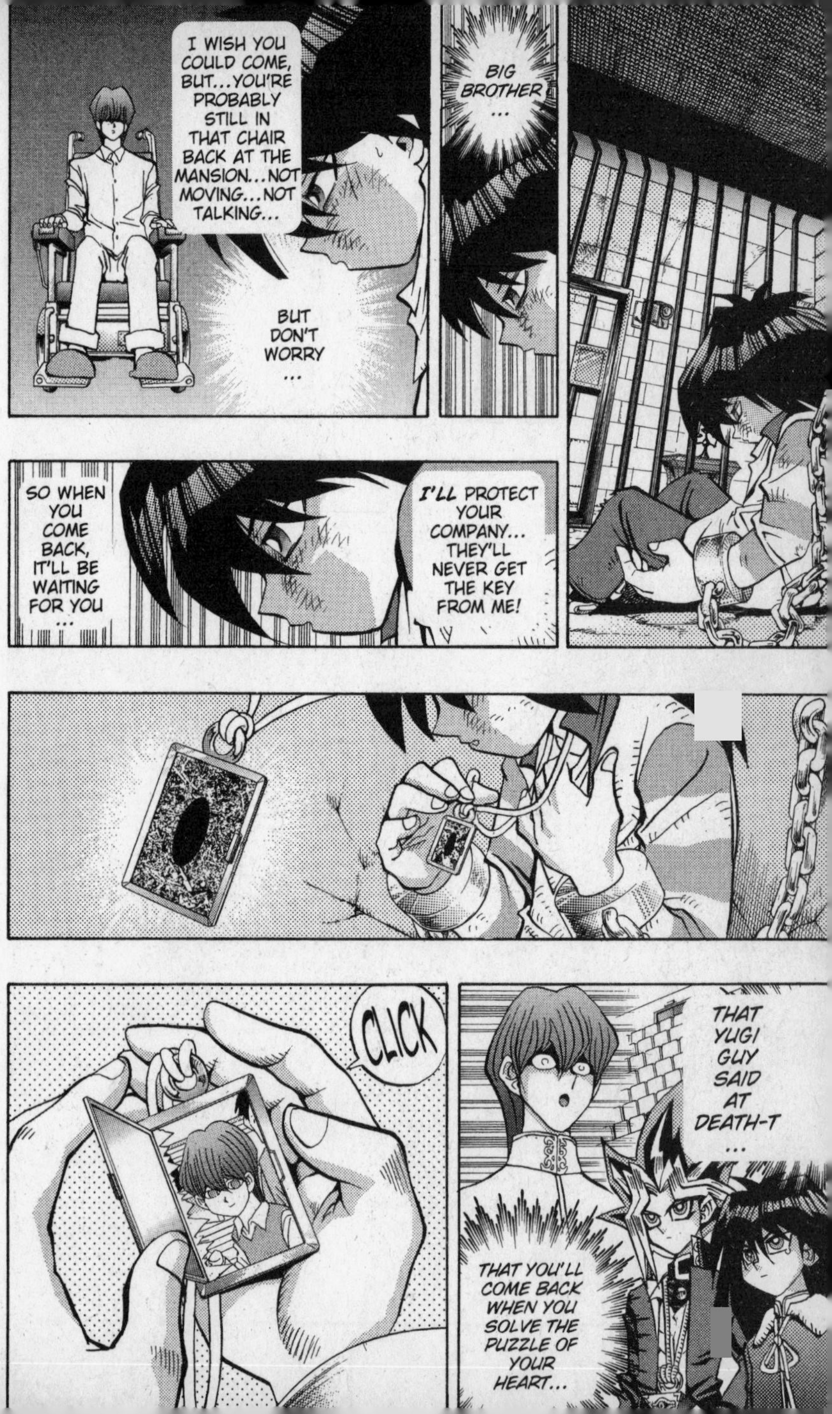
BIG BROTHER...
I WISH YOU COULD COME, BUT...YOU'RE PROBABLY STILL IN THAT CHAIR BACK AT THE MANSION...NOT MOVING...NOT TALKING...
BUT DON'T WORRY...
I'LL PROTECT YOUR COMPANY... THEY'LL NEVER GET THE KEY FROM ME!
SO WHEN YOU COME BACK, IT'LL BE WAITING FOR YOU...
THAT YUGI GUY SAID AT DEATH-T...
THAT YOU'LL COME BACK WHEN YOU SOLVE THE PUZZLE OF YOUR HEART...
CLICK

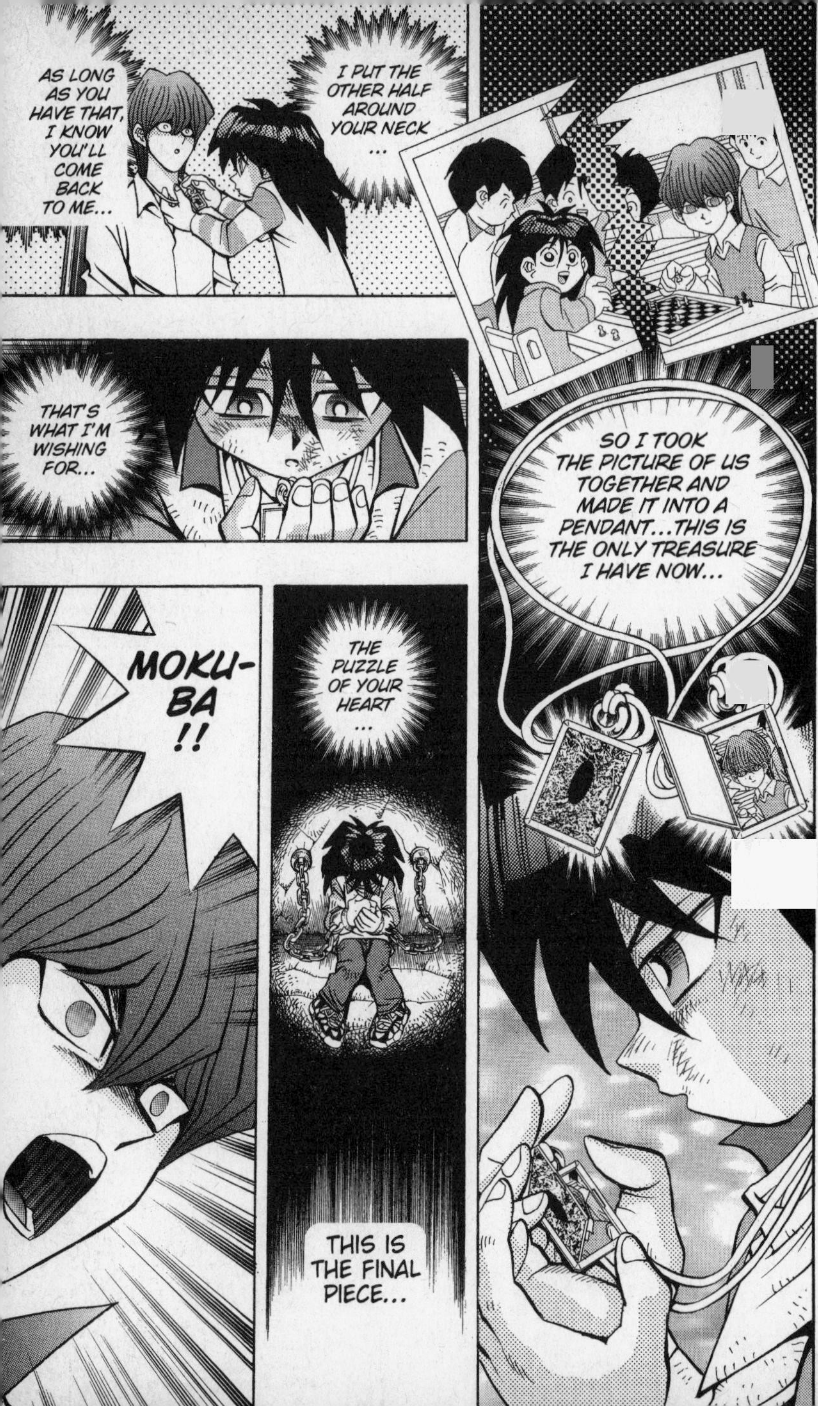
SO I TOOK THE PICTURE OF US TOGETHER AND MADE IT INTO A PENDANT...THIS IS THE ONLY TREASURE I HAVE NOW...
I PUT THE OTHER HALF AROUND YOUR NECK...
AS LONG AS YOU HAVE THAT, I KNOW YOU'LL COME BACK TO ME...
THAT'S WHAT I'M WISHING FOR...
THE PUZZLE OF YOUR HEART...
THIS IS THE FINAL PIECE...
MOKU-BA!!

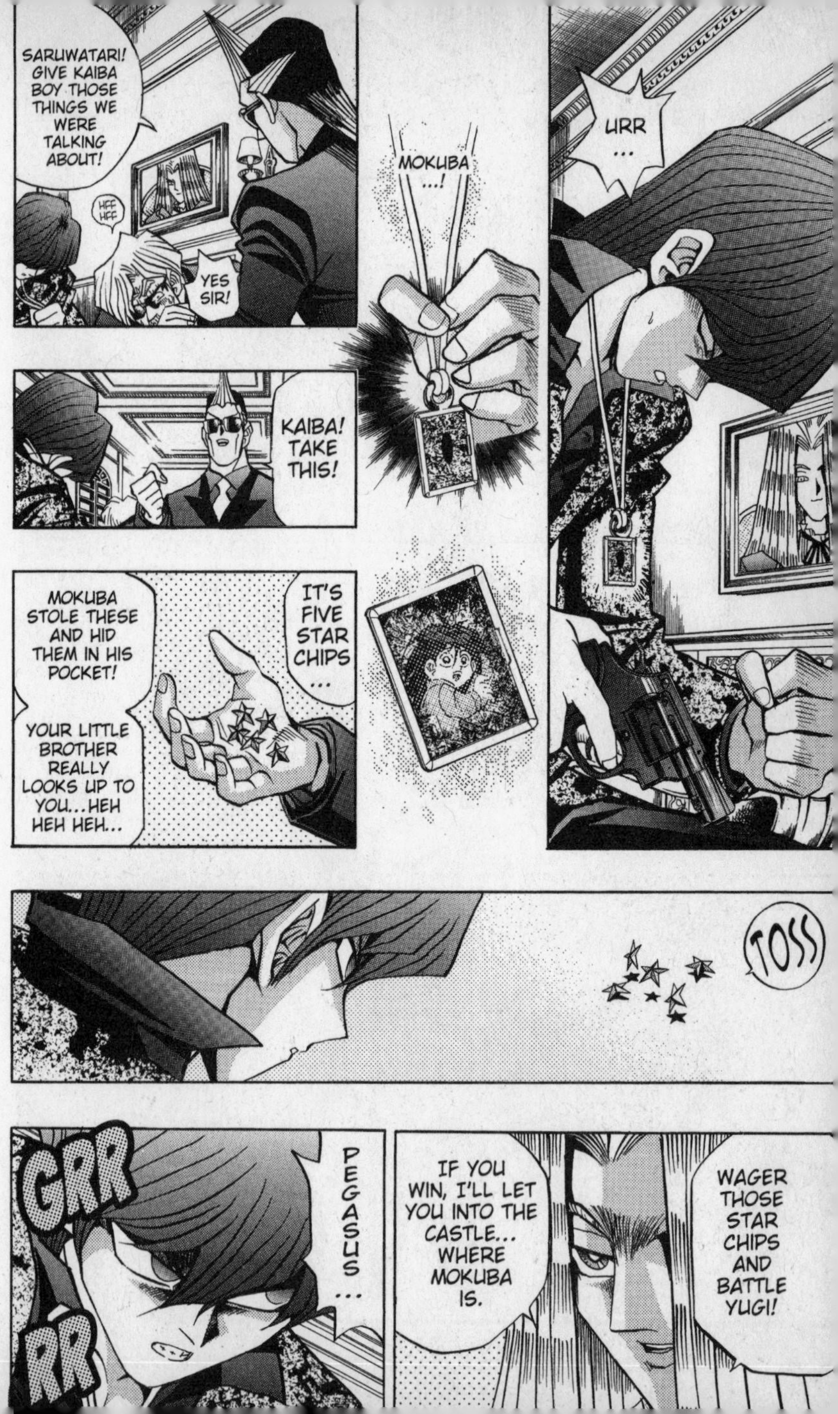
URR ...
MOKUBA ...!
SARUWATARI! GIVE KAIBA BOY THOSE THINGS WE WERE TALKING ABOUT!
YES SIR!
HFF HFF
KAIBA! TAKE THIS!
IT'S FIVE STAR CHIPS ...
MOKUBA STOLE THESE AND HID THEM IN HIS POCKET!
YOUR LITTLE BROTHER REALLY LOOKS UP TO YOU...HEH HEH HEH...
TOSS
WAGER THOSE STAR CHIPS AND BATTLE YUGI!
IF YOU WIN, I'LL LET YOU INTO THE CASTLE... WHERE MOKUBA IS.
PEGASUS ...
GRR RR

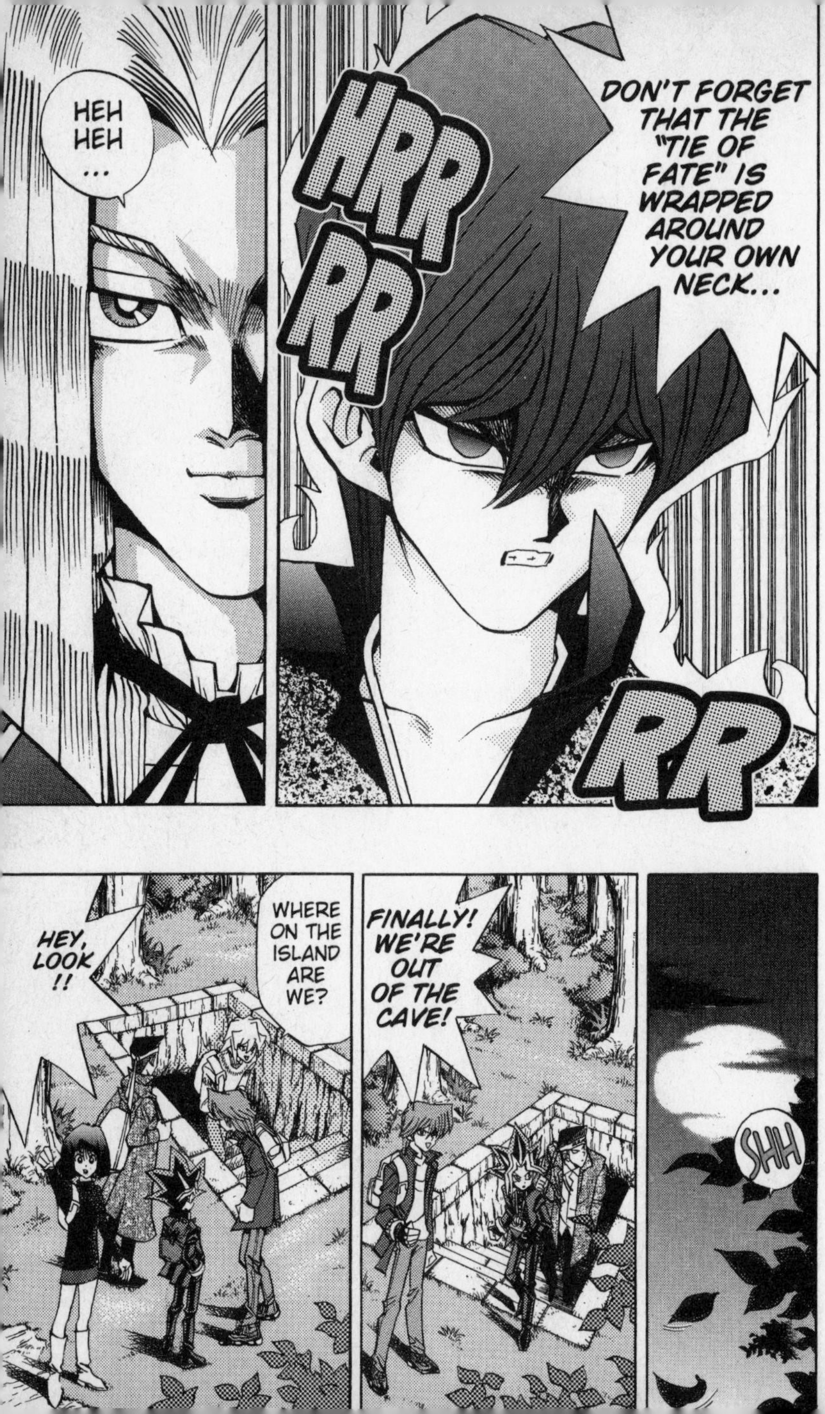
HRR RR
DON'T FORGET THAT THE "TIE OF FATE" IS WRAPPED AROUND YOUR OWN NECK...
RR
HEH HEH ...
SHH
FINALLY! WE'RE OUT OF THE CAVE!
WHERE ON THE ISLAND ARE WE?
HEY, LOOK!!

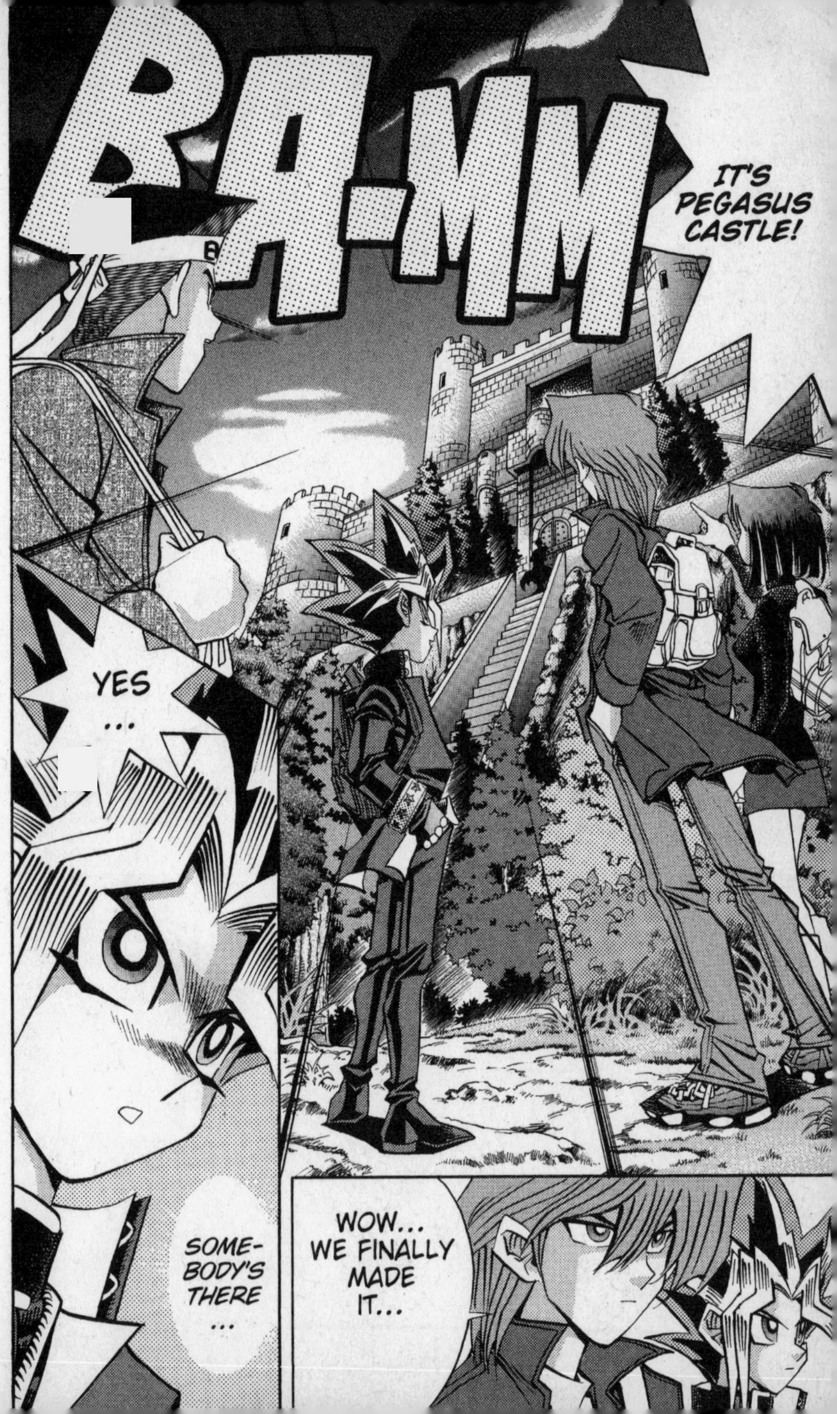
BA-MM
IT'S PEGASUS CASTLE!
WOW... WE FINALLY MADE IT...
YES...
SOME-BODY'S THERE...

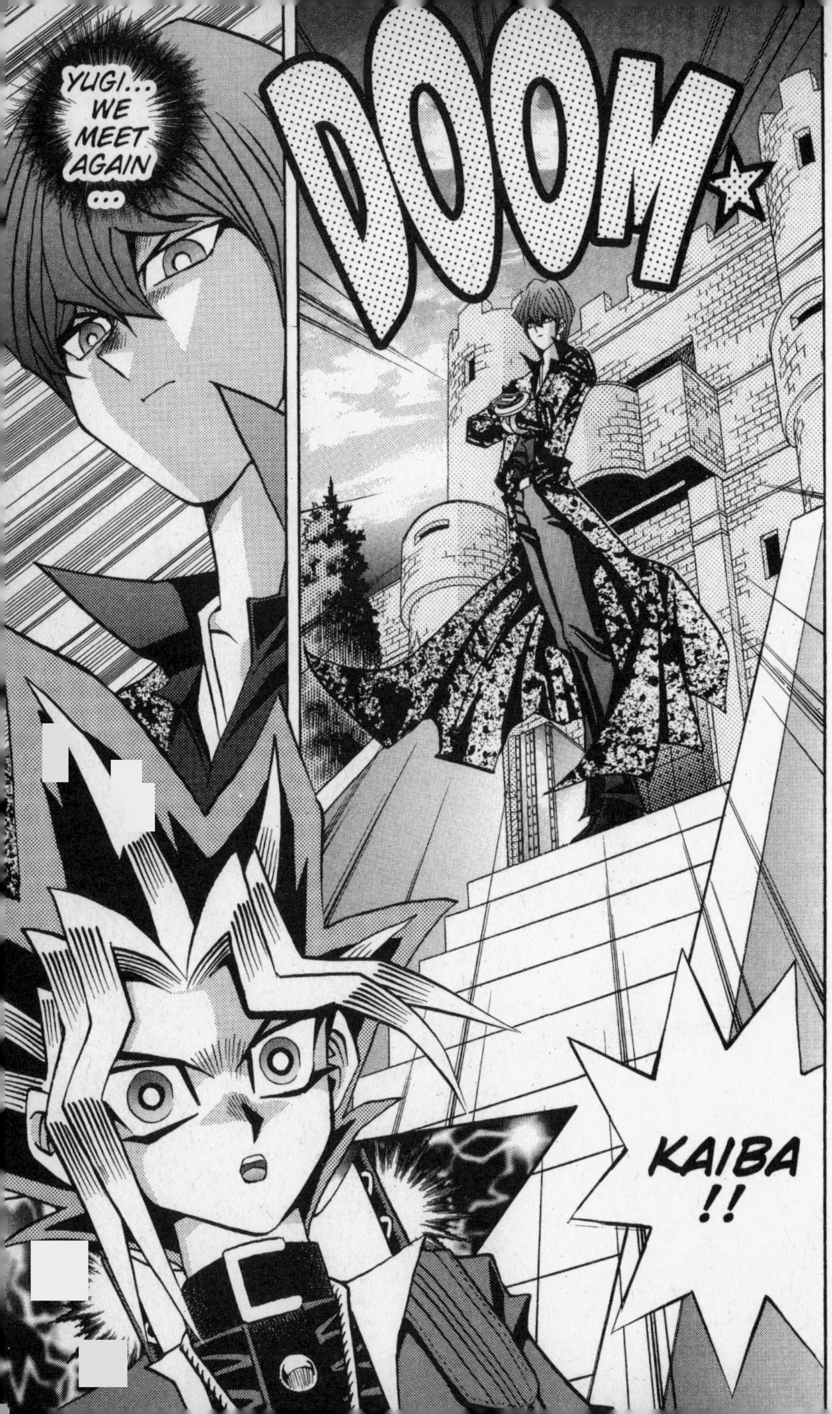
DOOM
YUGI... WE MEET AGAIN...
KAIBA!!

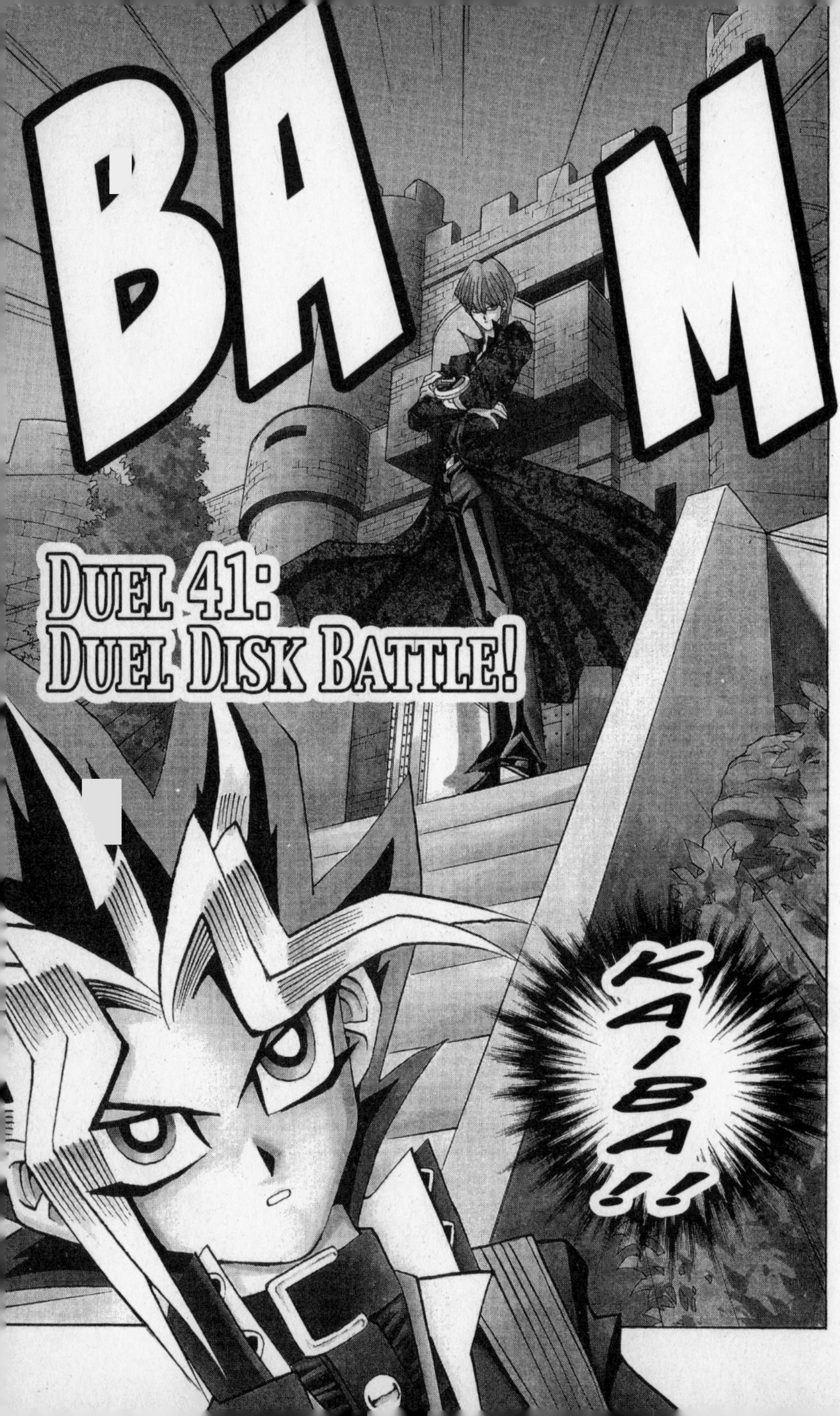
BAM
DUEL 41:
DUEL DISK BATTLE!
KAIBA!!

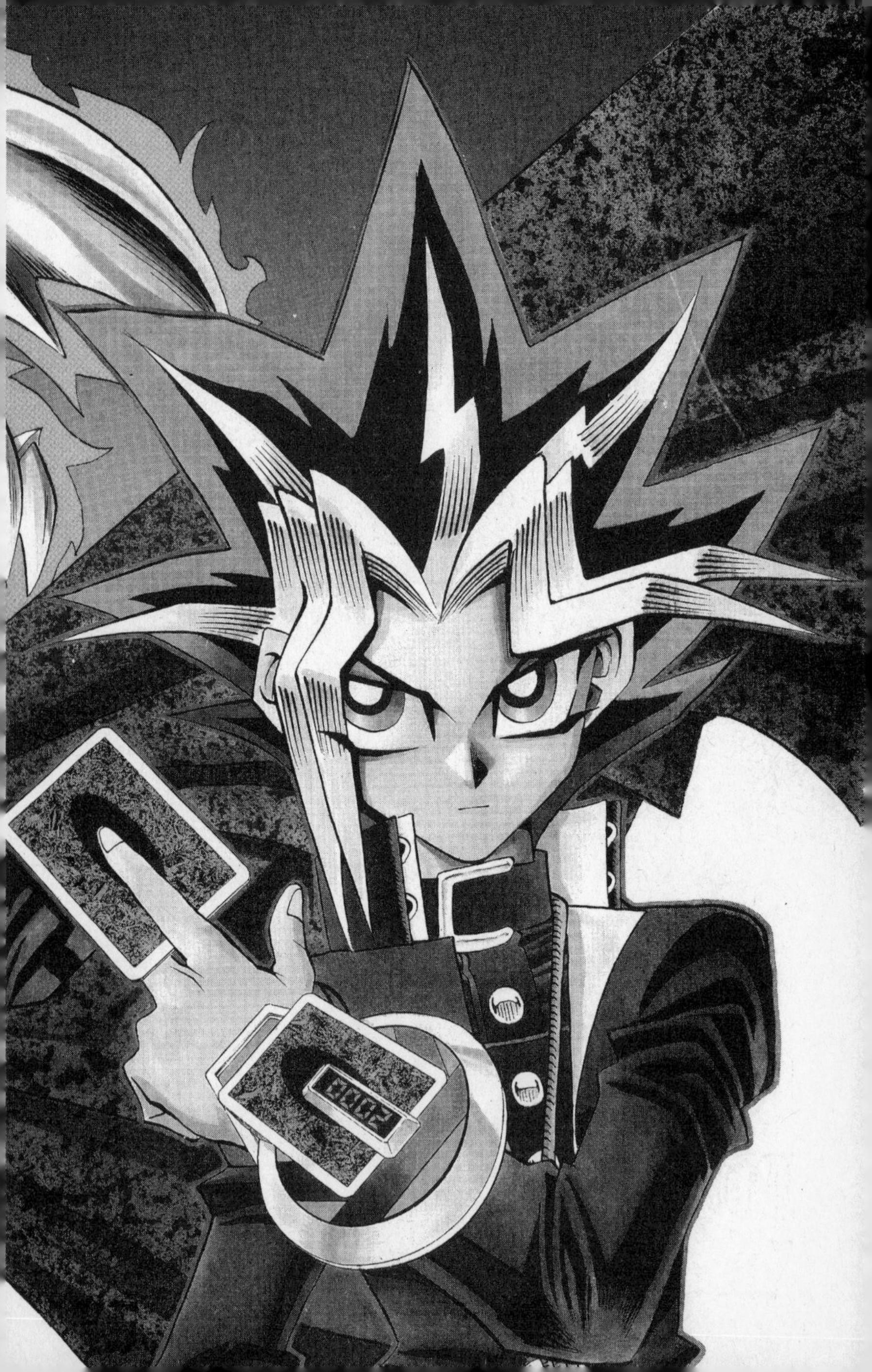

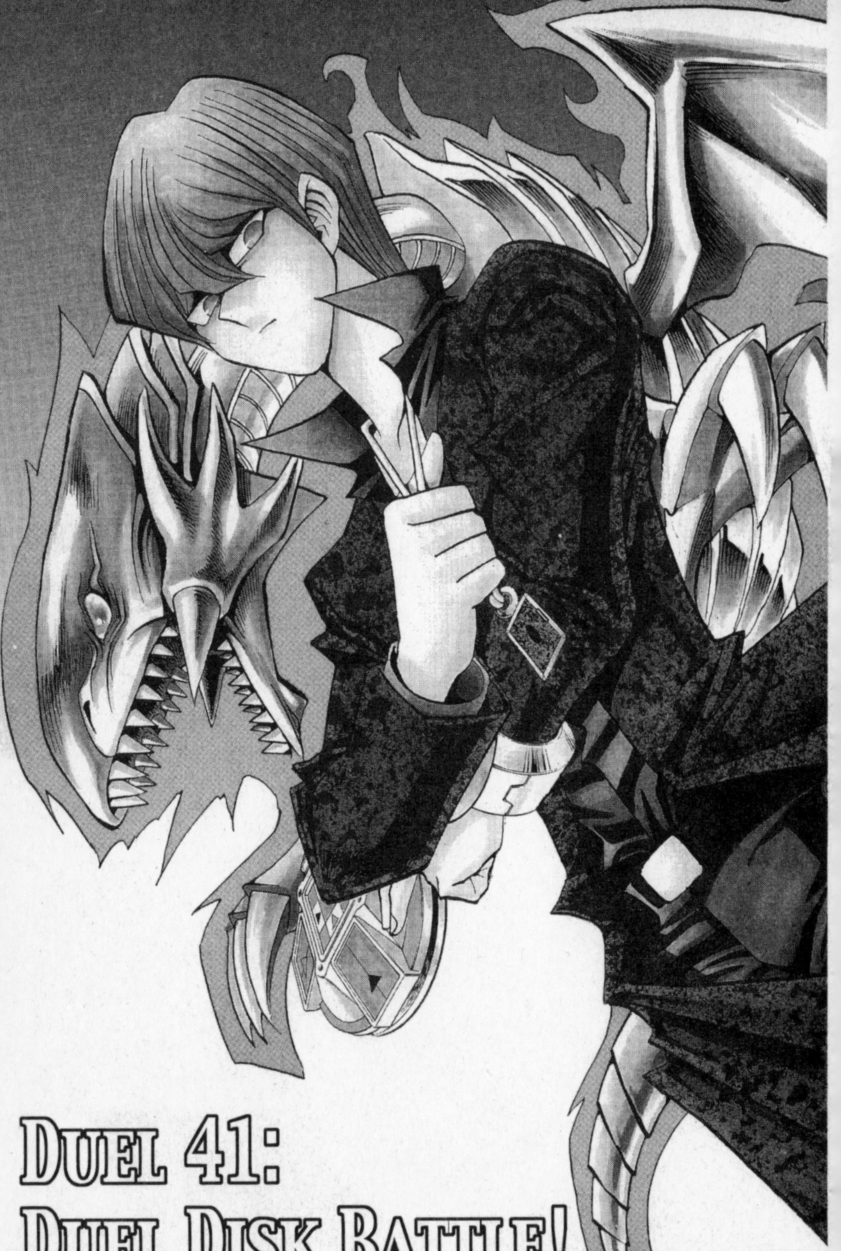

Duel 41: Duel Disk Battle!

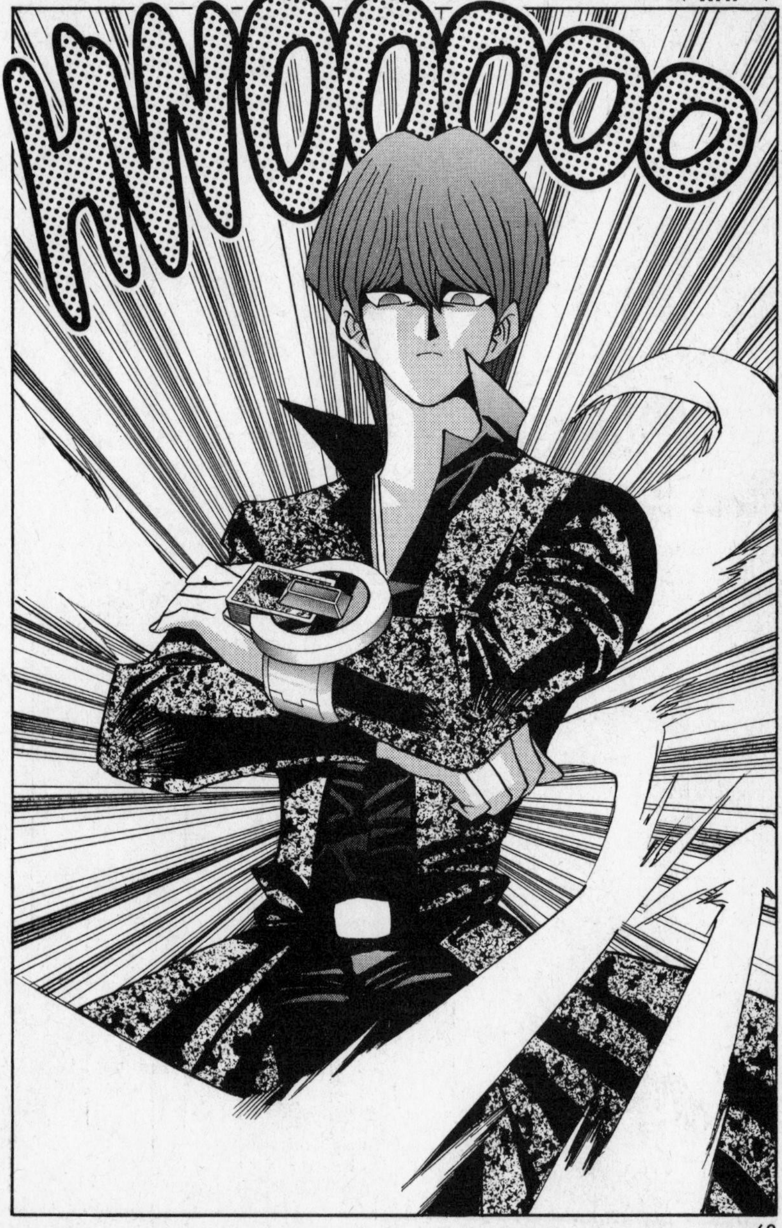
HWOOOOO

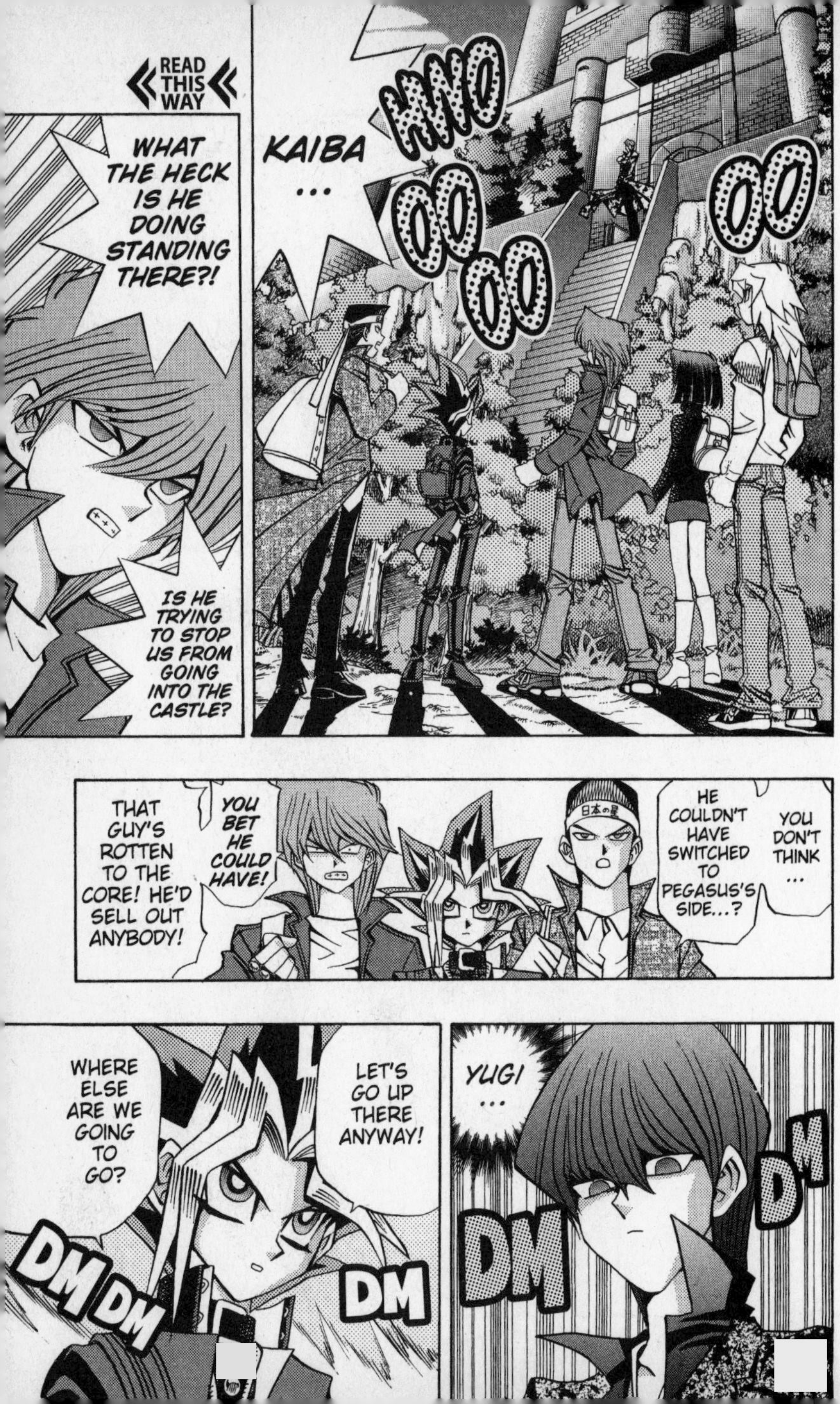
READ THIS WAY
WHOO OO OO OO
KAIBA ...
WHAT THE HECK IS HE DOING STANDING THERE?!
IS HE TRYING TO STOP US FROM GOING INTO THE CASTLE?
YOU DON'T THINK ...
HE COULDN'T HAVE SWITCHED TO PEGASUS'S SIDE...?
YOU BET HE COULD HAVE!
THAT GUY'S ROTTEN TO THE CORE! HE'D SELL OUT ANYBODY!
YUGI ...
DM DM
LET'S GO UP THERE ANYWAY!
WHERE ELSE ARE WE GOING TO GO?
DM
DM DM DM

READ THIS WAY

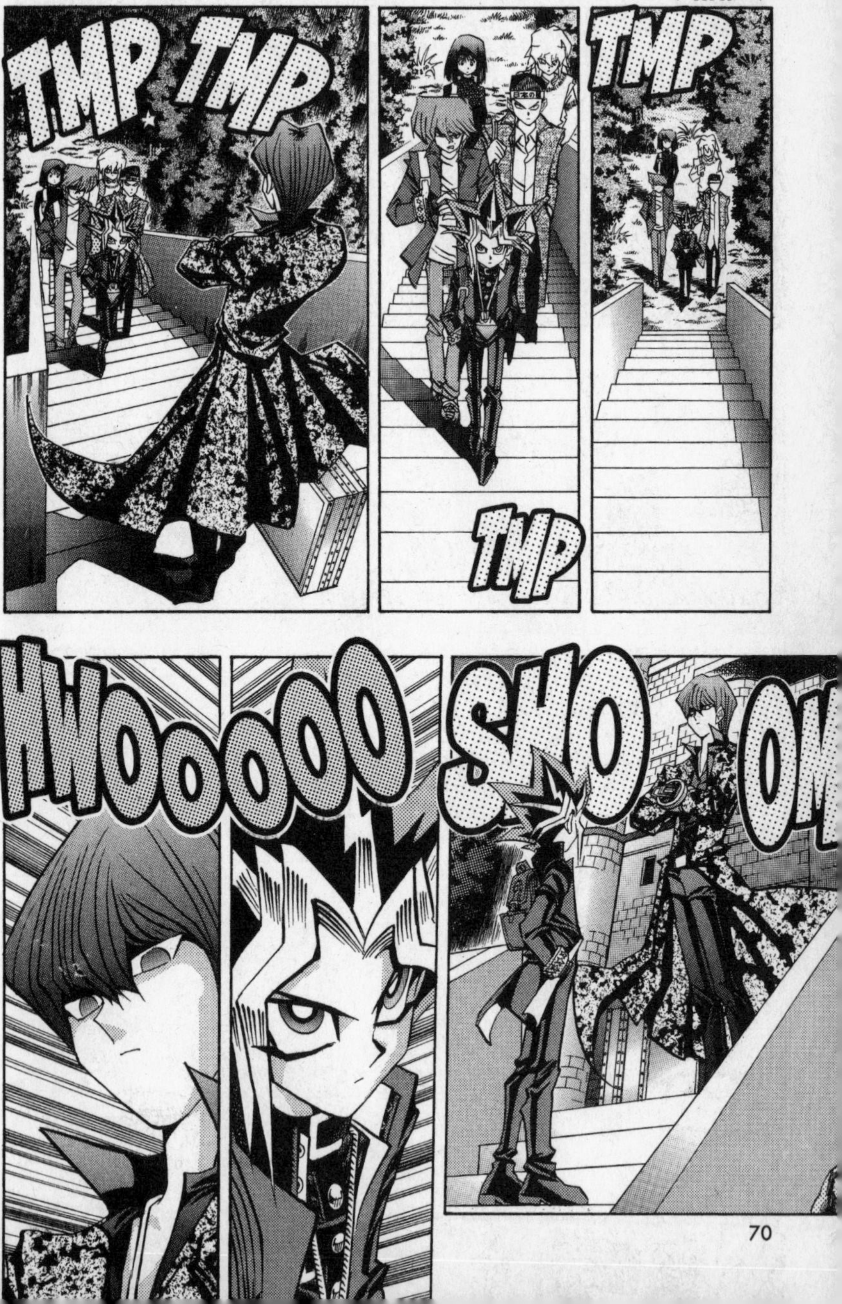
TMP
TMP
TMP TMP
HWOOOOOO SHO OM

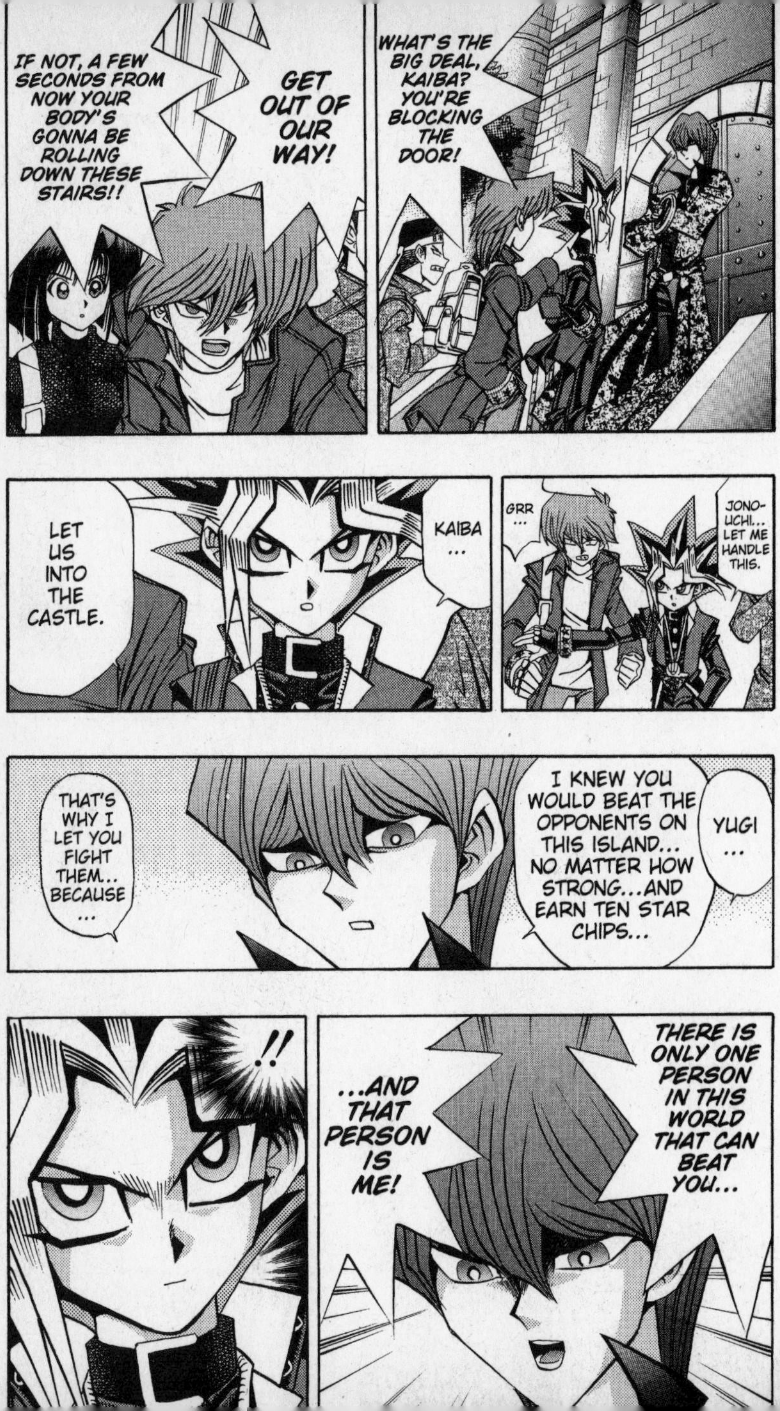
WHAT'S THE BIG DEAL, KAIBA? YOU'RE BLOCKING THE DOOR!
GET OUT OF OUR WAY!
IF NOT, A FEW SECONDS FROM NOW YOUR BODY'S GONNA BE ROLLING DOWN THESE STAIRS!!
JONO-UCHI... LET ME HANDLE THIS.
GRR ...
KAIBA ...
LET US INTO THE CASTLE.
YUGI ...
I KNEW YOU WOULD BEAT THE OPPONENTS ON THIS ISLAND... NO MATTER HOW STRONG...AND EARN TEN STAR CHIPS...
THAT'S WHY I LET YOU FIGHT THEM... BECAUSE ...
THERE IS ONLY ONE PERSON IN THIS WORLD THAT CAN BEAT YOU...
...AND THAT PERSON IS ME!
!!

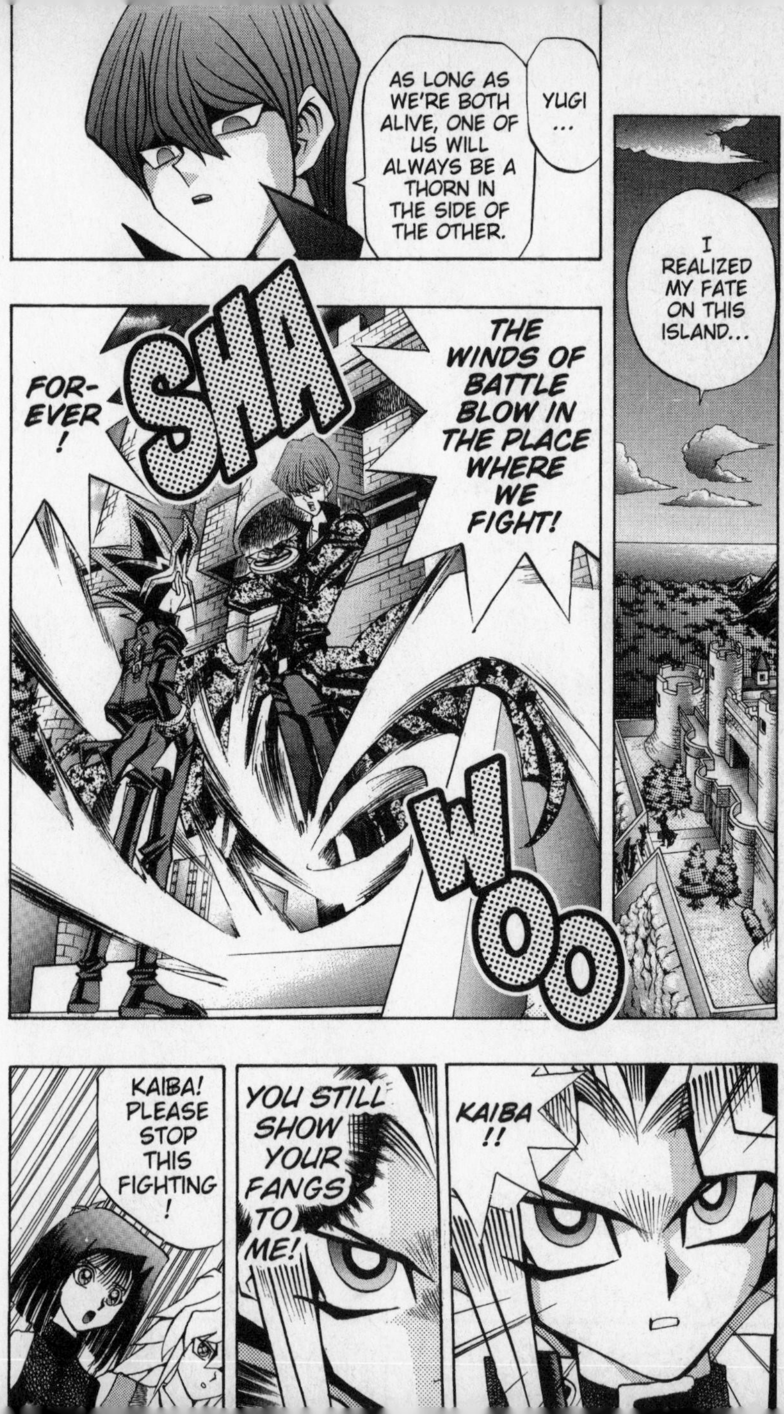
YUGI ...
AS LONG AS WE'RE BOTH ALIVE, ONE OF US WILL ALWAYS BE A THORN IN THE SIDE OF THE OTHER.
I REALIZED MY FATE ON THIS ISLAND...
THE WINDS OF BATTLE BLOW IN THE PLACE WHERE WE FIGHT!
SHA
FOR-EVER!
WOOO
KAIBA!!
YOU STILL SHOW YOUR FANGS TO ME!
KAIBA! PLEASE STOP THIS FIGHTING!

READ THIS WAY

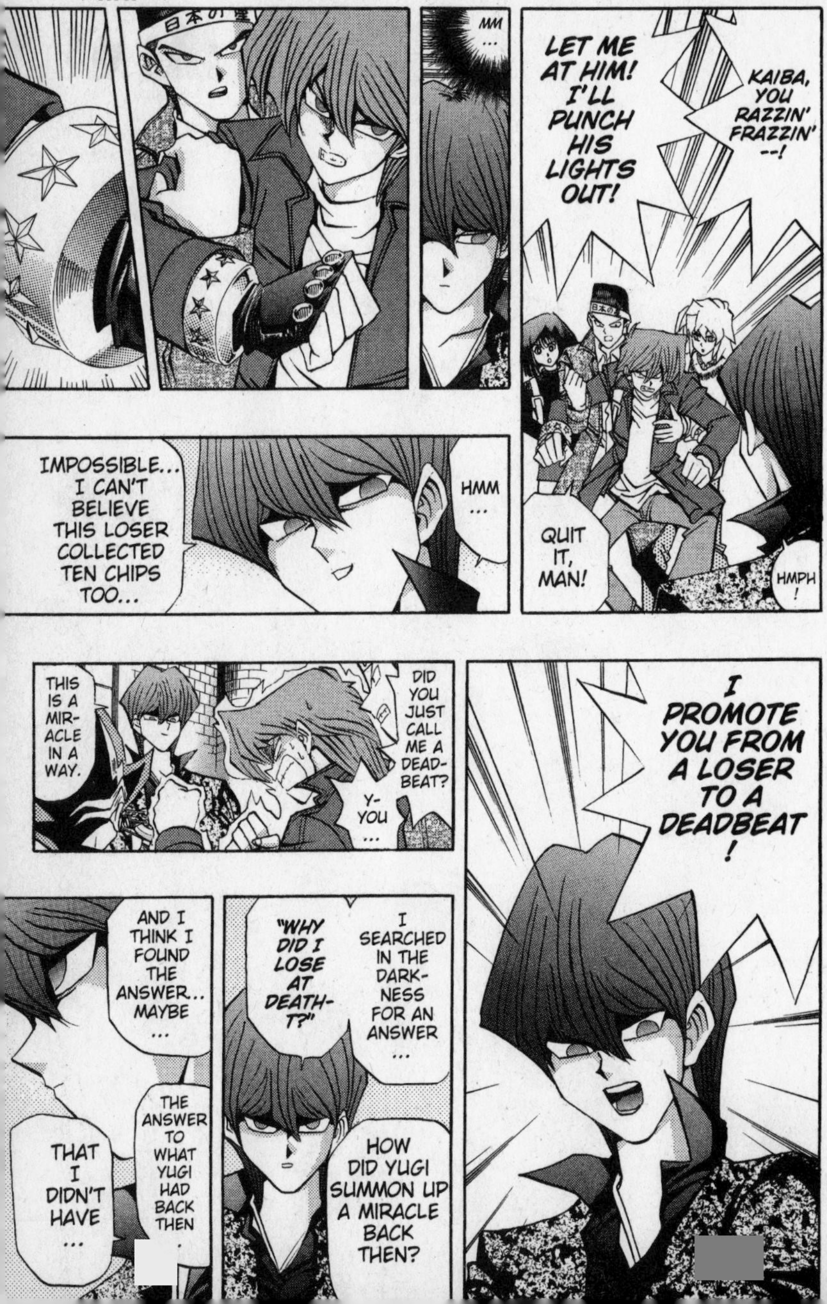
LET ME AT HIM! I'LL PUNCH HIS LIGHTS OUT!
KAIBA, YOU RAZZIN' FRAZZIN' --!
QUIT IT, MAN!
HMPH!
MM...
HMM...
IMPOSSIBLE... I CAN'T BELIEVE THIS LOSER COLLECTED TEN CHIPS TOO...
I PROMOTE YOU FROM A LOSER TO A DEADBEAT!
Y-YOU...
DID YOU JUST CALL ME A DEADBEAT?
THIS IS A MIRACLE IN A WAY.
I SEARCHED IN THE DARKNESS FOR AN ANSWER...
"WHY DID I LOSE AT DEATH-T?"
HOW DID YUGI SUMMON UP A MIRACLE BACK THEN?
AND I THINK I FOUND THE ANSWER... MAYBE...
THE ANSWER TO WHAT YUGI HAD BACK THEN.
THAT I DIDN'T HAVE...

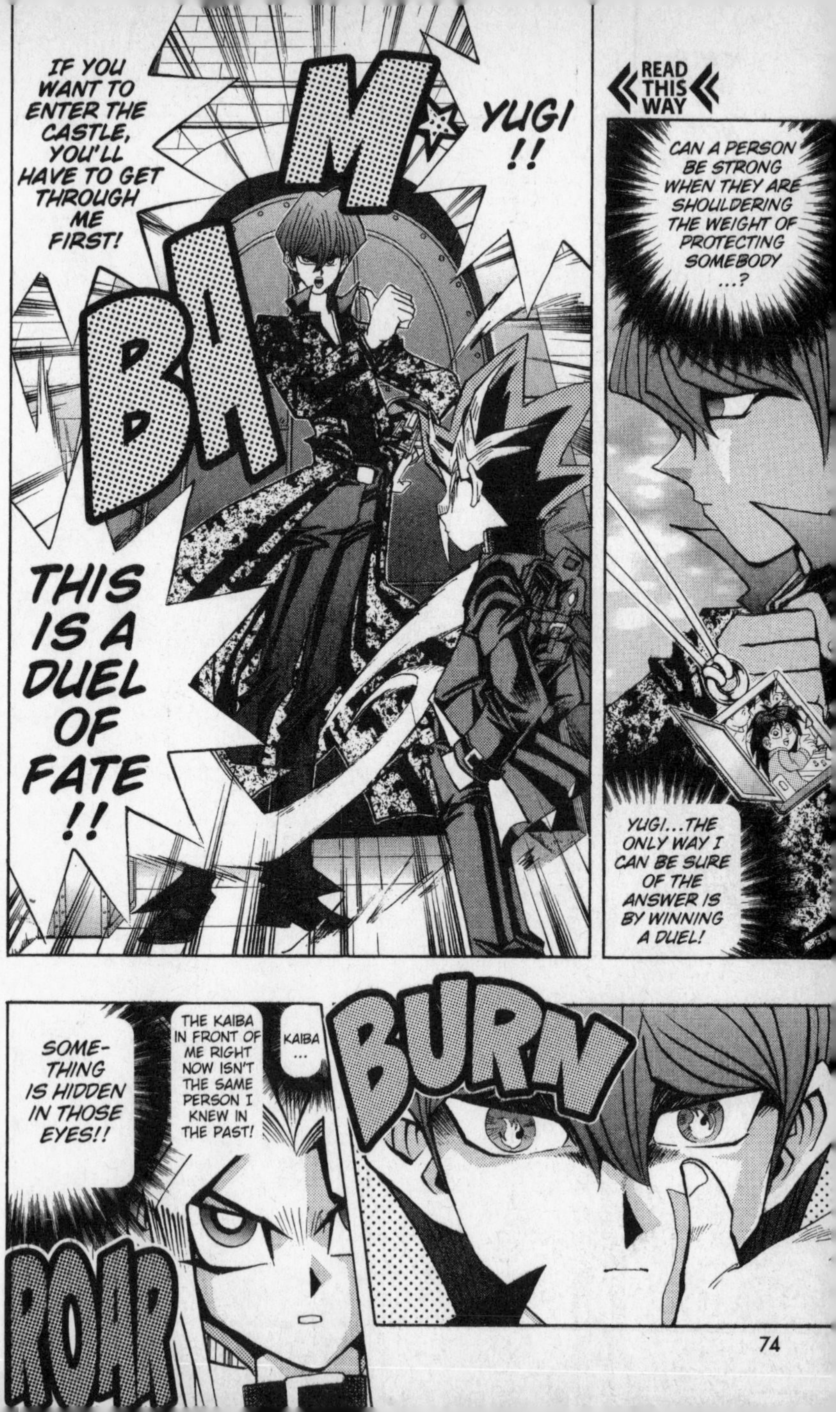
READ THIS WAY
CAN A PERSON BE STRONG WHEN THEY ARE SHOULDERING THE WEIGHT OF PROTECTING SOMEBODY ...?
YUGI...THE ONLY WAY I CAN BE SURE OF THE ANSWER IS BY WINNING A DUEL!
YUGI !!
BAM
IF YOU WANT TO ENTER THE CASTLE, YOU'LL HAVE TO GET THROUGH ME FIRST!
THIS IS A DUEL OF FATE !!
BURN
KAIBA ...
THE KAIBA IN FRONT OF ME RIGHT NOW ISN'T THE SAME PERSON I KNEW IN THE PAST!
SOME-THING IS HIDDEN IN THOSE EYES!!
ROAR

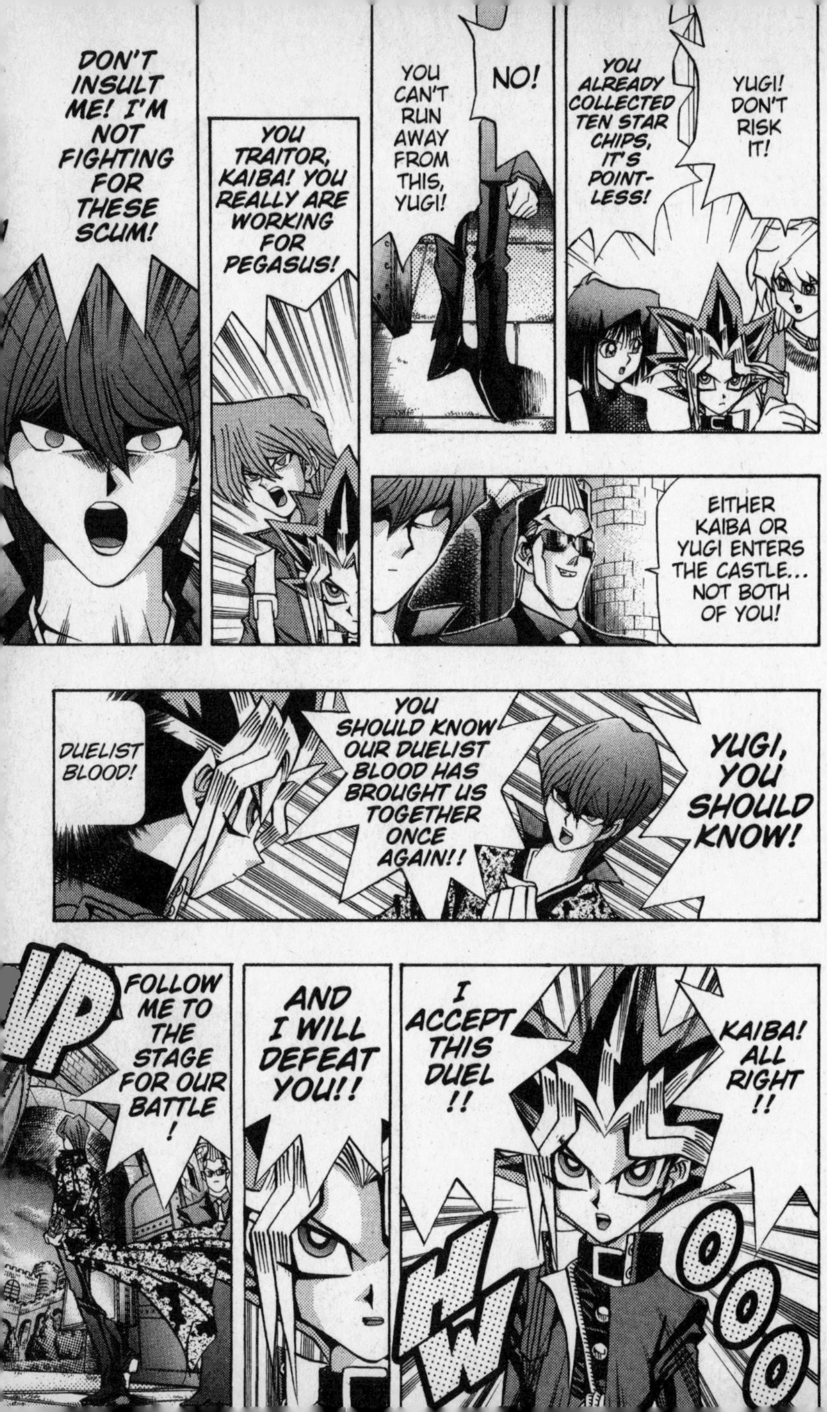
YUGI! DON'T RISK IT!
YOU ALREADY COLLECTED TEN STAR CHIPS, IT'S POINTLESS!
NO!
YOU CAN'T RUN AWAY FROM THIS, YUGI!
EITHER KAIBA OR YUGI ENTERS THE CASTLE... NOT BOTH OF YOU!
YOU TRAITOR, KAIBA! YOU REALLY ARE WORKING FOR PEGASUS!
DON'T INSULT ME! I'M NOT FIGHTING FOR THESE SCUM!
YUGI, YOU SHOULD KNOW!
YOU SHOULD KNOW OUR DUELIST BLOOD HAS BROUGHT US TOGETHER ONCE AGAIN!!
DUELIST BLOOD!
KAIBA! ALL RIGHT!!
I ACCEPT THIS DUEL!!
AND I WILL DEFEAT YOU!!
FOLLOW ME TO THE STAGE FOR OUR BATTLE!

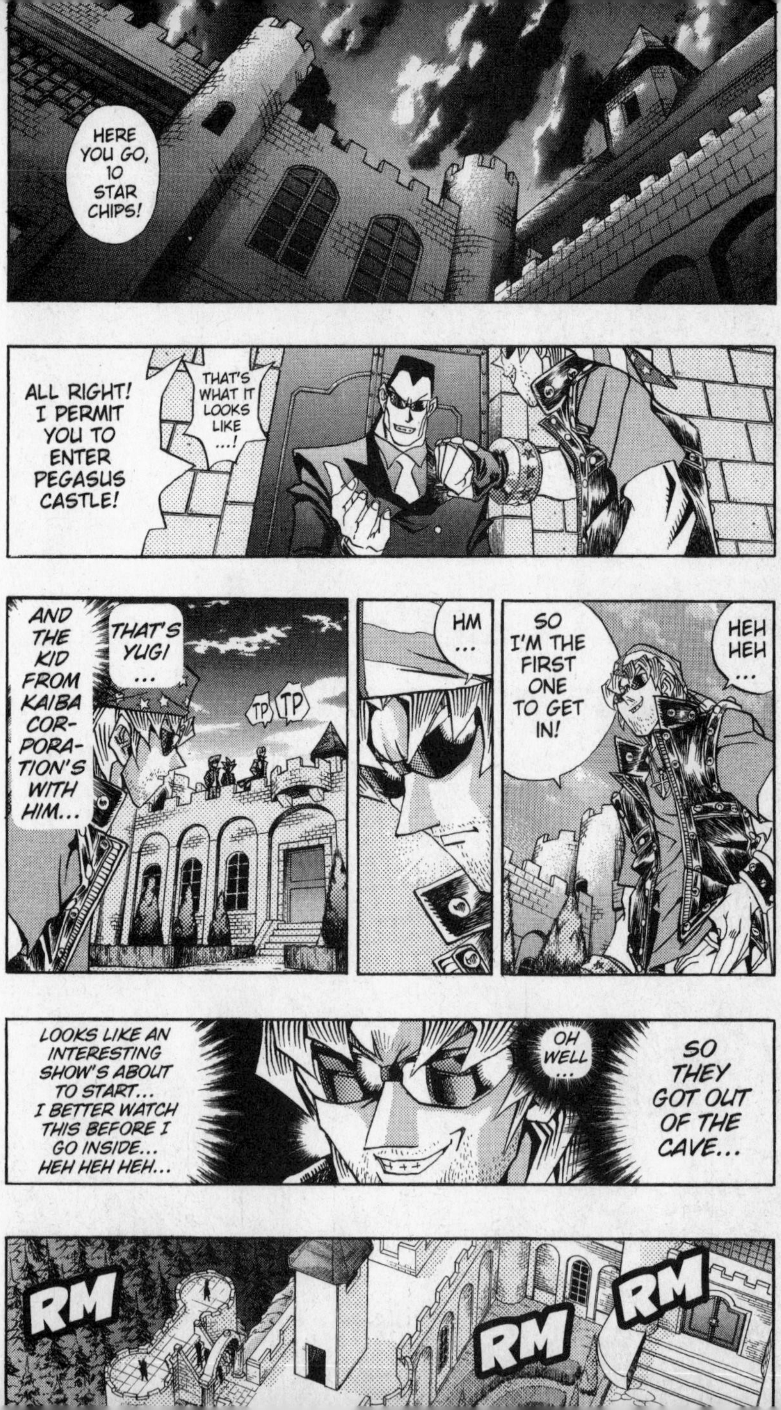
HERE YOU GO, 10 STAR CHIPS!
THAT'S WHAT IT LOOKS LIKE ...!
ALL RIGHT! I PERMIT YOU TO ENTER PEGASUS CASTLE!
HEH HEH ...
SO I'M THE FIRST ONE TO GET IN!
HM ...
THAT'S YUGI ...
TP TP
AND THE KID FROM KAIBA CORPORATION'S WITH HIM...
SO THEY GOT OUT OF THE CAVE...
OH WELL ...
LOOKS LIKE AN INTERESTING SHOW'S ABOUT TO START... I BETTER WATCH THIS BEFORE I GO INSIDE... HEH HEH HEH...
RM
RM
RM

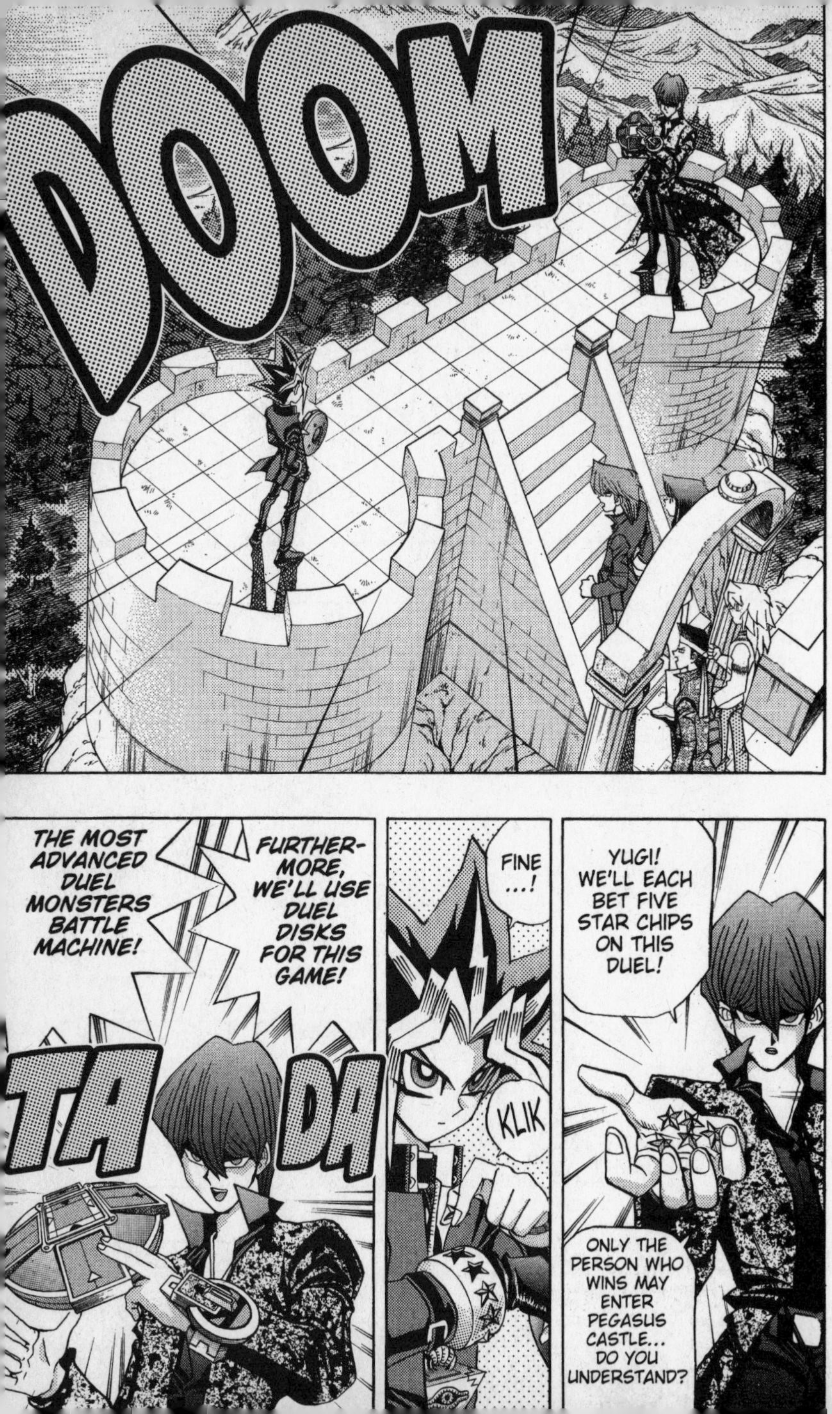
DOOM
YUGI! WE'LL EACH BET FIVE STAR CHIPS ON THIS DUEL!
ONLY THE PERSON WHO WINS MAY ENTER PEGASUS CASTLE... DO YOU UNDERSTAND?
FINE ...!
KLIK
FURTHER-MORE, WE'LL USE DUEL DISKS FOR THIS GAME!
THE MOST ADVANCED DUEL MONSTERS BATTLE MACHINE!
TA DA

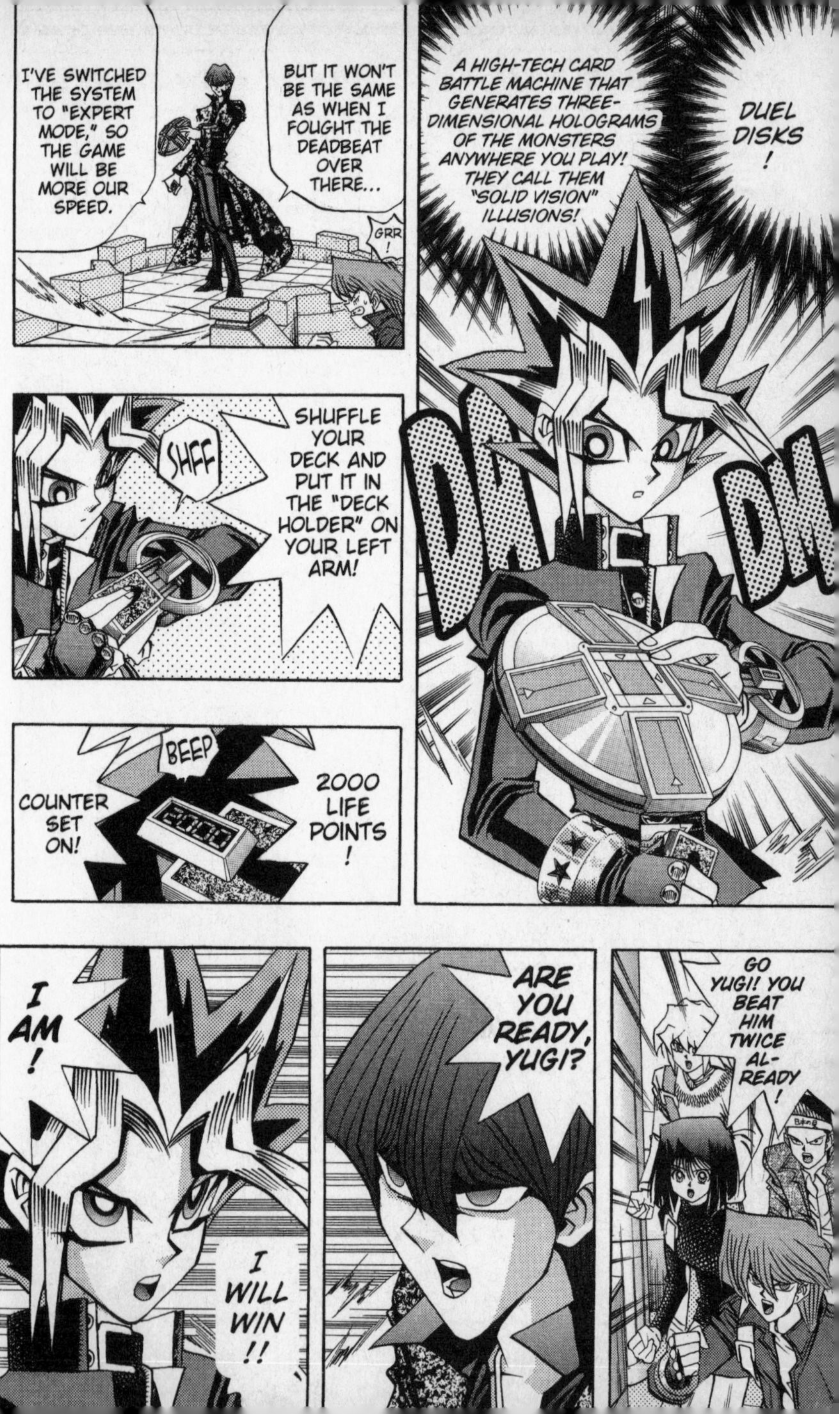
DUEL DISKS!
A HIGH-TECH CARD BATTLE MACHINE THAT GENERATES THREE-DIMENSIONAL HOLOGRAMS OF THE MONSTERS ANYWHERE YOU PLAY! THEY CALL THEM "SOLID VISION" ILLUSIONS!
DM DM
BUT IT WON'T BE THE SAME AS WHEN I FOUGHT THE DEADBEAT OVER THERE...
I'VE SWITCHED THE SYSTEM TO "EXPERT MODE," SO THE GAME WILL BE MORE OUR SPEED.
GRR!
SHUFFLE YOUR DECK AND PUT IT IN THE "DECK HOLDER" ON YOUR LEFT ARM!
SHFF
BEEP
2000 LIFE POINTS!
COUNTER SET ON!
GO YUGI! YOU BEAT HIM TWICE AL-READY!
ARE YOU READY, YUGI?
I AM!
I WILL WIN!!

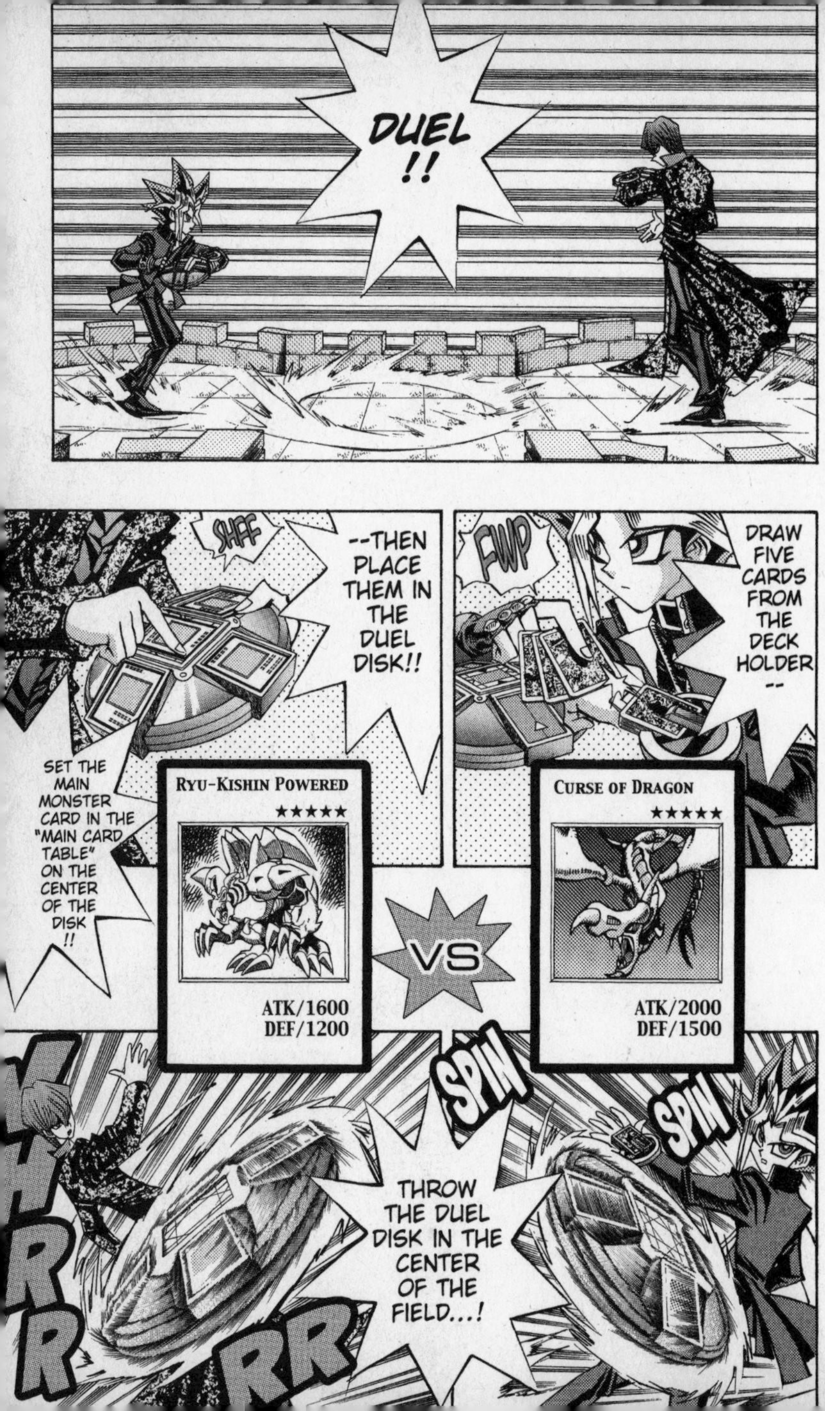
DUEL !!
FWP
DRAW FIVE CARDS FROM THE DECK HOLDER --
SHFF
--THEN PLACE THEM IN THE DUEL DISK!!
CURSE OF DRAGON
ATK/2000 DEF/1500
VS
RYU-KISHIN POWERED
ATK/1600 DEF/1200
SET THE MAIN MONSTER CARD IN THE "MAIN CARD TABLE" ON THE CENTER OF THE DISK !!
SPIN
SPIN
THROW THE DUEL DISK IN THE CENTER OF THE FIELD...!
RR

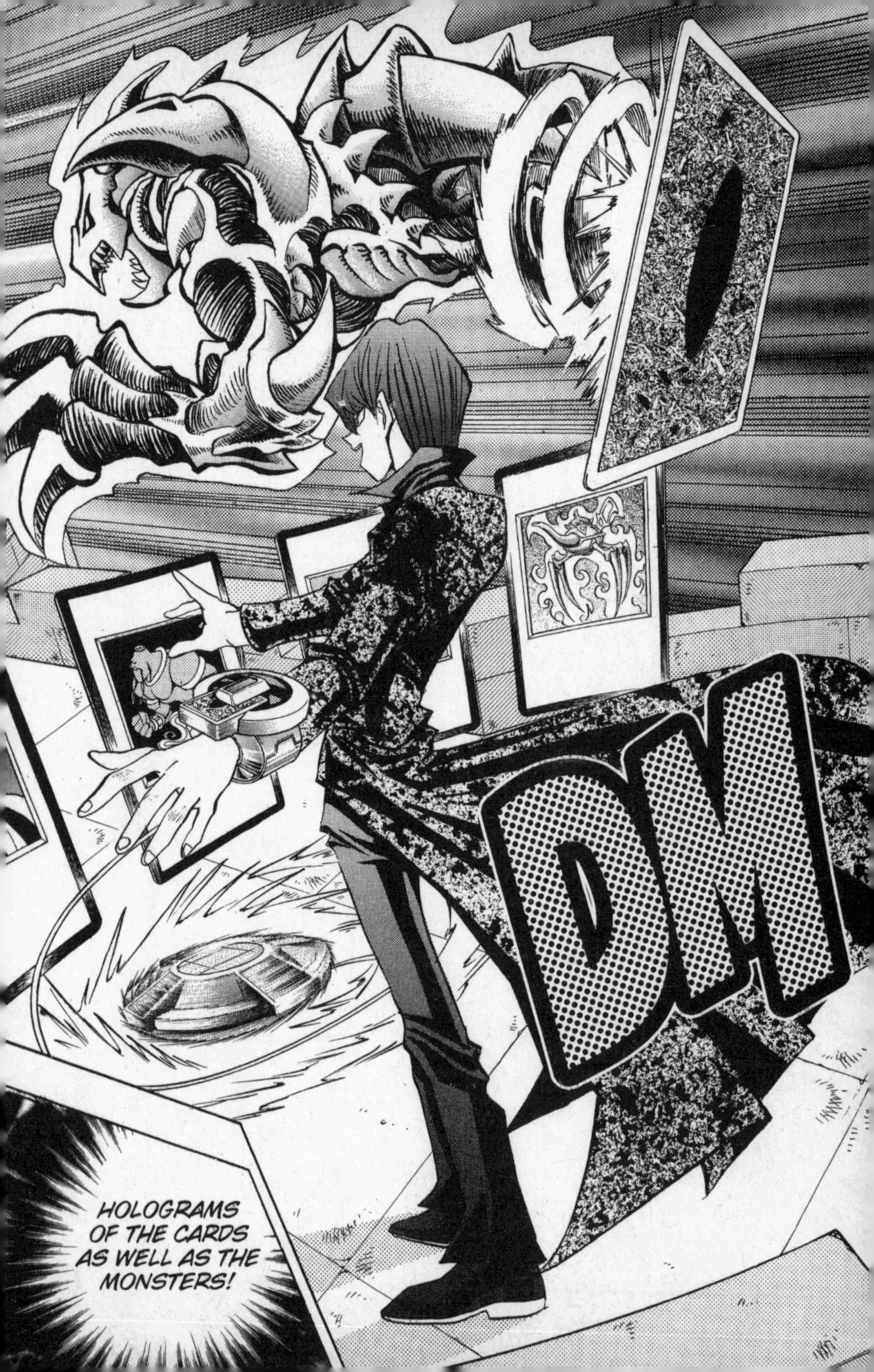
DM
HOLOGRAMS OF THE CARDS AS WELL AS THE MONSTERS!

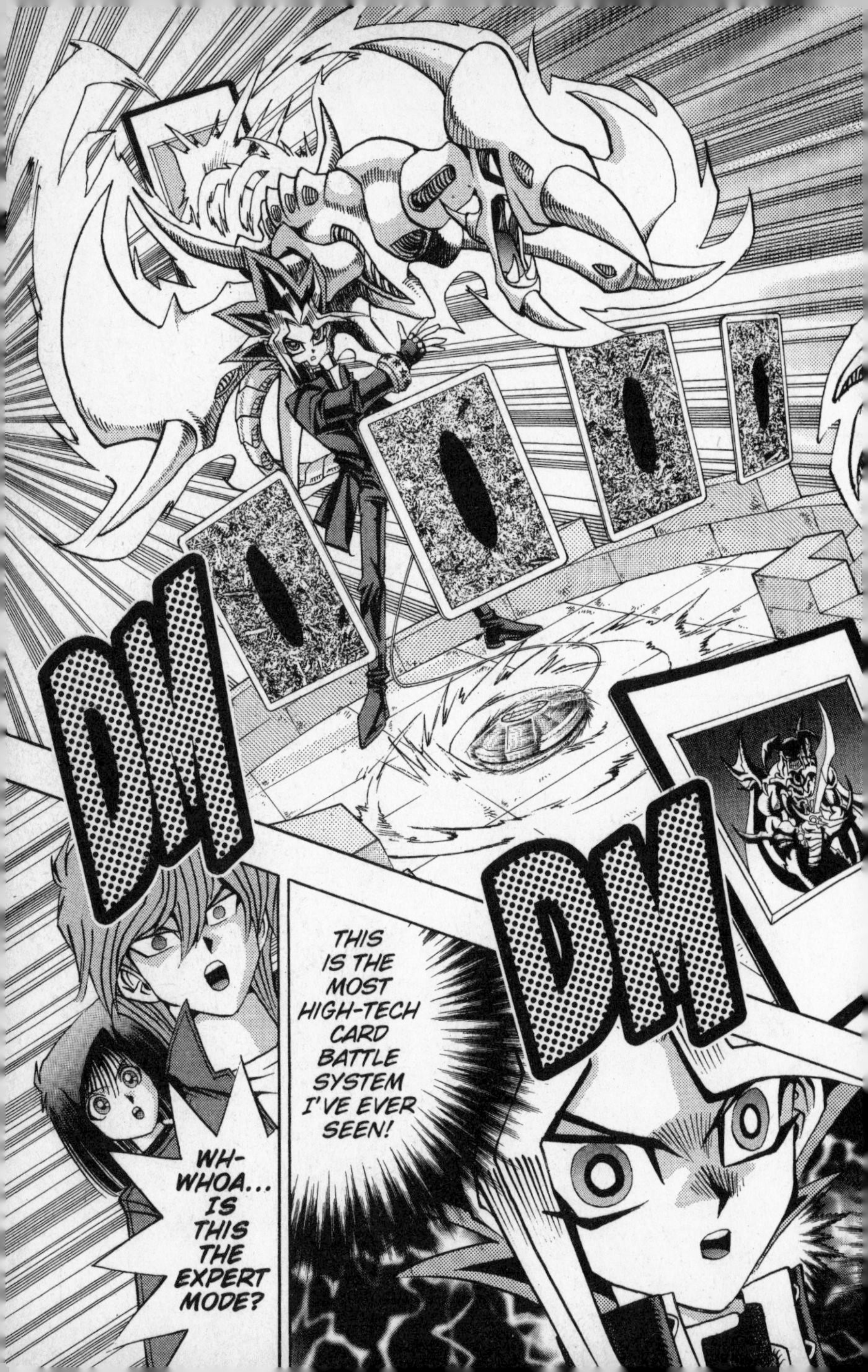
DM
DM
THIS IS THE MOST HIGH-TECH CARD BATTLE SYSTEM I'VE EVER SEEN!
WH-WHOA... IS THIS THE EXPERT MODE?

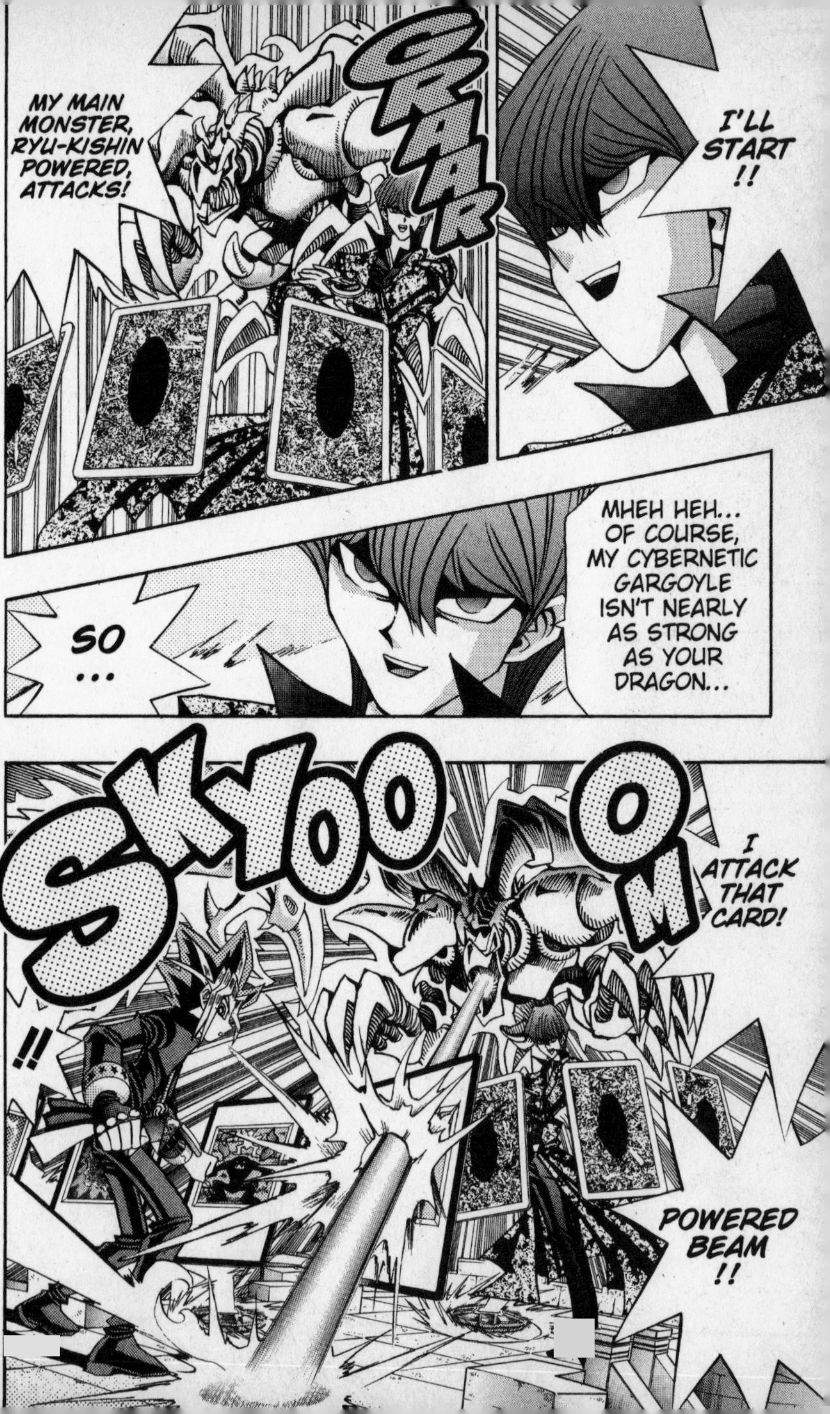
I'LL START!!
GRAAR
MY MAIN MONSTER, RYU-KISHIN POWERED, ATTACKS!
MHEH HEH... OF COURSE, MY CYBERNETIC GARGOYLE ISN'T NEARLY AS STRONG AS YOUR DRAGON...
SO...
SKYOOOM
I ATTACK THAT CARD!
!!
POWERED BEAM!!

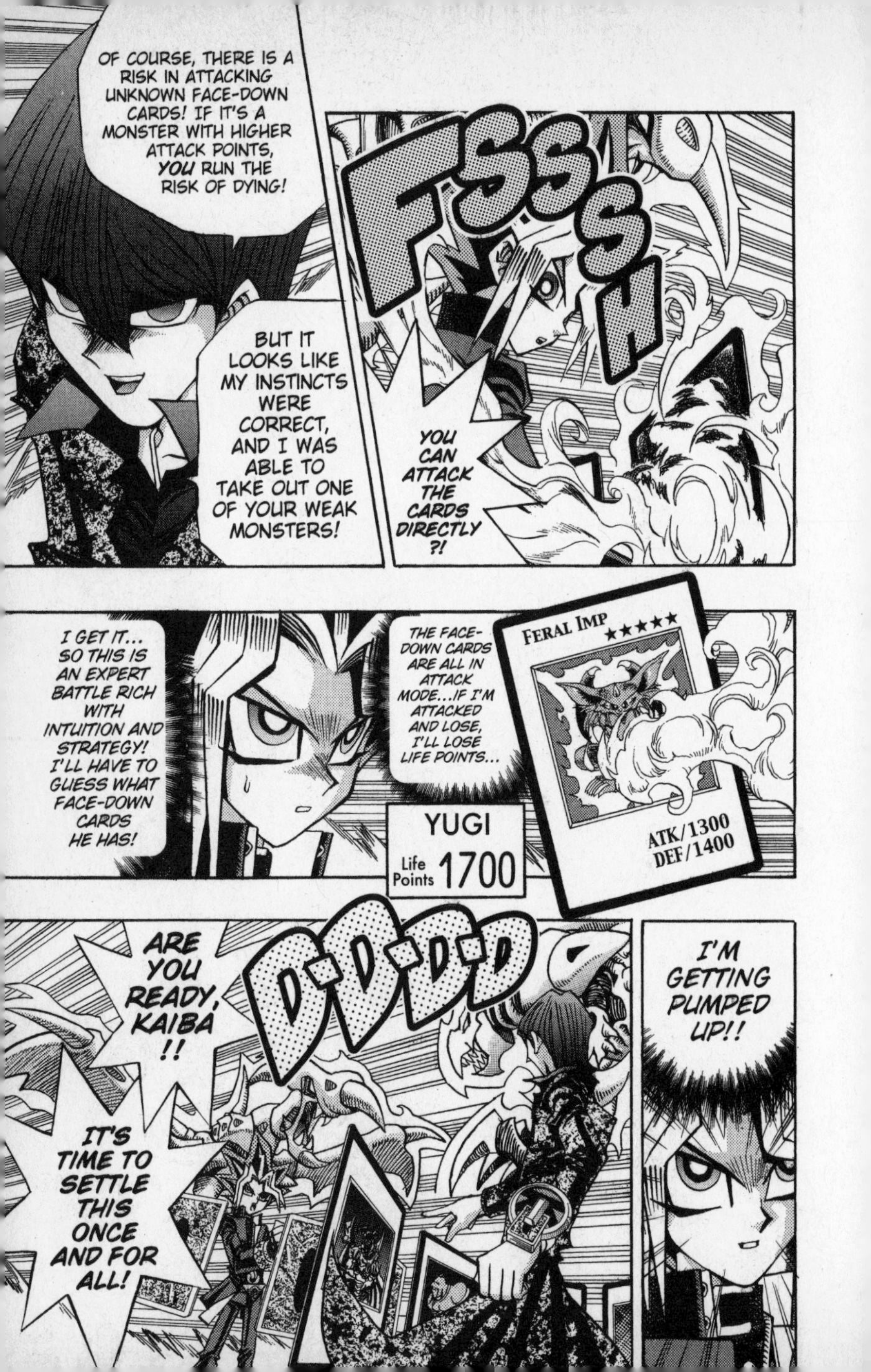
FSSSH
YOU CAN ATTACK THE CARDS DIRECTLY?!
OF COURSE, THERE IS A RISK IN ATTACKING UNKNOWN FACE-DOWN CARDS! IF IT'S A MONSTER WITH HIGHER ATTACK POINTS, YOU RUN THE RISK OF DYING!
BUT IT LOOKS LIKE MY INSTINCTS WERE CORRECT, AND I WAS ABLE TO TAKE OUT ONE OF YOUR WEAK MONSTERS!
FERAL IMP ★★★★★
ATK/1300
DEF/1400
THE FACE-DOWN CARDS ARE ALL IN ATTACK MODE...IF I'M ATTACKED AND LOSE, I'LL LOSE LIFE POINTS...
YUGI
Life Points 1700
I GET IT... SO THIS IS AN EXPERT BATTLE RICH WITH INTUITION AND STRATEGY! I'LL HAVE TO GUESS WHAT FACE-DOWN CARDS HE HAS!
I'M GETTING PUMPED UP!!
D-D-D-D
ARE YOU READY, KAIBA!!
IT'S TIME TO SETTLE THIS ONCE AND FOR ALL!

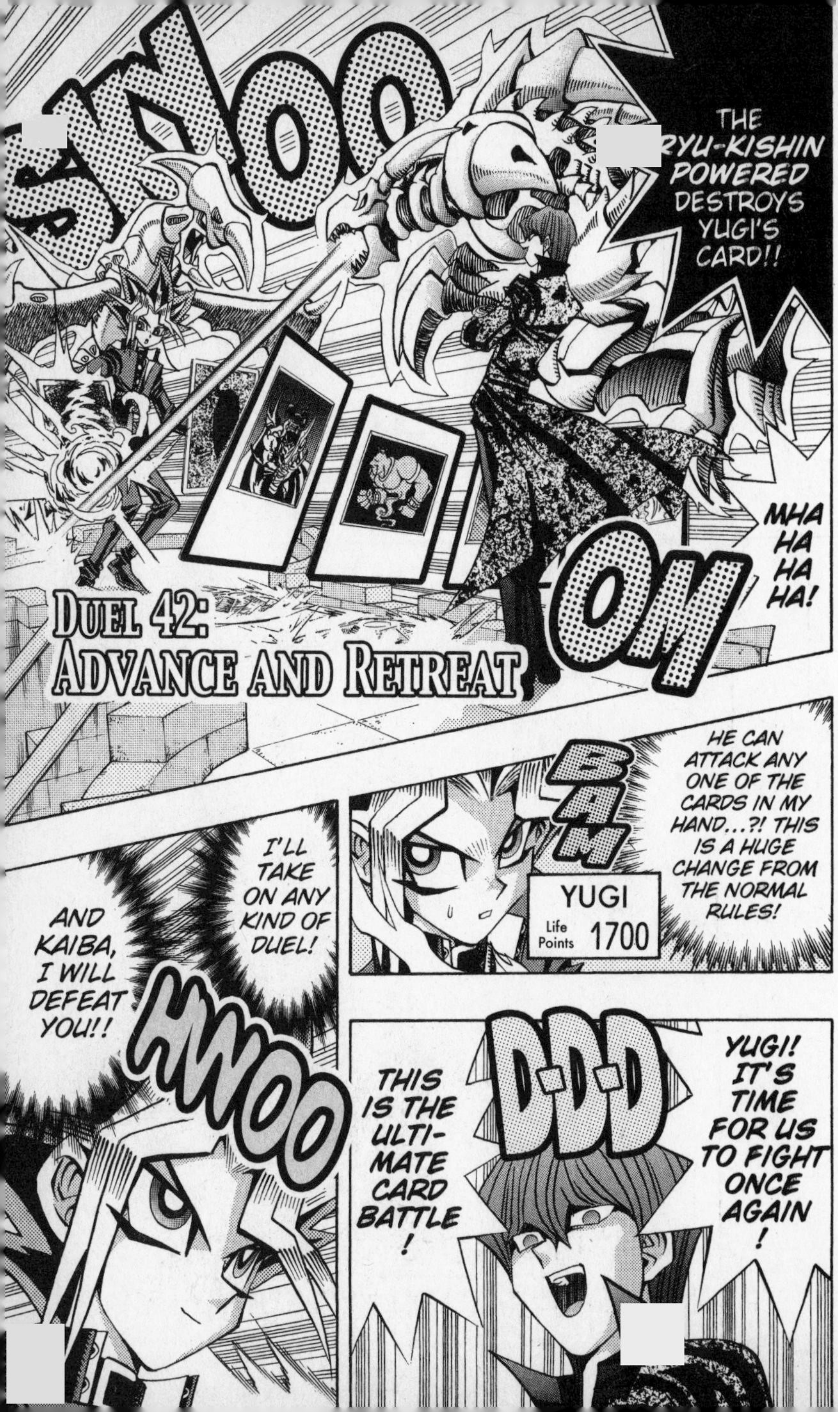
THE RYU-KISHIN POWERED DESTROYS YUGI'S CARD!!
MHA HA HA HA!
OM
DUEL 42: ADVANCE AND RETREAT
HE CAN ATTACK ANY ONE OF THE CARDS IN MY HAND...?! THIS IS A HUGE CHANGE FROM THE NORMAL RULES!
SAM
YUGI
Life Points 1700
YUGI! IT'S TIME FOR US TO FIGHT ONCE AGAIN!
D-D-D
THIS IS THE ULTI-MATE CARD BATTLE!
I'LL TAKE ON ANY KIND OF DUEL!
AND KAIBA, I WILL DEFEAT YOU!!
HWOO

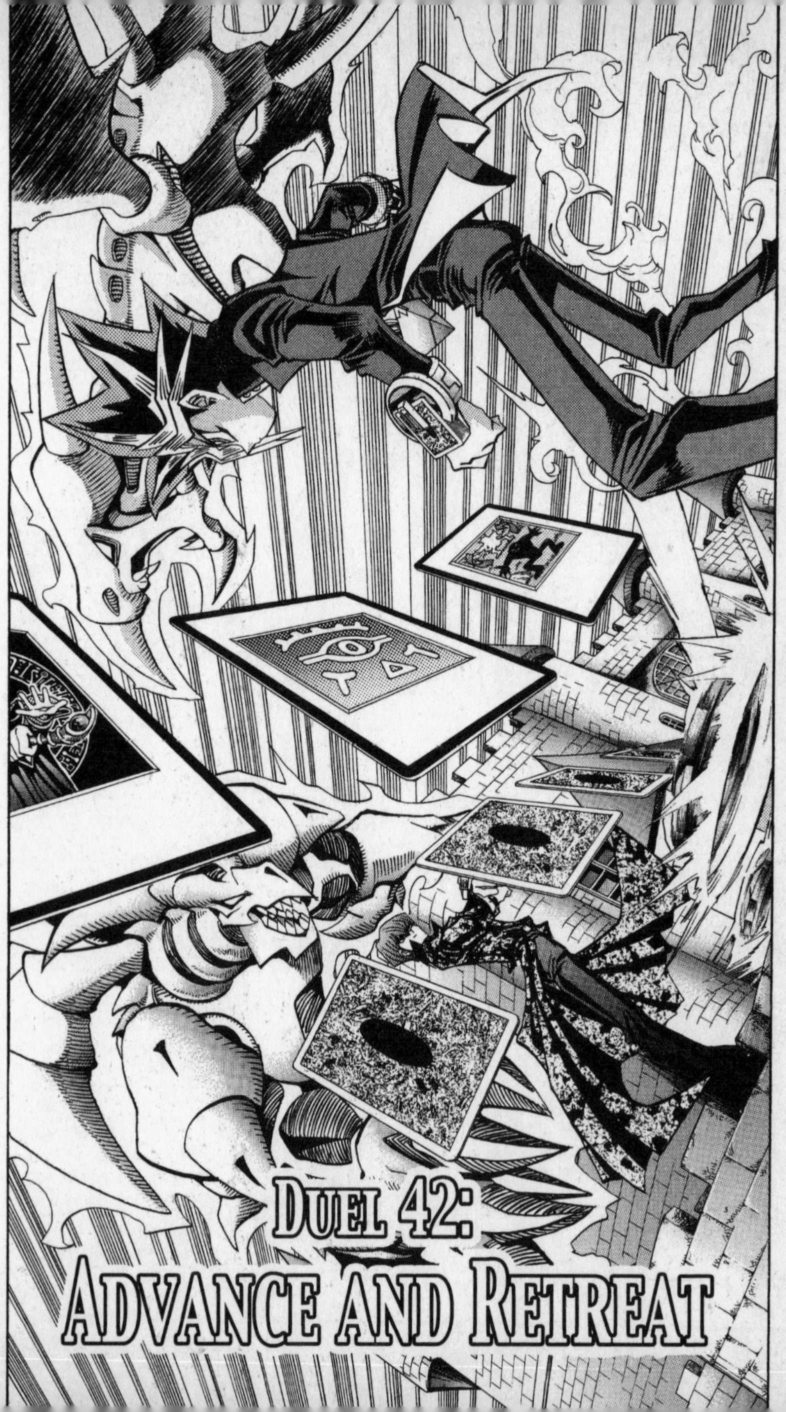
DUEL 42:
ADVANCE AND RETREAT

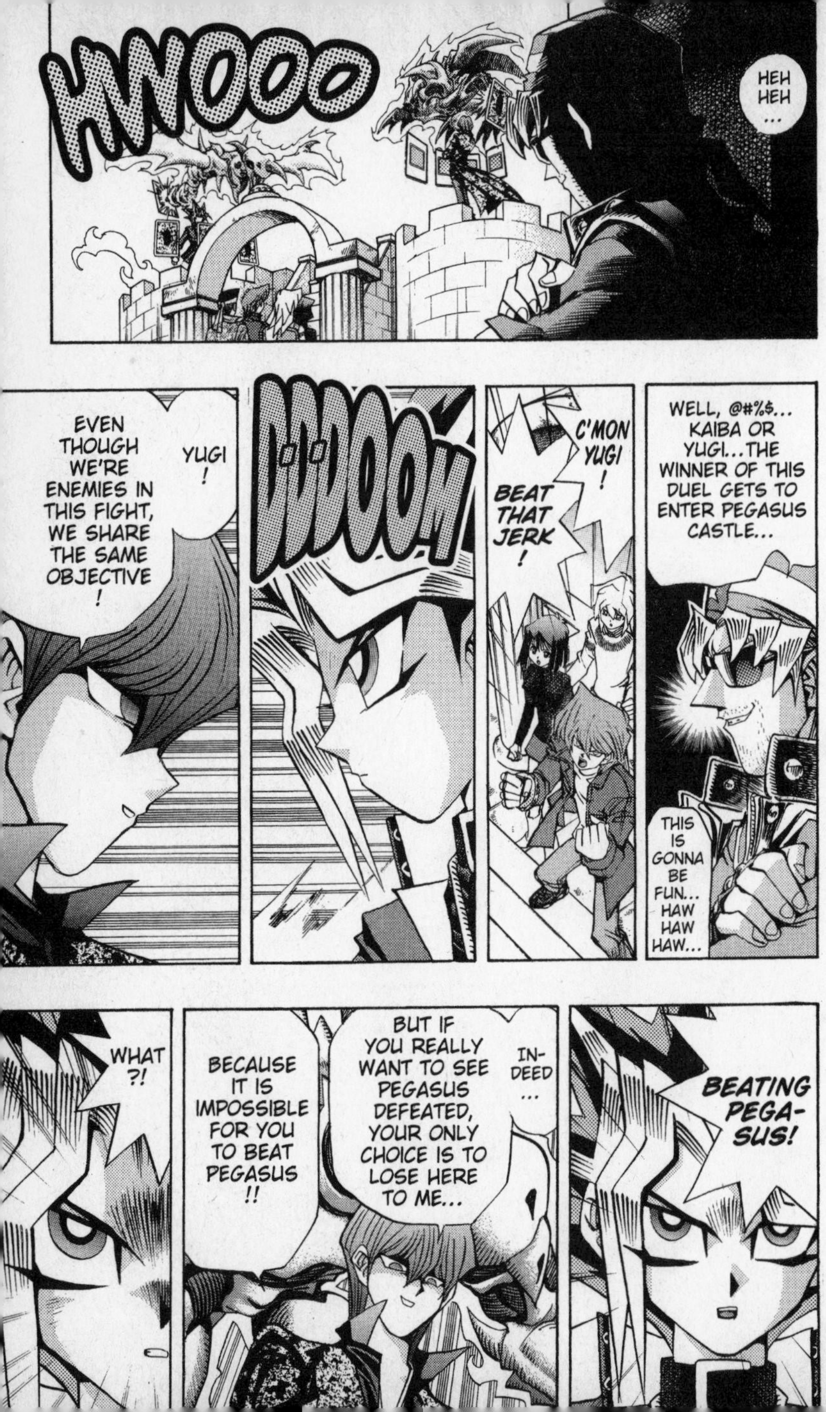
HWOOO
HEH HEH...
WELL, @#%$... KAIBA OR YUGI... THE WINNER OF THIS DUEL GETS TO ENTER PEGASUS CASTLE...
THIS IS GONNA BE FUN... HAW HAW HAW...
C'MON YUGI!
BEAT THAT JERK!
DDDOOM
YUGI!
EVEN THOUGH WE'RE ENEMIES IN THIS FIGHT, WE SHARE THE SAME OBJECTIVE!
BEATING PEGASUS!
IN-DEED...
BUT IF YOU REALLY WANT TO SEE PEGASUS DEFEATED, YOUR ONLY CHOICE IS TO LOSE HERE TO ME...
BECAUSE IT IS IMPOSSIBLE FOR YOU TO BEAT PEGASUS!!
WHAT?!

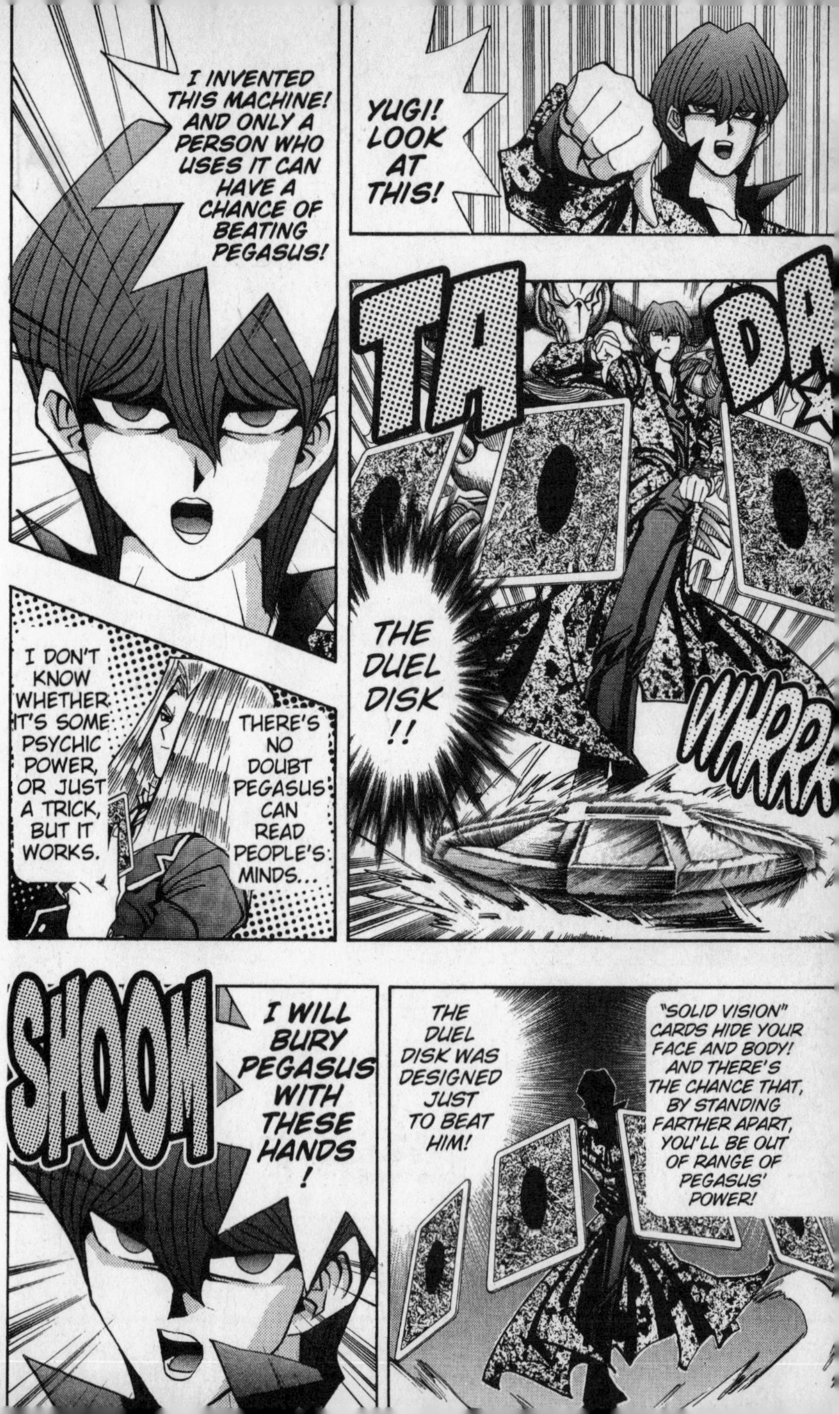
YUGI! LOOK AT THIS!
I INVENTED THIS MACHINE! AND ONLY A PERSON WHO USES IT CAN HAVE A CHANCE OF BEATING PEGASUS!
TA DA
THE DUEL DISK!!
WHRR
THERE'S NO DOUBT PEGASUS CAN READ PEOPLE'S MINDS...
I DON'T KNOW WHETHER IT'S SOME PSYCHIC POWER, OR JUST A TRICK, BUT IT WORKS.
"SOLID VISION" CARDS HIDE YOUR FACE AND BODY! AND THERE'S THE CHANCE THAT, BY STANDING FARTHER APART, YOU'LL BE OUT OF RANGE OF PEGASUS' POWER!
THE DUEL DISK WAS DESIGNED JUST TO BEAT HIM!
I WILL BURY PEGASUS WITH THESE HANDS!
SHOOM

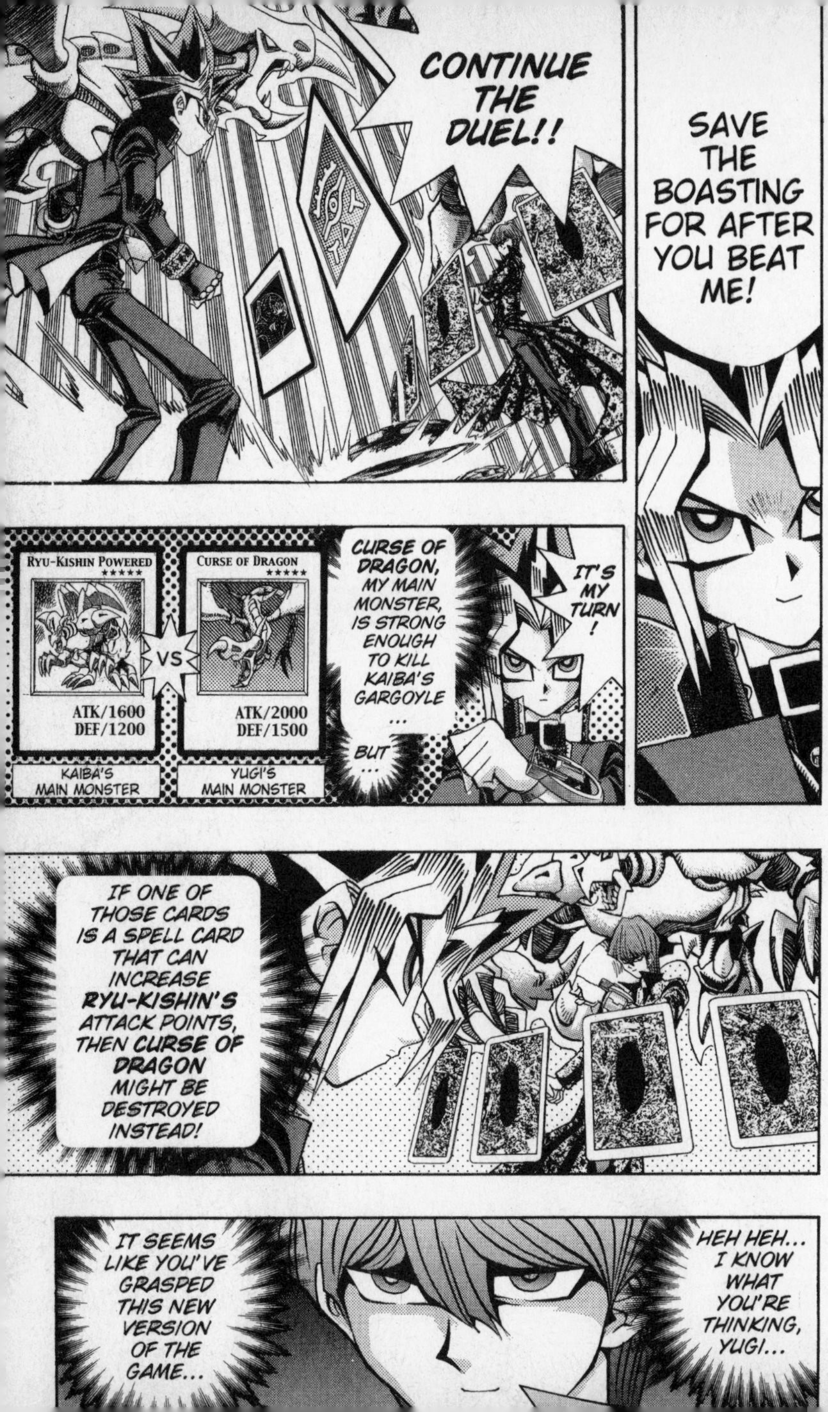
SAVE THE BOASTING FOR AFTER YOU BEAT ME!
CONTINUE THE DUEL!!
IT'S MY TURN!
CURSE OF DRAGON, MY MAIN MONSTER, IS STRONG ENOUGH TO KILL KAIBA'S GARGOYLE... BUT...
CURSE OF DRAGON
ATK/2000 DEF/1500
YUGI'S MAIN MONSTER
VS
RYU-KISHIN POWERED
ATK/1600 DEF/1200
KAIBA'S MAIN MONSTER
IF ONE OF THOSE CARDS IS A SPELL CARD THAT CAN INCREASE RYU-KISHIN'S ATTACK POINTS, THEN CURSE OF DRAGON MIGHT BE DESTROYED INSTEAD!
HEH HEH... I KNOW WHAT YOU'RE THINKING, YUGI...
IT SEEMS LIKE YOU'VE GRASPED THIS NEW VERSION OF THE GAME...

READ THIS WAY

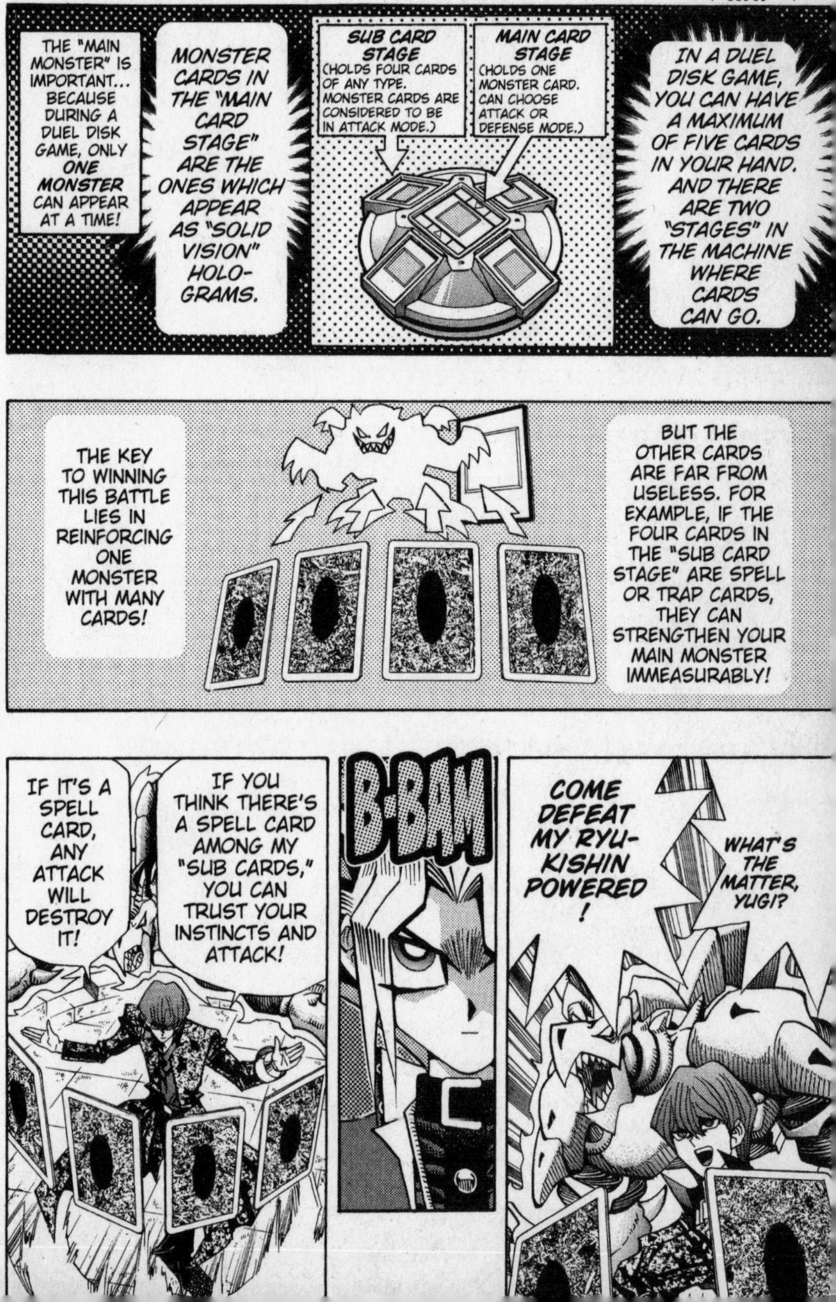
IN A DUEL DISK GAME, YOU CAN HAVE A MAXIMUM OF FIVE CARDS IN YOUR HAND. AND THERE ARE TWO "STAGES" IN THE MACHINE WHERE CARDS CAN GO.
MAIN CARD STAGE (HOLDS ONE MONSTER CARD. CAN CHOOSE ATTACK OR DEFENSE MODE.)
SUB CARD STAGE (HOLDS FOUR CARDS OF ANY TYPE. MONSTER CARDS ARE CONSIDERED TO BE IN ATTACK MODE.)
MONSTER CARDS IN THE "MAIN CARD STAGE" ARE THE ONES WHICH APPEAR AS "SOLID VISION" HOLO-GRAMS.
THE "MAIN MONSTER" IS IMPORTANT... BECAUSE DURING A DUEL DISK GAME, ONLY ONE MONSTER CAN APPEAR AT A TIME!
BUT THE OTHER CARDS ARE FAR FROM USELESS. FOR EXAMPLE, IF THE FOUR CARDS IN THE "SUB CARD STAGE" ARE SPELL OR TRAP CARDS, THEY CAN STRENGTHEN YOUR MAIN MONSTER IMMEASURABLY!
THE KEY TO WINNING THIS BATTLE LIES IN REINFORCING ONE MONSTER WITH MANY CARDS!
WHAT'S THE MATTER, YUGI?
COME DEFEAT MY RYU-KISHIN POWERED!
B-BAM
IF YOU THINK THERE'S A SPELL CARD AMONG MY "SUB CARDS," YOU CAN TRUST YOUR INSTINCTS AND ATTACK!
IF IT'S A SPELL CARD, ANY ATTACK WILL DESTROY IT!

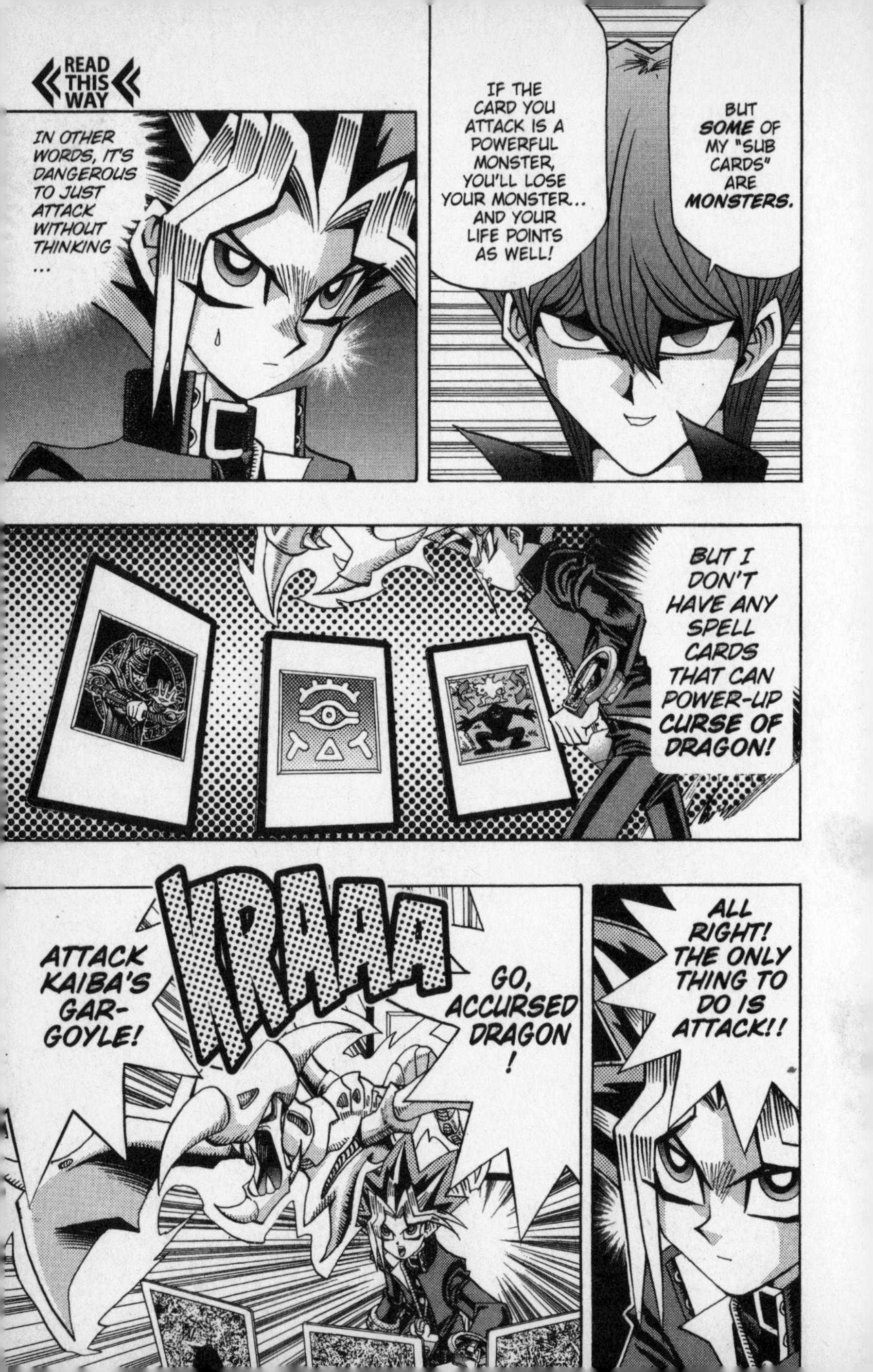
READ THIS WAY
BUT SOME OF MY "SUB CARDS" ARE MONSTERS.
IF THE CARD YOU ATTACK IS A POWERFUL MONSTER, YOU'LL LOSE YOUR MONSTER... AND YOUR LIFE POINTS AS WELL!
IN OTHER WORDS, IT'S DANGEROUS TO JUST ATTACK WITHOUT THINKING...
BUT I DON'T HAVE ANY SPELL CARDS THAT CAN POWER-UP CURSE OF DRAGON!
ALL RIGHT! THE ONLY THING TO DO IS ATTACK!!
VRAAA
GO, ACCURSED DRAGON!
ATTACK KAIBA'S GAR-GOYLE!

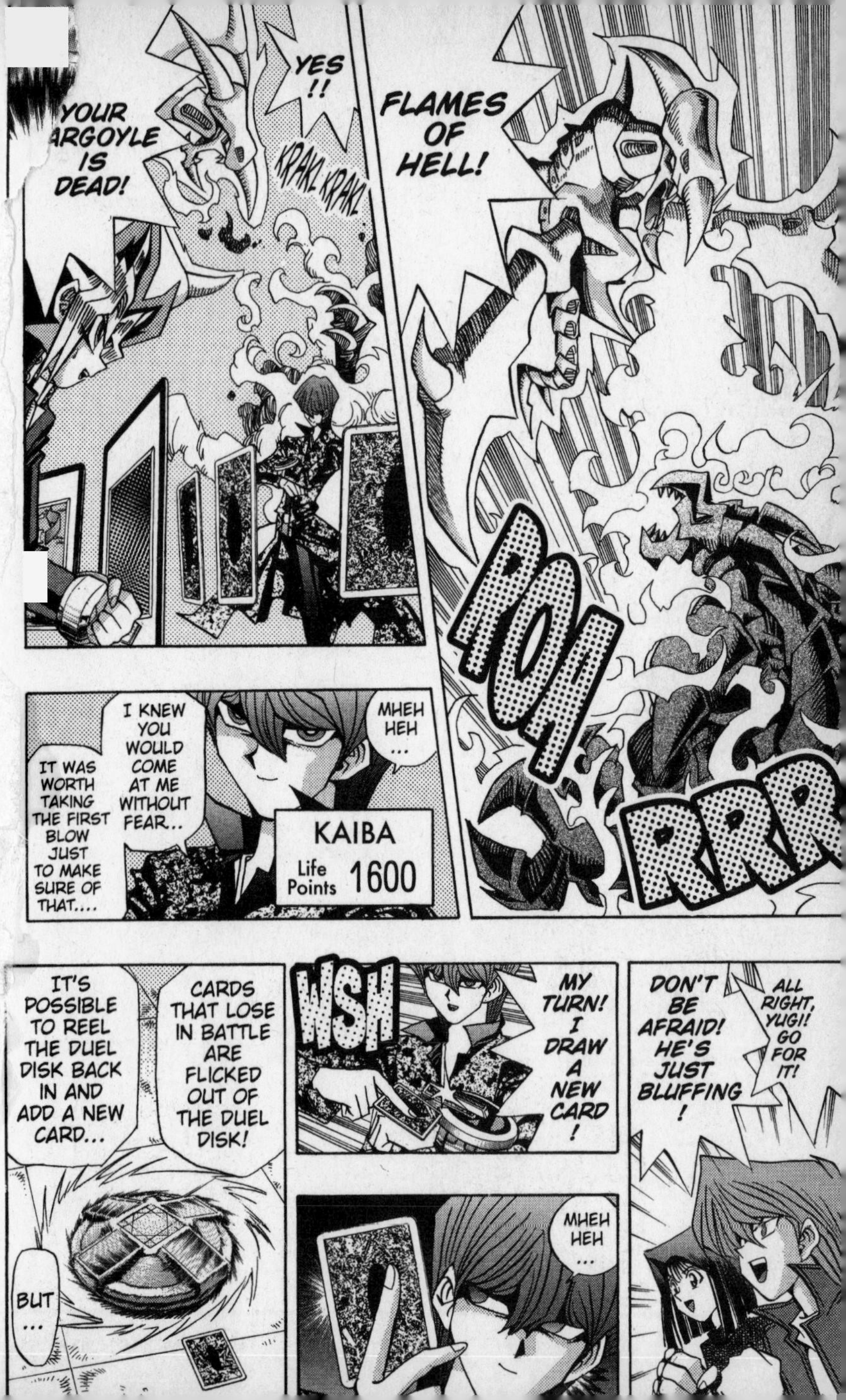
FLAMES OF HELL!
ROA!
RRR
YES!!
YOUR GARGOYLE IS DEAD!
KRAKL KRAKL
MHEH HEH...
I KNEW YOU WOULD COME AT ME WITHOUT FEAR..
IT WAS WORTH TAKING THE FIRST BLOW JUST TO MAKE SURE OF THAT....
KAIBA
Life Points 1600
ALL RIGHT, YUGI!! GO FOR IT!
DON'T BE AFRAID! HE'S JUST BLUFFING!
MY TURN! I DRAW A NEW CARD!
WSH
MHEH HEH...
CARDS THAT LOSE IN BATTLE ARE FLICKED OUT OF THE DUEL DISK!
IT'S POSSIBLE TO REEL THE DUEL DISK BACK IN AND ADD A NEW CARD...
BUT...

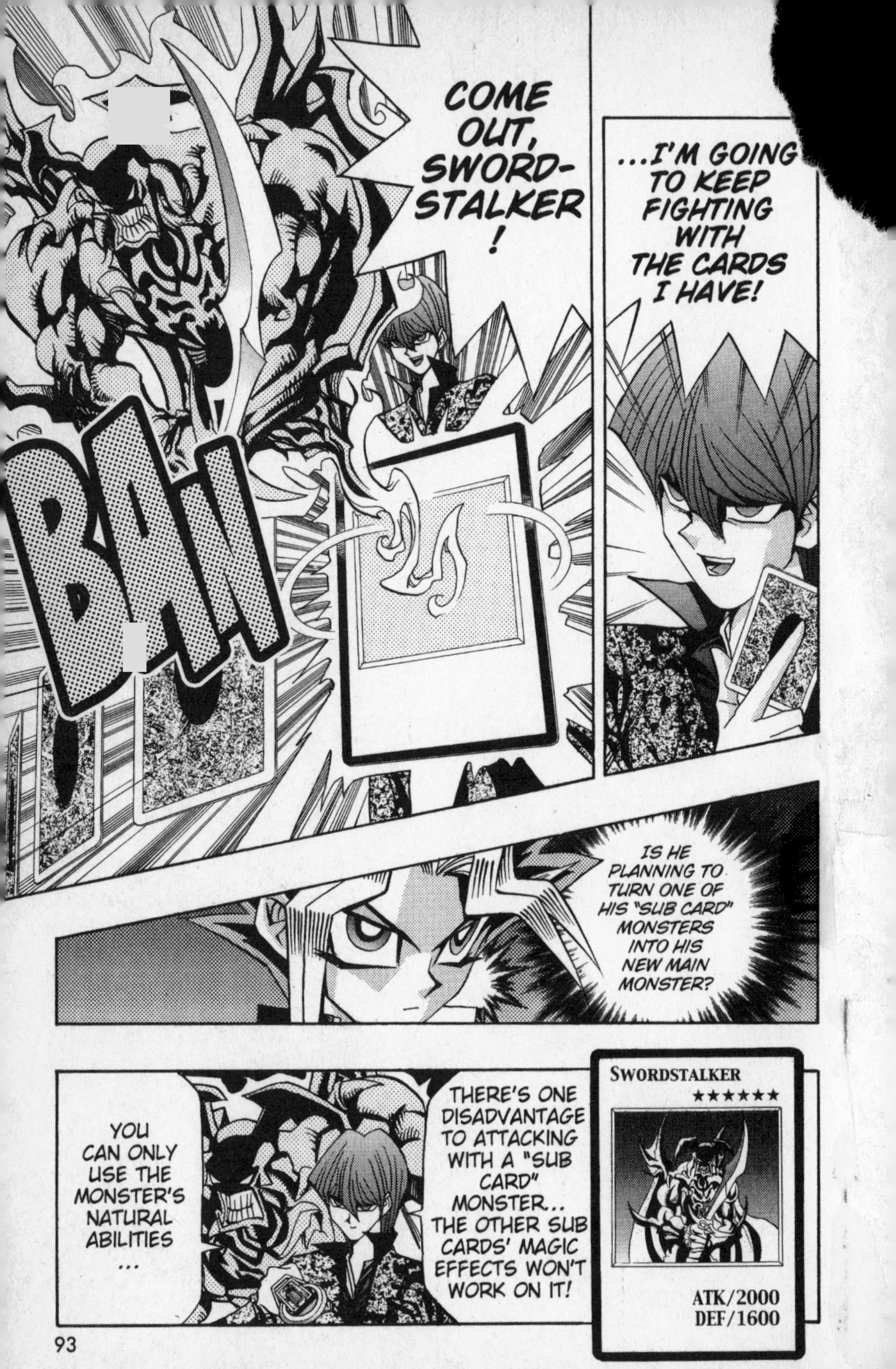
...I'M GOING TO KEEP FIGHTING WITH THE CARDS I HAVE!
COME OUT, SWORD-STALKER!
BAM
IS HE PLANNING TO TURN ONE OF HIS "SUB CARD" MONSTERS INTO HIS NEW MAIN MONSTER?
SWORDSTALKER
★★★★★★
ATK/2000
DEF/1600
THERE'S ONE DISADVANTAGE TO ATTACKING WITH A "SUB CARD" MONSTER... THE OTHER SUB CARDS' MAGIC EFFECTS WON'T WORK ON IT!
YOU CAN ONLY USE THE MONSTER'S NATURAL ABILITIES...

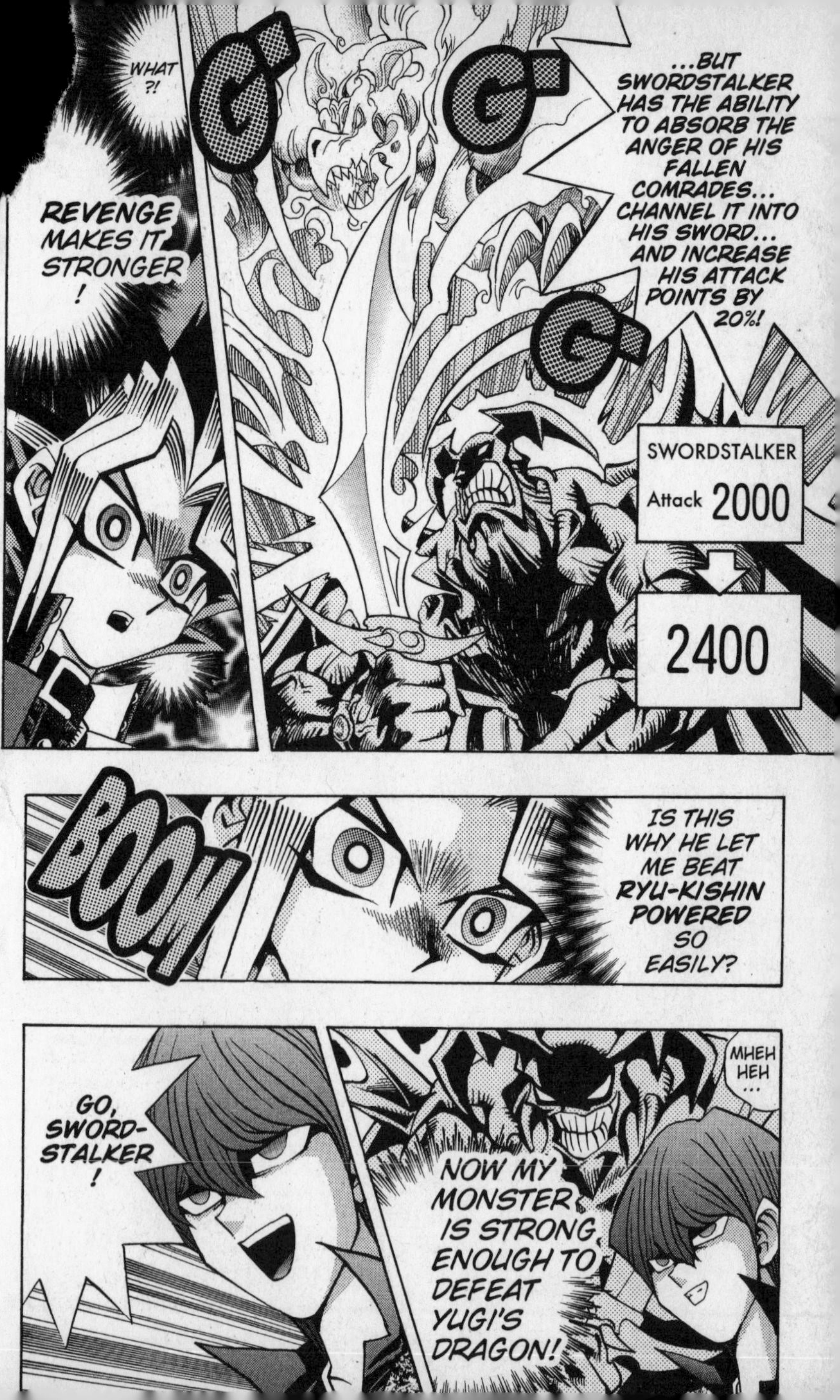
G
G
G
...BUT SWORDSTALKER HAS THE ABILITY TO ABSORB THE ANGER OF HIS FALLEN COMRADES... CHANNEL IT INTO HIS SWORD... AND INCREASE HIS ATTACK POINTS BY 20%!
SWORDSTALKER
Attack 2000
2400
WHAT ?!
REVENGE MAKES IT STRONGER !
IS THIS WHY HE LET ME BEAT RYU-KISHIN POWERED SO EASILY?
BOOM
MHEH HEH ...
NOW MY MONSTER IS STRONG ENOUGH TO DEFEAT YUGI'S DRAGON!
GO, SWORD-STALKER !

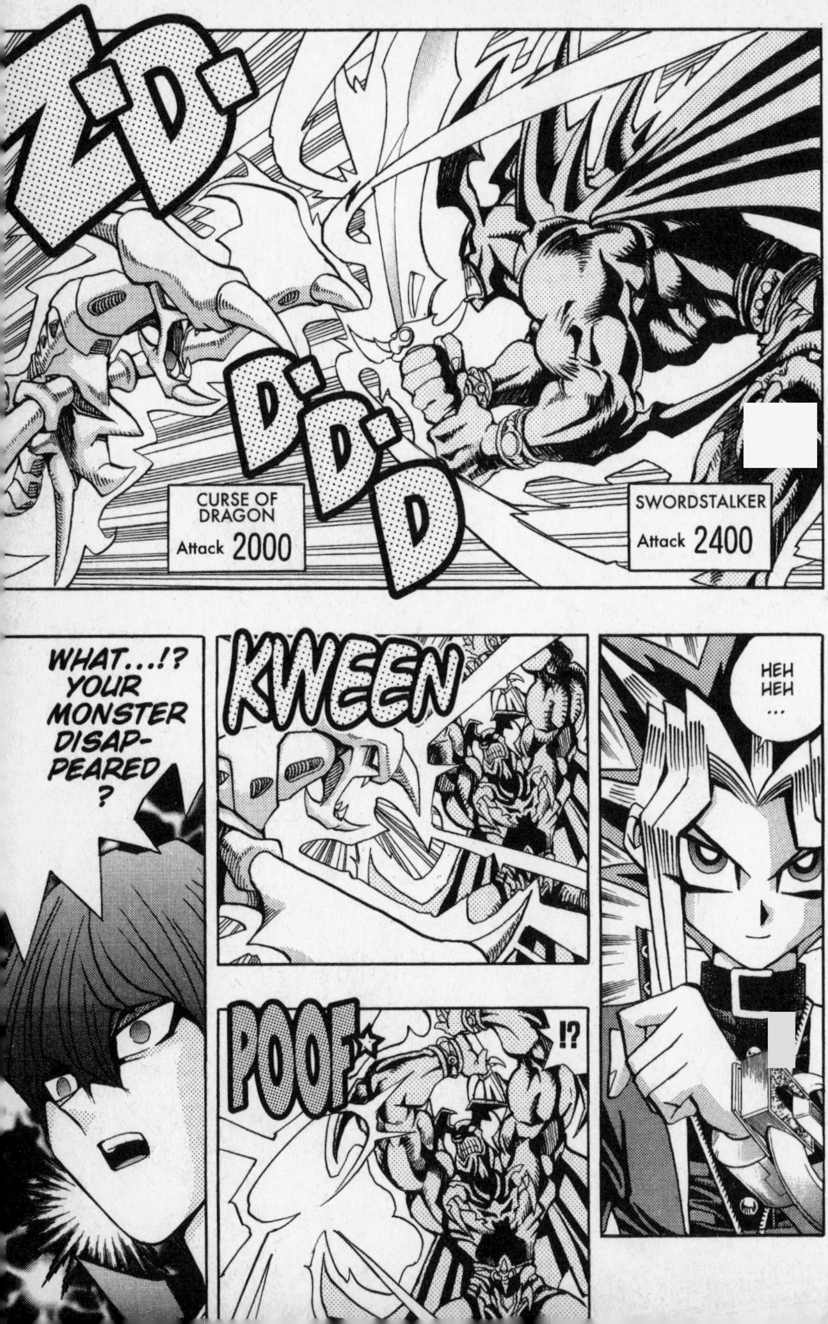
ZDD
DDD
SWORDSTALKER
Attack 2400
CURSE OF DRAGON
Attack 2000
HEH HEH ...
KWEEN
!?
POOF
WHAT...!? YOUR MONSTER DISAPPEARED ?

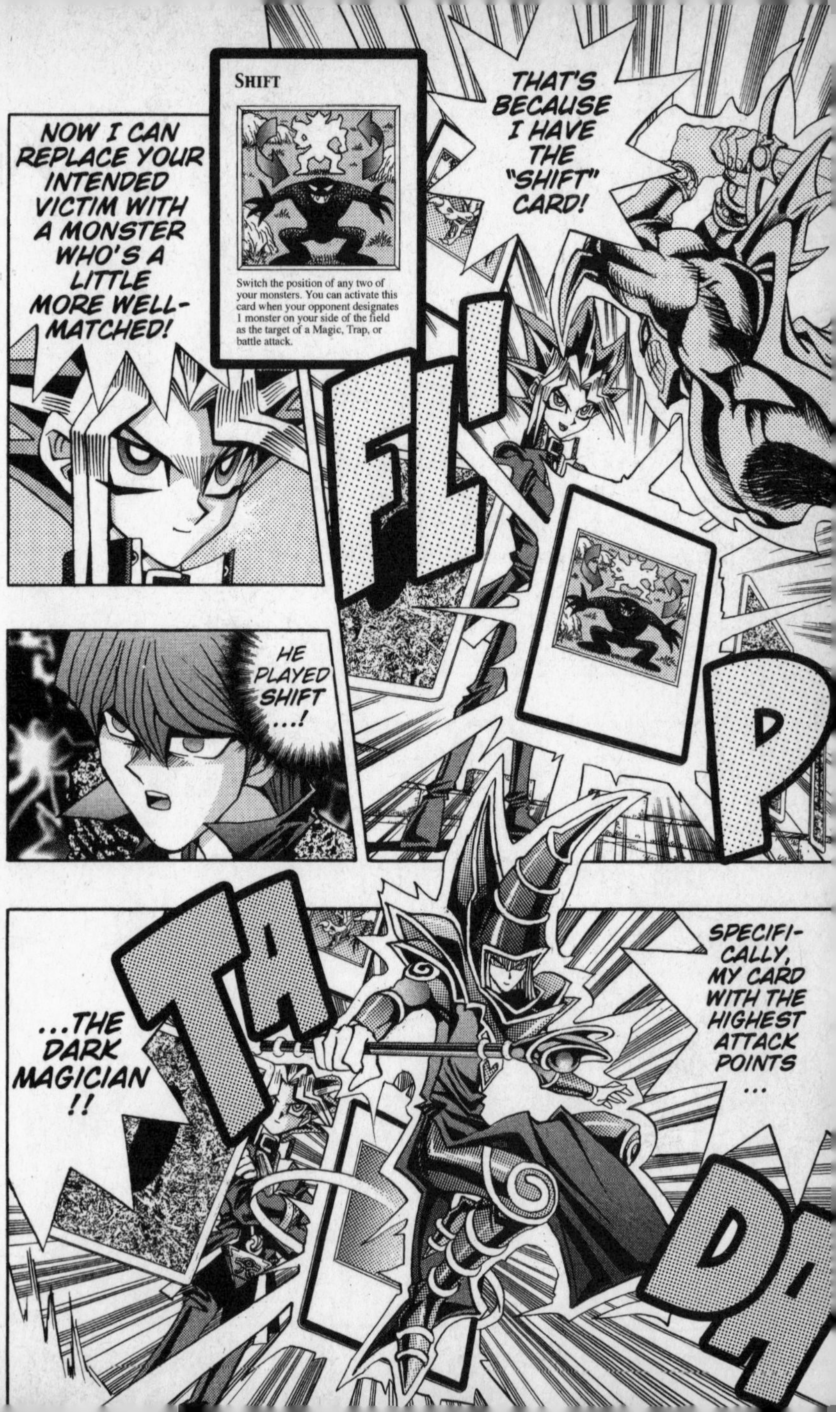
THAT'S BECAUSE I HAVE THE "SHIFT" CARD!
FL'P
SHIFT
Switch the position of any two of your monsters. You can activate this card when your opponent designates 1 monster on your side of the field as the target of a Magic, Trap, or battle attack.
NOW I CAN REPLACE YOUR INTENDED VICTIM WITH A MONSTER WHO'S A LITTLE MORE WELL-MATCHED!
HE PLAYED SHIFT ...!
SPECIFI-CALLY, MY CARD WITH THE HIGHEST ATTACK POINTS ...
...THE DARK MAGICIAN !!
TA
DA

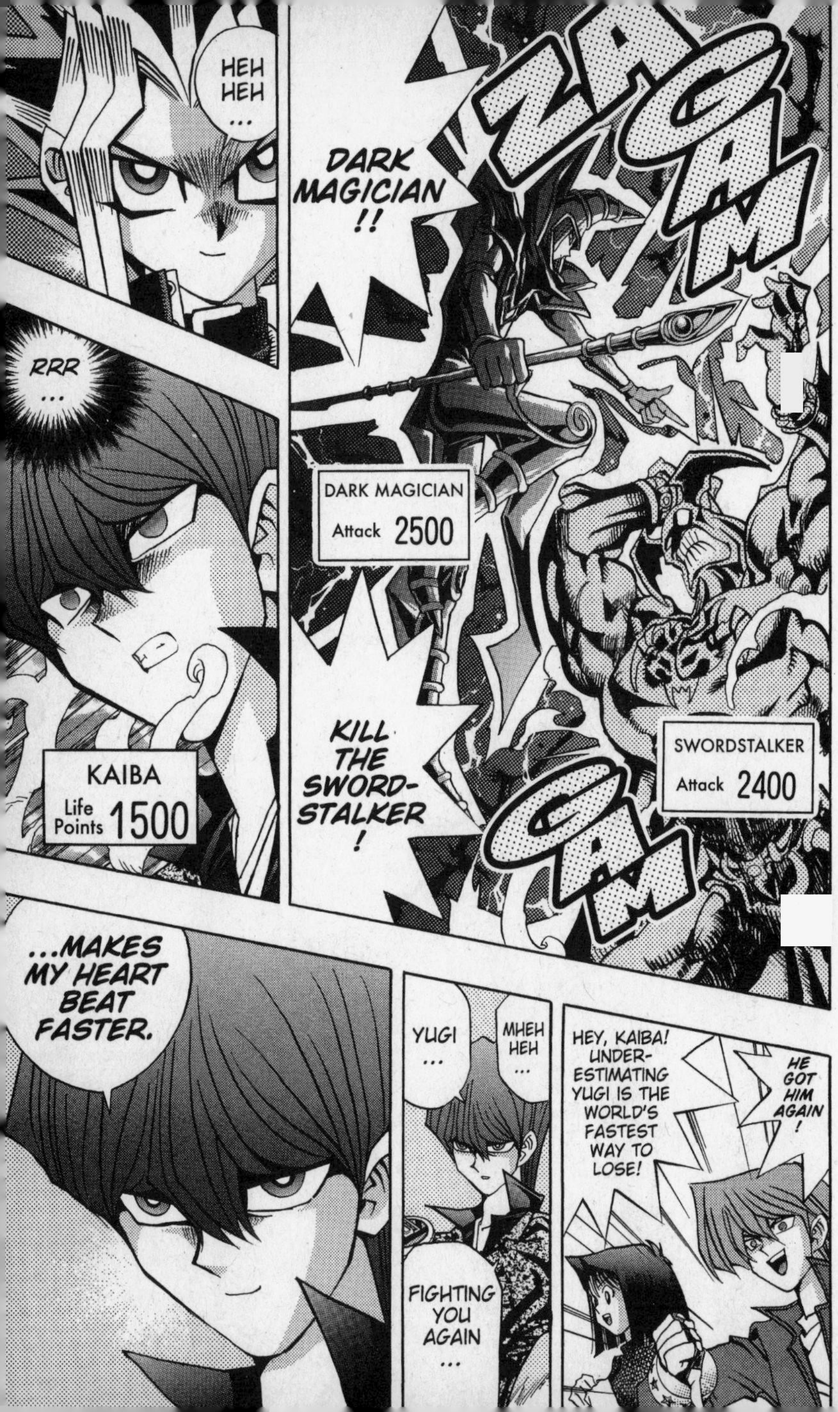
DARK MAGICIAN !!
ZAGAM
DARK MAGICIAN Attack 2500
KILL THE SWORD-STALKER !
SWORDSTALKER Attack 2400
GAM
HEH HEH ...
RRR ...
KAIBA Life Points 1500
HE GOT HIM AGAIN !
HEY, KAIBA! UNDER-ESTIMATING YUGI IS THE WORLD'S FASTEST WAY TO LOSE!
MHEH HEH ...
YUGI ...
FIGHTING YOU AGAIN ...
...MAKES MY HEART BEAT FASTER.

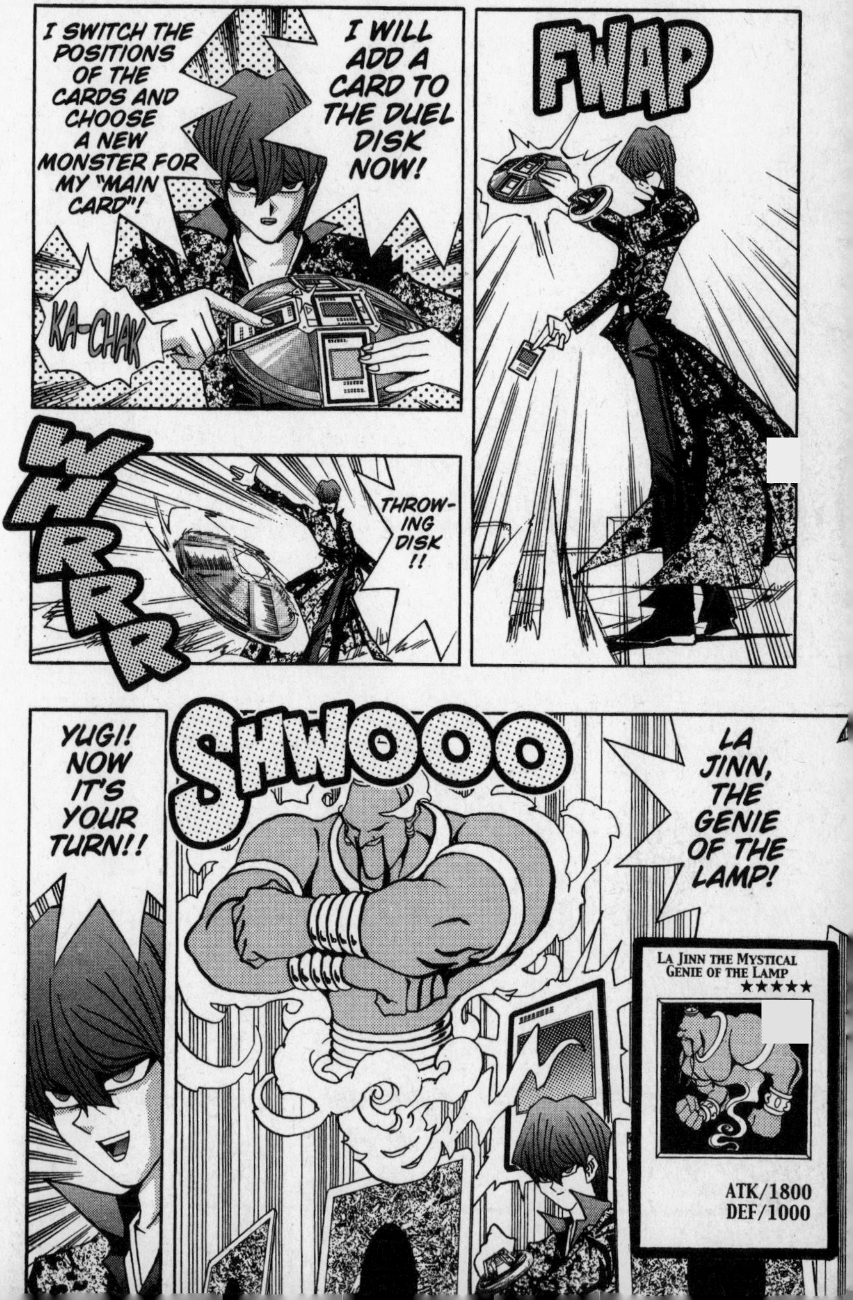
FWAP
I WILL ADD A CARD TO THE DUEL DISK NOW!
I SWITCH THE POSITIONS OF THE CARDS AND CHOOSE A NEW MONSTER FOR MY "MAIN CARD"!
KA-CHAK
THROWING DISK!!
WHRRR
LA JINN, THE GENIE OF THE LAMP!
SHWOOO
LA JINN THE MYSTICAL GENIE OF THE LAMP
★★★★★
ATK/1800
DEF/1000
YUGI! NOW IT'S YOUR TURN!!

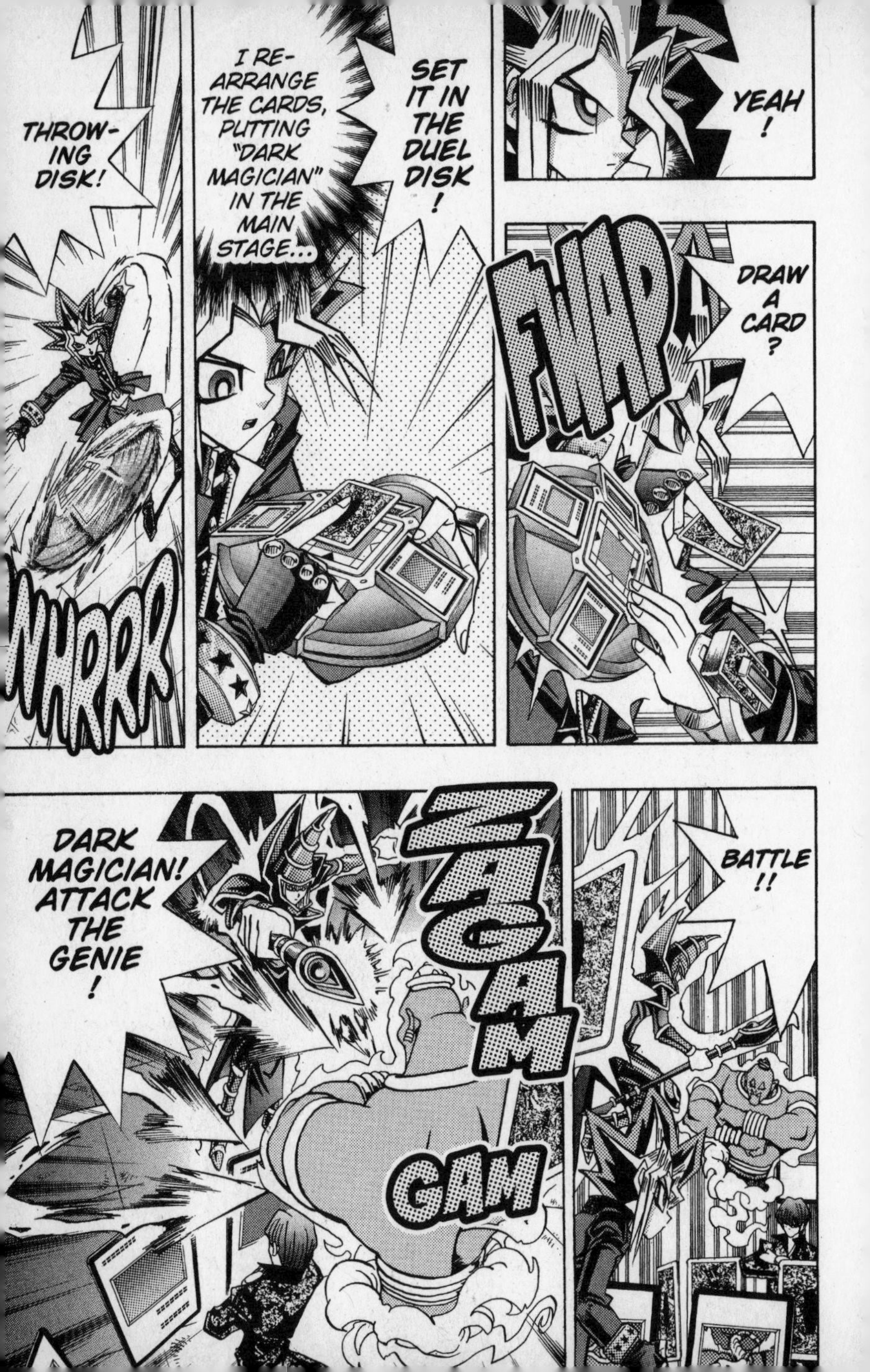
YEAH!
DRAW A CARD?
FWAP
SET IT IN THE DUEL DISK!
I RE-ARRANGE THE CARDS, PUTTING "DARK MAGICIAN" IN THE MAIN STAGE...
THROWING DISK!
WHRRR
BATTLE!!
ZAGAM
DARK MAGICIAN! ATTACK THE GENIE!
GAM

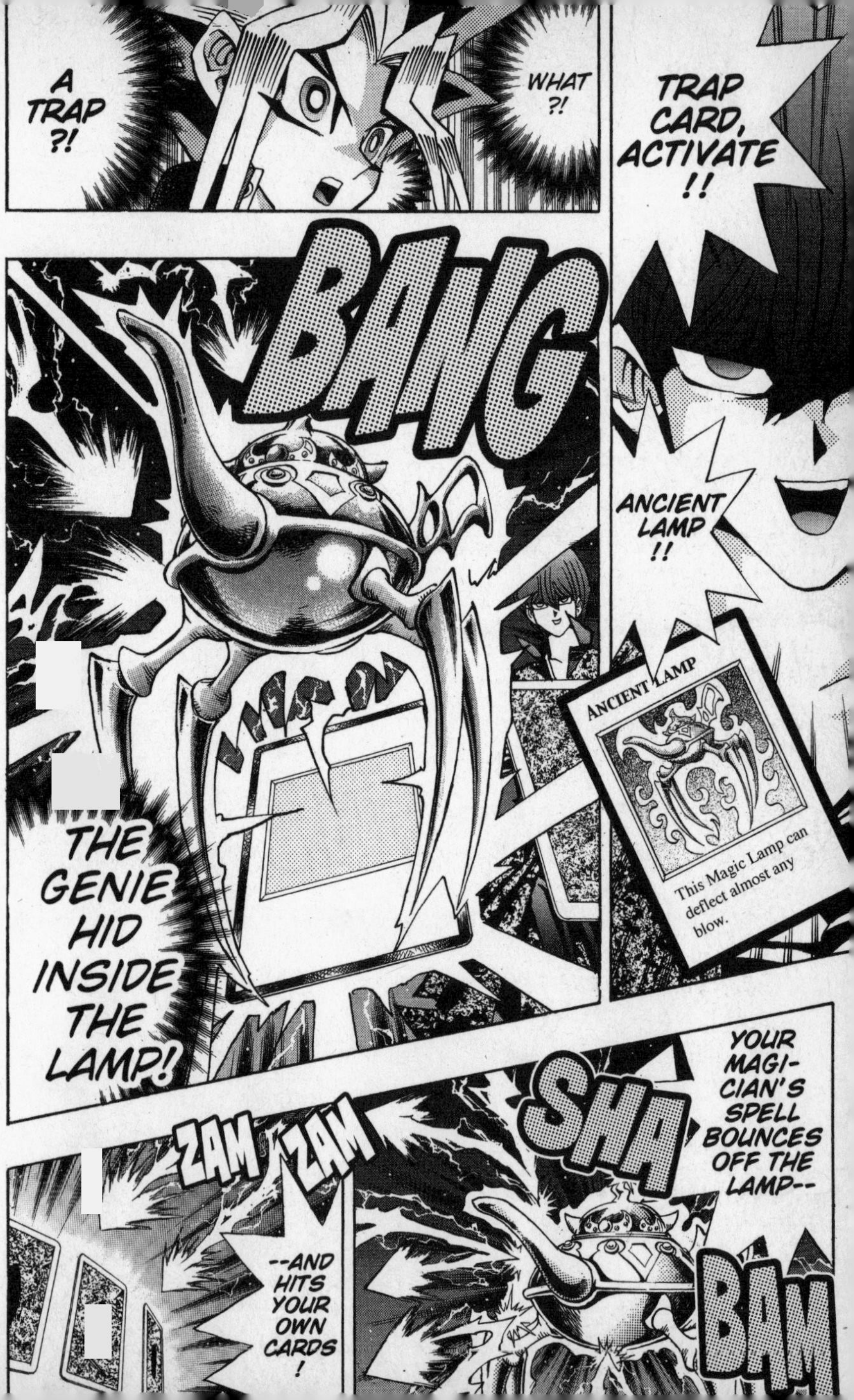
TRAP CARD, ACTIVATE !!
ANCIENT LAMP !!
ANCIENT LAMP
This Magic Lamp can deflect almost any blow.
WHAT ?!
A TRAP ?!
BANG
THE GENIE HID INSIDE THE LAMP!
YOUR MAGI- CIAN'S SPELL BOUNCES OFF THE LAMP--
SHA
BAM
ZAM
ZAM
--AND HITS YOUR OWN CARDS !

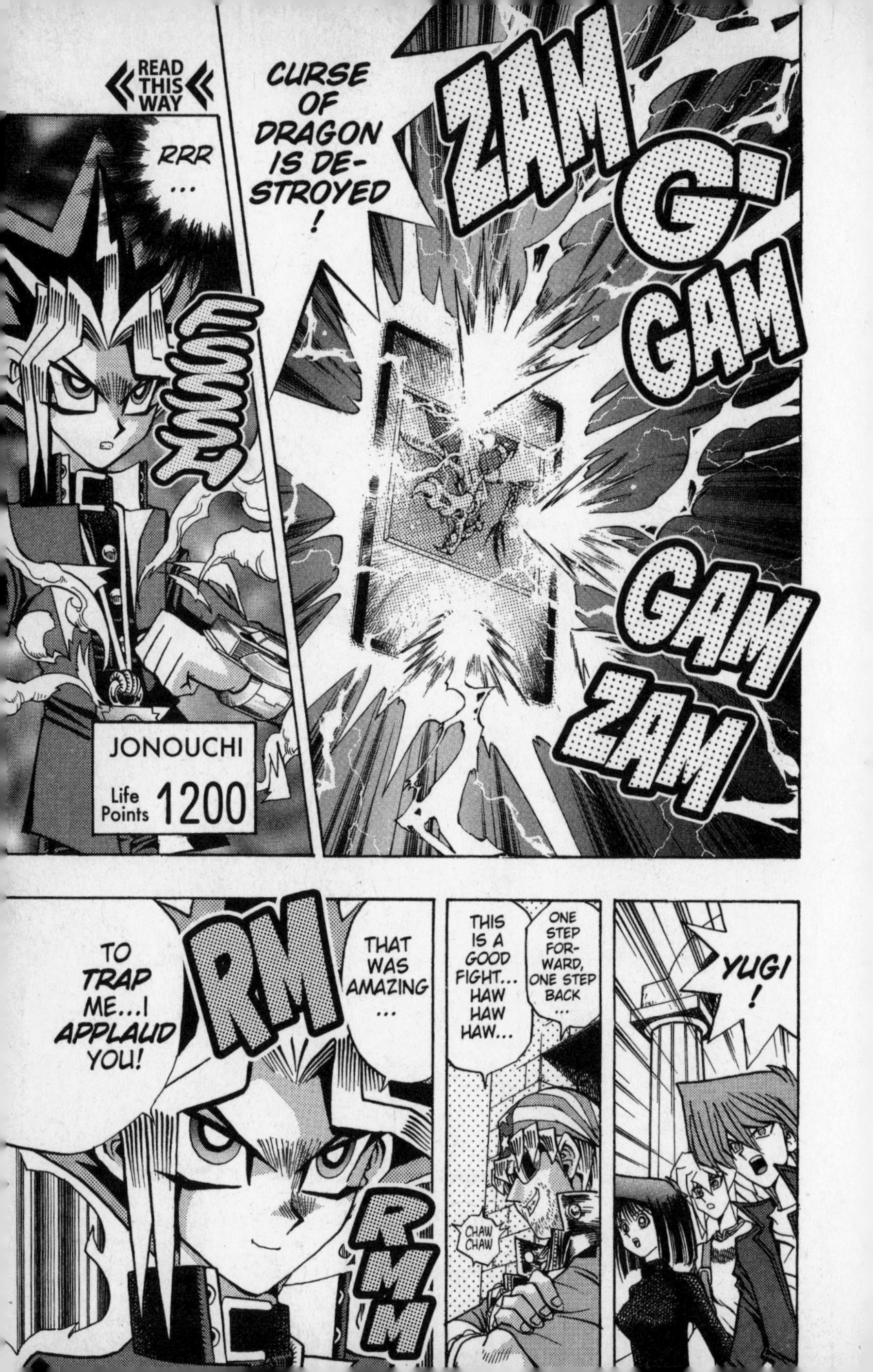
ZAM G' GAM
CURSE OF DRAGON IS DESTROYED!
GAM ZAM
READ THIS WAY
RRR...
JONOUCHI
Life Points 1200
YUGI!
ONE STEP FORWARD, ONE STEP BACK...
THIS IS A GOOD FIGHT... HAW HAW HAW...
CHAW CHAW
THAT WAS AMAZING...
RM
TO TRAP ME...I APPLAUD YOU!
RMM

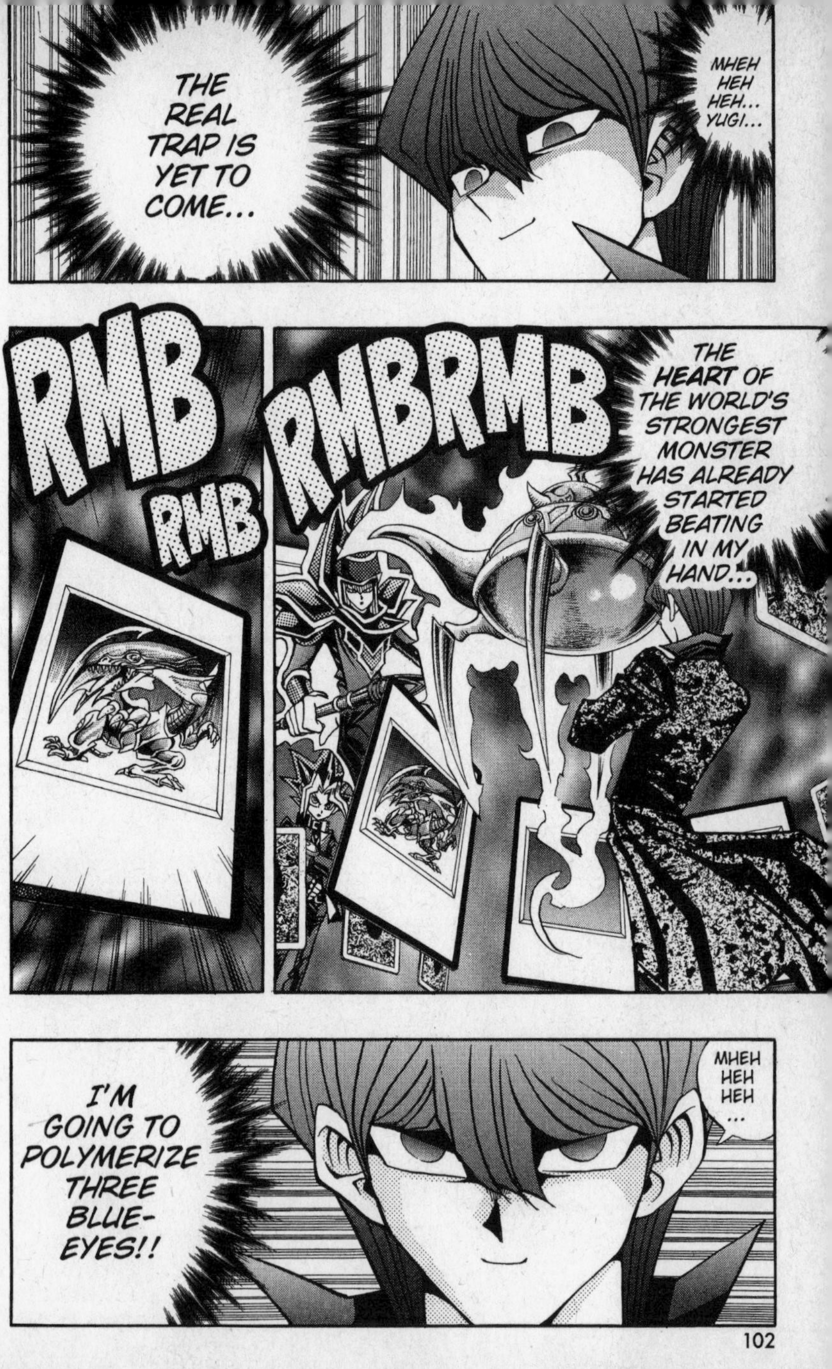
MHEH HEH HEH... YUGI...
THE REAL TRAP IS YET TO COME...
THE HEART OF THE WORLD'S STRONGEST MONSTER HAS ALREADY STARTED BEATING IN MY HAND...
RMBRMB
RMB
RMB
MHEH HEH HEH ...
I'M GOING TO POLYMERIZE THREE BLUE-EYES!!

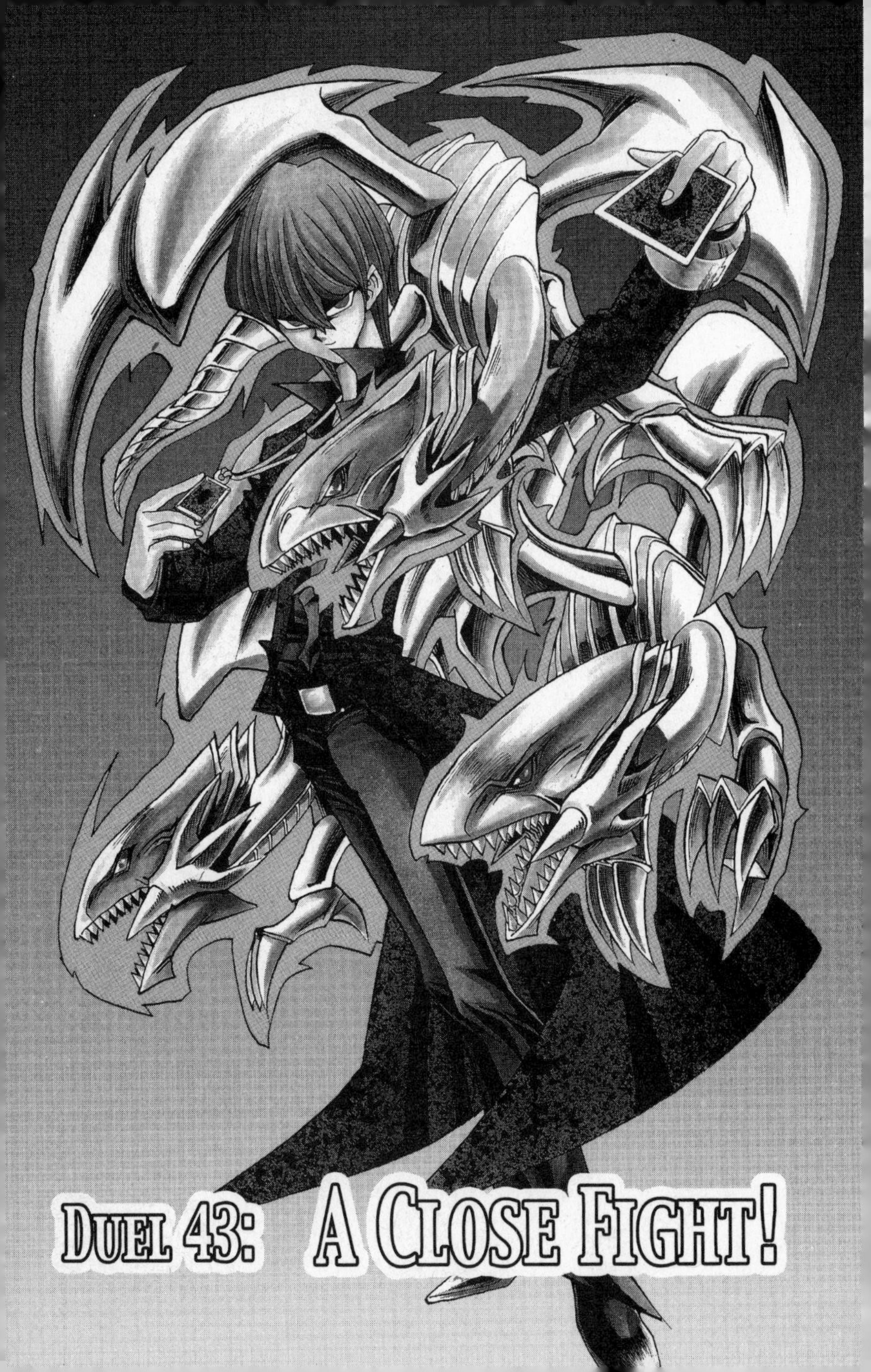

Duel 43: A Close Fight!

READ THIS WAY

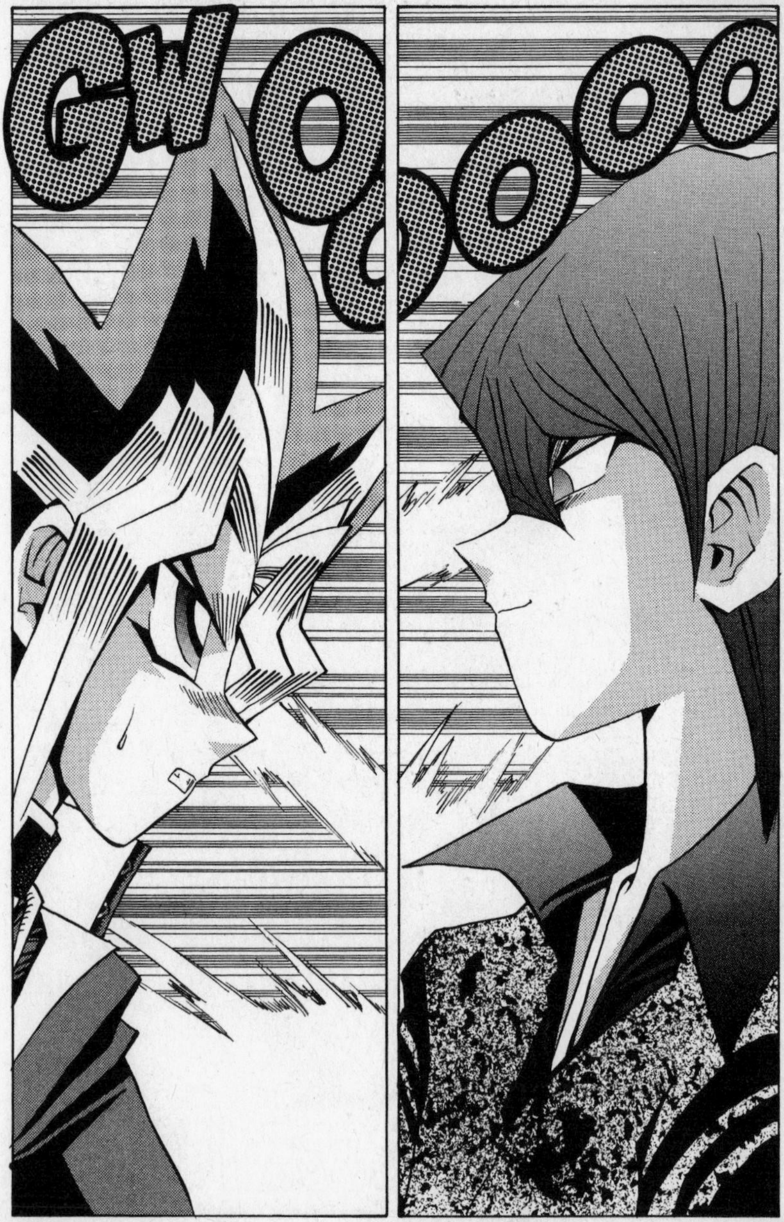

GWOOOOOOO

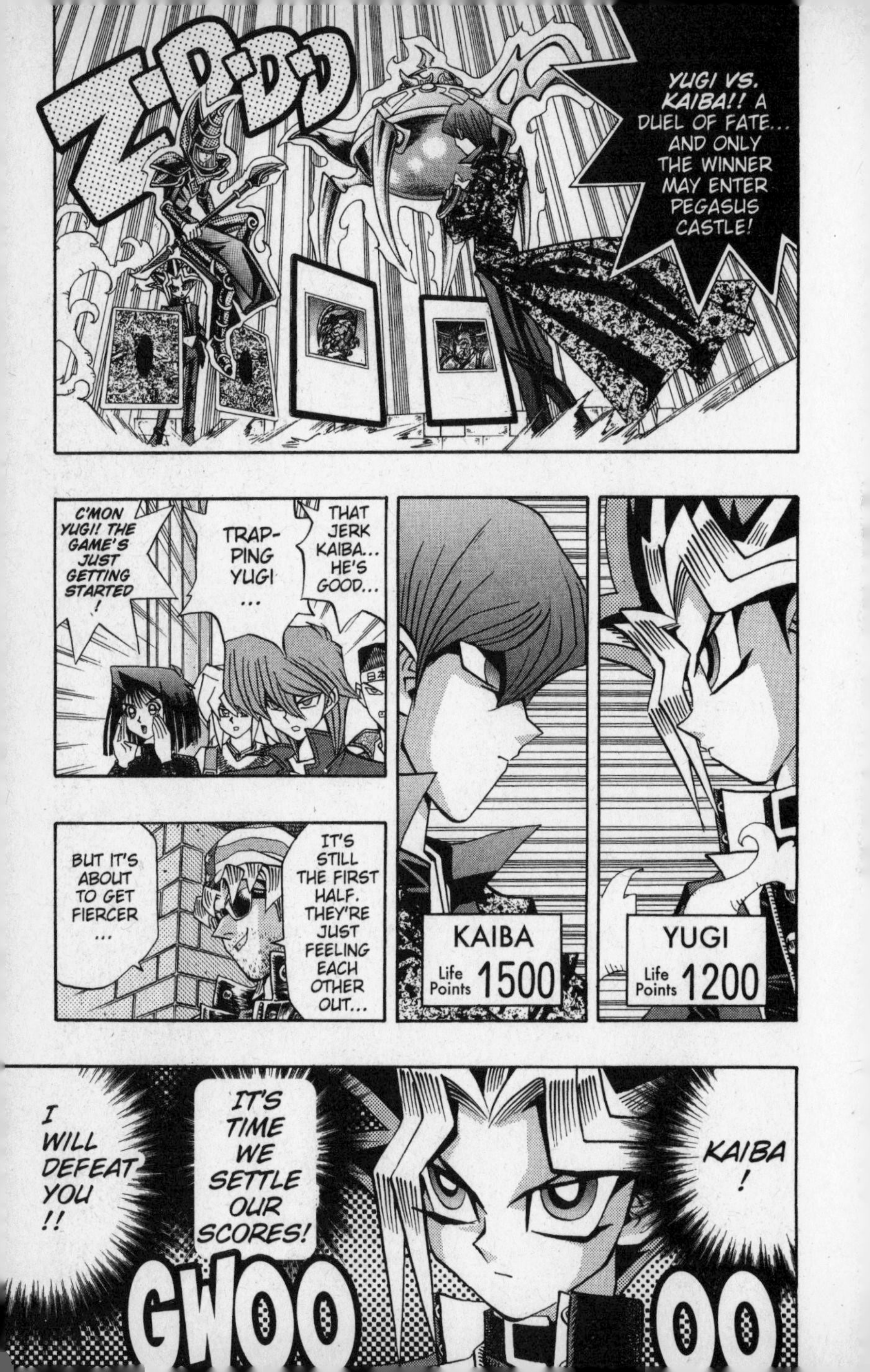
YUGI VS. KAIBA!! A DUEL OF FATE... AND ONLY THE WINNER MAY ENTER PEGASUS CASTLE!
Z-D-D-D
YUGI
Life Points 1200
KAIBA
Life Points 1500
THAT JERK KAIBA... HE'S GOOD...
TRAP-PING YUGI...
C'MON YUGI! THE GAME'S JUST GETTING STARTED!
IT'S STILL THE FIRST HALF. THEY'RE JUST FEELING EACH OTHER OUT...
BUT IT'S ABOUT TO GET FIERCER...
KAIBA!
IT'S TIME WE SETTLE OUR SCORES!
I WILL DEFEAT YOU!!
GWOO
OO

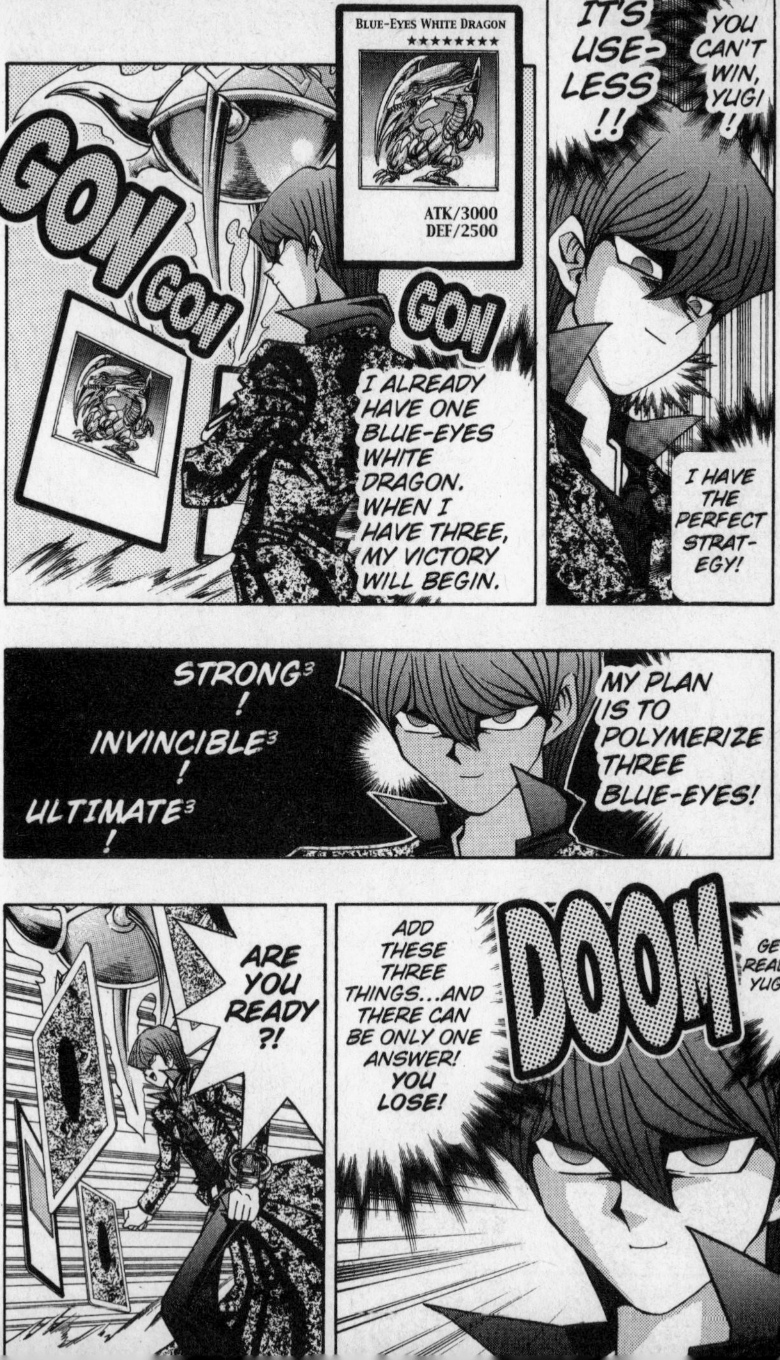

YOU CAN'T WIN, YUGI!
IT'S USE-LESS!!
I HAVE THE PERFECT STRAT-EGY!
BLUE-EYES WHITE DRAGON
ATK/3000
DEF/2500
GON
GON GON
I ALREADY HAVE ONE BLUE-EYES WHITE DRAGON. WHEN I HAVE THREE, MY VICTORY WILL BEGIN.
MY PLAN IS TO POLYMERIZE THREE BLUE-EYES!
STRONG^3!
INVINCIBLE^3!
ULTIMATE^3!
GET READY, YUGI!
DOOM
ADD THESE THREE THINGS...AND THERE CAN BE ONLY ONE ANSWER! YOU LOSE!
ARE YOU READY?!

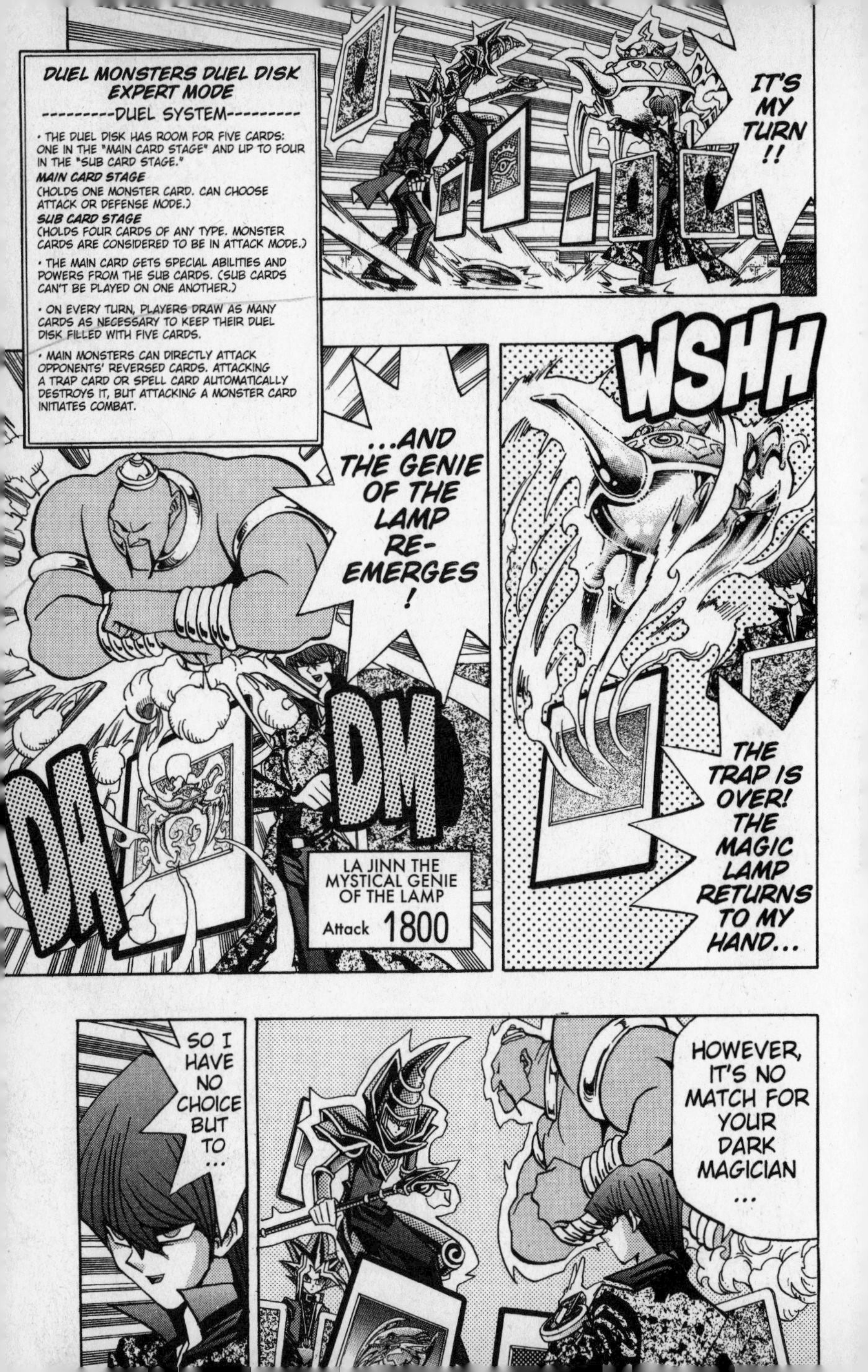
IT'S MY TURN !!
DUEL MONSTERS DUEL DISK EXPERT MODE
---------DUEL SYSTEM---------
• THE DUEL DISK HAS ROOM FOR FIVE CARDS: ONE IN THE "MAIN CARD STAGE" AND UP TO FOUR IN THE "SUB CARD STAGE."
MAIN CARD STAGE
(HOLDS ONE MONSTER CARD. CAN CHOOSE ATTACK OR DEFENSE MODE.)
SUB CARD STAGE
(HOLDS FOUR CARDS OF ANY TYPE. MONSTER CARDS ARE CONSIDERED TO BE IN ATTACK MODE.)
• THE MAIN CARD GETS SPECIAL ABILITIES AND POWERS FROM THE SUB CARDS. (SUB CARDS CAN'T BE PLAYED ON ONE ANOTHER.)
• ON EVERY TURN, PLAYERS DRAW AS MANY CARDS AS NECESSARY TO KEEP THEIR DUEL DISK FILLED WITH FIVE CARDS.
• MAIN MONSTERS CAN DIRECTLY ATTACK OPPONENTS' REVERSED CARDS. ATTACKING A TRAP CARD OR SPELL CARD AUTOMATICALLY DESTROYS IT, BUT ATTACKING A MONSTER CARD INITIATES COMBAT.
WSHH
THE TRAP IS OVER! THE MAGIC LAMP RETURNS TO MY HAND...
...AND THE GENIE OF THE LAMP RE-EMERGES !
DM
DA
LA JINN THE MYSTICAL GENIE OF THE LAMP
Attack 1800
HOWEVER, IT'S NO MATCH FOR YOUR DARK MAGICIAN ...
SO I HAVE NO CHOICE BUT TO ...

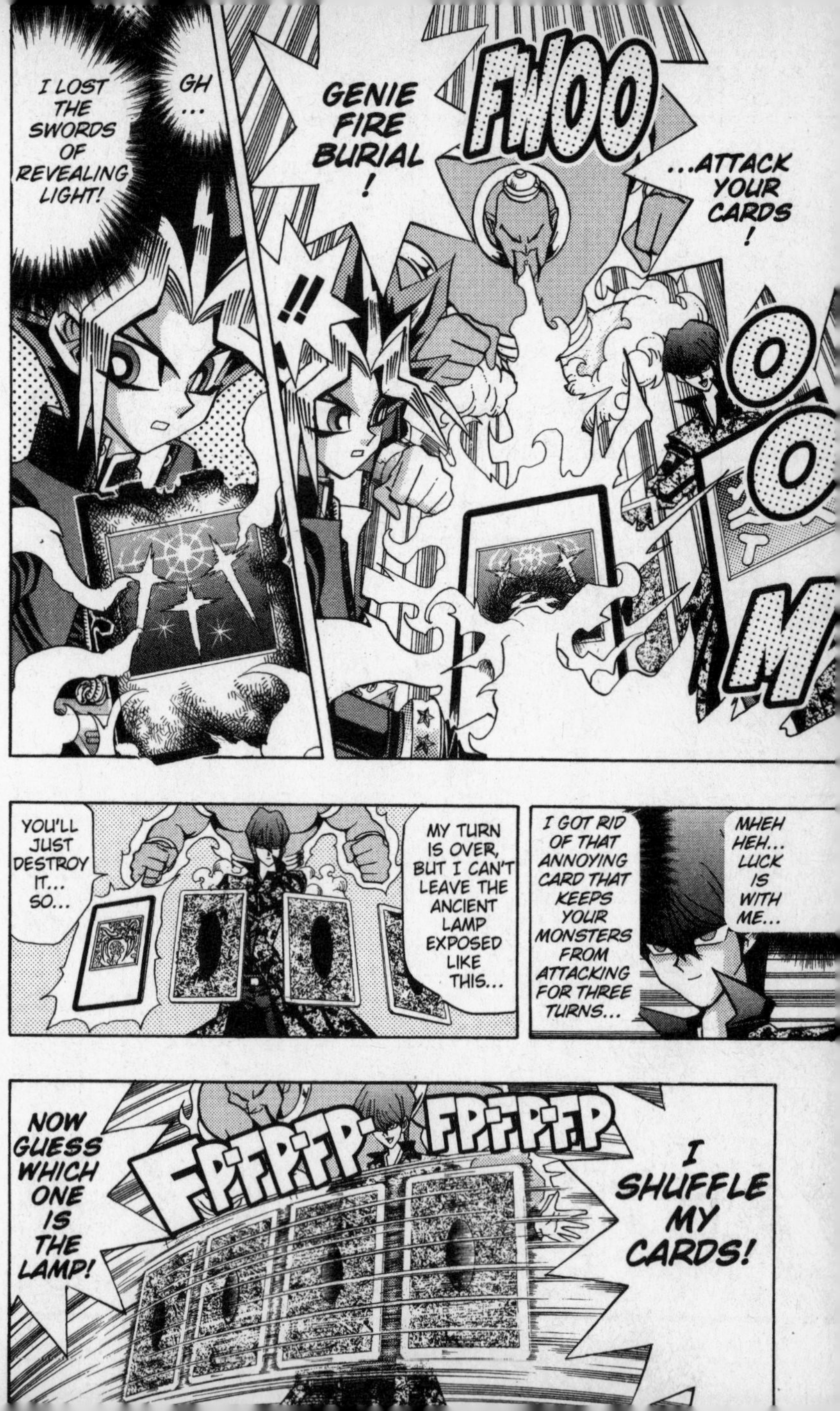
GENIE FIRE BURIAL!
FWOOOOOM
...ATTACK YOUR CARDS!
!!
GH...
I LOST THE SWORDS OF REVEALING LIGHT!
MHEH HEH... LUCK IS WITH ME...
I GOT RID OF THAT ANNOYING CARD THAT KEEPS YOUR MONSTERS FROM ATTACKING FOR THREE TURNS...
MY TURN IS OVER, BUT I CAN'T LEAVE THE ANCIENT LAMP EXPOSED LIKE THIS...
YOU'LL JUST DESTROY IT... SO...
I SHUFFLE MY CARDS!
NOW GUESS WHICH ONE IS THE LAMP!

READ THIS WAY

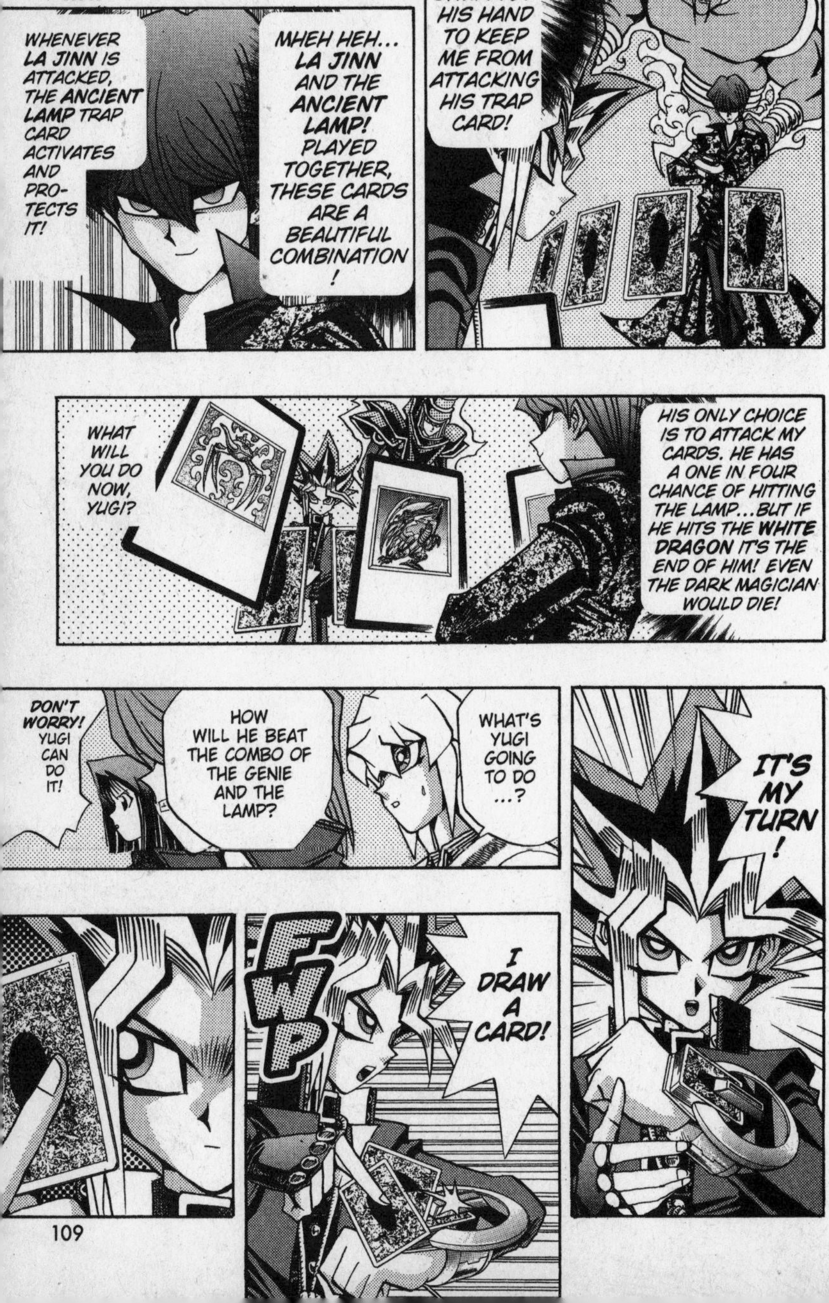

HE SHUFFLED HIS HAND TO KEEP ME FROM ATTACKING HIS TRAP CARD!
MHEH HEH... LA JINN AND THE ANCIENT LAMP! PLAYED TOGETHER, THESE CARDS ARE A BEAUTIFUL COMBINATION!
WHENEVER LA JINN IS ATTACKED, THE ANCIENT LAMP TRAP CARD ACTIVATES AND PRO-TECTS IT!
HIS ONLY CHOICE IS TO ATTACK MY CARDS. HE HAS A ONE IN FOUR CHANCE OF HITTING THE LAMP...BUT IF HE HITS THE WHITE DRAGON IT'S THE END OF HIM! EVEN THE DARK MAGICIAN WOULD DIE!
WHAT WILL YOU DO NOW, YUGI?
IT'S MY TURN!
WHAT'S YUGI GOING TO DO ...?
HOW WILL HE BEAT THE COMBO OF THE GENIE AND THE LAMP?
DON'T WORRY! YUGI CAN DO IT!
I DRAW A CARD!
FWP

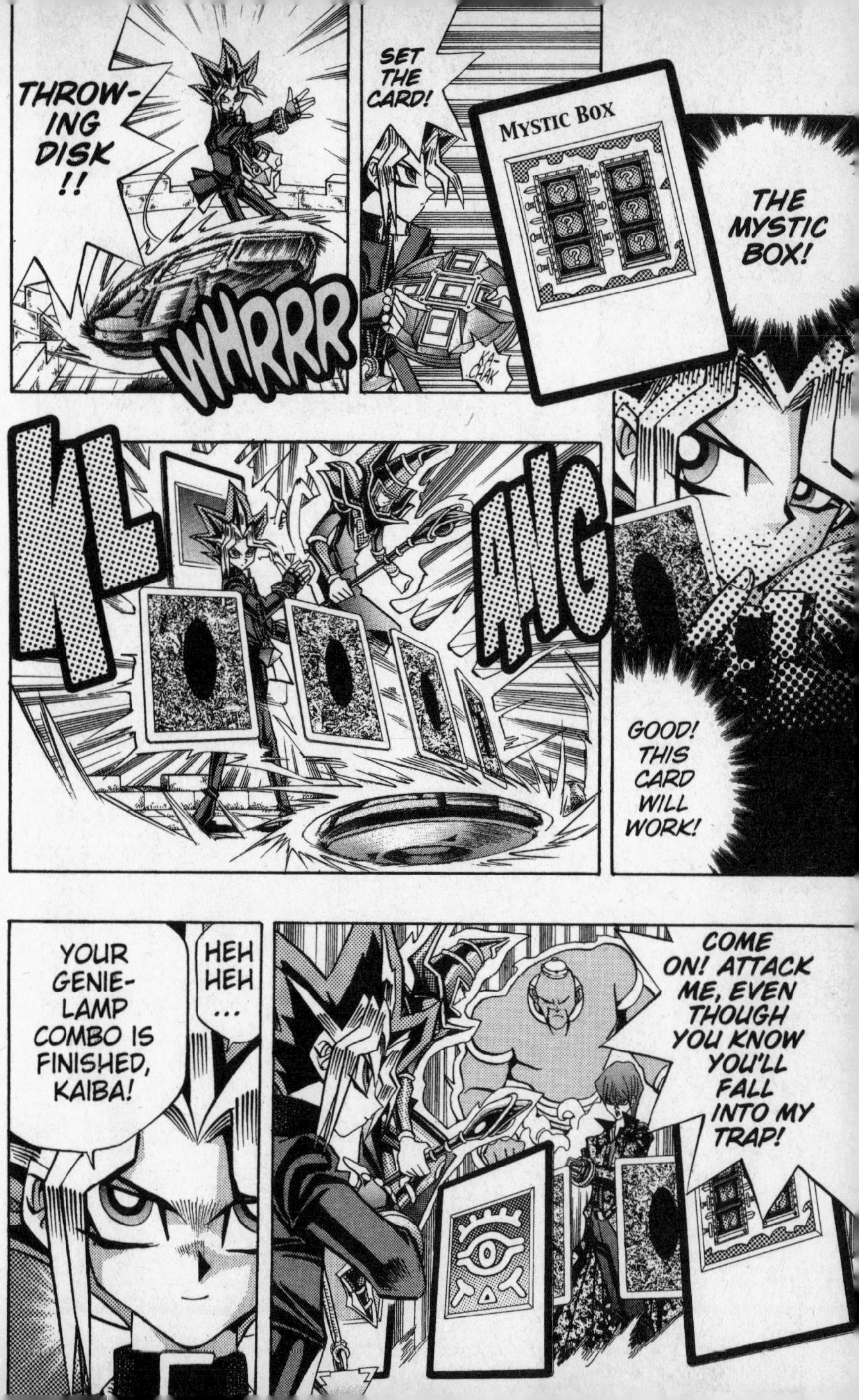
MYSTIC BOX
THE MYSTIC BOX!
SET THE CARD!
KA-CHAK
THROWING-DISK!!
WHRRR
GOOD! THIS CARD WILL WORK!
KLANG
COME ON! ATTACK ME, EVEN THOUGH YOU KNOW YOU'LL FALL INTO MY TRAP!
HEH HEH ...
YOUR GENIE-LAMP COMBO IS FINISHED, KAIBA!

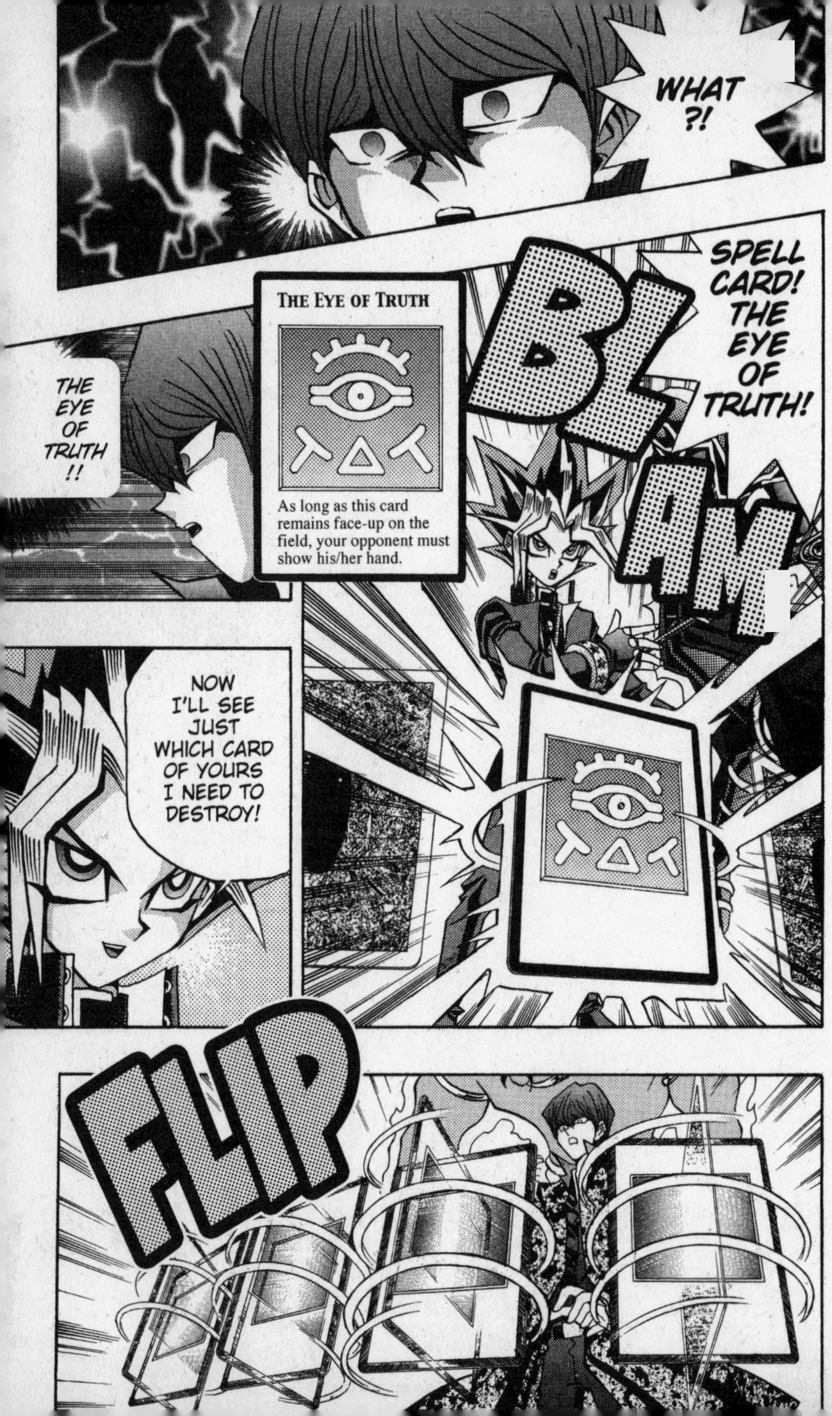
WHAT ?!
SPELL CARD! THE EYE OF TRUTH!
BLAM!
THE EYE OF TRUTH
As long as this card remains face-up on the field, your opponent must show his/her hand.
THE EYE OF TRUTH !!
NOW I'LL SEE JUST WHICH CARD OF YOURS I NEED TO DESTROY!
FLIP

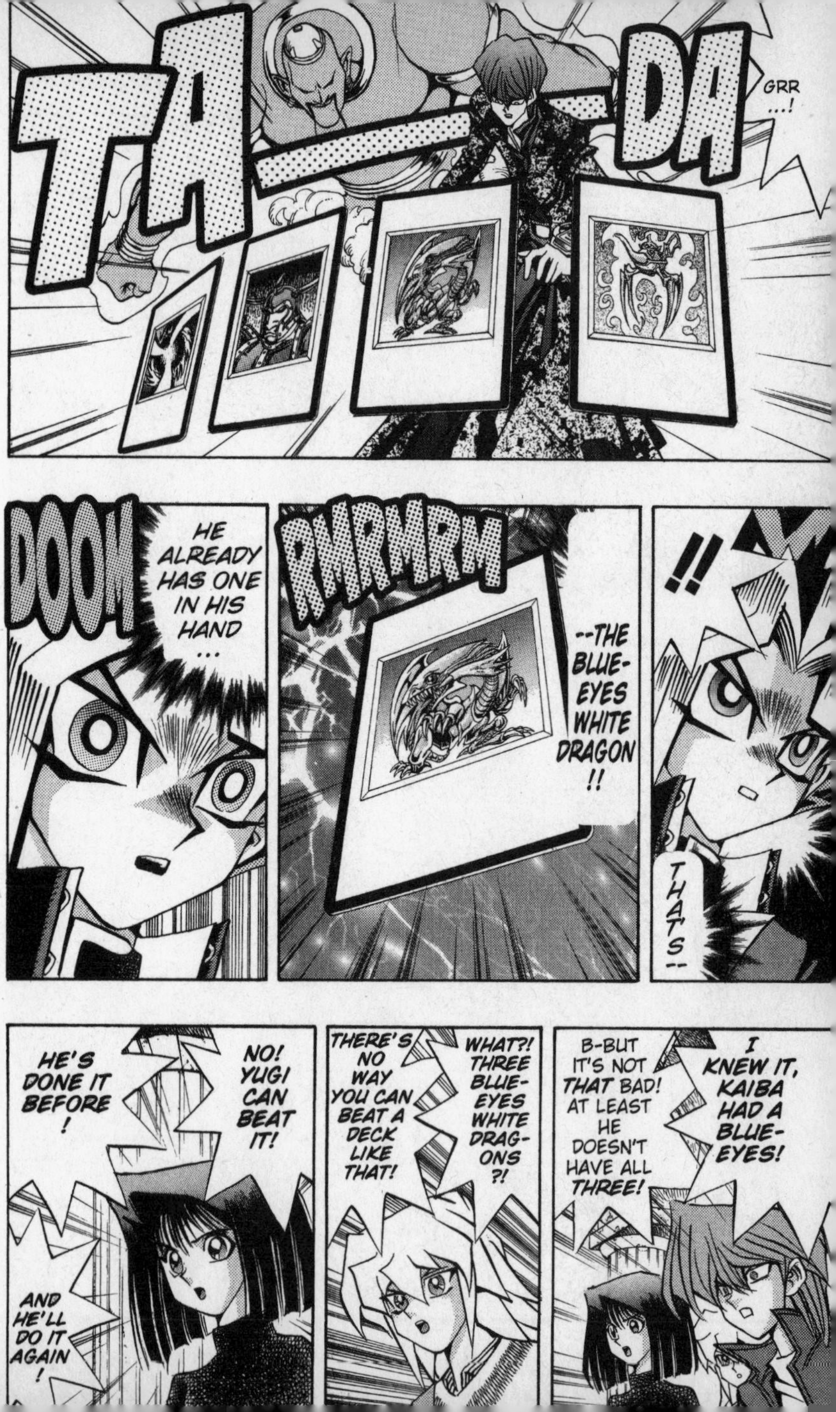
TA—DA
GRR ...!
!!
THAT'S--
RMRMRM
--THE BLUE-EYES WHITE DRAGON !!
DOOM
HE ALREADY HAS ONE IN HIS HAND ...
I KNEW IT, KAIBA HAD A BLUE-EYES!
B-BUT IT'S NOT THAT BAD! AT LEAST HE DOESN'T HAVE ALL THREE!
WHAT?! THREE BLUE-EYES WHITE DRAG-ONS ?!
THERE'S NO WAY YOU CAN BEAT A DECK LIKE THAT!
NO! YUGI CAN BEAT IT!
HE'S DONE IT BEFORE !
AND HE'LL DO IT AGAIN !

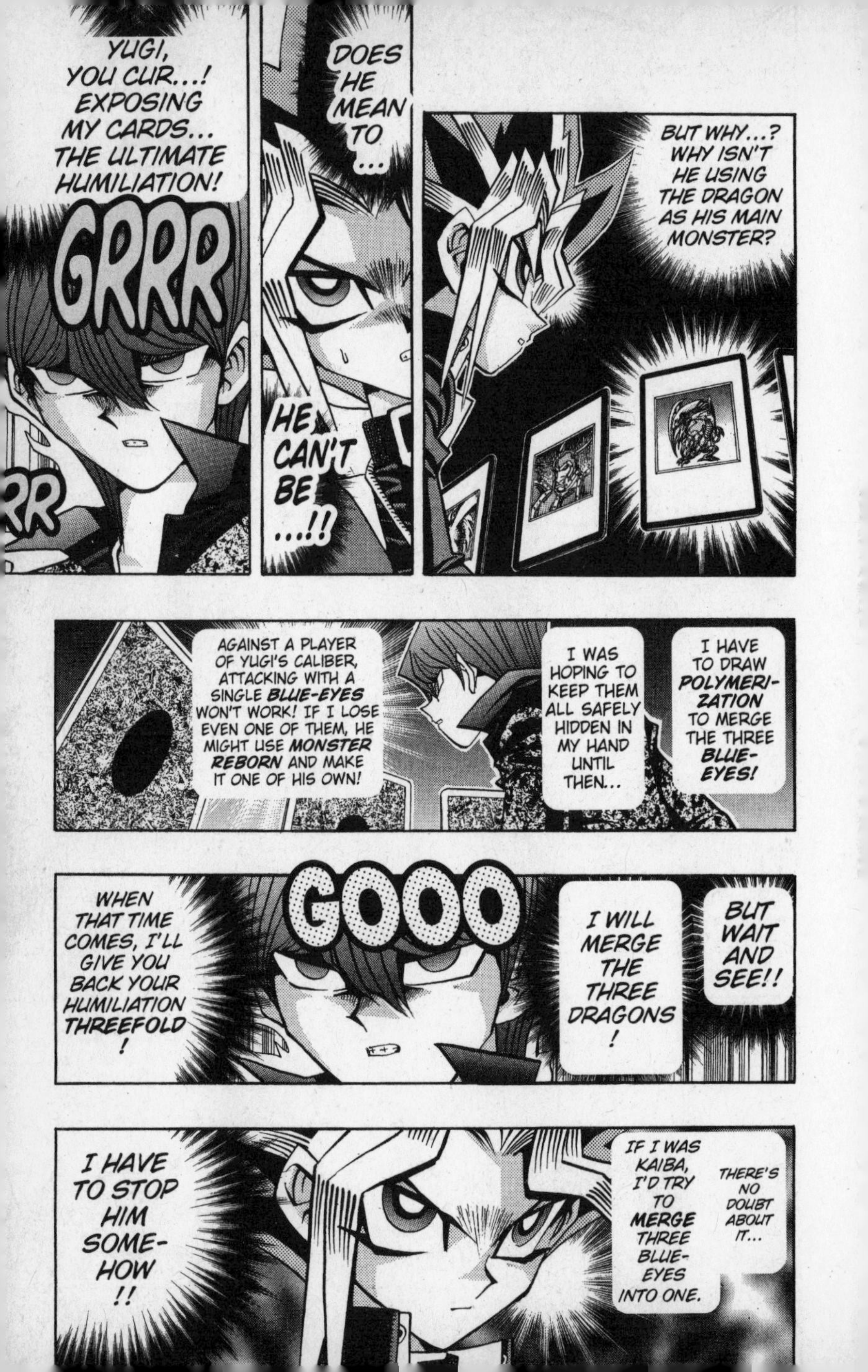
BUT WHY...? WHY ISN'T HE USING THE DRAGON AS HIS MAIN MONSTER?
DOES HE MEAN TO ...
HE CAN'T BE ...!!
YUGI, YOU CUR...! EXPOSING MY CARDS... THE ULTIMATE HUMILIATION!
GRRR
RR
I HAVE TO DRAW POLYMERIZATION TO MERGE THE THREE BLUE-EYES!
I WAS HOPING TO KEEP THEM ALL SAFELY HIDDEN IN MY HAND UNTIL THEN...
AGAINST A PLAYER OF YUGI'S CALIBER, ATTACKING WITH A SINGLE BLUE-EYES WON'T WORK! IF I LOSE EVEN ONE OF THEM, HE MIGHT USE MONSTER REBORN AND MAKE IT ONE OF HIS OWN!
BUT WAIT AND SEE!!
I WILL MERGE THE THREE DRAGONS!
GOOO
WHEN THAT TIME COMES, I'LL GIVE YOU BACK YOUR HUMILIATION THREEFOLD!
THERE'S NO DOUBT ABOUT IT...
IF I WAS KAIBA, I'D TRY TO MERGE THREE BLUE-EYES INTO ONE.
I HAVE TO STOP HIM SOME-HOW!!

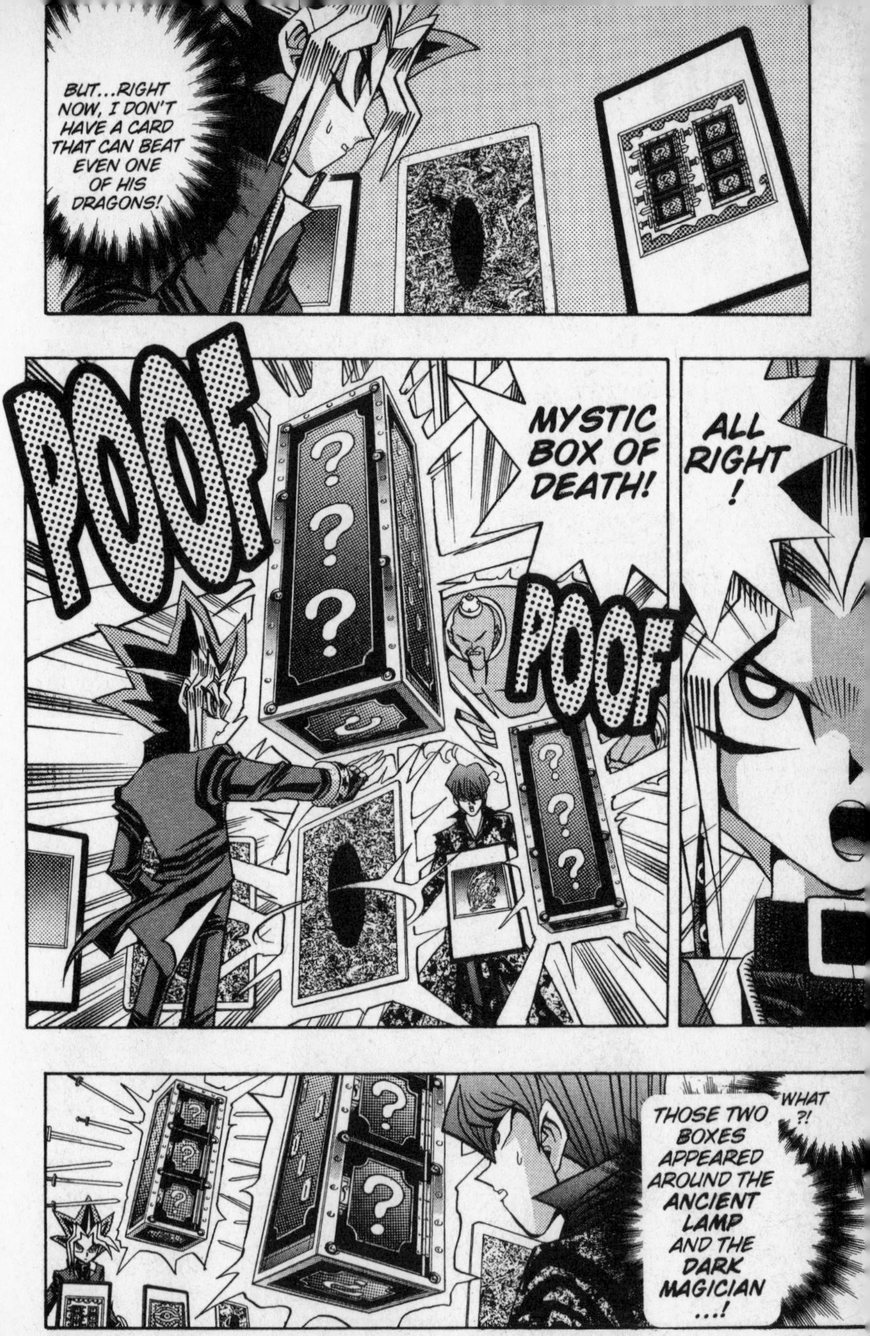
BUT...RIGHT NOW, I DON'T HAVE A CARD THAT CAN BEAT EVEN ONE OF HIS DRAGONS!
ALL RIGHT!
MYSTIC BOX OF DEATH!
POOF
POOF
WHAT?!
THOSE TWO BOXES APPEARED AROUND THE ANCIENT LAMP AND THE DARK MAGICIAN...!

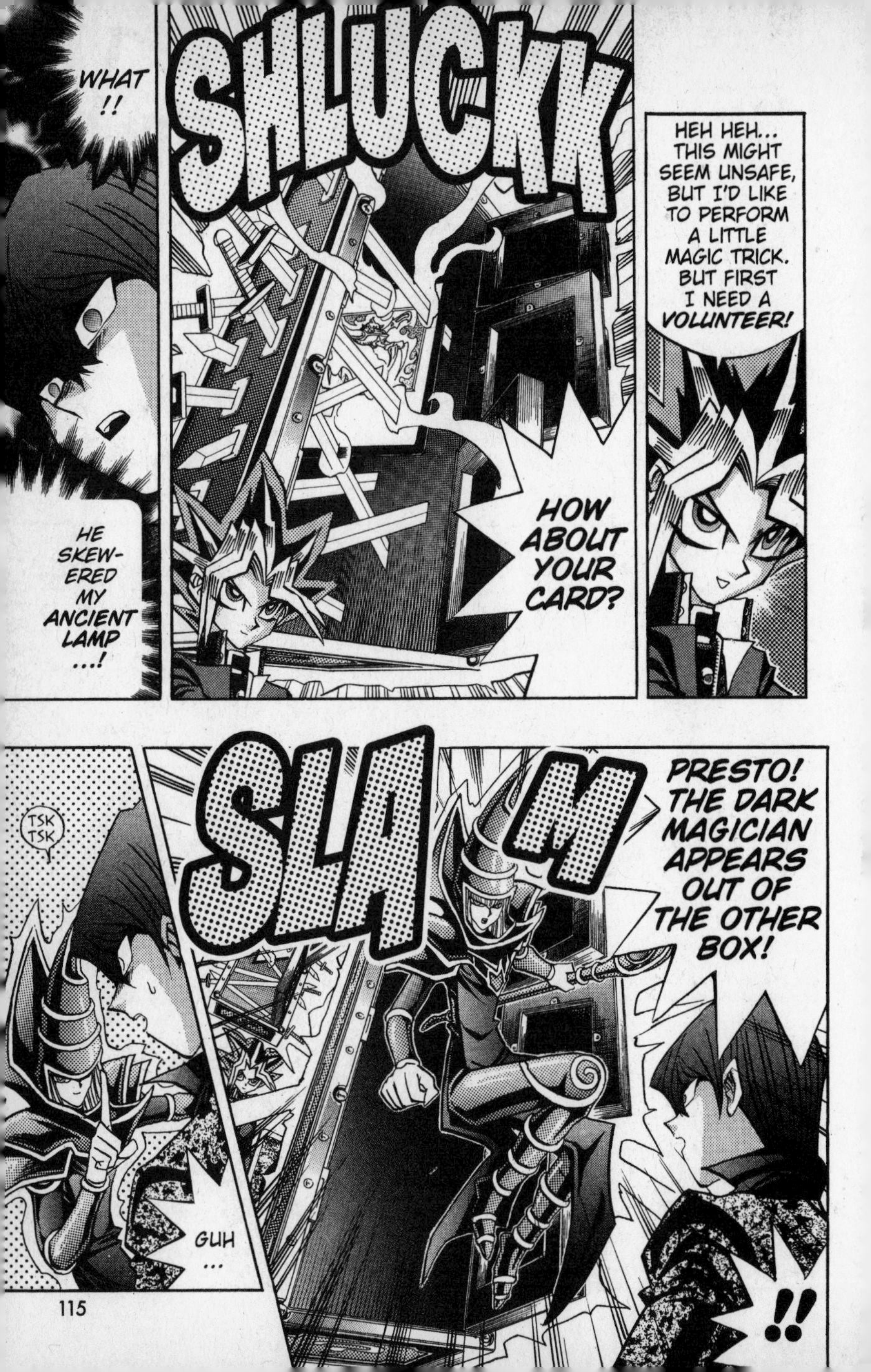
HEH HEH... THIS MIGHT SEEM UNSAFE, BUT I'D LIKE TO PERFORM A LITTLE MAGIC TRICK. BUT FIRST I NEED A VOLUNTEER!
SHLUCKK
HOW ABOUT YOUR CARD?
WHAT !!
HE SKEW-ERED MY ANCIENT LAMP ...!
SLAM
PRESTO! THE DARK MAGICIAN APPEARS OUT OF THE OTHER BOX!
!!
TSK TSK
GUH ...

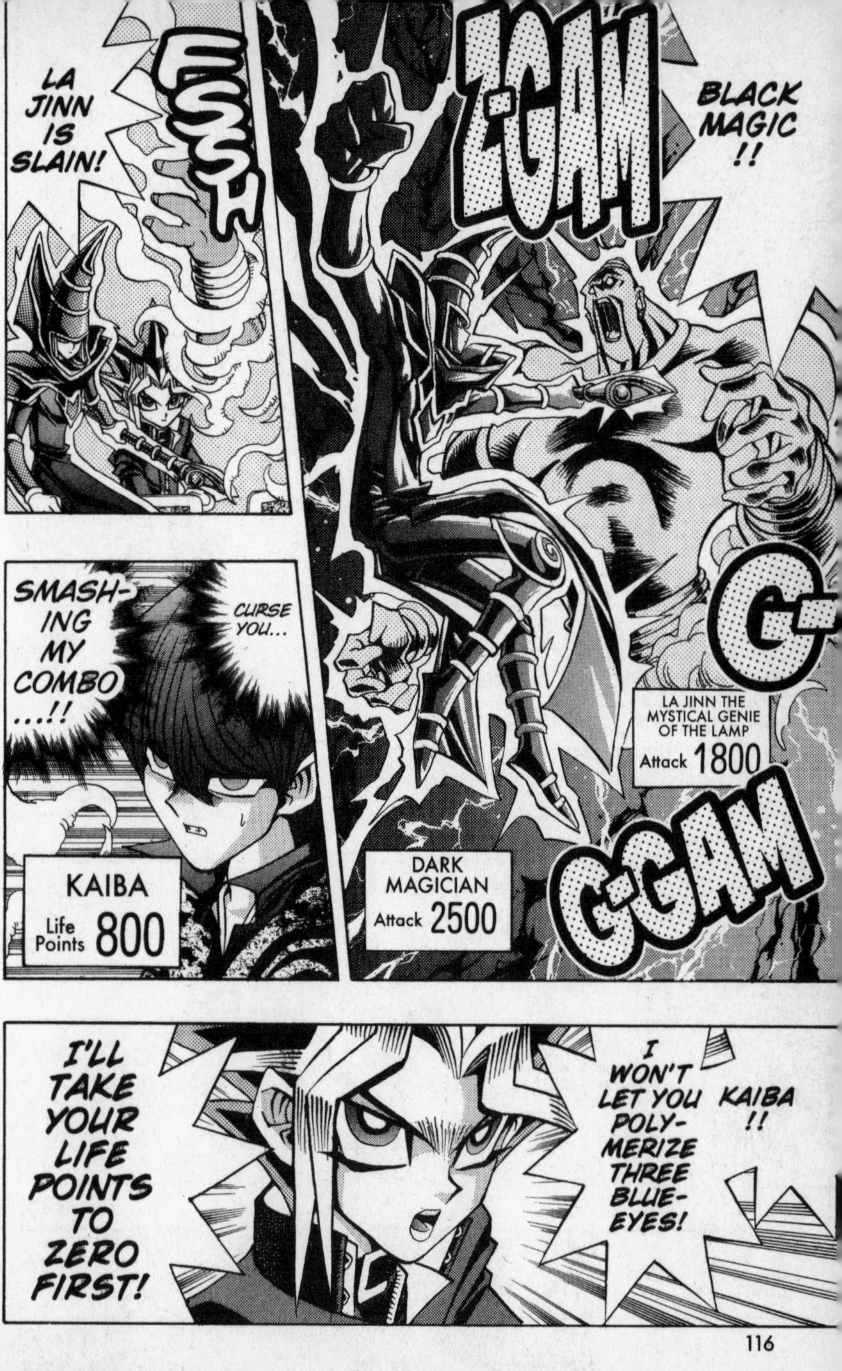

BLACK MAGIC !!
Z-GAM
G-
LA JINN THE MYSTICAL GENIE OF THE LAMP Attack 1800
G-GAM
DARK MAGICIAN Attack 2500
LA JINN IS SLAIN!
FSSH
CURSE YOU...
SMASHING MY COMBO ...!!
KAIBA Life Points 800
KAIBA !!
I WON'T LET YOU POLYMERIZE THREE BLUE-EYES!
I'LL TAKE YOUR LIFE POINTS TO ZERO FIRST!

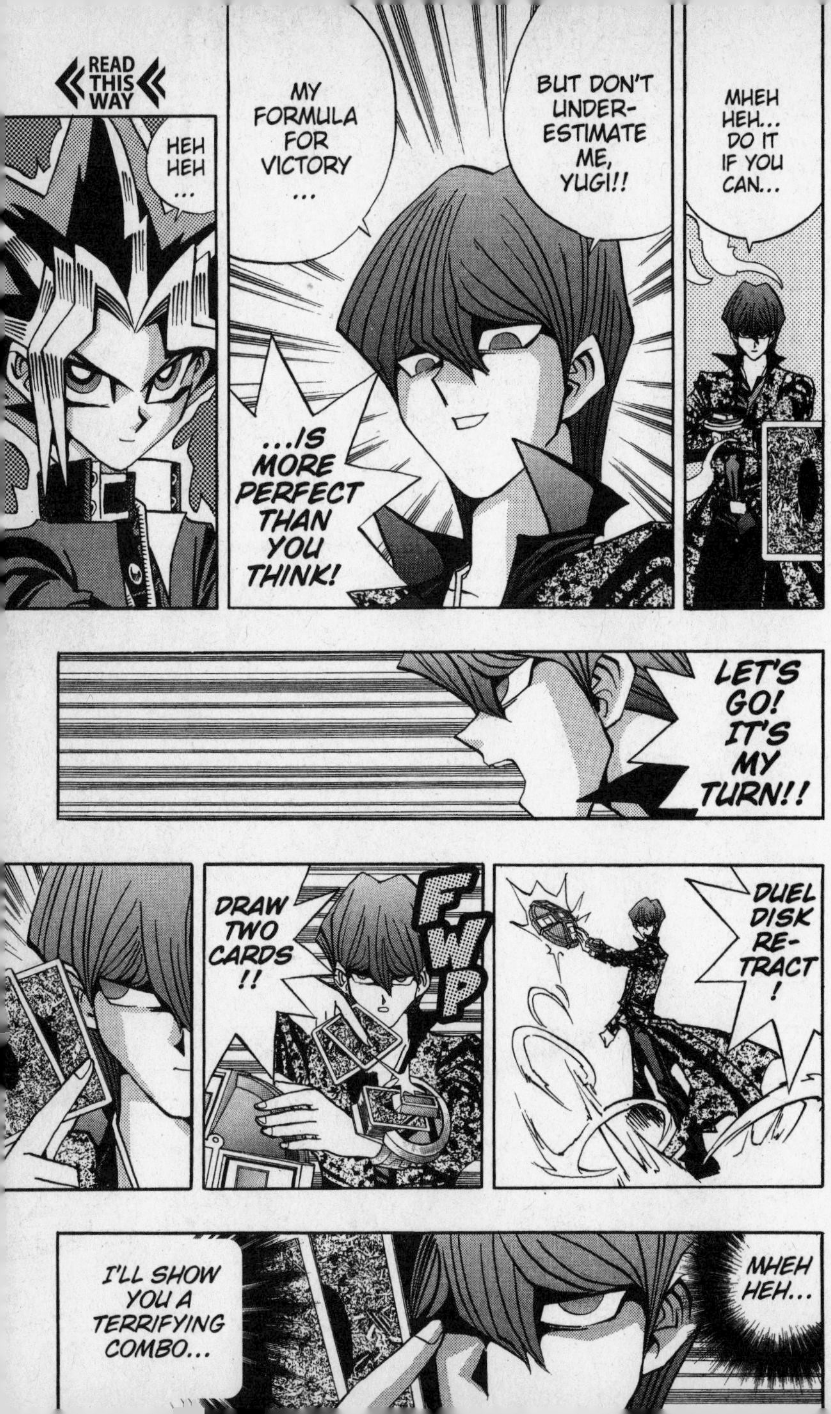
READ THIS WAY
MHEH HEH... DO IT IF YOU CAN...
BUT DON'T UNDER-ESTIMATE ME, YUGI!!
MY FORMULA FOR VICTORY ...
...IS MORE PERFECT THAN YOU THINK!
HEH HEH ...
LET'S GO! IT'S MY TURN!!
DUEL DISK RE-TRACT!
FWP
DRAW TWO CARDS!!
MHEH HEH...
I'LL SHOW YOU A TERRIFYING COMBO...

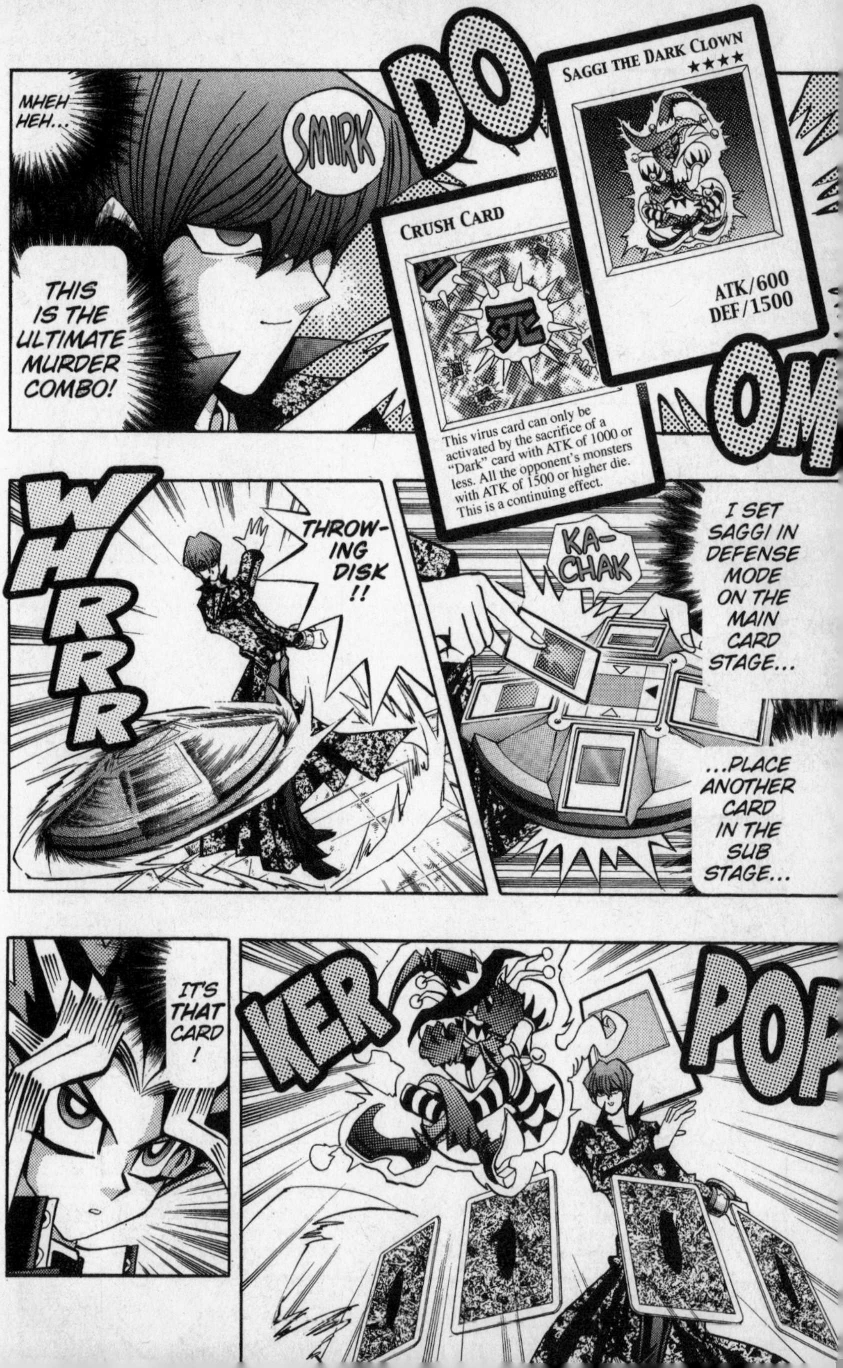
DO-
OM
Saggi the Dark Clown
★★★★
ATK/600
DEF/1500
Crush Card
This virus card can only be activated by the sacrifice of a "Dark" card with ATK of 1000 or less. All the opponent's monsters with ATK of 1500 or higher die. This is a continuing effect.
SMIRK
MHEH HEH...
THIS IS THE ULTIMATE MURDER COMBO!
KA-CHAK
I SET SAGGI IN DEFENSE MODE ON THE MAIN CARD STAGE...
...PLACE ANOTHER CARD IN THE SUB STAGE...
WHRRR
THROWING DISK!!
KER
POP
IT'S THAT CARD!

READ THIS WAY

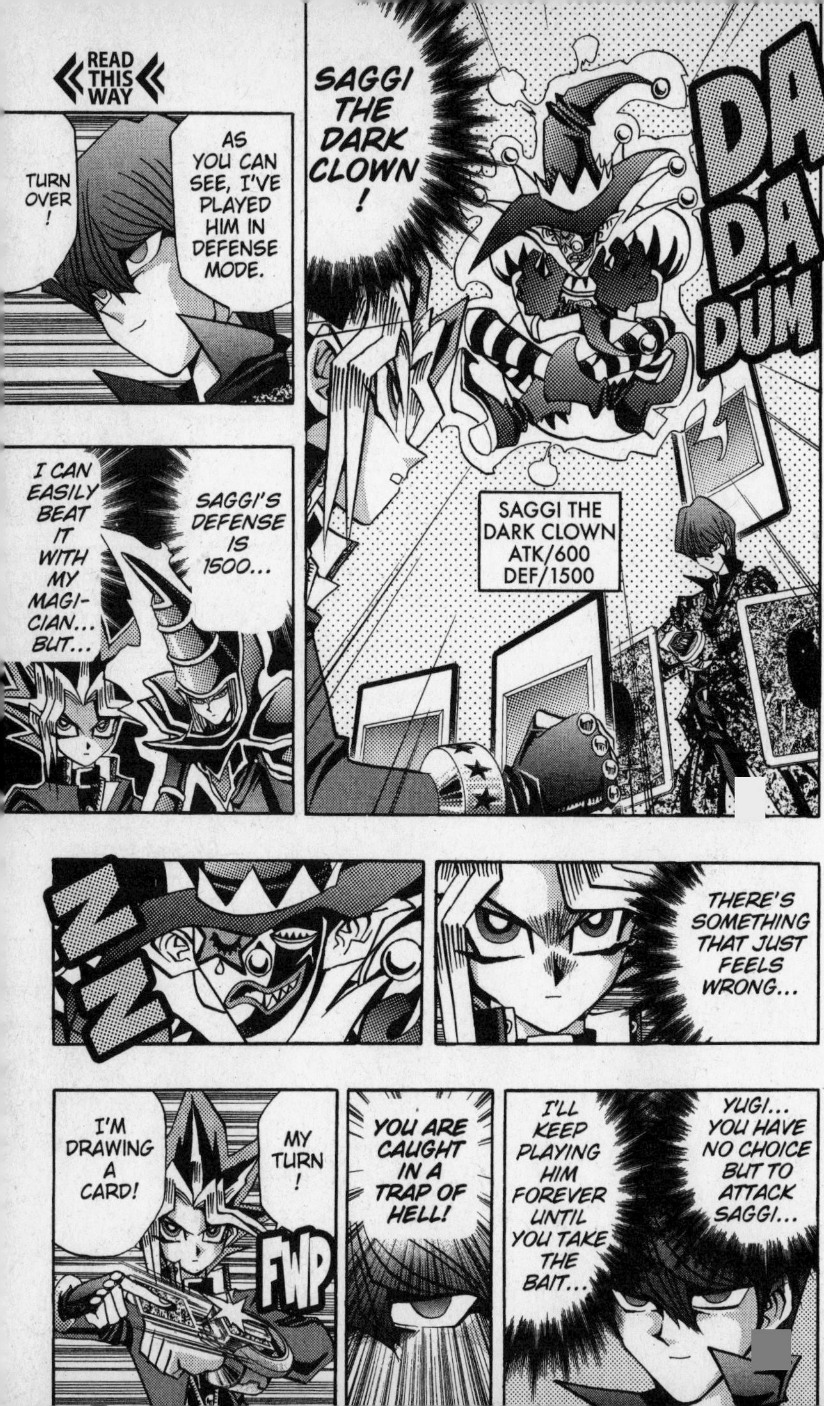
DA DA DUM
SAGGI THE DARK CLOWN!
SAGGI THE DARK CLOWN ATK/600 DEF/1500
AS YOU CAN SEE, I'VE PLAYED HIM IN DEFENSE MODE.
TURN OVER!
SAGGI'S DEFENSE IS 1500...
I CAN EASILY BEAT IT WITH MY MAGICIAN... BUT...
THERE'S SOMETHING THAT JUST FEELS WRONG...
YUGI... YOU HAVE NO CHOICE BUT TO ATTACK SAGGI...
I'LL KEEP PLAYING HIM FOREVER UNTIL YOU TAKE THE BAIT...
YOU ARE CAUGHT IN A TRAP OF HELL!
MY TURN!
FWP
I'M DRAWING A CARD!

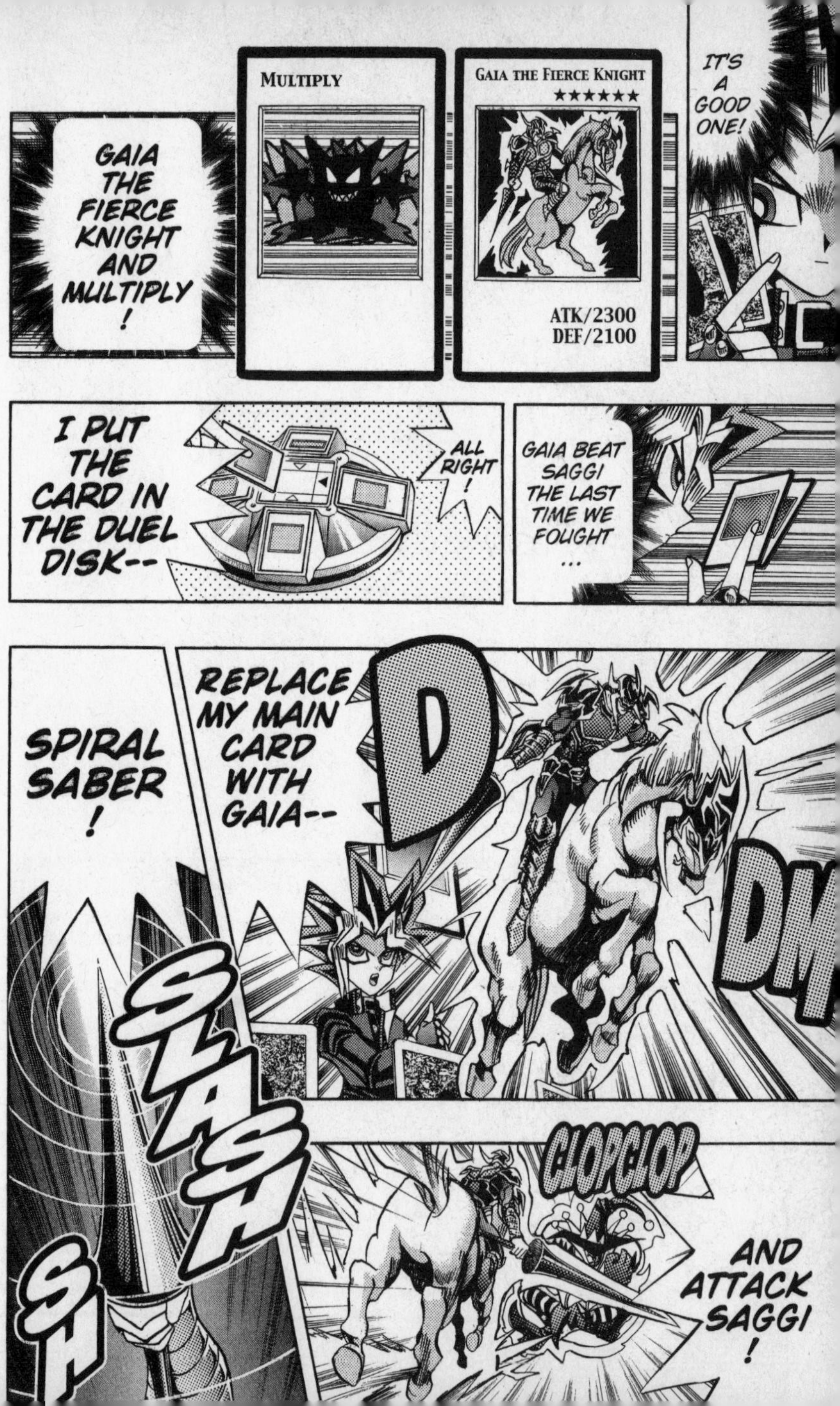
IT'S A GOOD ONE!
GAIA THE FIERCE KNIGHT
★★★★★★
ATK/2300
DEF/2100
MULTIPLY
GAIA THE FIERCE KNIGHT AND MULTIPLY!
GAIA BEAT SAGGI THE LAST TIME WE FOUGHT...
ALL RIGHT!
I PUT THE CARD IN THE DUEL DISK--
DM
REPLACE MY MAIN CARD WITH GAIA--
D
CLOPCLOP
AND ATTACK SAGGI!
SPIRAL SABER!
SLASH
SH

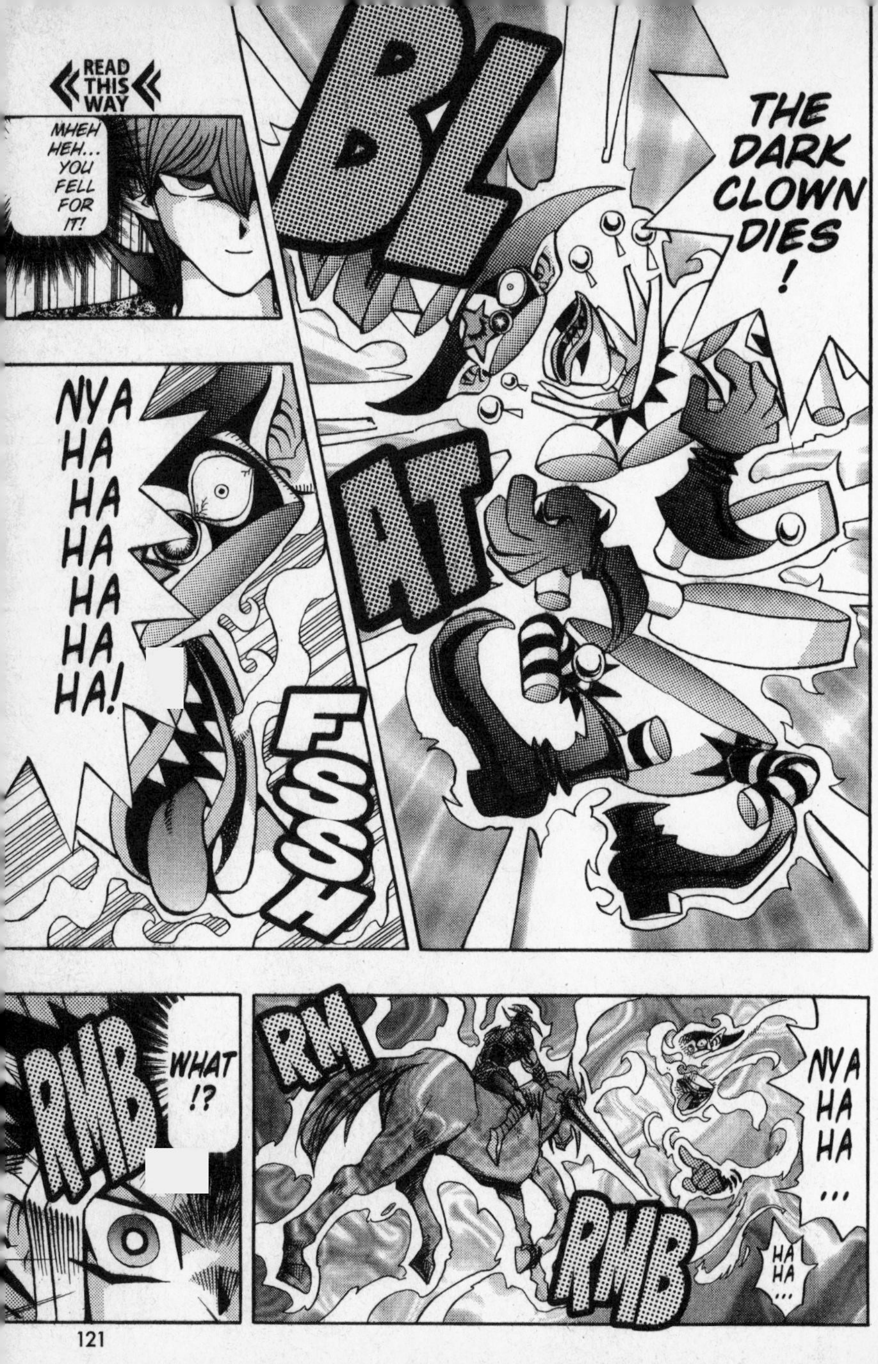
READ THIS WAY
BLAT
THE DARK CLOWN DIES!
FSSH
MHEH HEH... YOU FELL FOR IT!
NYA HA HA HA HA HA HA HA HA HA HA HA HA HA!
RM
NYA HA HA...
HA HA...
RMB
RMB
WHAT!?

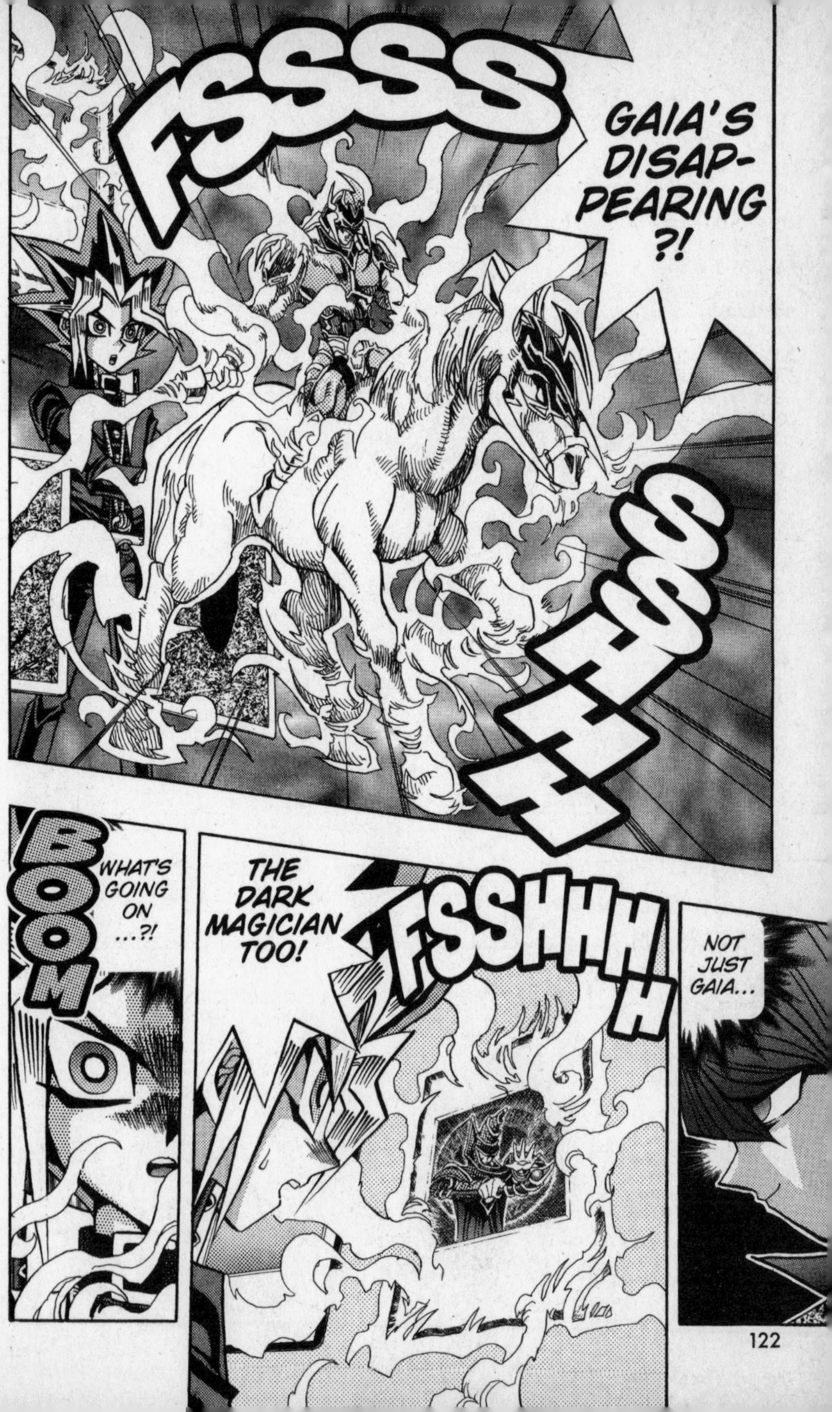
FSSSS
GAIA'S DISAP-PEARING ?!
SSHHHH
NOT JUST GAIA...
THE DARK MAGICIAN TOO!
FSSHHHH
WHAT'S GOING ON ...?!
BOOM

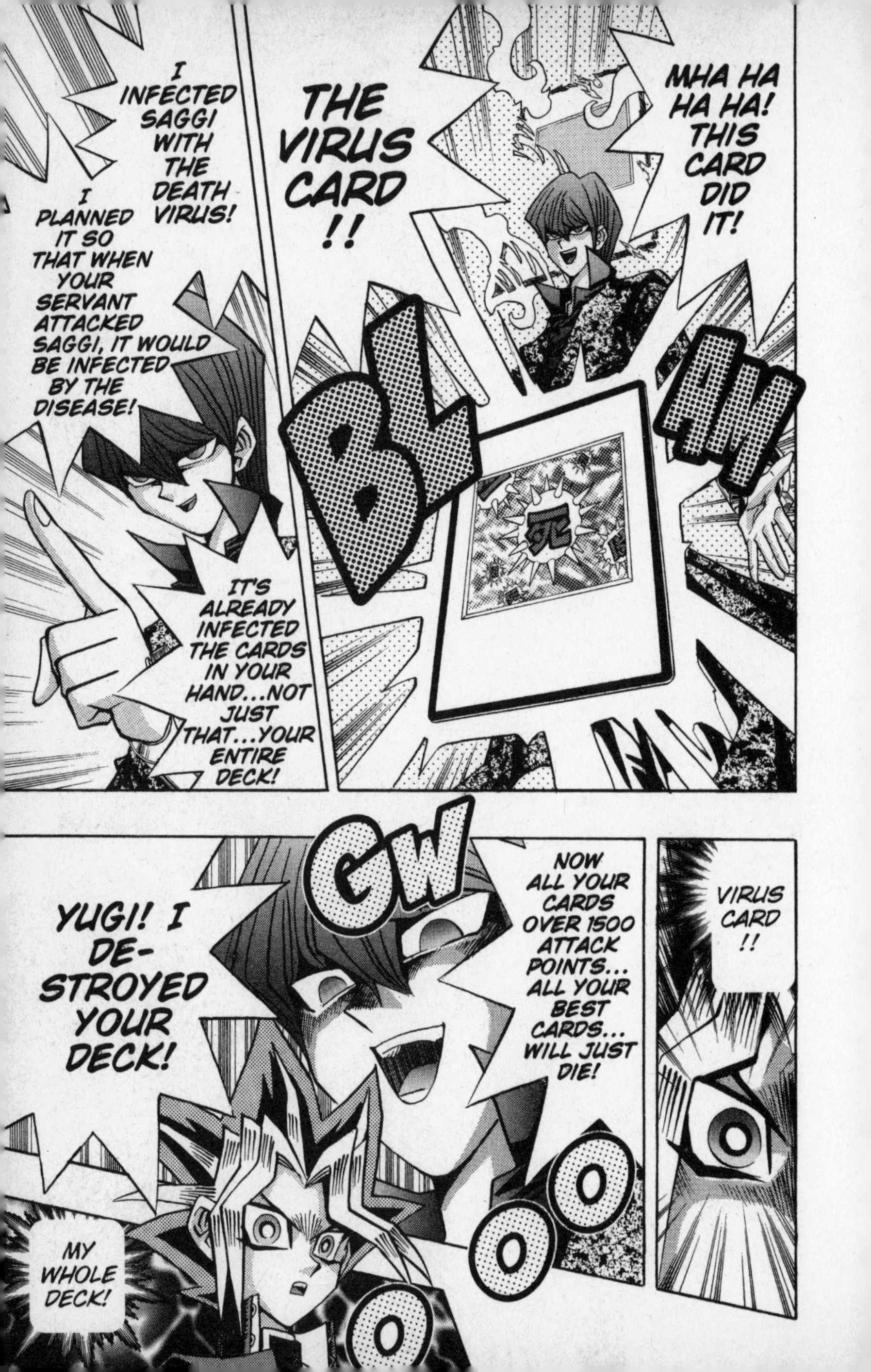
MHA HA HA HA! THIS CARD DID IT!
THE VIRUS CARD!!
BLAM
I INFECTED SAGGI WITH THE DEATH VIRUS!
I PLANNED IT SO THAT WHEN YOUR SERVANT ATTACKED SAGGI, IT WOULD BE INFECTED BY THE DISEASE!
IT'S ALREADY INFECTED THE CARDS IN YOUR HAND...NOT JUST THAT...YOUR ENTIRE DECK!
VIRUS CARD!!
GWOOOOO
NOW ALL YOUR CARDS OVER 1500 ATTACK POINTS... ALL YOUR BEST CARDS... WILL JUST DIE!
YUGI! I DE-STROYED YOUR DECK!
MY WHOLE DECK!

Duel 44: Hang in There!

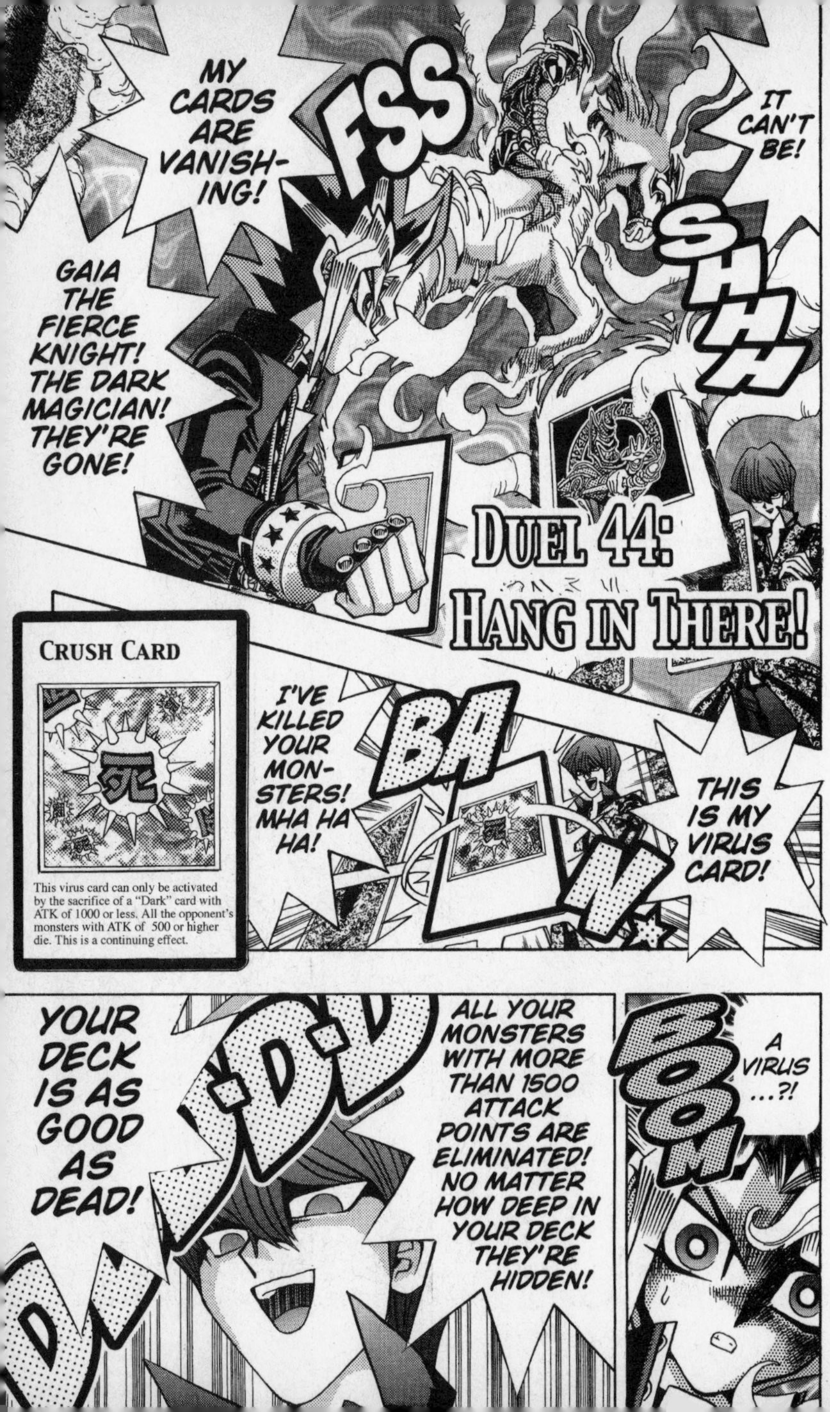
IT CAN'T BE!
SHHH
FSS
MY CARDS ARE VANISHING!
GAIA THE FIERCE KNIGHT! THE DARK MAGICIAN! THEY'RE GONE!
DUEL 44: HANG IN THERE!
THIS IS MY VIRUS CARD!
BAN
I'VE KILLED YOUR MONSTERS! MHA HA HA!
CRUSH CARD
This virus card can only be activated by the sacrifice of a "Dark" card with ATK of 1000 or less. All the opponent's monsters with ATK of 500 or higher die. This is a continuing effect.
BOOM
A VIRUS ...?!
ALL YOUR MONSTERS WITH MORE THAN 1500 ATTACK POINTS ARE ELIMINATED! NO MATTER HOW DEEP IN YOUR DECK THEY'RE HIDDEN!
YOUR DECK IS AS GOOD AS DEAD!
D D D

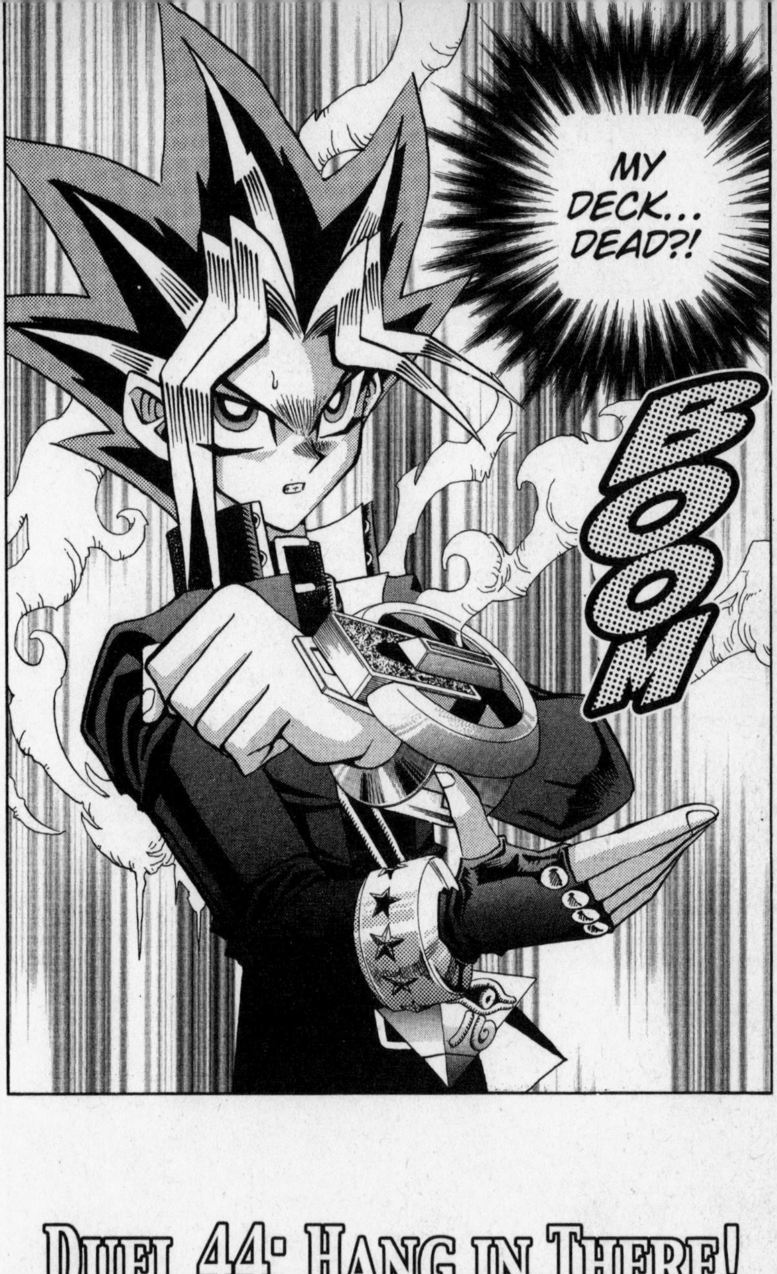
MY DECK... DEAD?!
BOOM!

Duel 44: Hang in There!

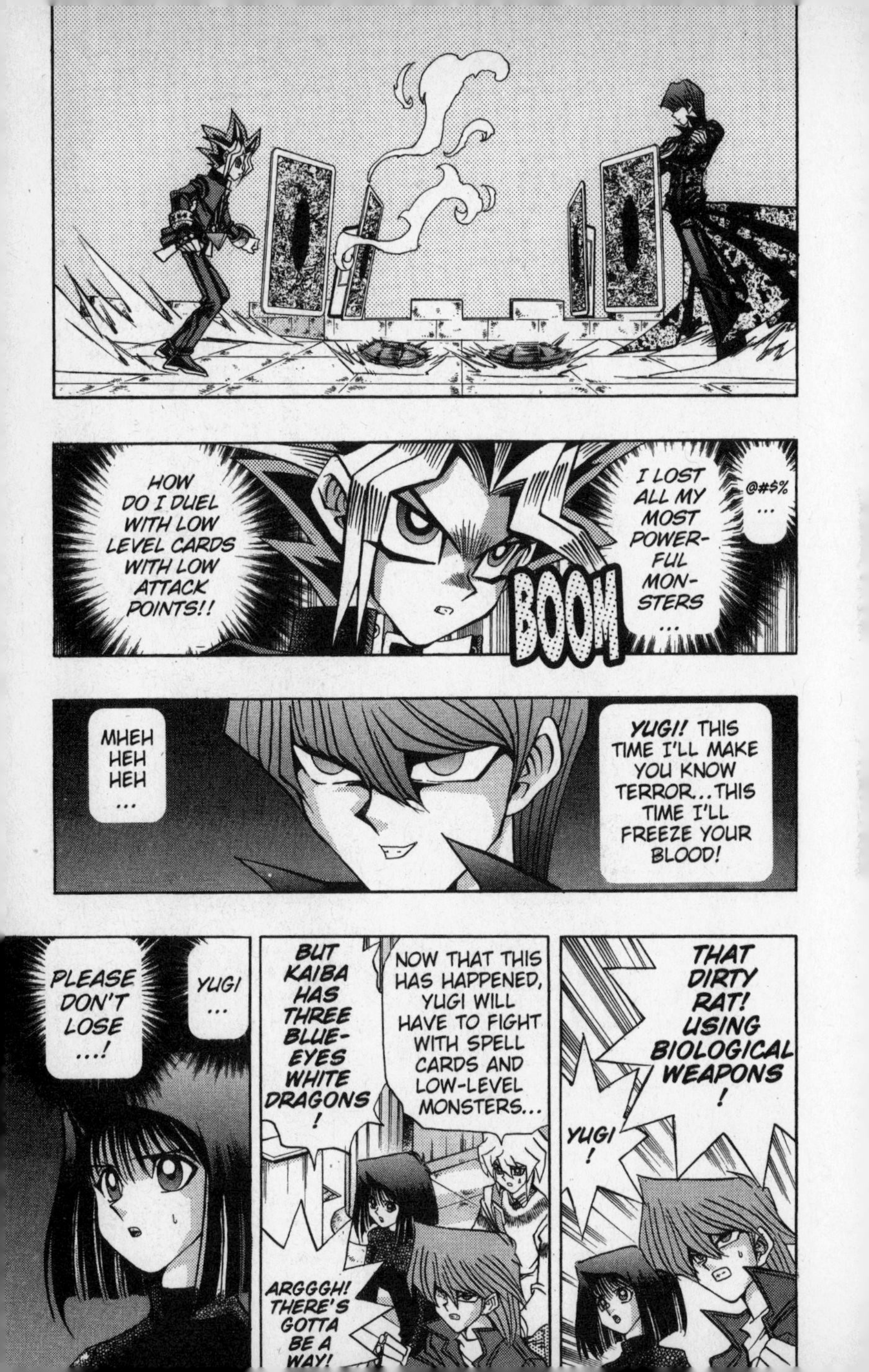
@#$% ...
I LOST ALL MY MOST POWERFUL MONSTERS ...
BOOM
HOW DO I DUEL WITH LOW LEVEL CARDS WITH LOW ATTACK POINTS!!
YUGI! THIS TIME I'LL MAKE YOU KNOW TERROR...THIS TIME I'LL FREEZE YOUR BLOOD!
MHEH HEH HEH ...
THAT DIRTY RAT! USING BIOLOGICAL WEAPONS !
YUGI !
NOW THAT THIS HAS HAPPENED, YUGI WILL HAVE TO FIGHT WITH SPELL CARDS AND LOW-LEVEL MONSTERS...
BUT KAIBA HAS THREE BLUE-EYES WHITE DRAGONS !
ARGGGH! THERE'S GOTTA BE A WAY!
YUGI ...
PLEASE DON'T LOSE ...!

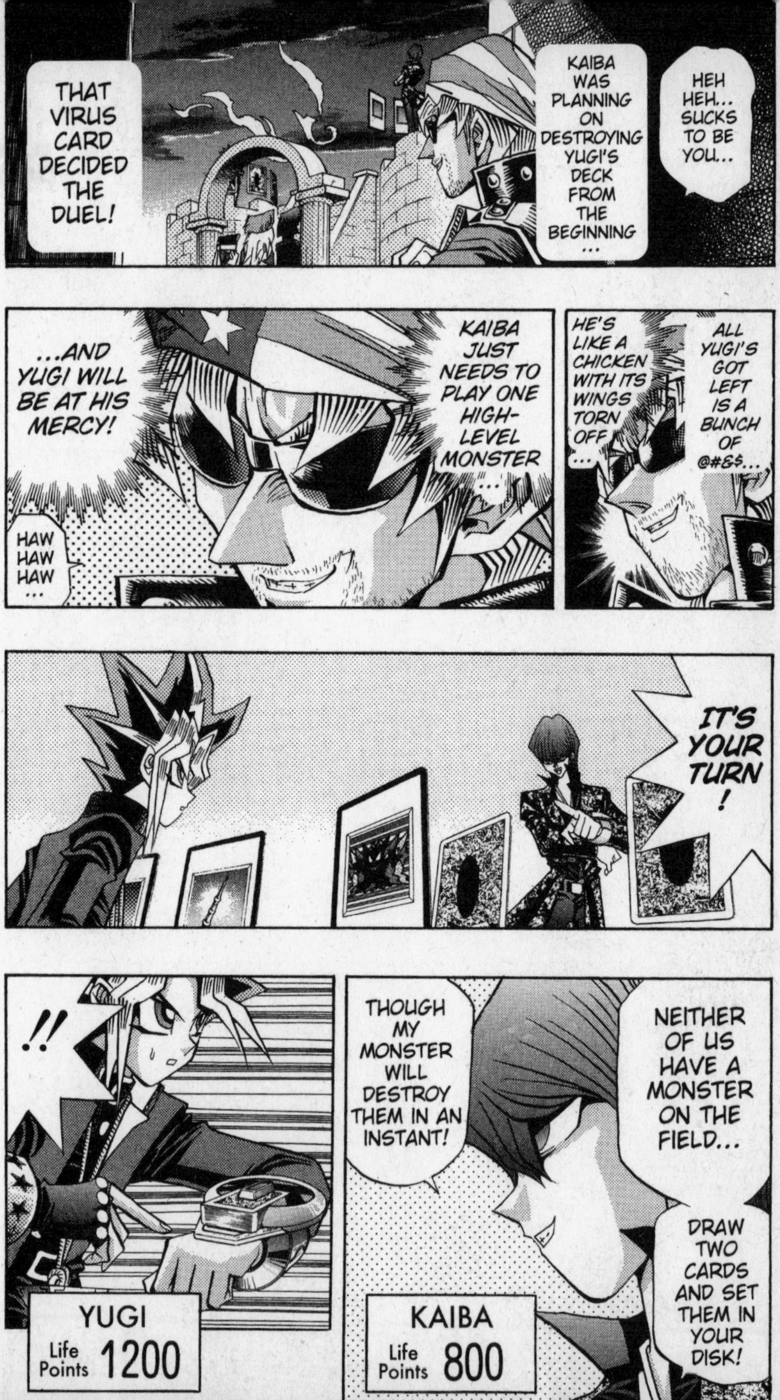
HEH HEH... SUCKS TO BE YOU...
KAIBA WAS PLANNING ON DESTROYING YUGI'S DECK FROM THE BEGINNING...
THAT VIRUS CARD DECIDED THE DUEL!
ALL YUGI'S GOT LEFT IS A BUNCH OF @#&$...
HE'S LIKE A CHICKEN WITH ITS WINGS TORN OFF...
KAIBA JUST NEEDS TO PLAY ONE HIGH-LEVEL MONSTER...
...AND YUGI WILL BE AT HIS MERCY!
HAW HAW HAW...
IT'S YOUR TURN!
NEITHER OF US HAVE A MONSTER ON THE FIELD...
THOUGH MY MONSTER WILL DESTROY THEM IN AN INSTANT!
DRAW TWO CARDS AND SET THEM IN YOUR DISK!
KAIBA Life Points 800
!!
YUGI Life Points 1200

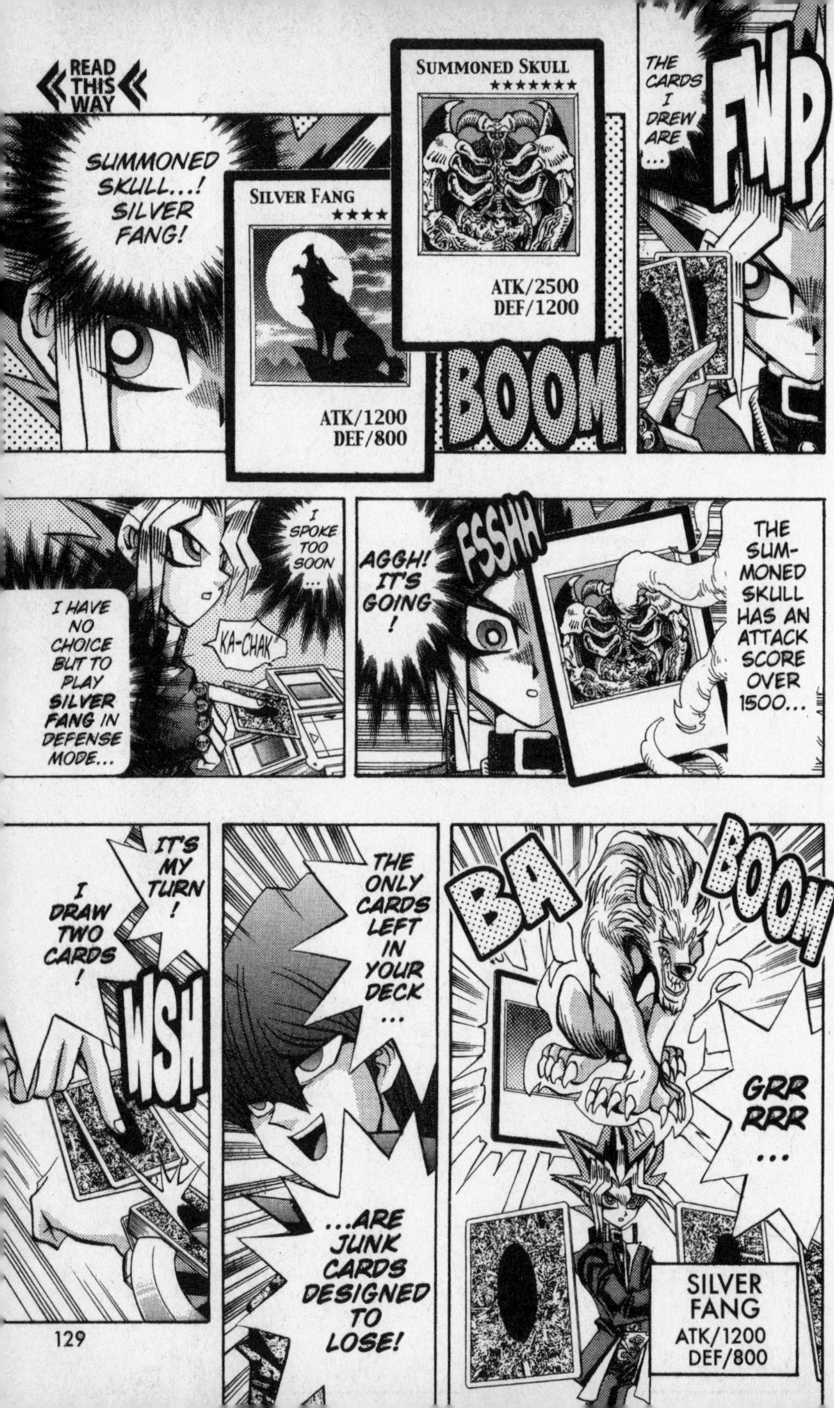
READ THIS WAY
THE CARDS I DREW ARE...
FWP
SUMMONED SKULL
ATK/2500
DEF/1200
SILVER FANG
ATK/1200
DEF/800
BOOM
SUMMONED SKULL...! SILVER FANG!
THE SUMMONED SKULL HAS AN ATTACK SCORE OVER 1500...
FSSHH
AGGH! IT'S GOING!
I SPOKE TOO SOON...
KA-CHAK
I HAVE NO CHOICE BUT TO PLAY SILVER FANG IN DEFENSE MODE...
BA
BOOM
GRR RRR...
SILVER FANG
ATK/1200
DEF/800
THE ONLY CARDS LEFT IN YOUR DECK...
...ARE JUNK CARDS DESIGNED TO LOSE!
IT'S MY TURN!
I DRAW TWO CARDS!
WSH

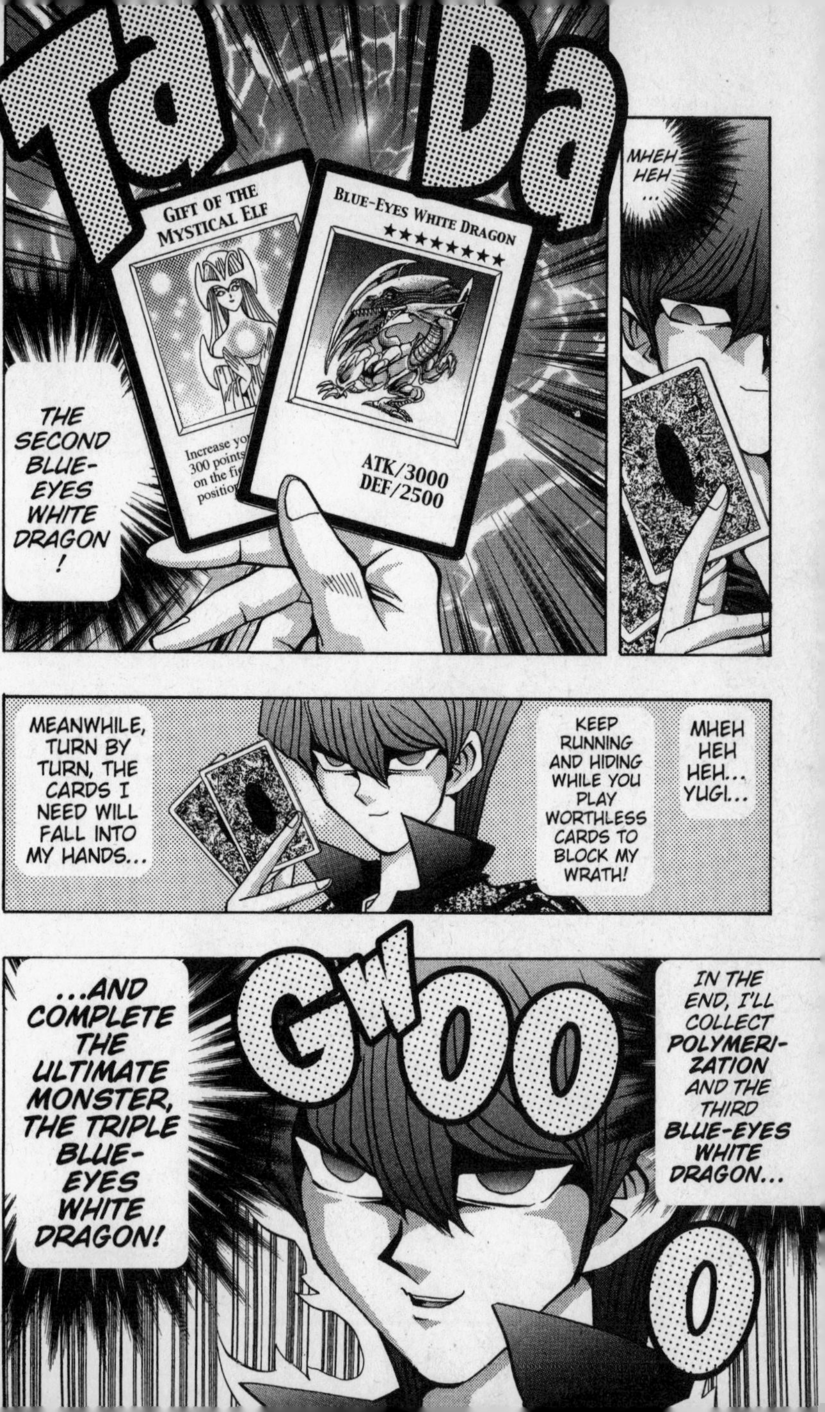
MHEH HEH...
TA DA
GIFT OF THE MYSTICAL ELF
BLUE-EYES WHITE DRAGON
ATK/3000 DEF/2500
THE SECOND BLUE-EYES WHITE DRAGON!
MHEH HEH HEH... YUGI...
KEEP RUNNING AND HIDING WHILE YOU PLAY WORTHLESS CARDS TO BLOCK MY WRATH!
MEANWHILE, TURN BY TURN, THE CARDS I NEED WILL FALL INTO MY HANDS...
IN THE END, I'LL COLLECT POLYMERIZATION AND THE THIRD BLUE-EYES WHITE DRAGON...
GWOOOO
...AND COMPLETE THE ULTIMATE MONSTER, THE TRIPLE BLUE-EYES WHITE DRAGON!

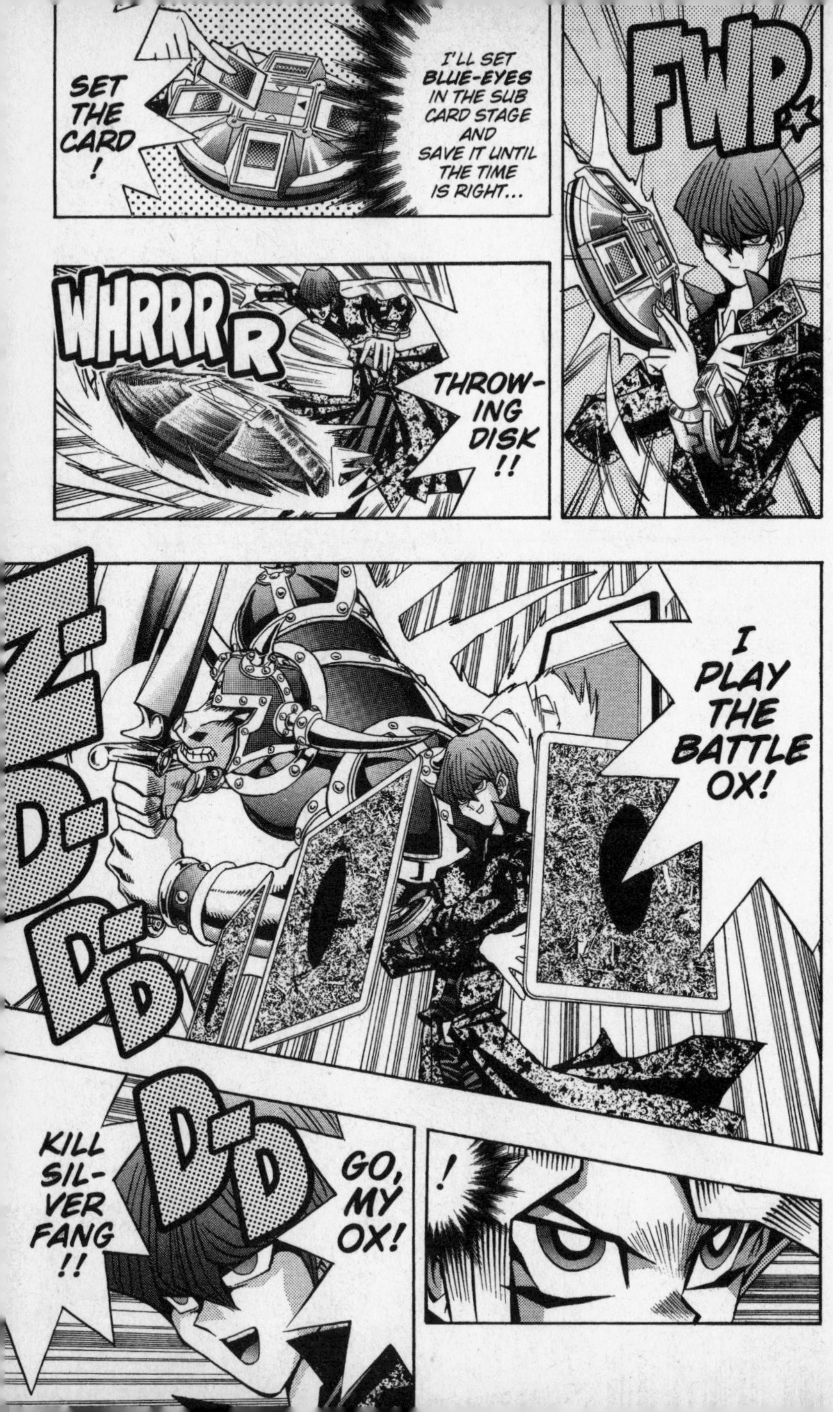
FWP
I'LL SET BLUE-EYES IN THE SUB CARD STAGE AND SAVE IT UNTIL THE TIME IS RIGHT...
SET THE CARD!
THROWING-DISK!!
WHRRRR R
I PLAY THE BATTLE OX!
Z-D-D-D
!
GO, MY OX!
D-D
KILL SIL-VER FANG!!

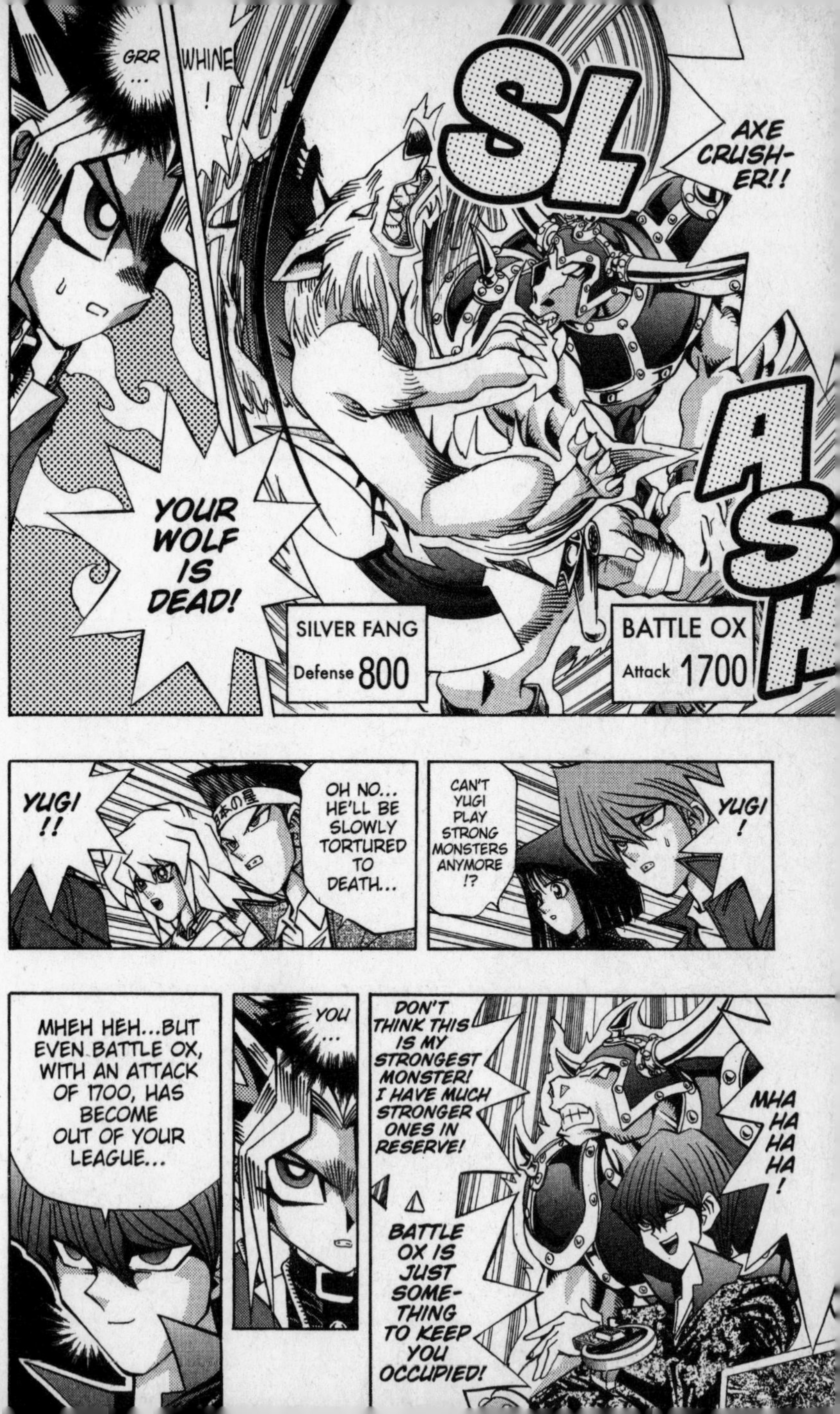
AXE CRUSHER!!
SLASH
WHINE !
GRR ...
YOUR WOLF IS DEAD!
BATTLE OX Attack 1700
SILVER FANG Defense 800
YUGI !
CAN'T YUGI PLAY STRONG MONSTERS ANYMORE !?
OH NO... HE'LL BE SLOWLY TORTURED TO DEATH...
YUGI !!
MHA HA HA HA !
DON'T THINK THIS IS MY STRONGEST MONSTER! I HAVE MUCH STRONGER ONES IN RESERVE!
BATTLE OX IS JUST SOMETHING TO KEEP YOU OCCUPIED!
YOU ...
MHEH HEH...BUT EVEN BATTLE OX, WITH AN ATTACK OF 1700, HAS BECOME OUT OF YOUR LEAGUE...

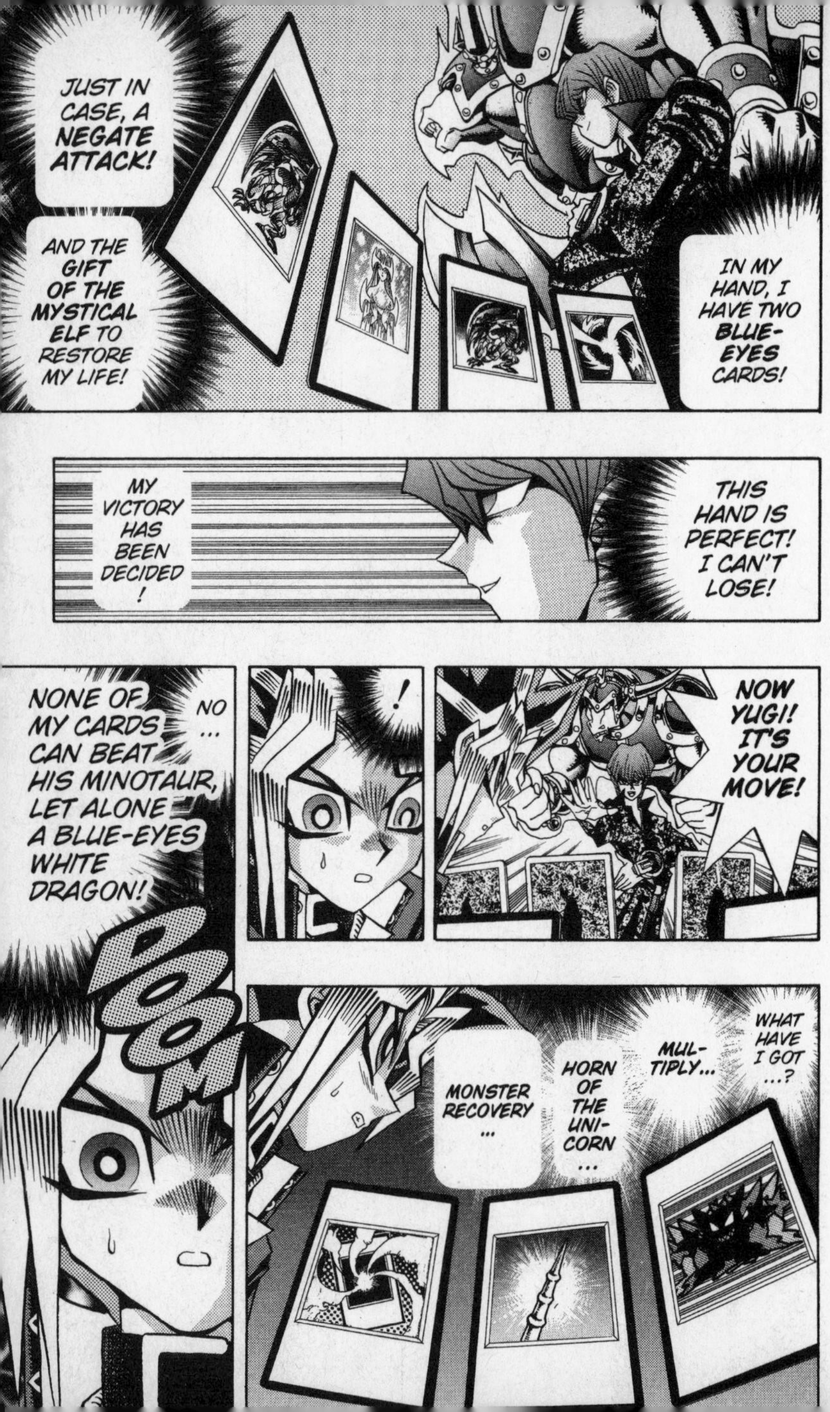
IN MY HAND, I HAVE TWO BLUE-EYES CARDS!
JUST IN CASE, A NEGATE ATTACK!
AND THE GIFT OF THE MYSTICAL ELF TO RESTORE MY LIFE!
THIS HAND IS PERFECT! I CAN'T LOSE!
MY VICTORY HAS BEEN DECIDED!
NOW YUGI! IT'S YOUR MOVE!
!
NO ...
NONE OF MY CARDS CAN BEAT HIS MINOTAUR, LET ALONE A BLUE-EYES WHITE DRAGON!
WHAT HAVE I GOT ...?
MUL-TIPLY...
HORN OF THE UNI-CORN ...
MONSTER RECOVERY ...
DOOOM

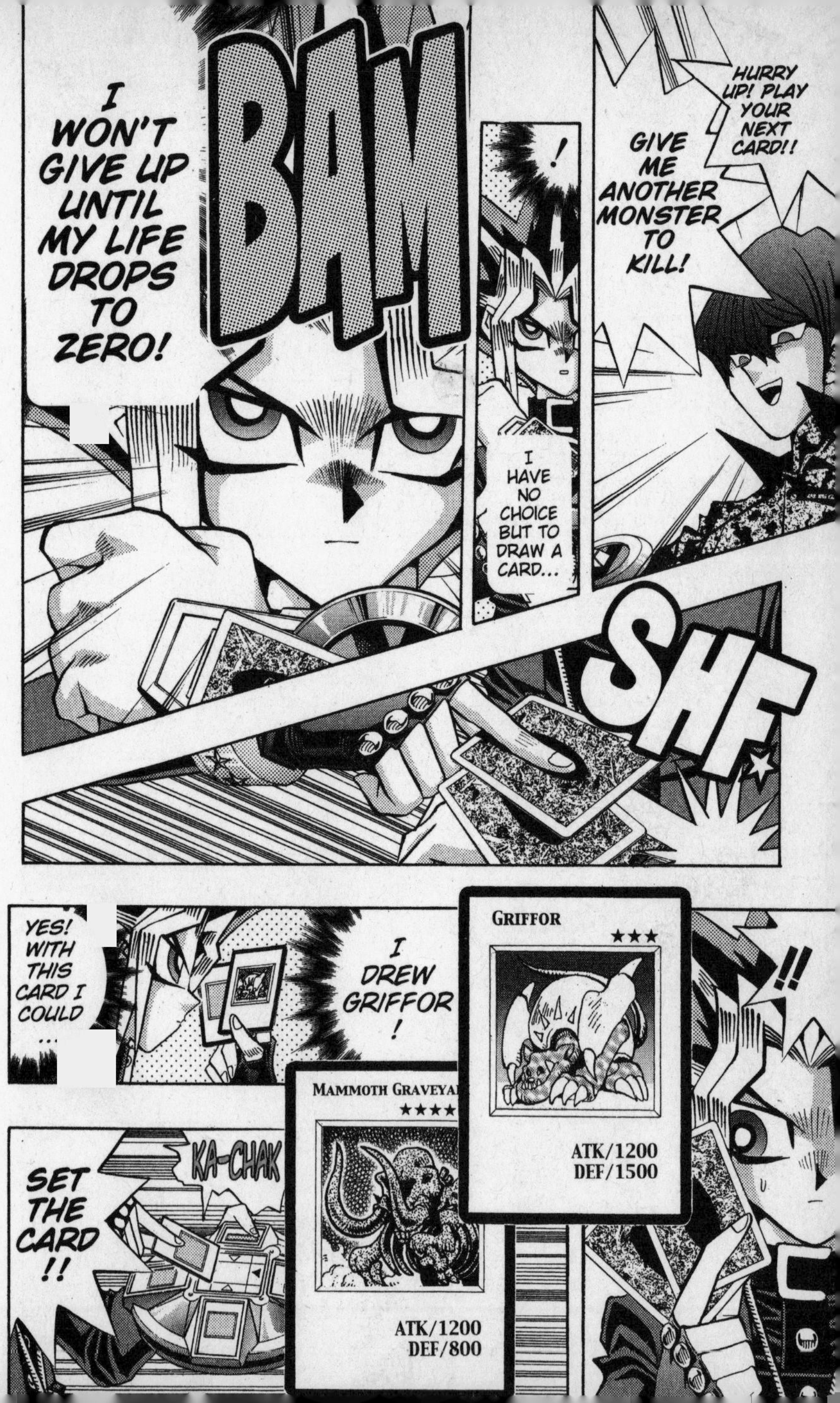
HURRY UP! PLAY YOUR NEXT CARD!!
GIVE ME ANOTHER MONSTER TO KILL!
!
I HAVE NO CHOICE BUT TO DRAW A CARD...
BAM
I WON'T GIVE UP UNTIL MY LIFE DROPS TO ZERO!
SHF
!!
GRIFFOR
ATK/1200
DEF/1500
MAMMOTH GRAVEYAR
ATK/1200
DEF/800
I DREW GRIFFOR!
YES! WITH THIS CARD I COULD...
KA-CHAK
SET THE CARD!!

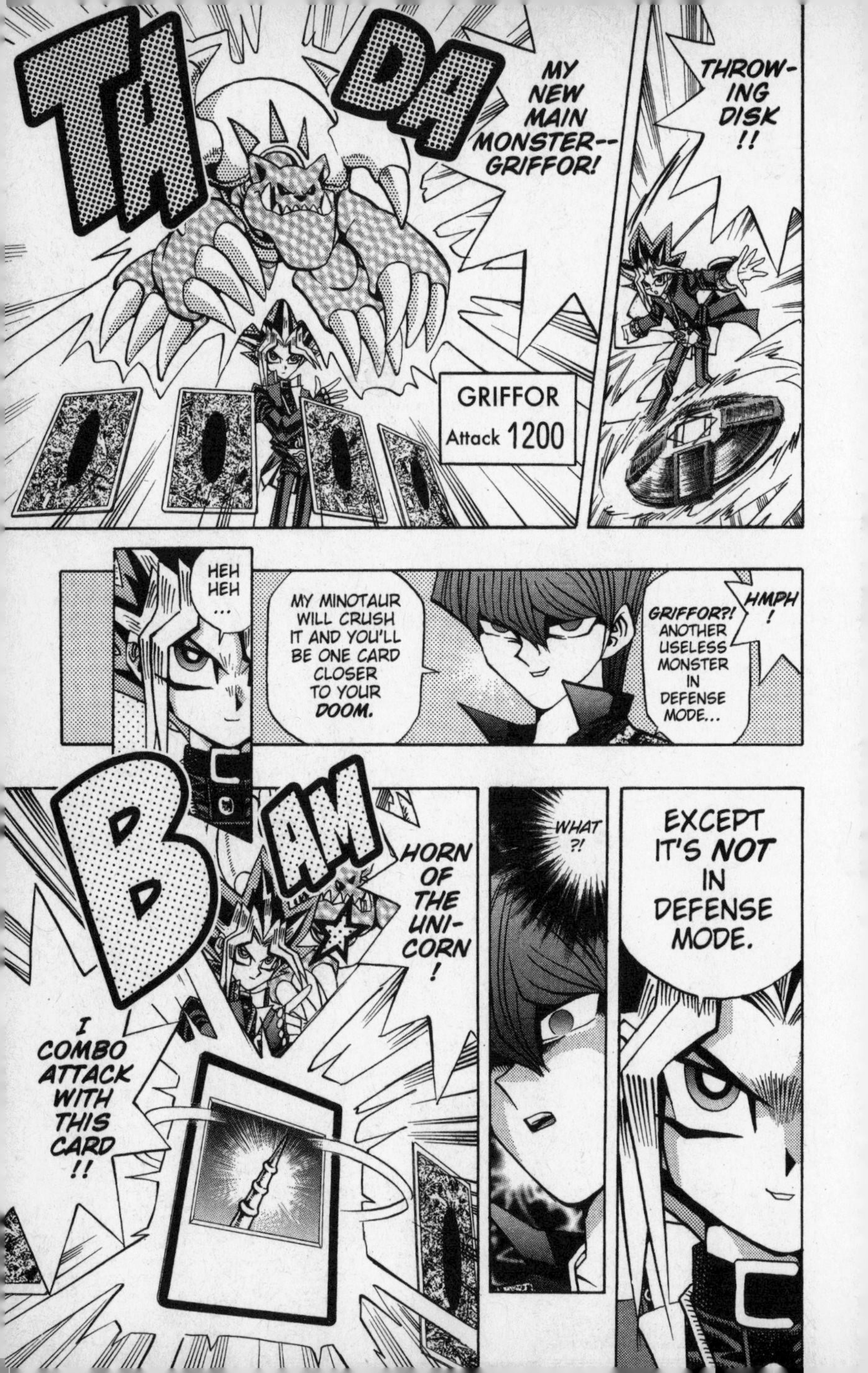
THROWING DISK!!
MY NEW MAIN MONSTER--GRIFFOR!
TA DA
GRIFFOR Attack 1200
HMPH!
GRIFFOR?! ANOTHER USELESS MONSTER IN DEFENSE MODE...
MY MINOTAUR WILL CRUSH IT AND YOU'LL BE ONE CARD CLOSER TO YOUR DOOM.
HEH HEH ...
EXCEPT IT'S NOT IN DEFENSE MODE.
WHAT?!
BAM
HORN OF THE UNI-CORN!
I COMBO ATTACK WITH THIS CARD!!

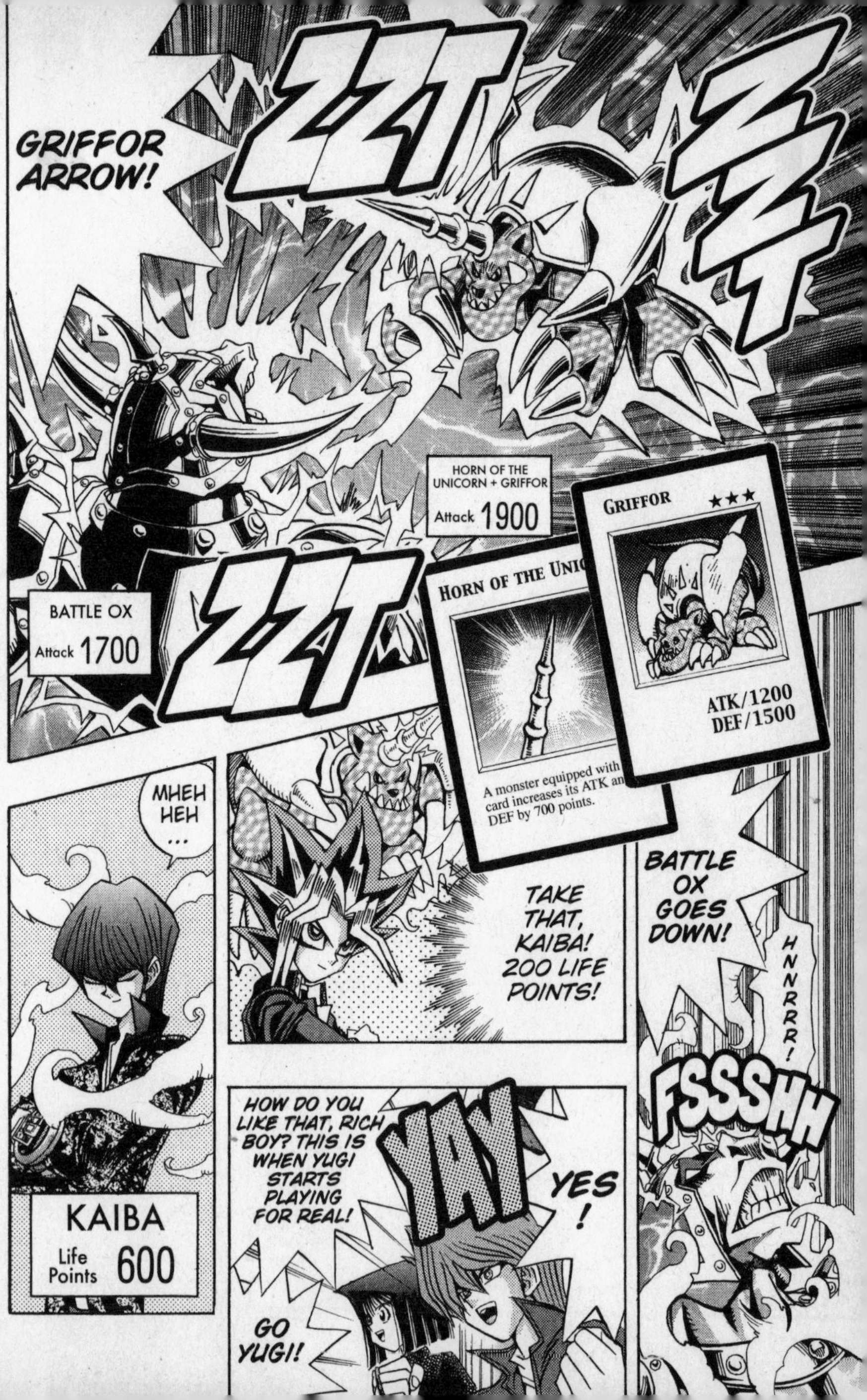
ZZT
ZZT
GRIFFOR ARROW!
HORN OF THE UNICORN + GRIFFOR
Attack 1900
GRIFFOR ★★★
ATK/1200
DEF/1500
HORN OF THE UNIC
A monster equipped with
card increases its ATK an
DEF by 700 points.
ZZT
BATTLE OX
Attack 1700
BATTLE OX GOES DOWN!
HNNRRR!
FSSSHH
TAKE THAT, KAIBA! 200 LIFE POINTS!
HOW DO YOU LIKE THAT, RICH BOY? THIS IS WHEN YUGI STARTS PLAYING FOR REAL!
YAY
YES!
GO YUGI!
MHEH HEH ...
KAIBA
Life Points 600

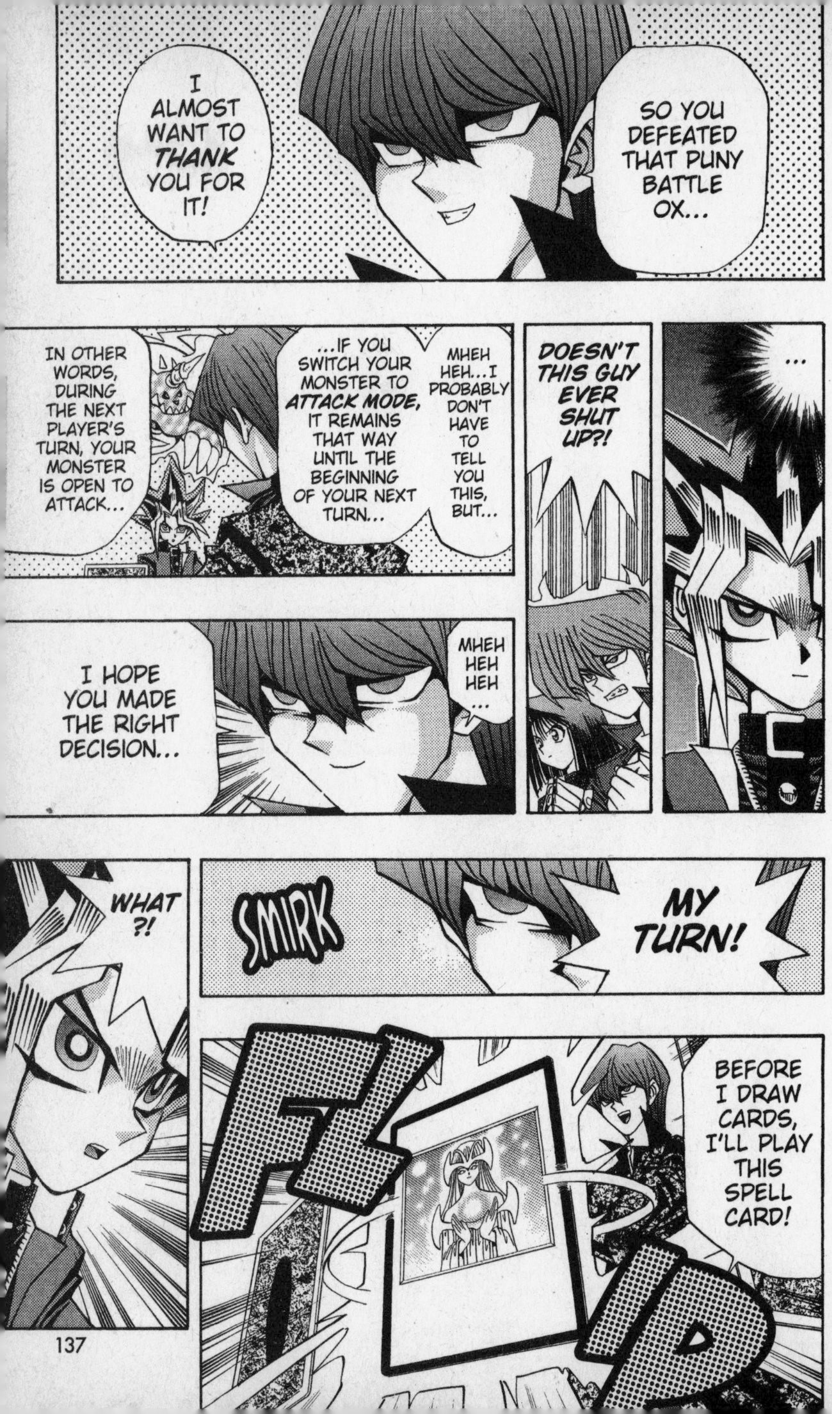
SO YOU DEFEATED THAT PUNY BATTLE OX...
I ALMOST WANT TO *THANK* YOU FOR IT!
...
DOESN'T THIS GUY EVER SHUT UP?!
MHEH HEH...I PROBABLY DON'T HAVE TO TELL YOU THIS, BUT...
...IF YOU SWITCH YOUR MONSTER TO *ATTACK MODE*, IT REMAINS THAT WAY UNTIL THE BEGINNING OF YOUR NEXT TURN...
IN OTHER WORDS, DURING THE NEXT PLAYER'S TURN, YOUR MONSTER IS OPEN TO ATTACK...
MHEH HEH HEH ...
I HOPE YOU MADE THE RIGHT DECISION...
MY TURN!
SMIRK
BEFORE I DRAW CARDS, I'LL PLAY THIS SPELL CARD!
FLIP
WHAT ?!

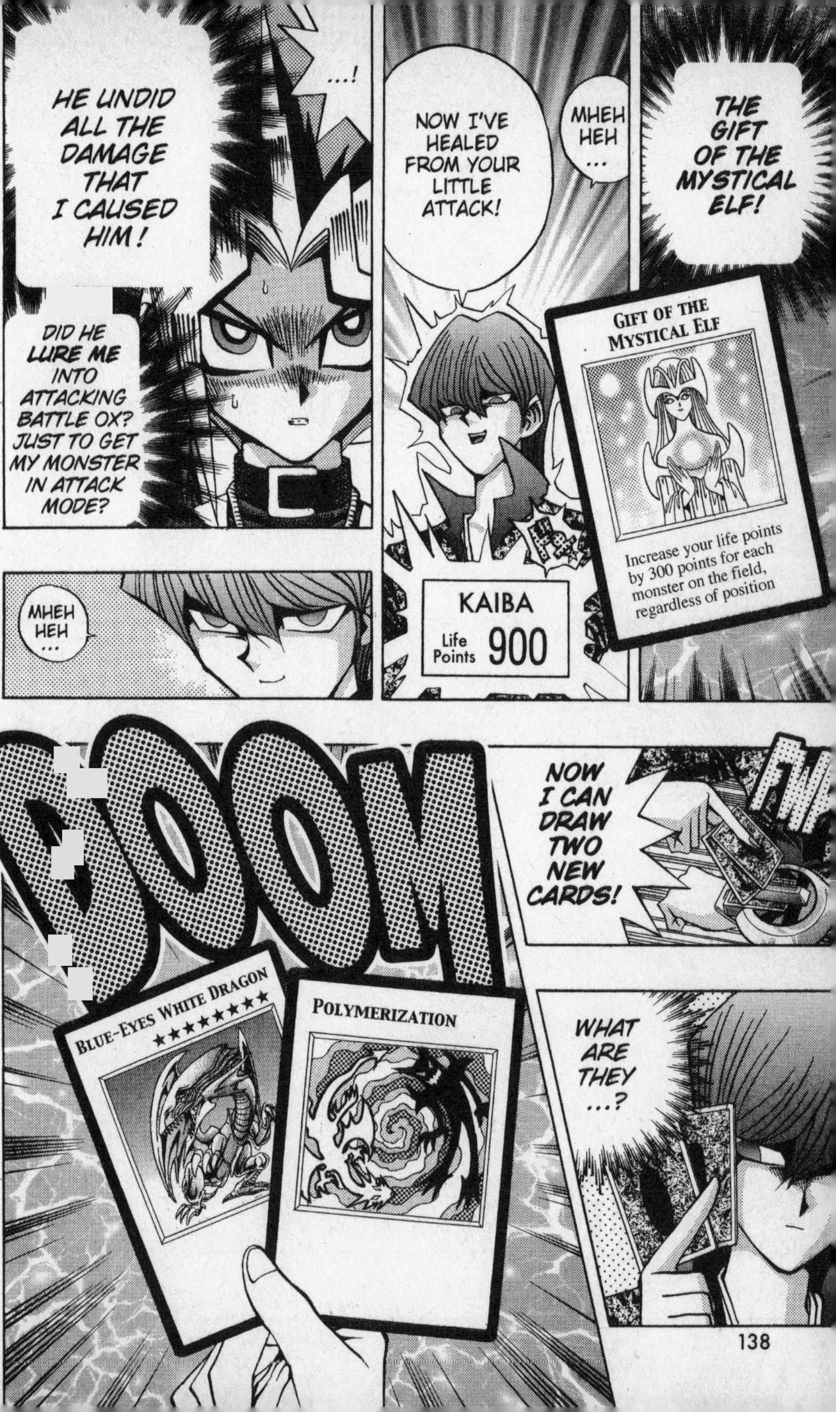
THE GIFT OF THE MYSTICAL ELF!
Gift of the Mystical Elf
Increase your life points by 300 points for each monster on the field, regardless of position
MHEH HEH ...
NOW I'VE HEALED FROM YOUR LITTLE ATTACK!
...!
HE UNDID ALL THE DAMAGE THAT I CAUSED HIM!
DID HE LURE ME INTO ATTACKING BATTLE OX? JUST TO GET MY MONSTER IN ATTACK MODE?
KAIBA
Life Points 900
MHEH HEH ...
NOW I CAN DRAW TWO NEW CARDS!
WHAT ARE THEY ...?
DOOM
Blue-Eyes White Dragon
★★★★★★★★
Polymerization

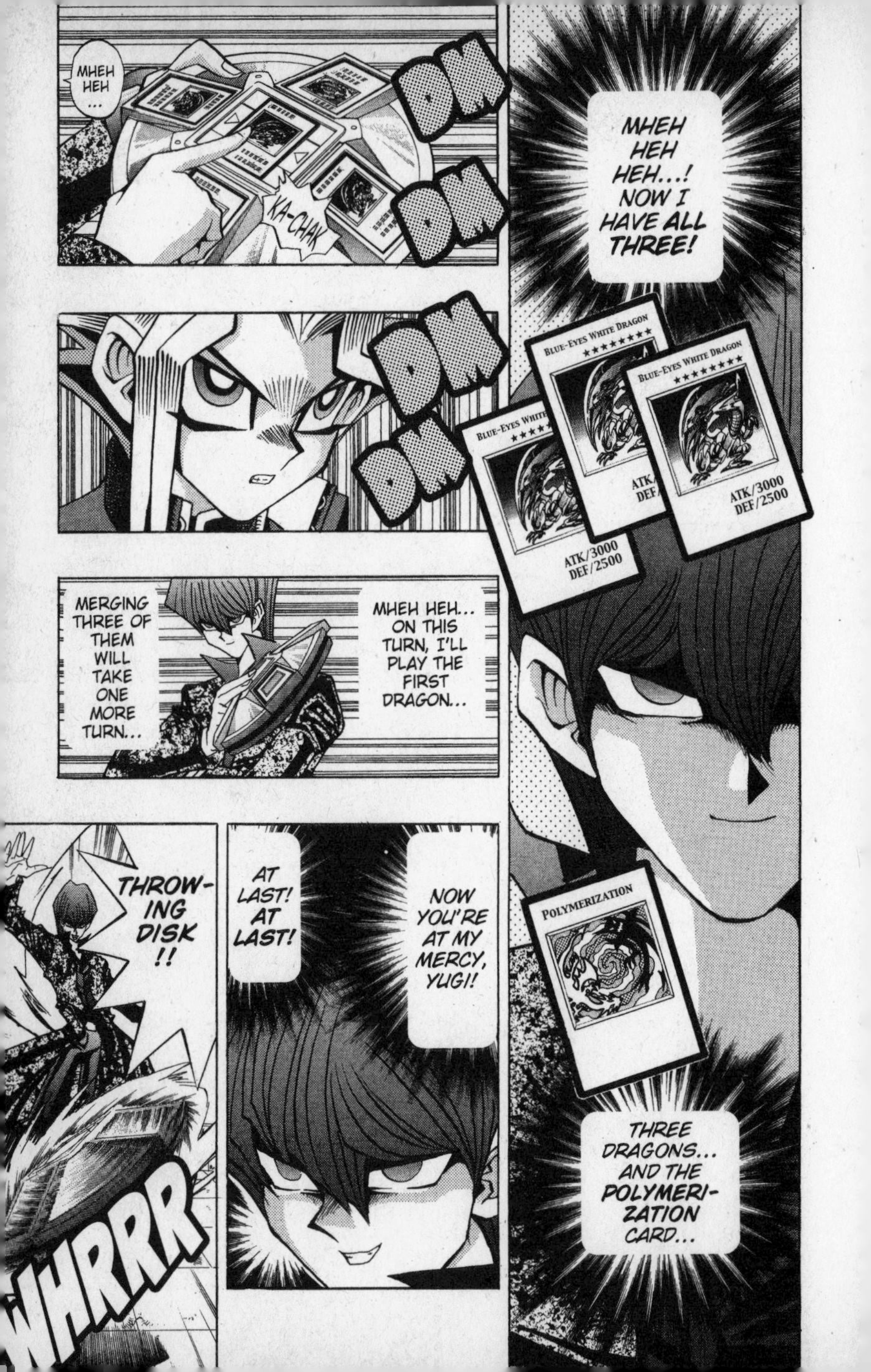
MHEH HEH HEH...! NOW I HAVE ALL THREE!
Blue-Eyes White Dragon
ATK/3000 DEF/2500
Blue-Eyes White Dragon
ATK/3000 DEF/2500
Polymerization
THREE DRAGONS... AND THE POLYMERIZATION CARD...
DOM
DOM
KA-CHAK
MHEH HEH ...
DOM
DOM
MHEH HEH... ON THIS TURN, I'LL PLAY THE FIRST DRAGON...
MERGING THREE OF THEM WILL TAKE ONE MORE TURN...
NOW YOU'RE AT MY MERCY, YUGI!
AT LAST! AT LAST!
THROWING DISK !!
WHRRR

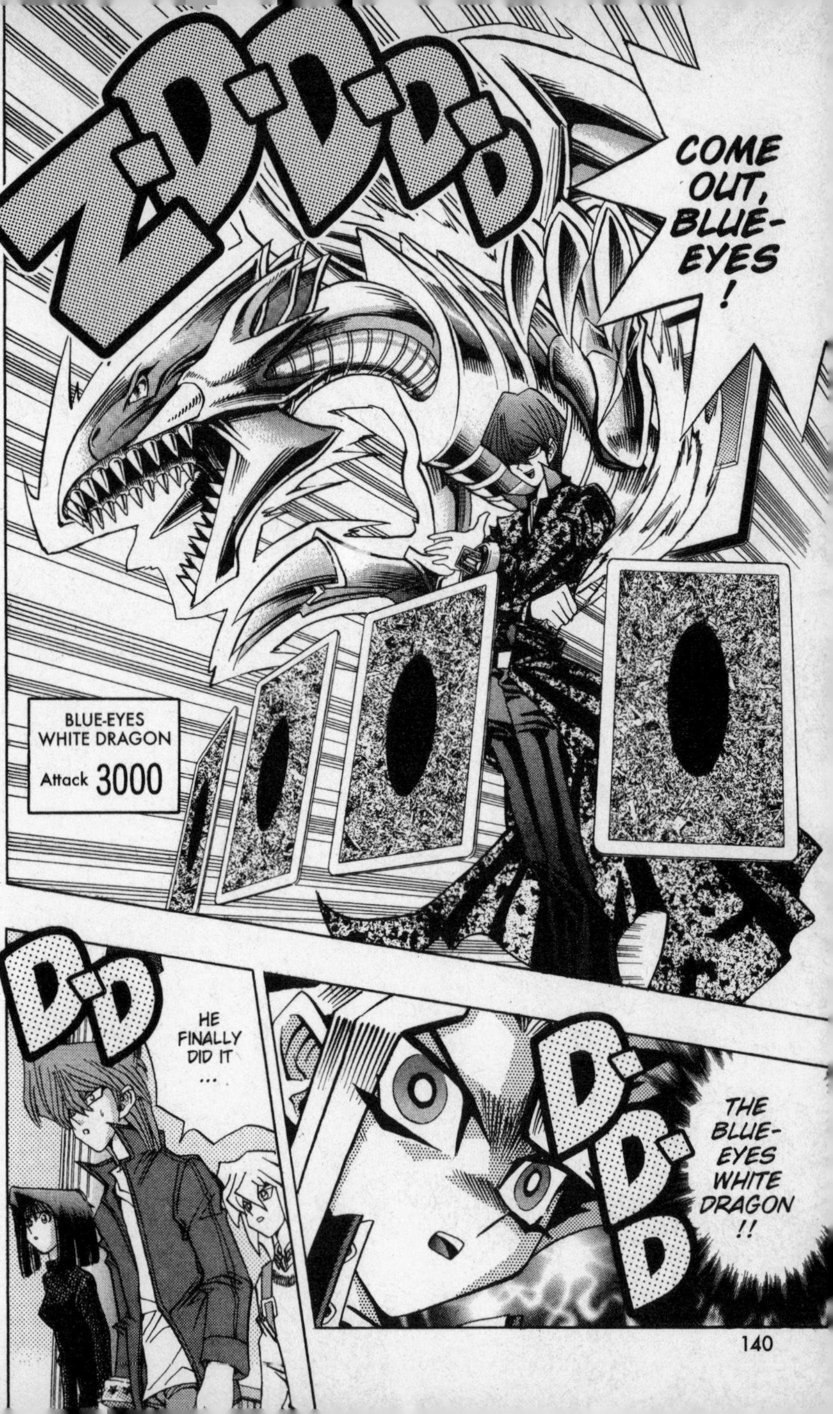
Z-D-D-D
COME OUT, BLUE-EYES!
BLUE-EYES WHITE DRAGON
Attack 3000
D-D-D
THE BLUE-EYES WHITE DRAGON!!
D-D
HE FINALLY DID IT ...

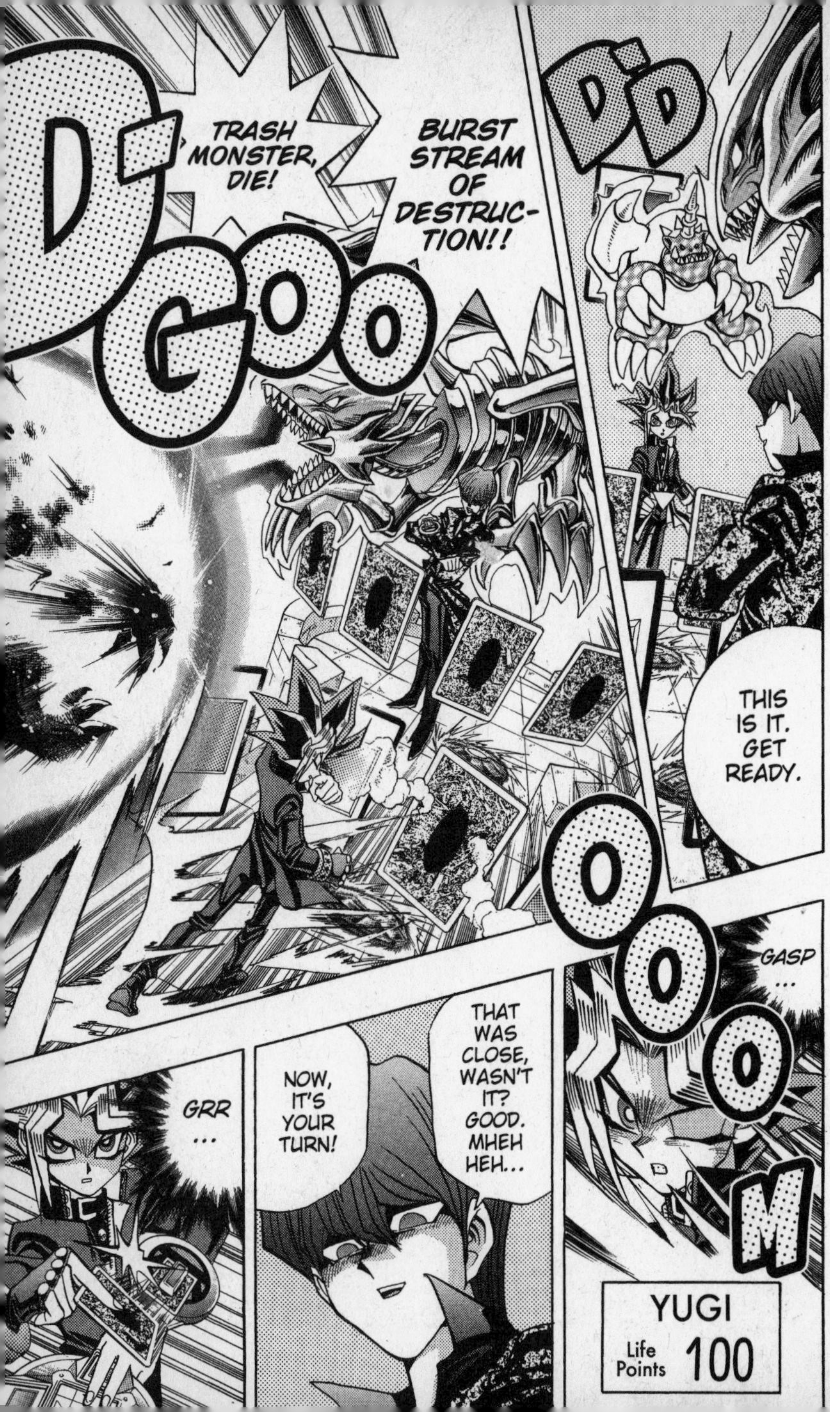
D-D
THIS IS IT. GET READY.
BURST STREAM OF DESTRUCTION!!
TRASH MONSTER, DIE!
D-GOO
OOOOM
GASP ...
YUGI
Life Points 100
THAT WAS CLOSE, WASN'T IT? GOOD. MHEH HEH...
NOW, IT'S YOUR TURN!
GRR ...

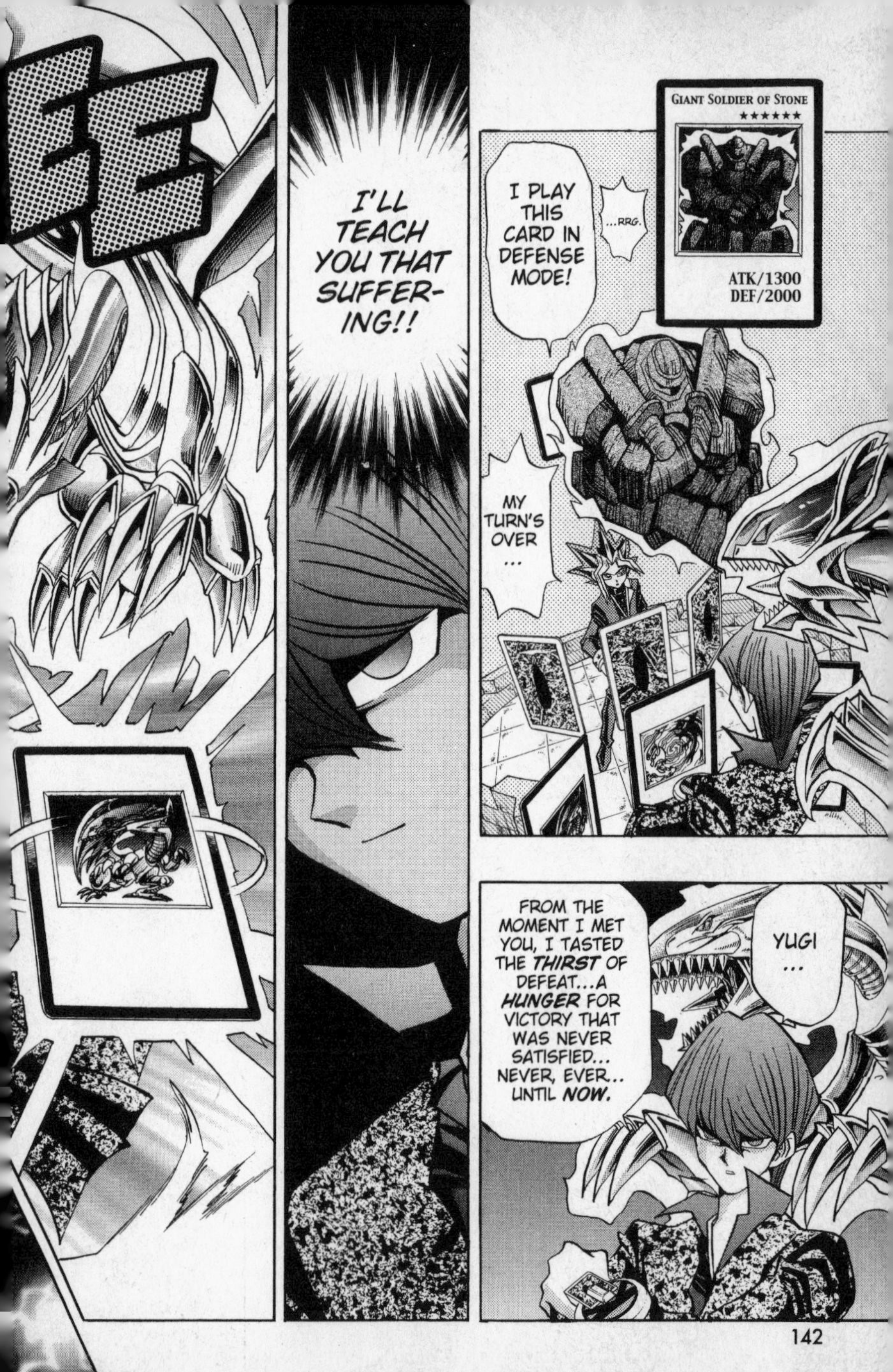
GIANT SOLDIER OF STONE
★★★★★★
ATK/1300
DEF/2000
...RRG.
I PLAY THIS CARD IN DEFENSE MODE!
MY TURN'S OVER ...
YUGI ...
FROM THE MOMENT I MET YOU, I TASTED THE ***THIRST*** OF DEFEAT...A ***HUNGER*** FOR VICTORY THAT WAS NEVER SATISFIED... NEVER, EVER... UNTIL ***NOW.***
I'LL TEACH YOU THAT SUFFER-ING!!

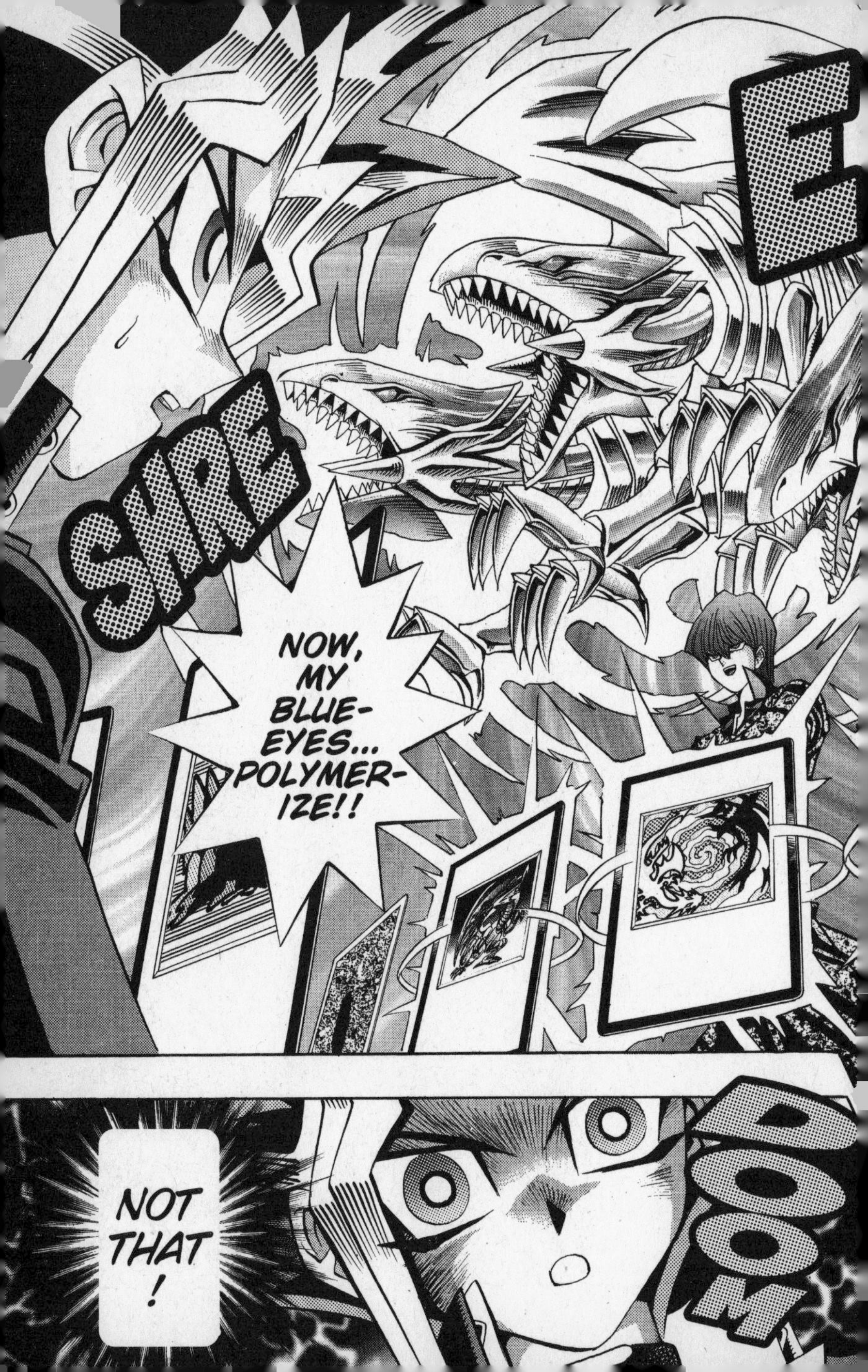
E
SHRE!
NOW, MY BLUE-EYES... POLYMERIZE!!
DOOM
NOT THAT!

BLUE-EYES WHITE DRAGON
★★★★★★★★

ATTACK 3000
DEFENSE 2500

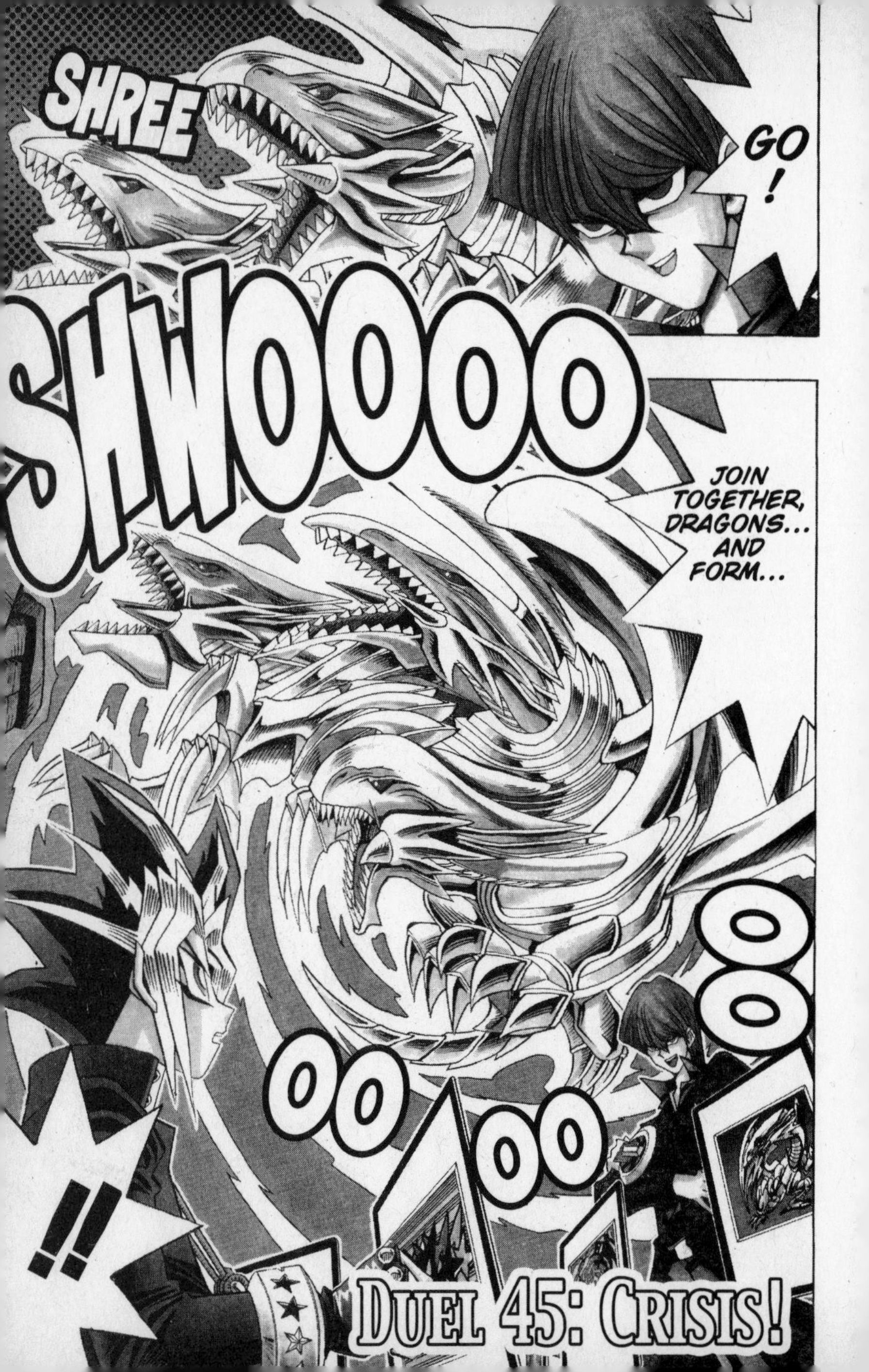
GO!
SHREE
SHWOOOO
JOIN TOGETHER, DRAGONS... AND FORM...
OO OO OO
!!
Duel 45: Crisis!

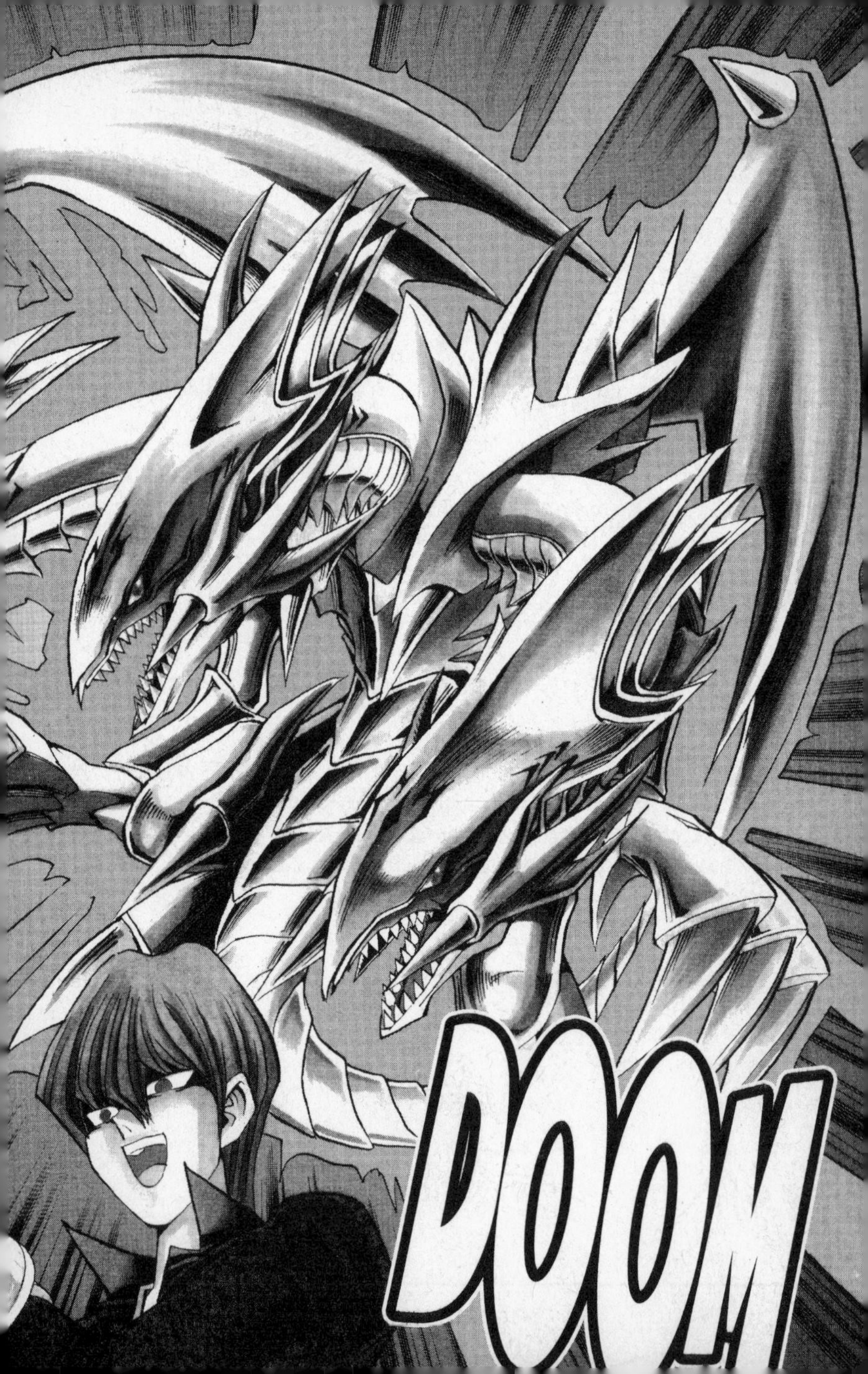
DOOM

Duel 45: Crisis!

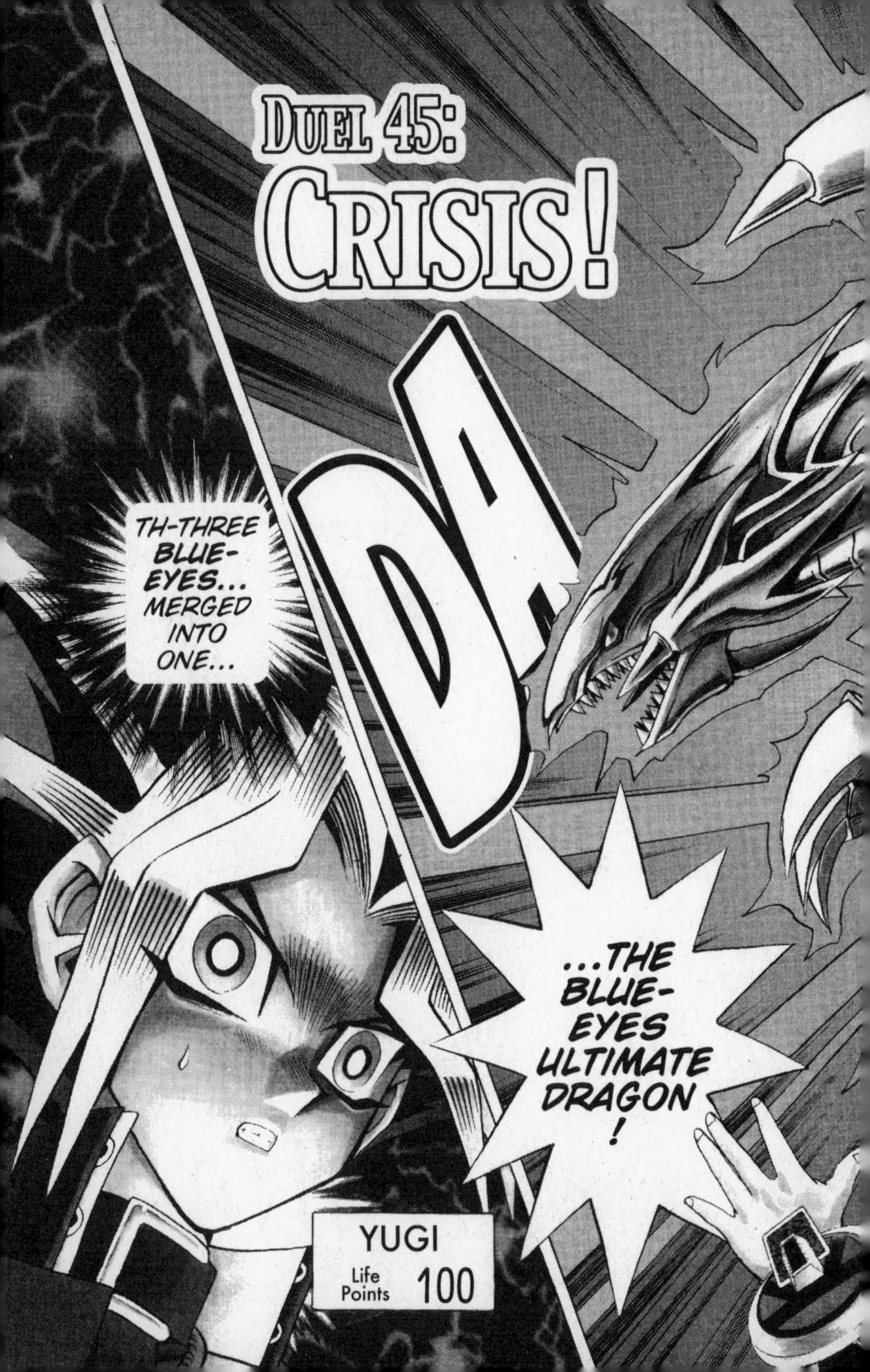
TH-THREE BLUE-EYES... MERGED INTO ONE...
DA
...THE BLUE-EYES ULTIMATE DRAGON!
YUGI
Life Points 100

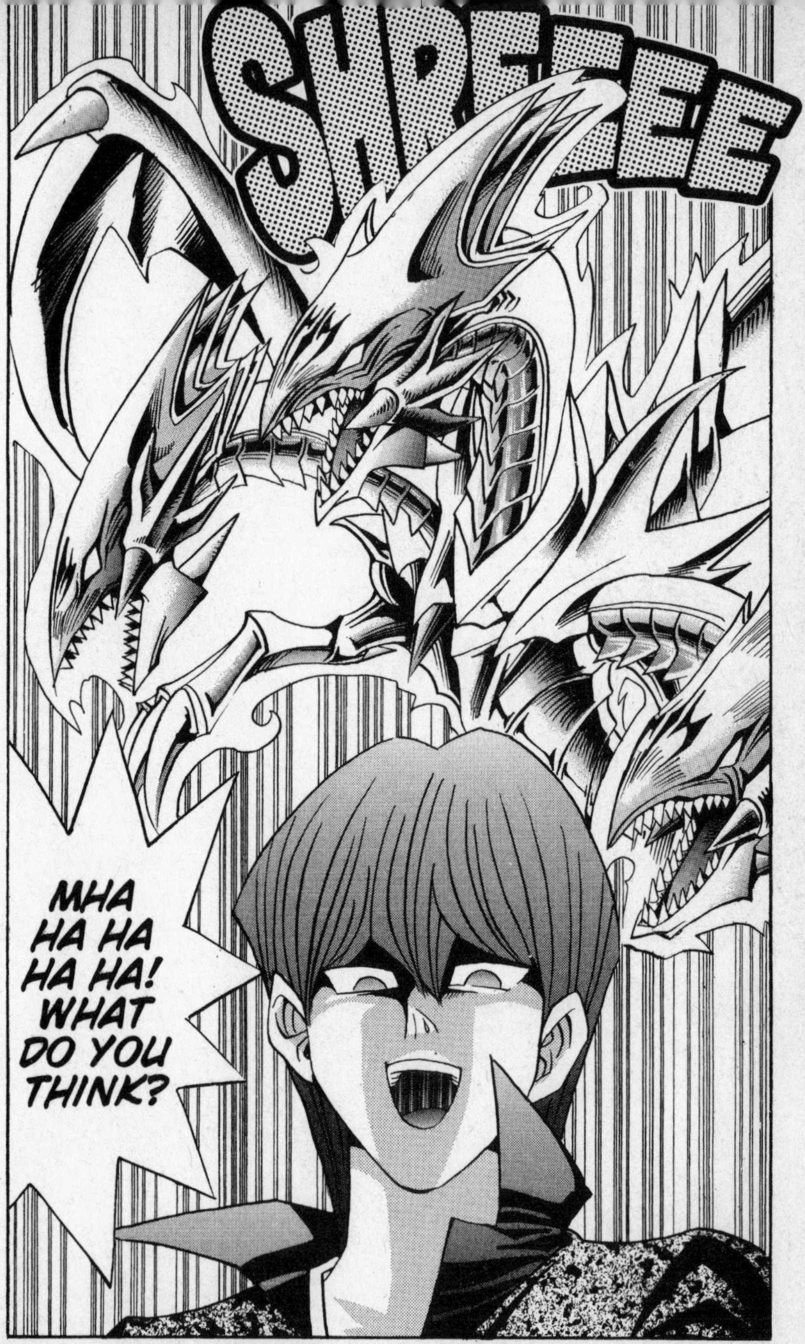
SHREEEE
MHA HA HA HA HA! WHAT DO YOU THINK?

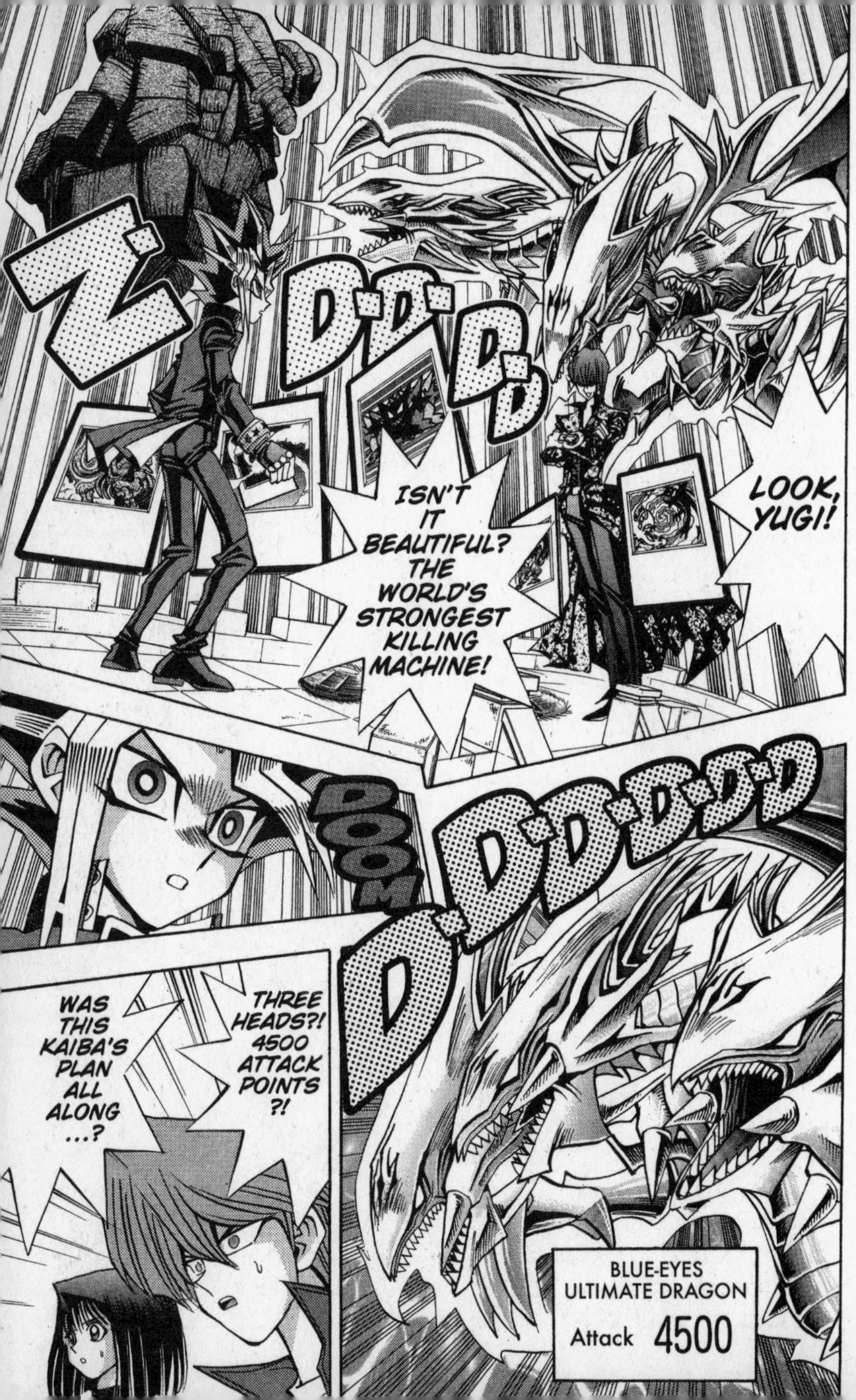
LOOK, YUGI!
ISN'T IT BEAUTIFUL? THE WORLD'S STRONGEST KILLING MACHINE!
ZD-D-D-D
DOOM
D-D-D-D-D-D
BLUE-EYES ULTIMATE DRAGON
Attack 4500
THREE HEADS?! 4500 ATTACK POINTS?!
WAS THIS KAIBA'S PLAN ALL ALONG ...?

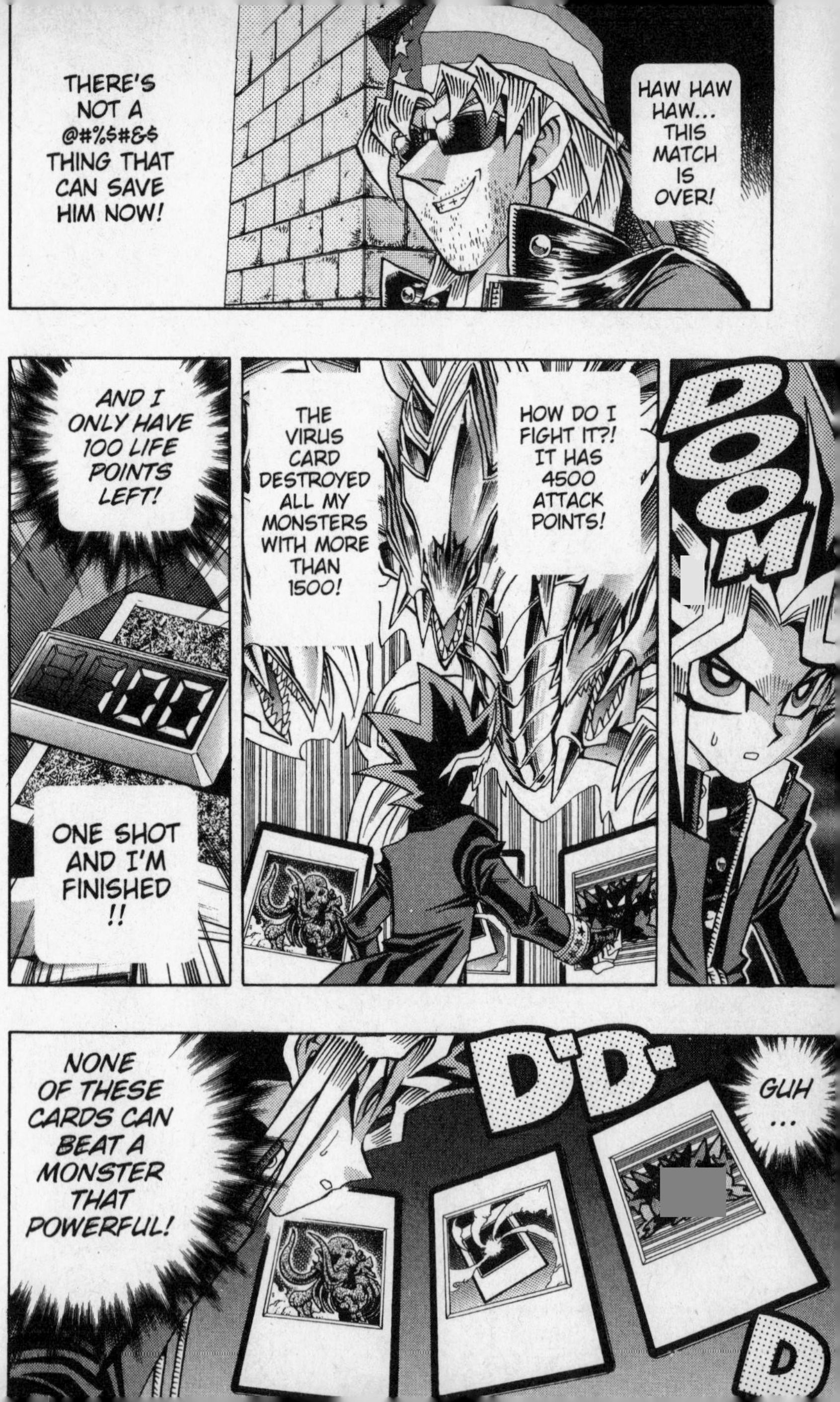
HAW HAW HAW... THIS MATCH IS OVER!
THERE'S NOT A @#%$#&$ THING THAT CAN SAVE HIM NOW!
DOOM
HOW DO I FIGHT IT?! IT HAS 4500 ATTACK POINTS!
THE VIRUS CARD DESTROYED ALL MY MONSTERS WITH MORE THAN 1500!
AND I ONLY HAVE 100 LIFE POINTS LEFT!
ONE SHOT AND I'M FINISHED!!
GUH...
D·D·
D
NONE OF THESE CARDS CAN BEAT A MONSTER THAT POWERFUL!

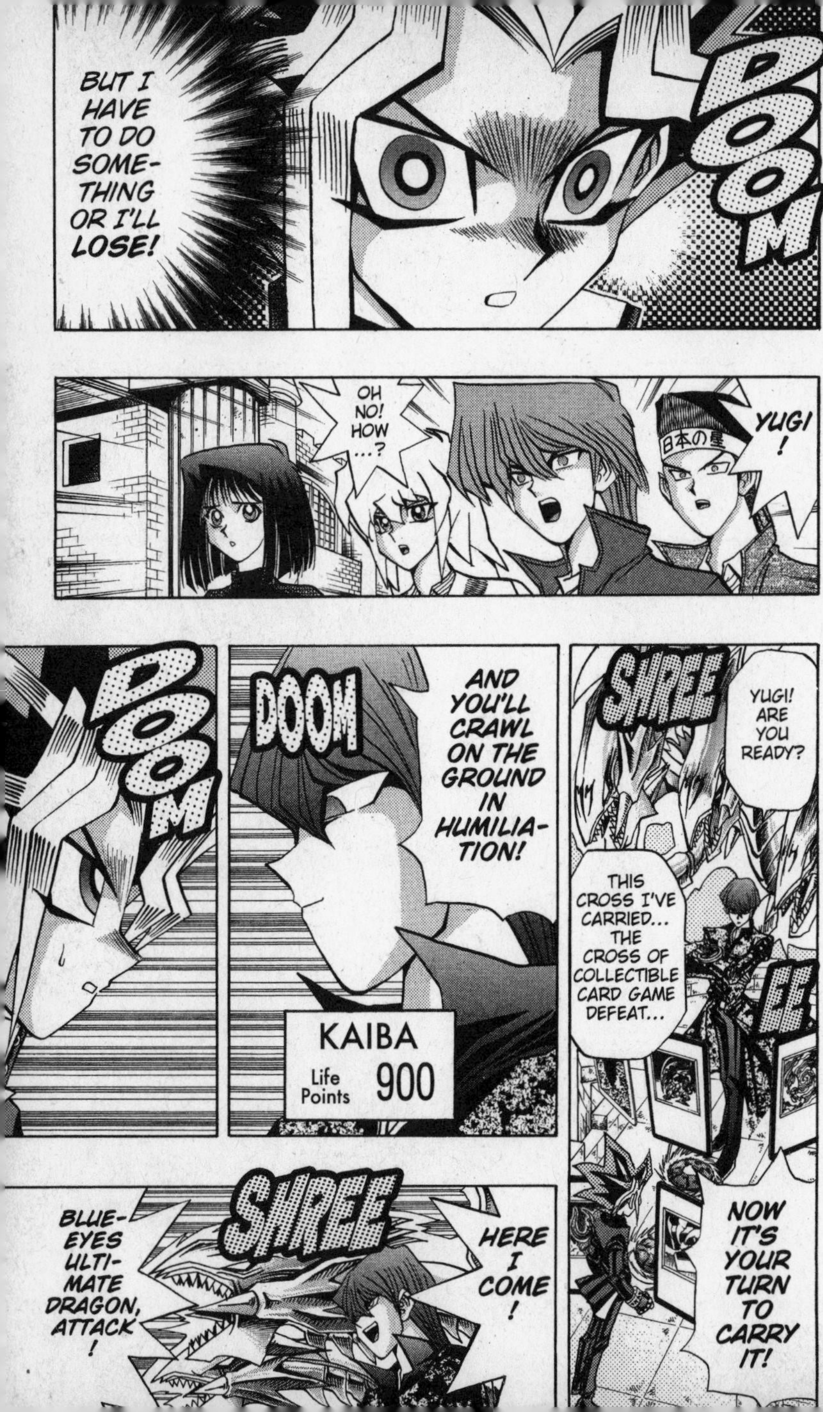
DOOM
BUT I HAVE TO DO SOMETHING OR I'LL LOSE!
YUGI!
日本の星
OH NO! HOW ...?
SHREE
YUGI! ARE YOU READY?
THIS CROSS I'VE CARRIED... THE CROSS OF COLLECTIBLE CARD GAME DEFEAT...
EE
NOW IT'S YOUR TURN TO CARRY IT!
AND YOU'LL CRAWL ON THE GROUND IN HUMILIATION!
DOOM
KAIBA
Life Points 900
DOOM
SHREE
HERE I COME!
BLUE-EYES ULTIMATE DRAGON, ATTACK!

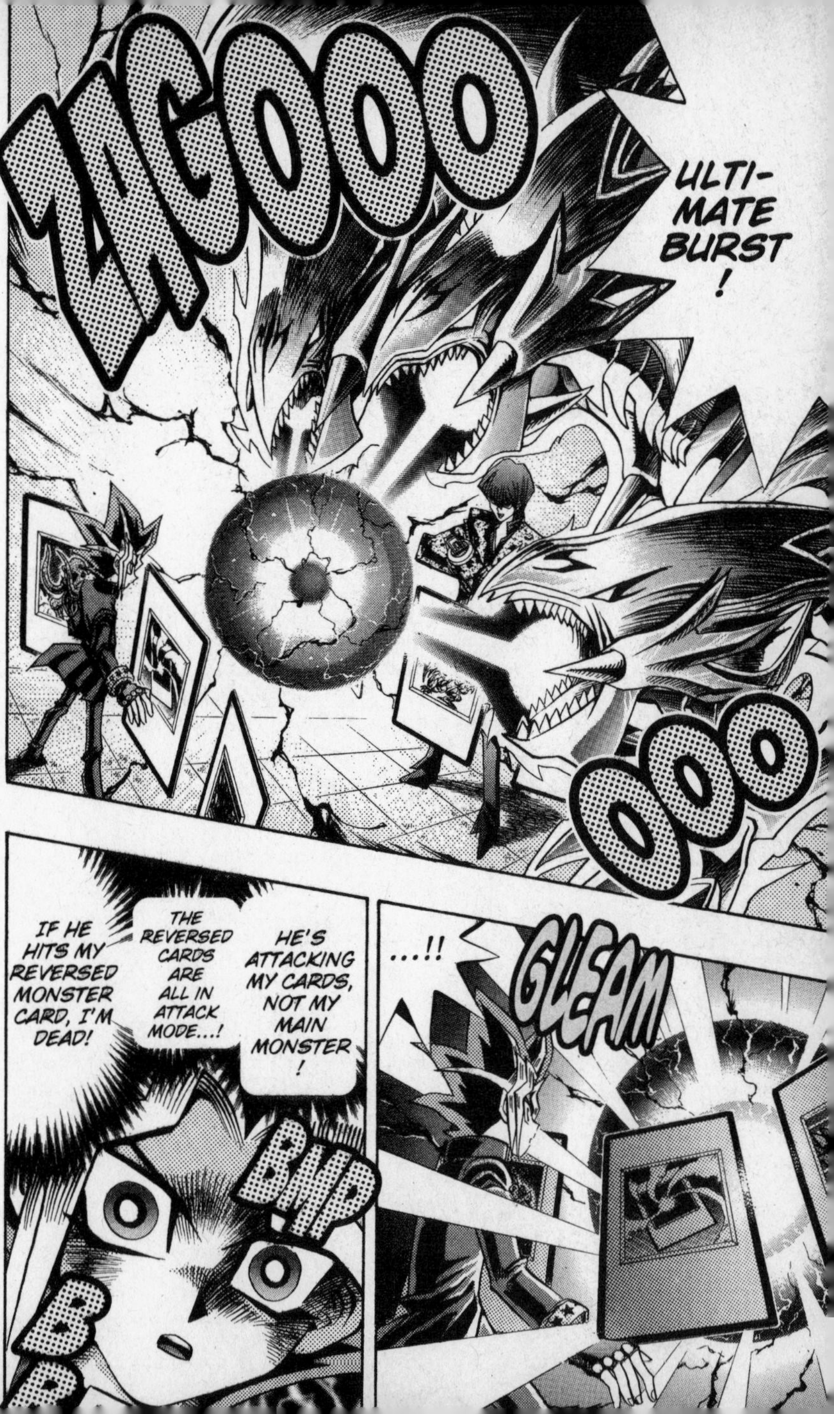
ZAGOOOO
ULTI-MATE BURST!
OOOO
...!!
GLEAM
HE'S ATTACKING MY CARDS, NOT MY MAIN MONSTER!
THE REVERSED CARDS ARE ALL IN ATTACK MODE...!
IF HE HITS MY REVERSED MONSTER CARD, I'M DEAD!
BMP

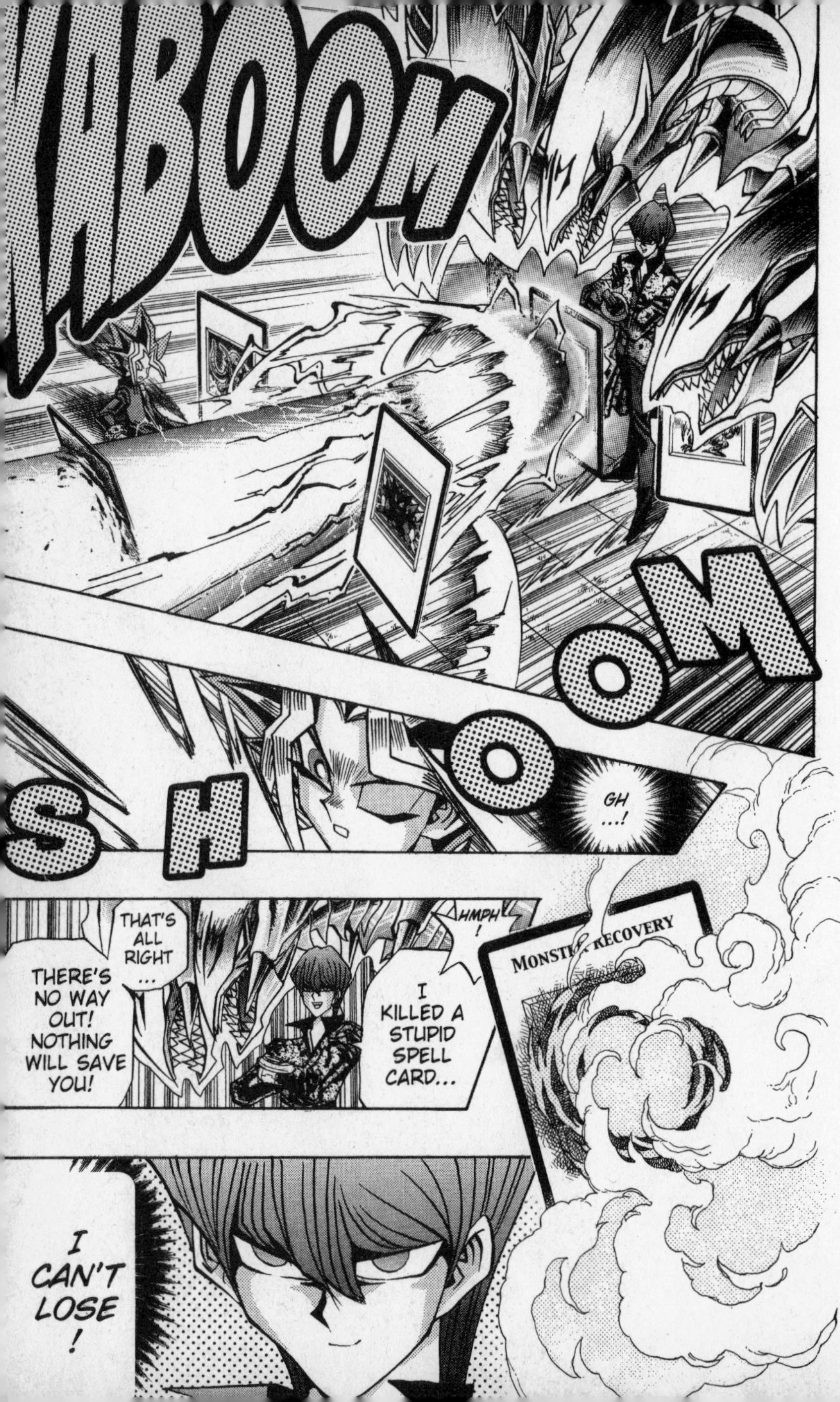
ABOOM
SHOOM
GH ...!
MONST RECOVERY
HMPH!
I KILLED A STUPID SPELL CARD...
THAT'S ALL RIGHT ...
THERE'S NO WAY OUT! NOTHING WILL SAVE YOU!
I CAN'T LOSE!

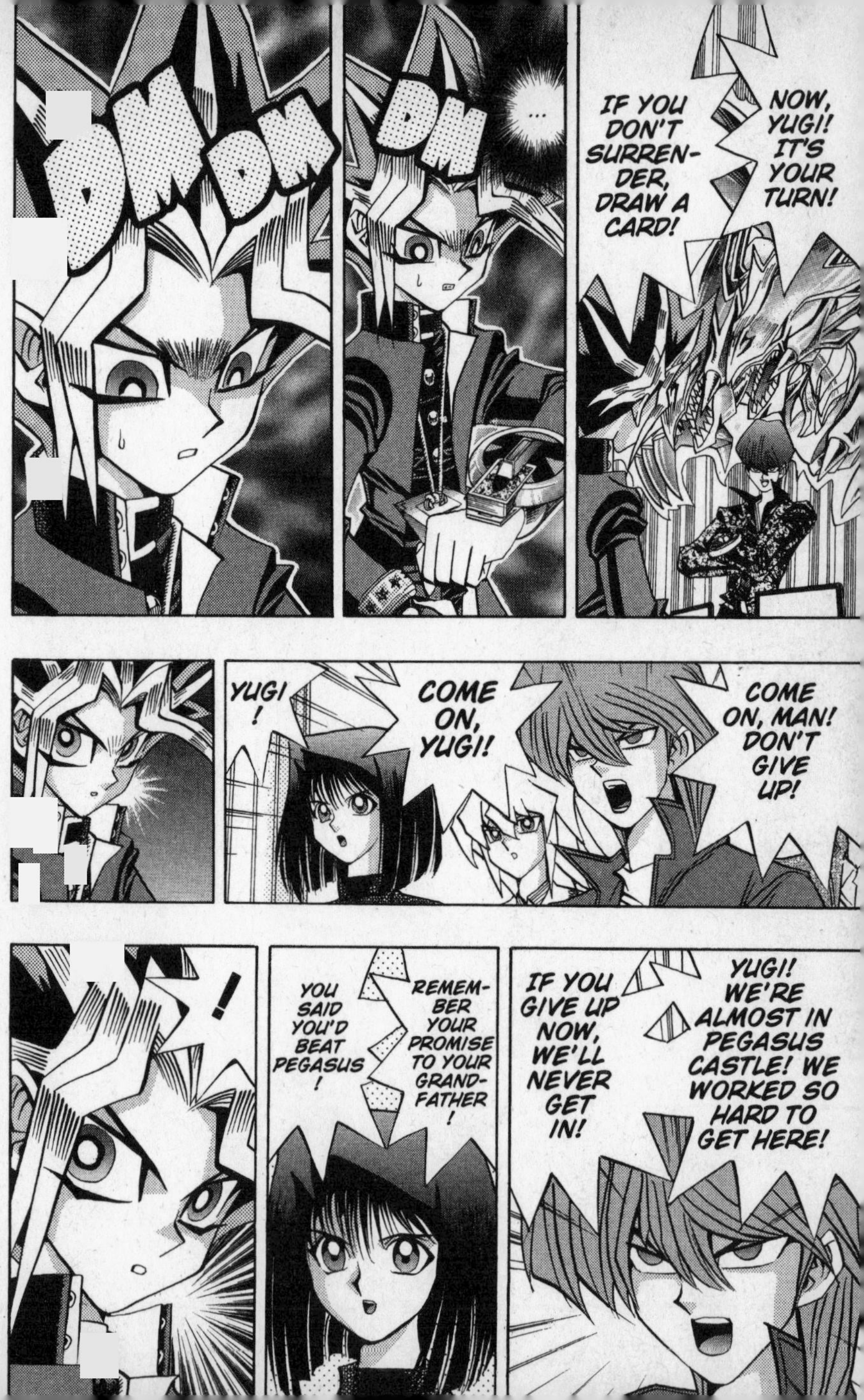
NOW, YUGI! IT'S YOUR TURN!
IF YOU DON'T SURREN-DER, DRAW A CARD!
...
DM
DM DM DM
COME ON, MAN! DON'T GIVE UP!
COME ON, YUGI!
YUGI!
YUGI! WE'RE ALMOST IN PEGASUS CASTLE! WE WORKED SO HARD TO GET HERE!
IF YOU GIVE UP NOW, WE'LL NEVER GET IN!
REMEM-BER YOUR PROMISE TO YOUR GRAND-FATHER!
YOU SAID YOU'D BEAT PEGASUS!
!

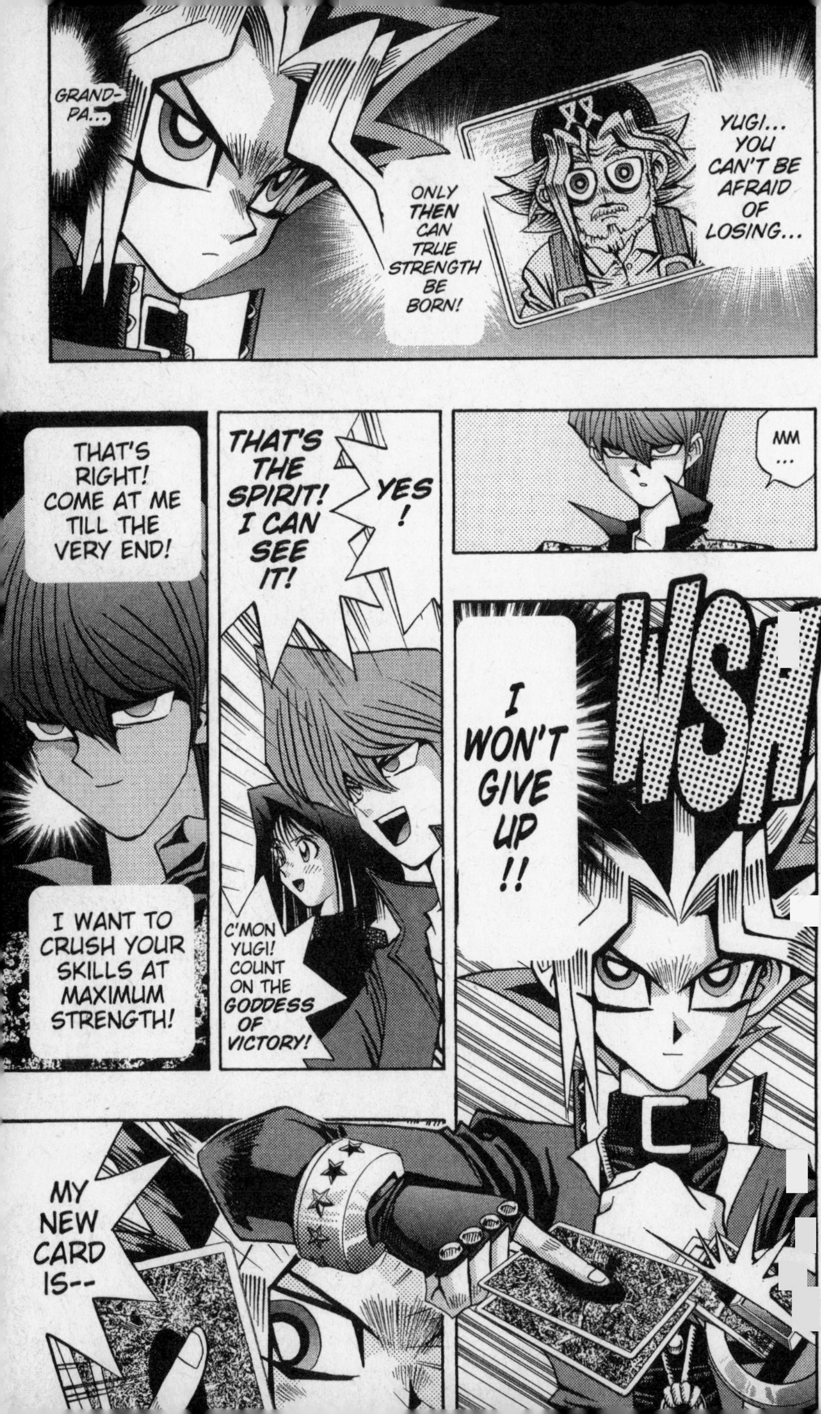
YUGI... YOU CAN'T BE AFRAID OF LOSING...
ONLY THEN CAN TRUE STRENGTH BE BORN!
GRAND-PA...
MM...
WSH!
I WON'T GIVE UP!!
YES!
THAT'S THE SPIRIT! I CAN SEE IT!
C'MON YUGI! COUNT ON THE GODDESS OF VICTORY!
THAT'S RIGHT! COME AT ME TILL THE VERY END!
I WANT TO CRUSH YOUR SKILLS AT MAXIMUM STRENGTH!
MY NEW CARD IS--

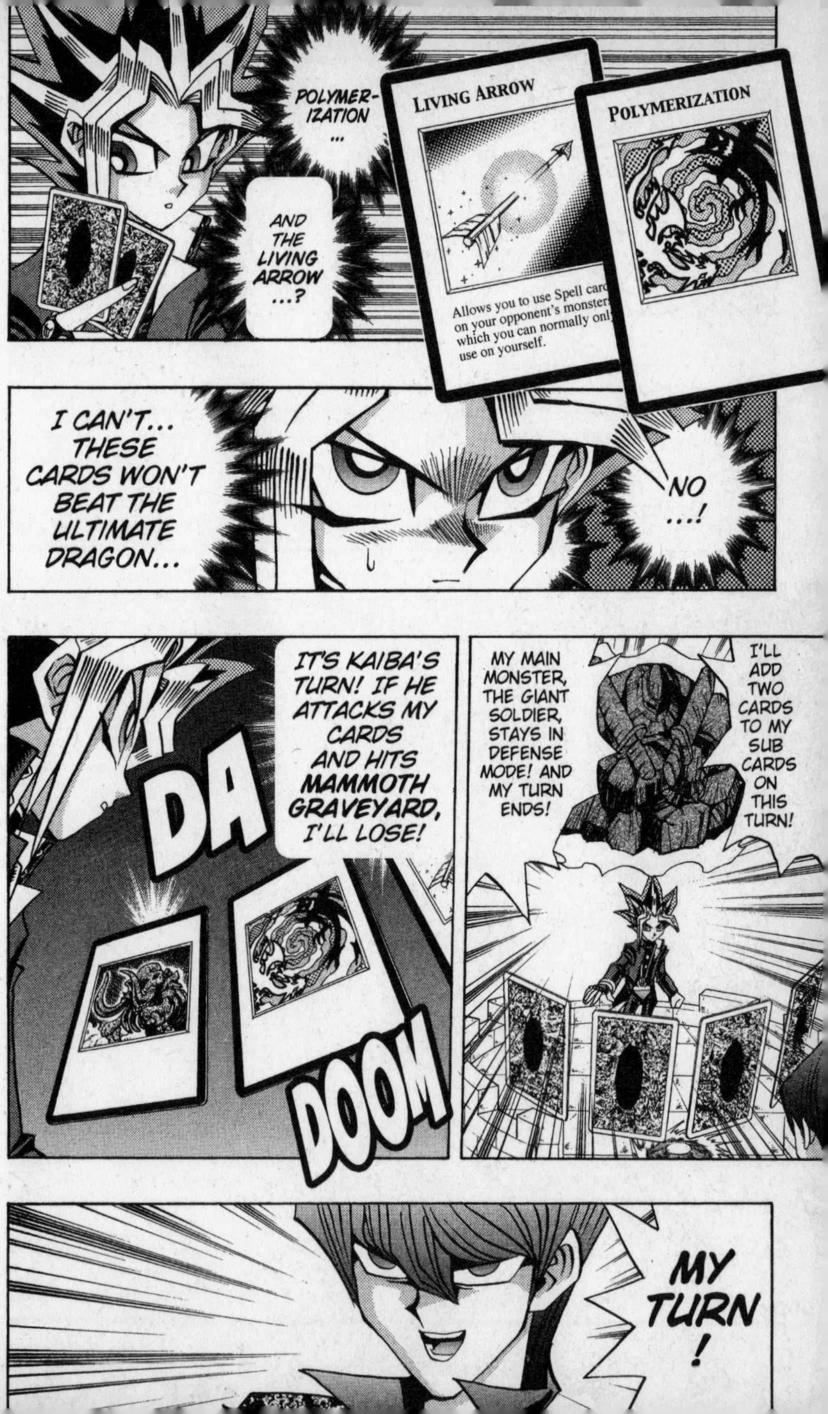
POLYMERIZATION
LIVING ARROW
POLYMER-IZATION...
Allows you to use Spell card on your opponent's monster which you can normally onl use on yourself.
AND THE LIVING ARROW...?
NO...!
I CAN'T... THESE CARDS WON'T BEAT THE ULTIMATE DRAGON...
I'LL ADD TWO CARDS TO MY SUB CARDS ON THIS TURN!
MY MAIN MONSTER, THE GIANT SOLDIER, STAYS IN DEFENSE MODE! AND MY TURN ENDS!
IT'S KAIBA'S TURN! IF HE ATTACKS MY CARDS AND HITS MAMMOTH GRAVEYARD, I'LL LOSE!
DA
DOOM
MY TURN!

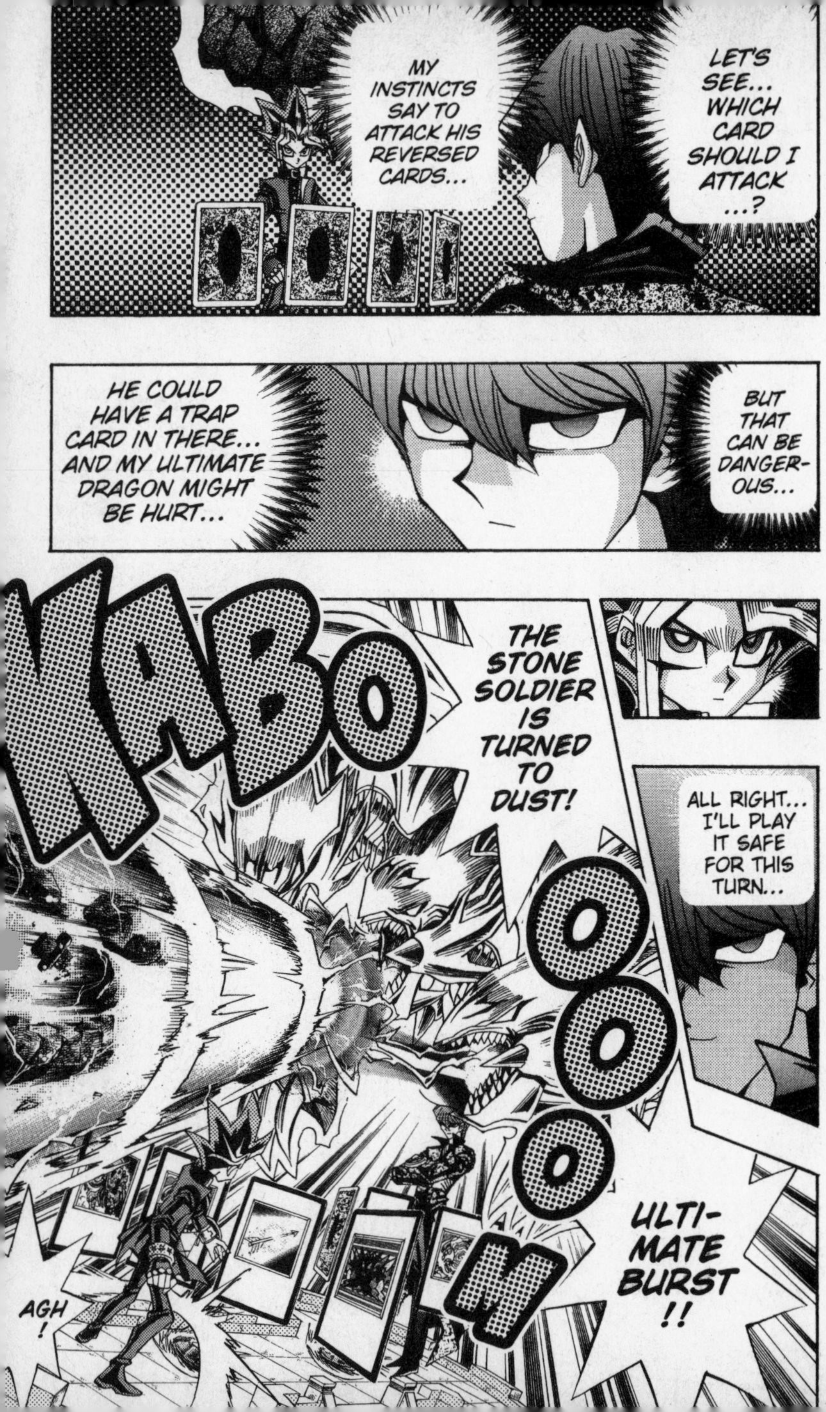
LET'S SEE... WHICH CARD SHOULD I ATTACK ...?
MY INSTINCTS SAY TO ATTACK HIS REVERSED CARDS...
BUT THAT CAN BE DANGER-OUS...
HE COULD HAVE A TRAP CARD IN THERE... AND MY ULTIMATE DRAGON MIGHT BE HURT...
ALL RIGHT... I'LL PLAY IT SAFE FOR THIS TURN...
THE STONE SOLDIER IS TURNED TO DUST!
KABOOOOM
ULTI-MATE BURST !!
AGH !

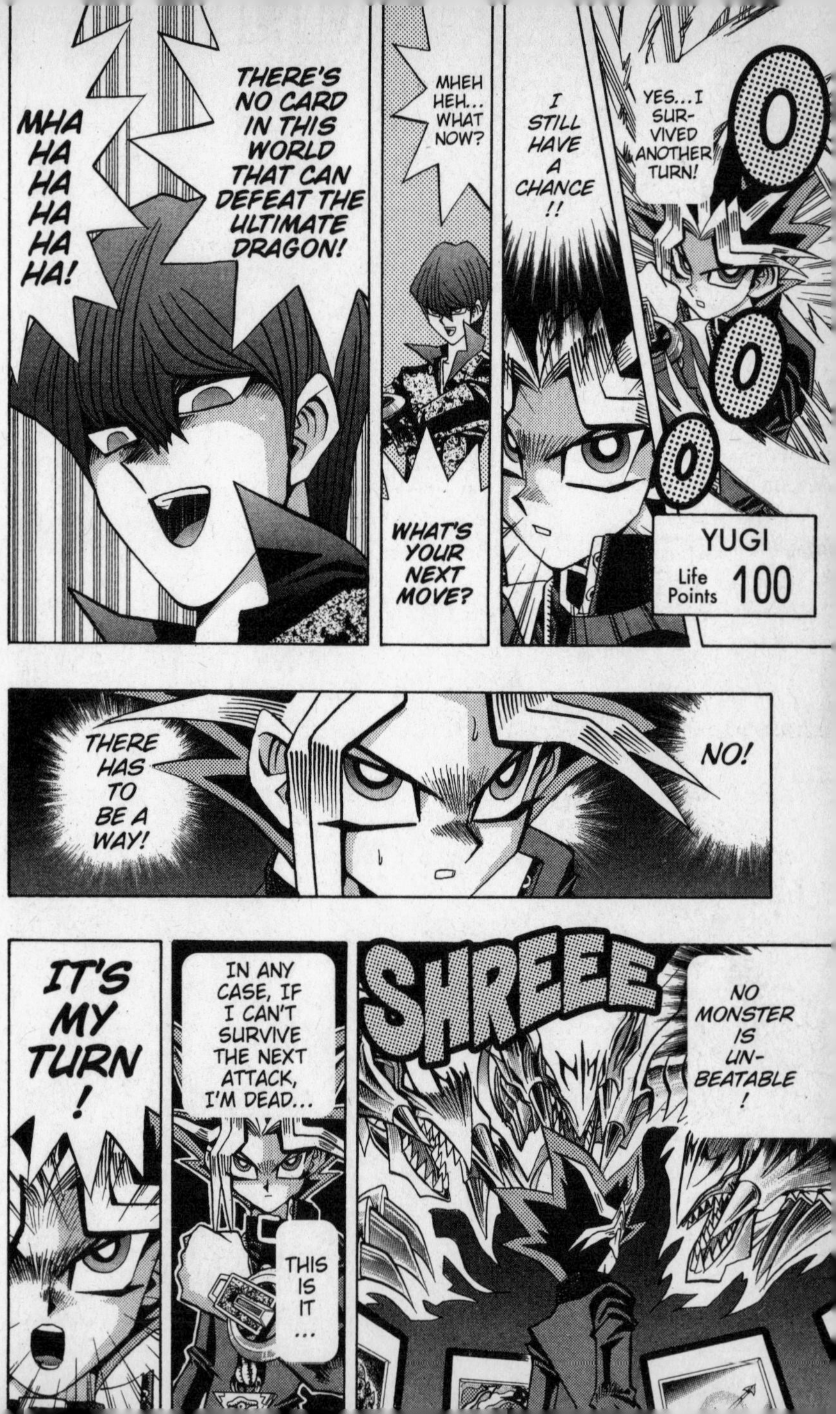
YES...I SURVIVED ANOTHER TURN!
I STILL HAVE A CHANCE!!
YUGI Life Points 100
MHEH HEH... WHAT NOW?
WHAT'S YOUR NEXT MOVE?
THERE'S NO CARD IN THIS WORLD THAT CAN DEFEAT THE ULTIMATE DRAGON!
MHA HA HA HA HA HA!
NO!
THERE HAS TO BE A WAY!
NO MONSTER IS UN-BEATABLE!
SHREEE
IN ANY CASE, IF I CAN'T SURVIVE THE NEXT ATTACK, I'M DEAD...
THIS IS IT...
IT'S MY TURN!

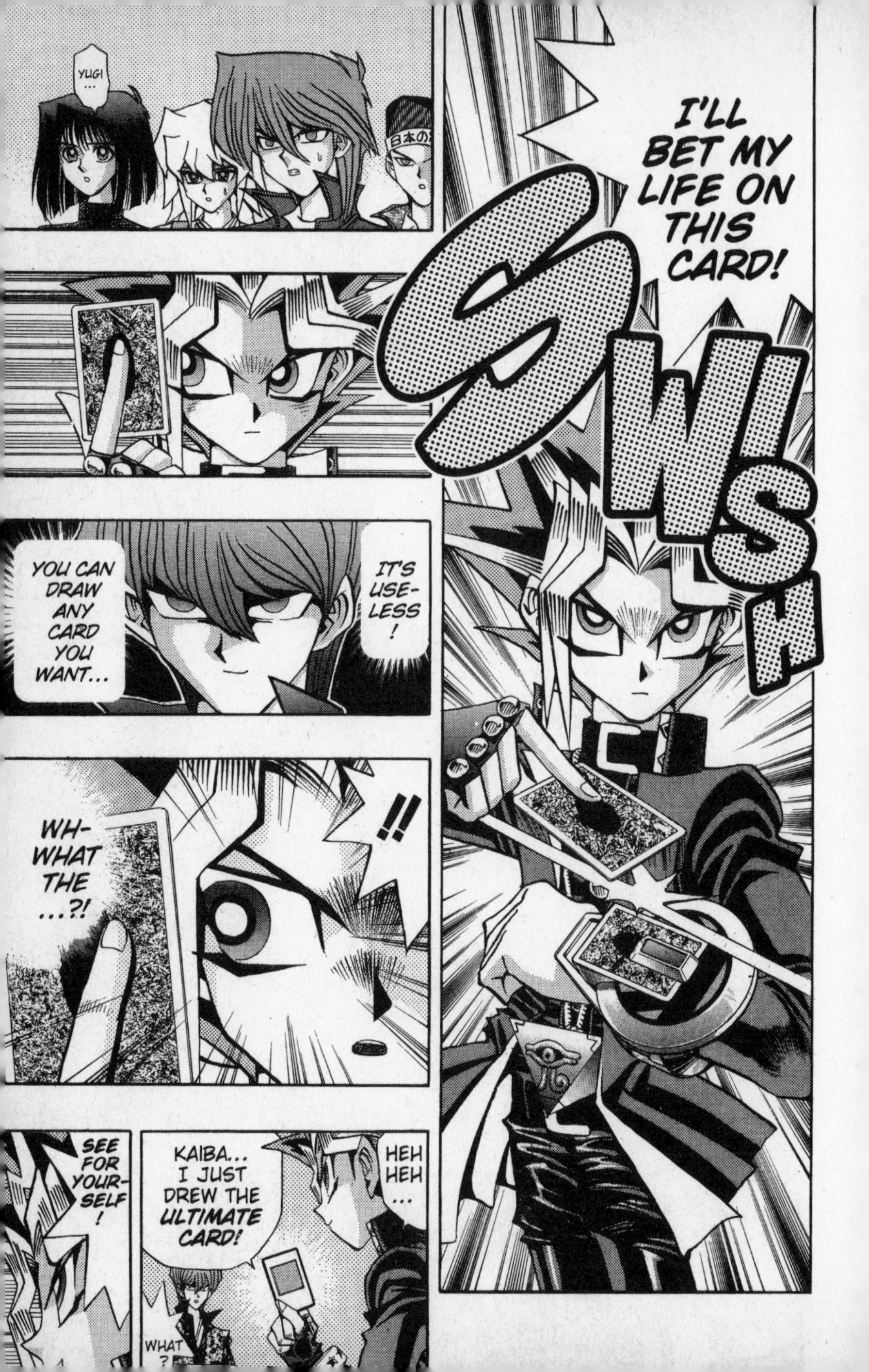
I'LL BET MY LIFE ON THIS CARD!
SWISH
YUGI...
IT'S USELESS!
YOU CAN DRAW ANY CARD YOU WANT...
!!
WH-WHAT THE...?!
HEH HEH...
KAIBA... I JUST DREW THE ULTIMATE CARD!
WHAT?
SEE FOR YOURSELF!

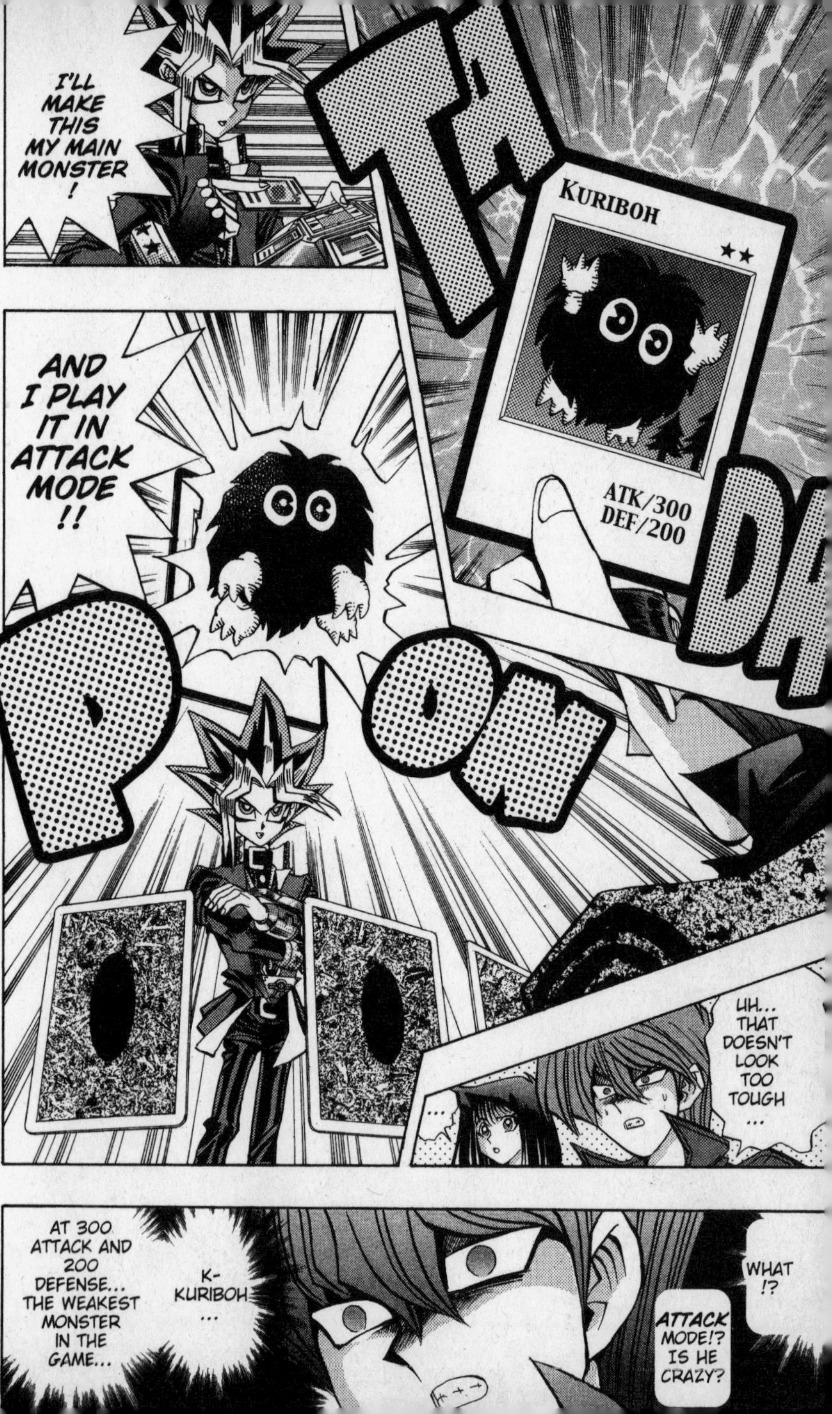
THA
KURIBOH
ATK/300
DEF/200
DA
I'LL MAKE THIS MY MAIN MONSTER!
AND I PLAY IT IN ATTACK MODE!!
POP
UH... THAT DOESN'T LOOK TOO TOUGH...
...
WHAT!?
ATTACK MODE!? IS HE CRAZY?
K-KURIBOH...
AT 300 ATTACK AND 200 DEFENSE... THE WEAKEST MONSTER IN THE GAME...

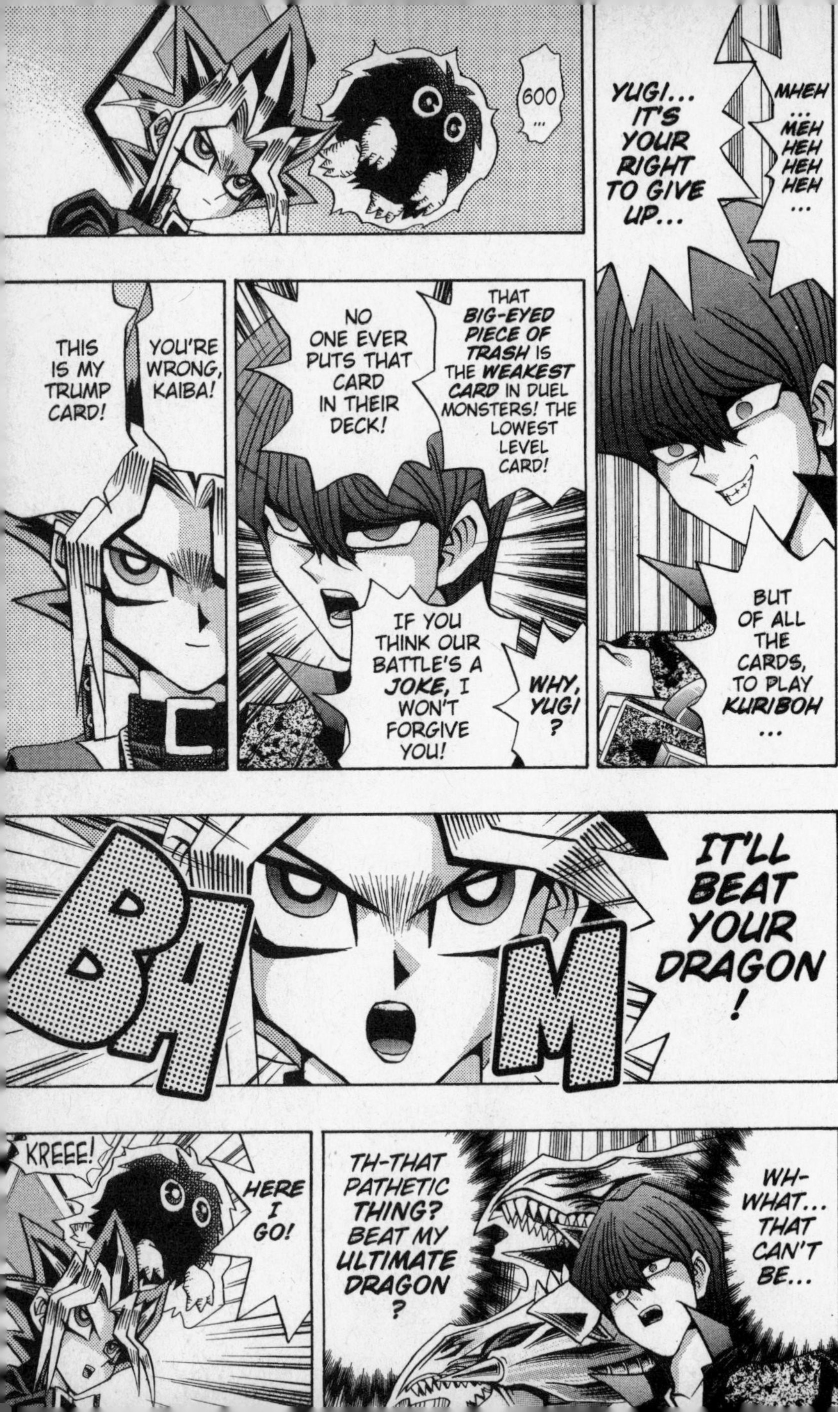
YUGI... IT'S YOUR RIGHT TO GIVE UP...
MHEH... MEH HEH HEH HEH...
BUT OF ALL THE CARDS, TO PLAY KURIBOH...
600...
THAT BIG-EYED PIECE OF TRASH IS THE WEAKEST CARD IN DUEL MONSTERS! THE LOWEST LEVEL CARD!
NO ONE EVER PUTS THAT CARD IN THEIR DECK!
WHY, YUGI?
IF YOU THINK OUR BATTLE'S A JOKE, I WON'T FORGIVE YOU!
YOU'RE WRONG, KAIBA!
THIS IS MY TRUMP CARD!
IT'LL BEAT YOUR DRAGON!
BAM
WH-WHAT... THAT CAN'T BE...
TH-THAT PATHETIC THING? BEAT MY ULTIMATE DRAGON?
HERE I GO!
KREEE!

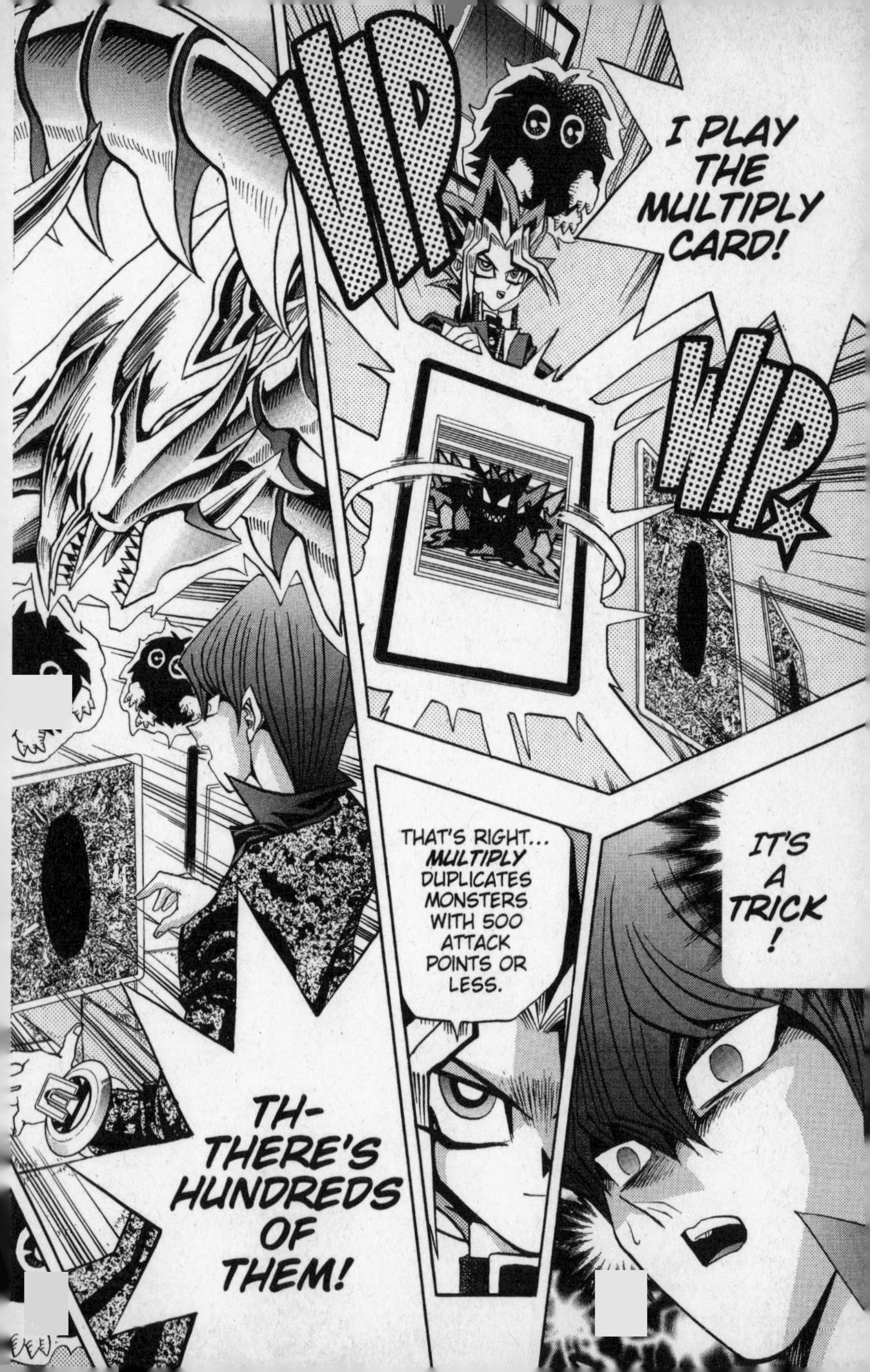
WIP
I PLAY THE MULTIPLY CARD!
WIP
IT'S A TRICK!
THAT'S RIGHT... MULTIPLY DUPLICATES MONSTERS WITH 500 ATTACK POINTS OR LESS.
TH-THERE'S HUNDREDS OF THEM!

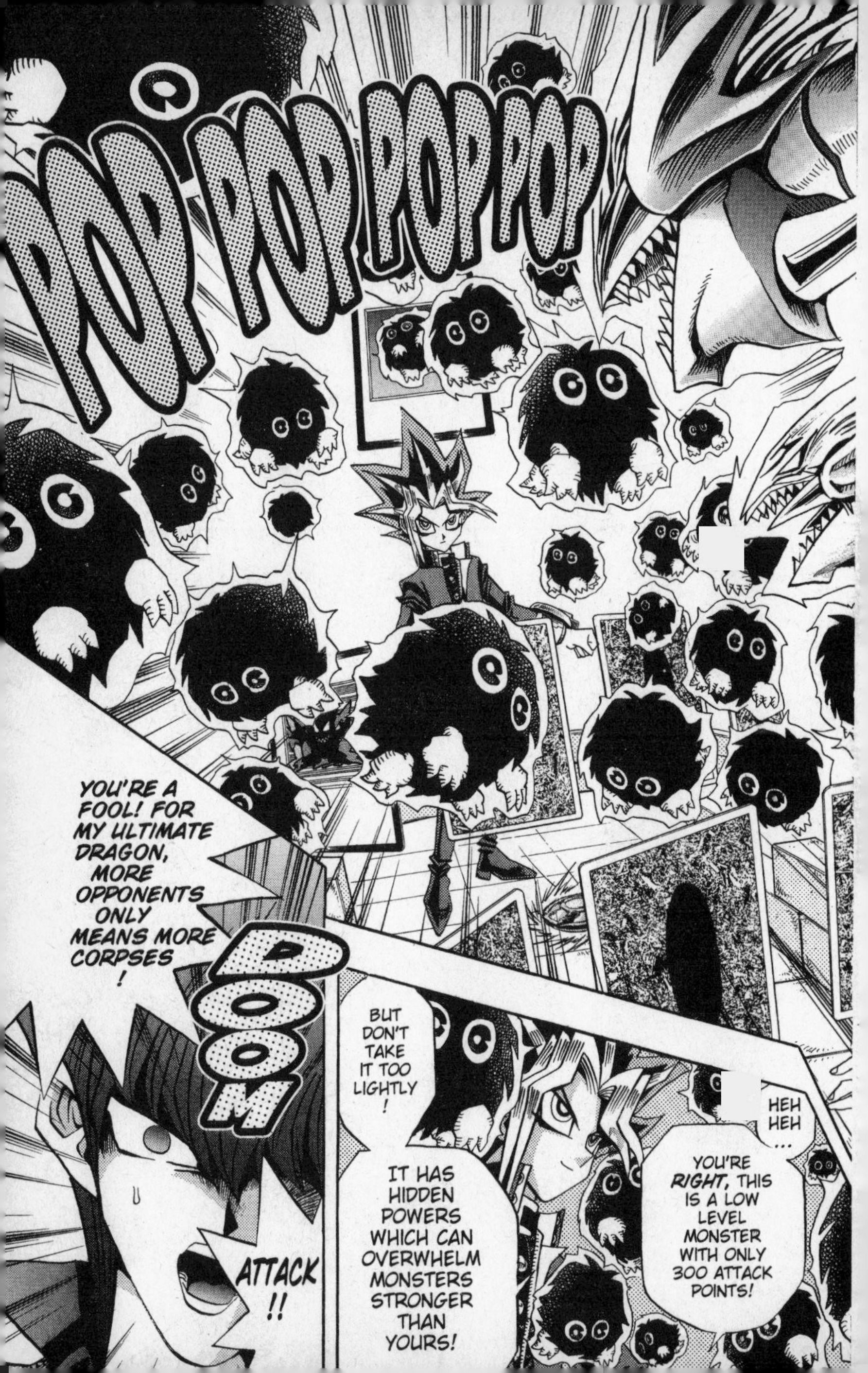
POP POP POP POP
HEH HEH...
YOU'RE RIGHT, THIS IS A LOW LEVEL MONSTER WITH ONLY 300 ATTACK POINTS!
BUT DON'T TAKE IT TOO LIGHTLY!
IT HAS HIDDEN POWERS WHICH CAN OVERWHELM MONSTERS STRONGER THAN YOURS!
YOU'RE A FOOL! FOR MY ULTIMATE DRAGON, MORE OPPONENTS ONLY MEANS MORE CORPSES!
DOOM
ATTACK!!

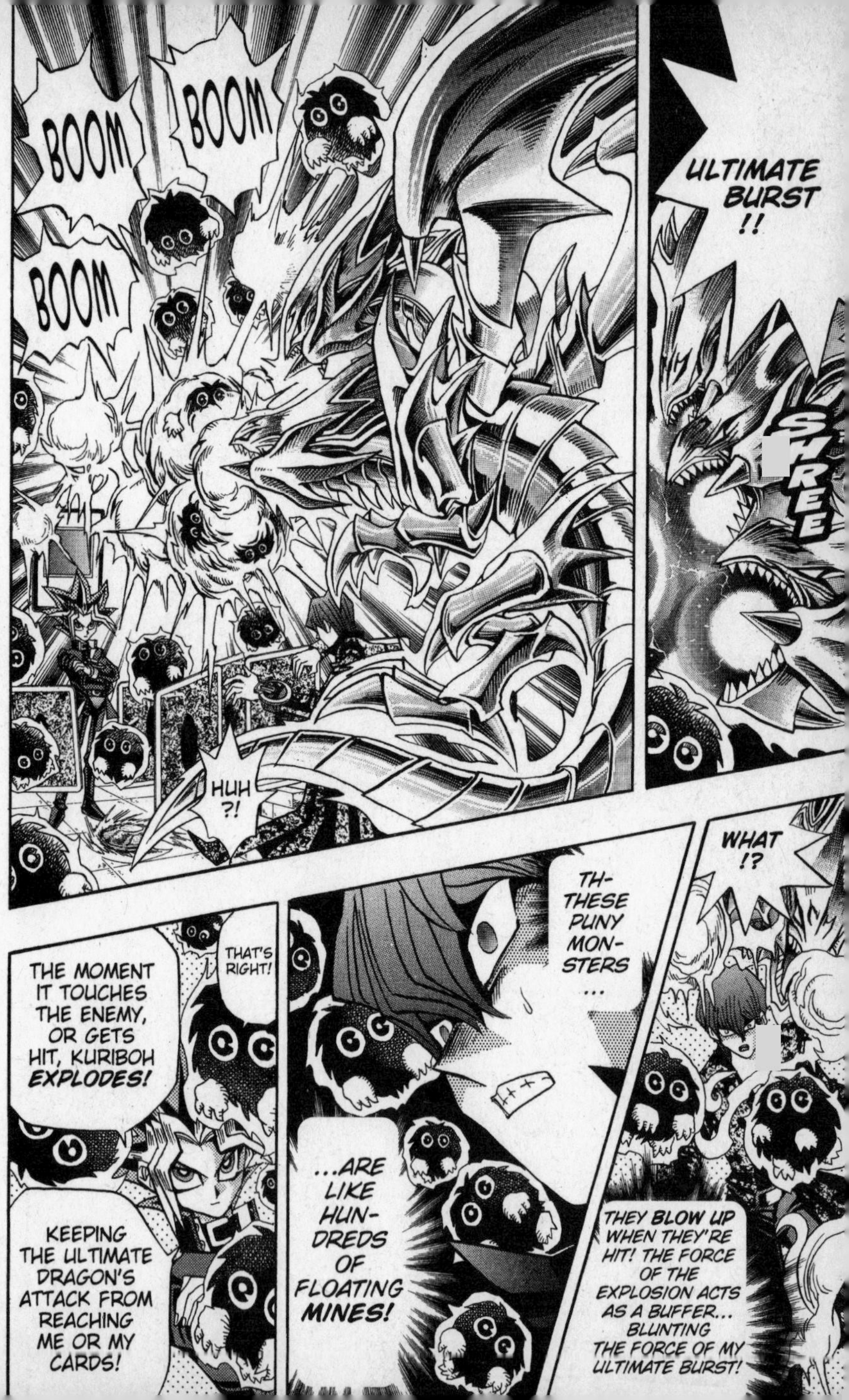
ULTIMATE BURST !!
SHREE
BOOM
BOOM
BOOM
HUH ?!
WHAT !?
TH- THESE PUNY MONSTERS ...
...ARE LIKE HUNDREDS OF FLOATING MINES!
THEY BLOW UP WHEN THEY'RE HIT! THE FORCE OF THE EXPLOSION ACTS AS A BUFFER... BLUNTING THE FORCE OF MY ULTIMATE BURST!
THAT'S RIGHT!
THE MOMENT IT TOUCHES THE ENEMY, OR GETS HIT, KURIBOH EXPLODES!
KEEPING THE ULTIMATE DRAGON'S ATTACK FROM REACHING ME OR MY CARDS!

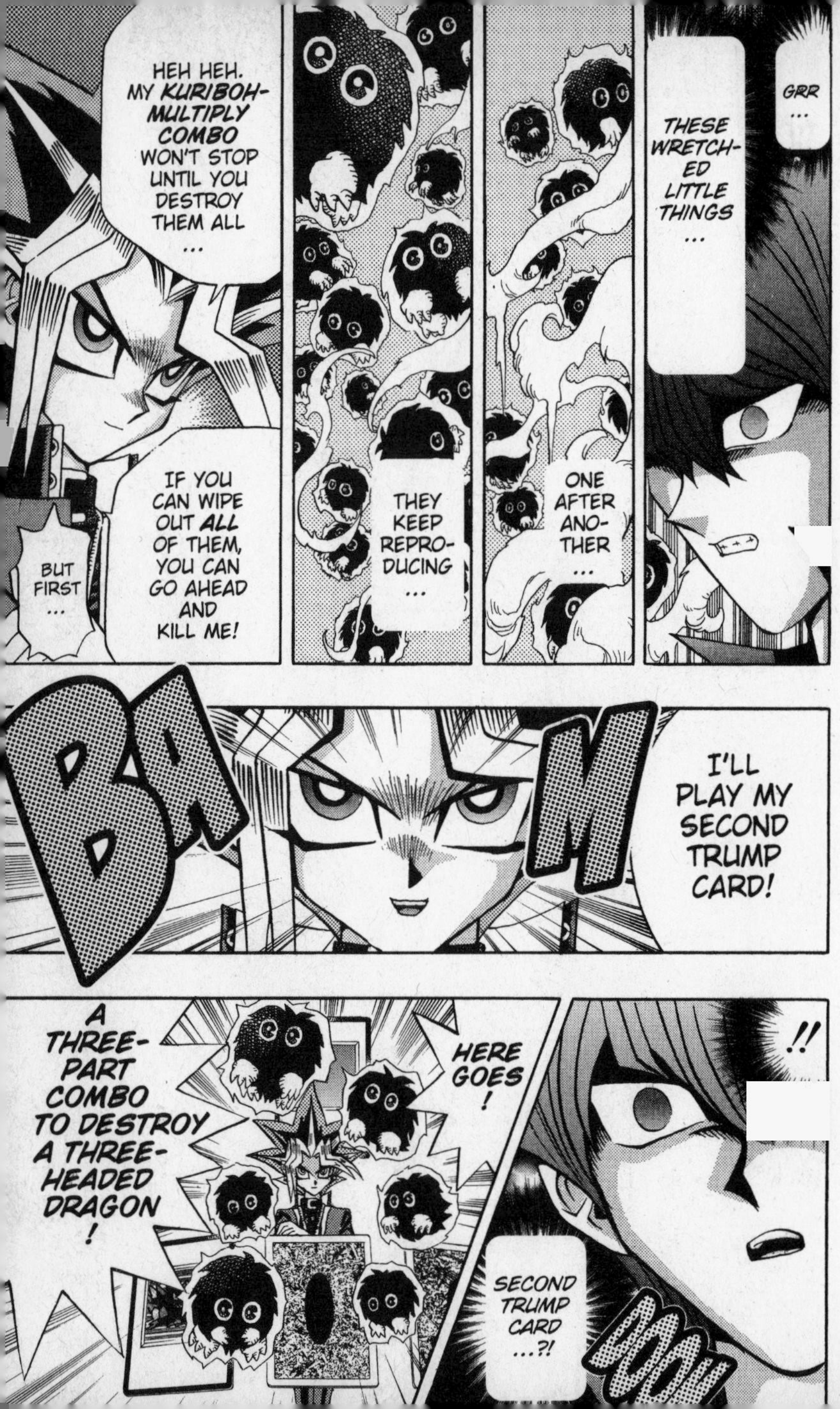
GRR ...
THESE WRETCHED LITTLE THINGS ...
ONE AFTER ANOTHER ...
THEY KEEP REPRODUCING ...
HEH HEH. MY *KURIBOH-MULTIPLY COMBO* WON'T STOP UNTIL YOU DESTROY THEM ALL ...
IF YOU CAN WIPE OUT *ALL* OF THEM, YOU CAN GO AHEAD AND KILL ME!
BUT FIRST ...
I'LL PLAY MY SECOND TRUMP CARD!
BAM
!!
SECOND TRUMP CARD ...?!
HERE GOES!
A THREE-PART COMBO TO DESTROY A THREE-HEADED DRAGON!

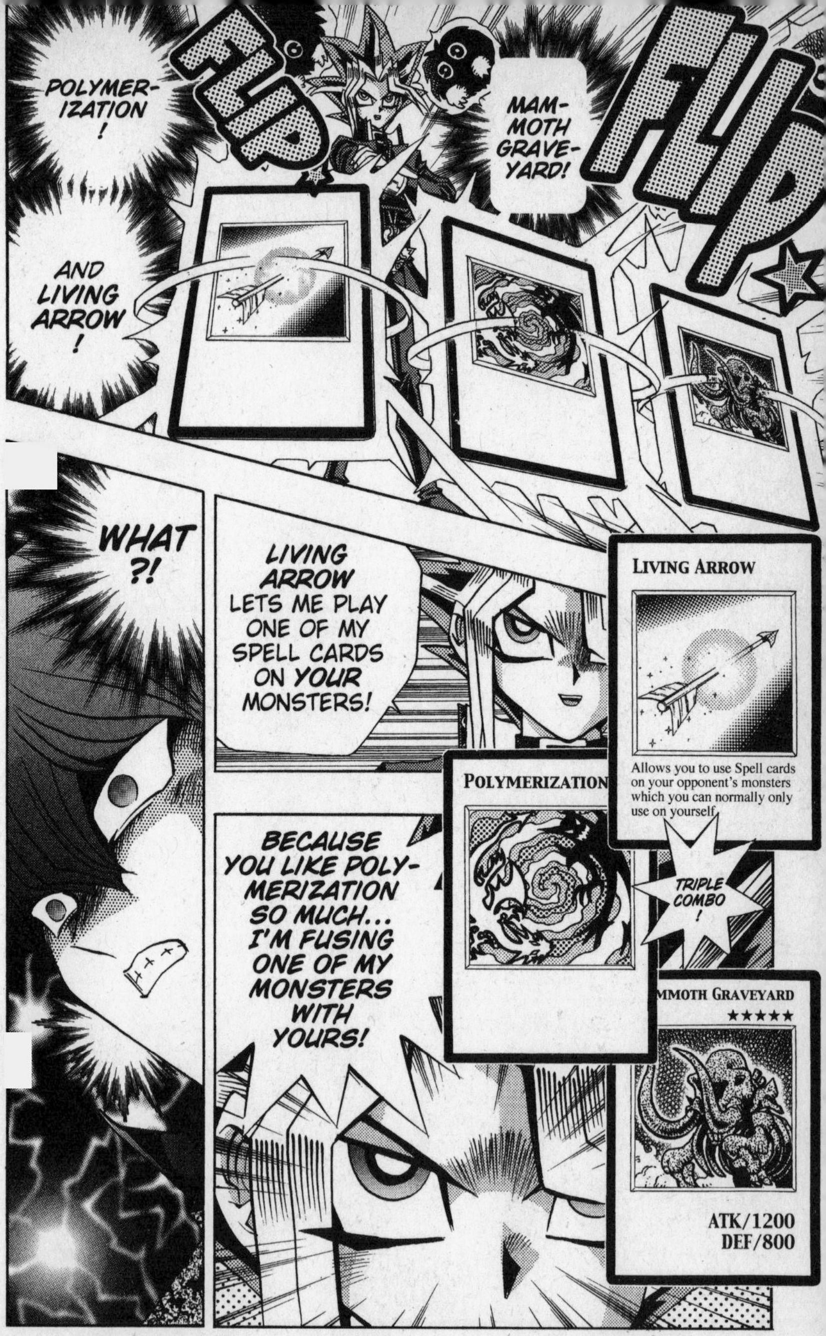
FLIP
MAM-MOTH GRAVE-YARD!
FLIP
POLYMER-IZATION!
AND LIVING ARROW!
LIVING ARROW
Allows you to use Spell cards on your opponent's monsters which you can normally only use on yourself.
LIVING ARROW LETS ME PLAY ONE OF MY SPELL CARDS ON YOUR MONSTERS!
POLYMERIZATION
TRIPLE COMBO!
MMOTH GRAVEYARD
★★★★★
ATK/1200
DEF/800
BECAUSE YOU LIKE POLY-MERIZATION SO MUCH... I'M FUSING ONE OF MY MONSTERS WITH YOURS!
WHAT?!

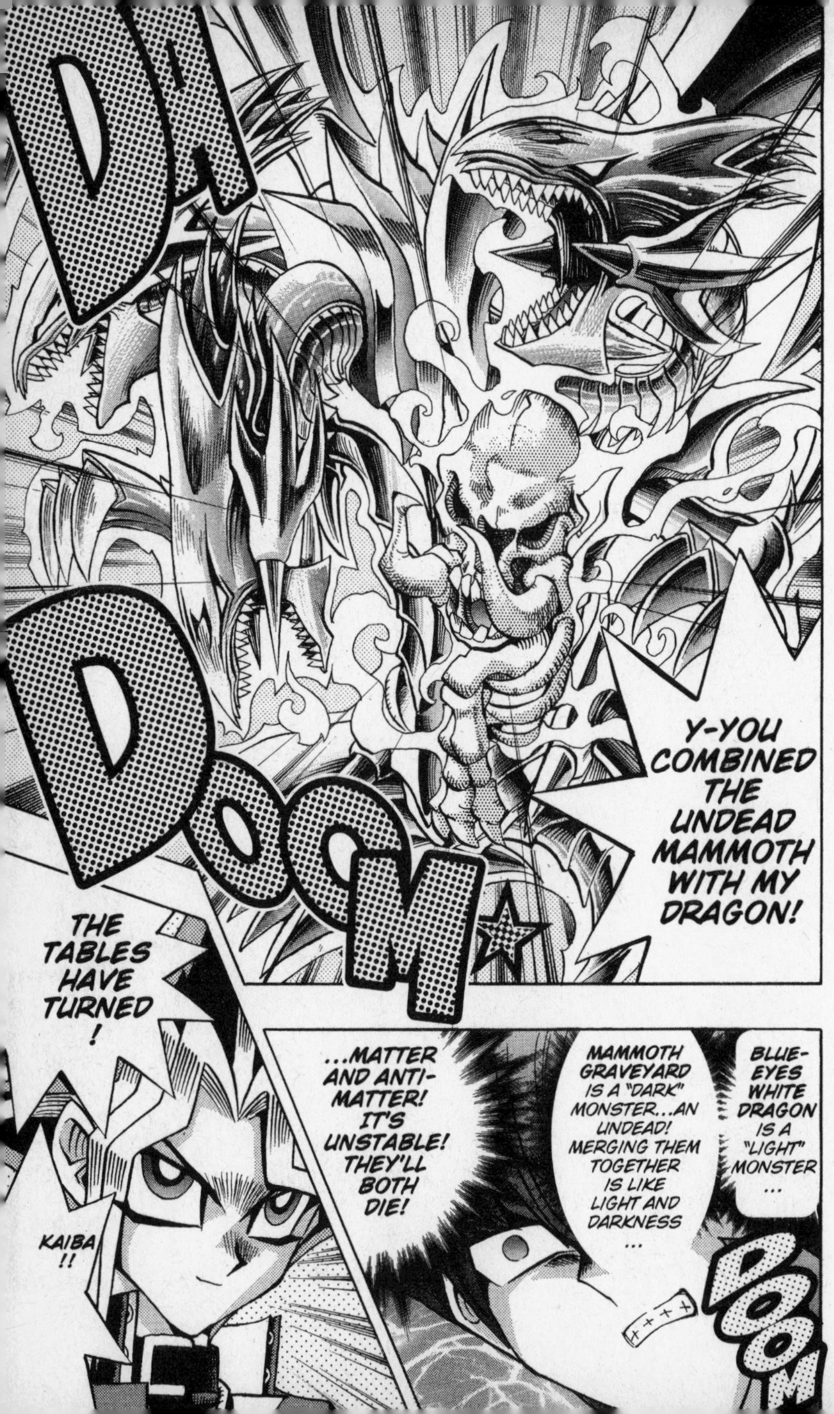
DOOM
Y-YOU COMBINED THE UNDEAD MAMMOTH WITH MY DRAGON!
BLUE-EYES WHITE DRAGON IS A "LIGHT" MONSTER...
MAMMOTH GRAVEYARD IS A "DARK" MONSTER...AN UNDEAD! MERGING THEM TOGETHER IS LIKE LIGHT AND DARKNESS...
...MATTER AND ANTI-MATTER! IT'S UNSTABLE! THEY'LL BOTH DIE!
DOOM
THE TABLES HAVE TURNED!
KAIBA!!

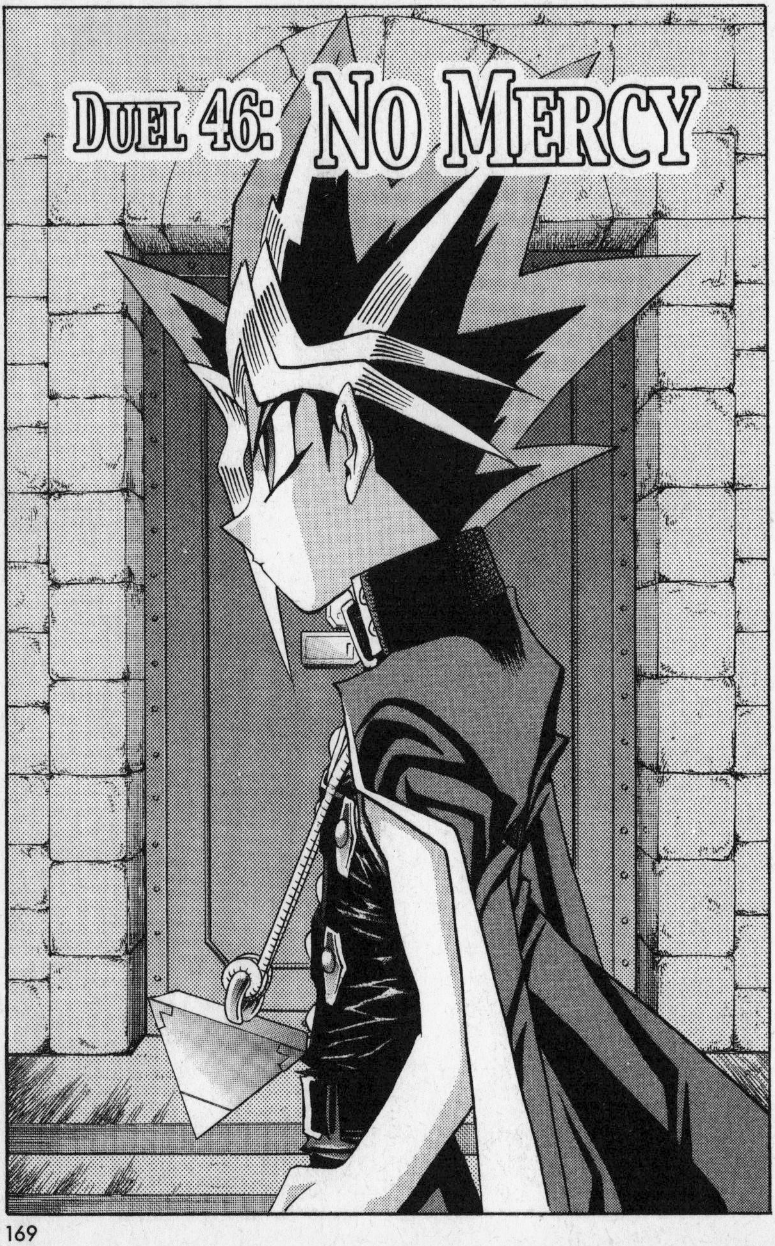
DUEL 46: NO MERCY

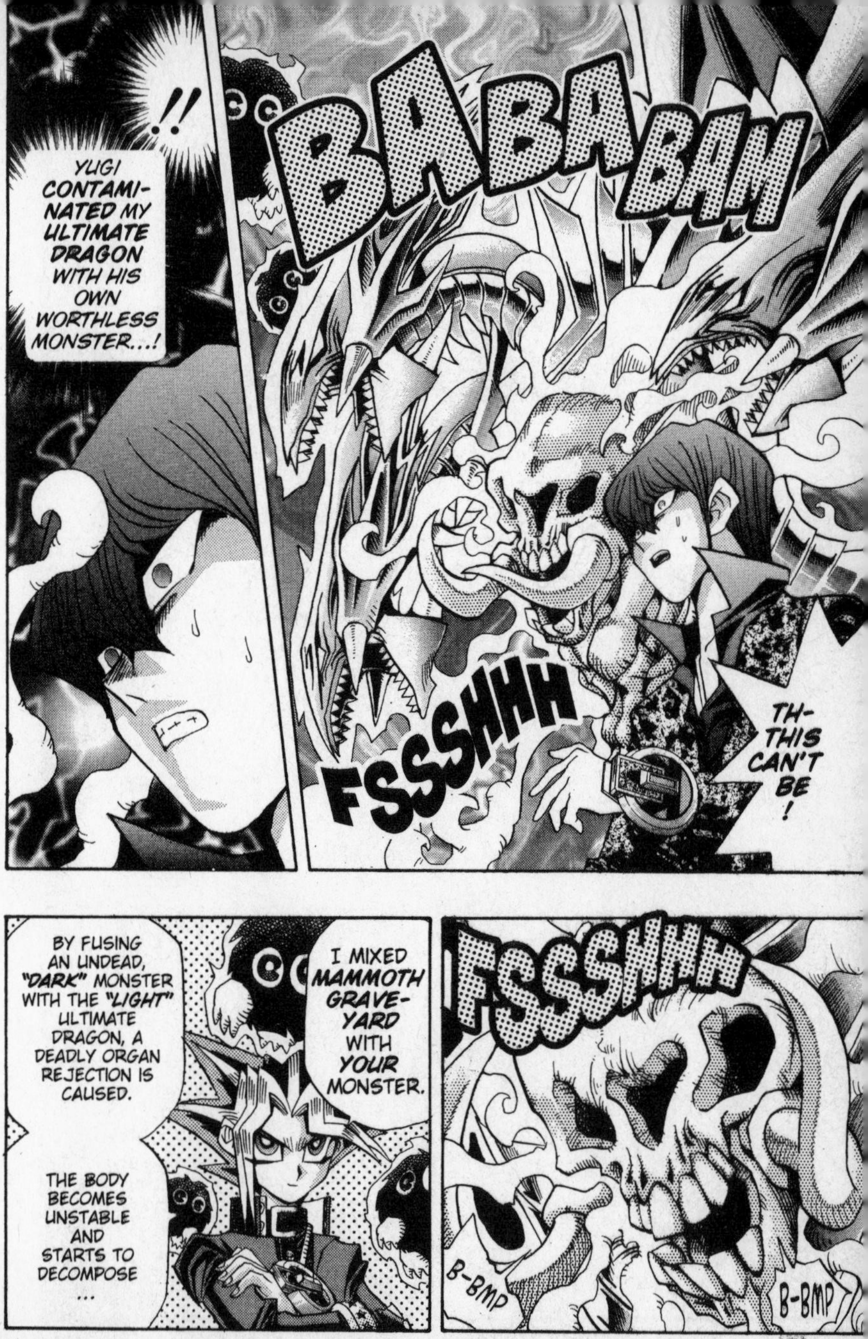
BABABAM
FSSSHHH
TH-THIS CAN'T BE!
!!
YUGI CONTAMINATED MY ULTIMATE DRAGON WITH HIS OWN WORTHLESS MONSTER...!
FSSSHHH
B-BMP
B-BMP
I MIXED MAMMOTH GRAVEYARD WITH YOUR MONSTER.
BY FUSING AN UNDEAD, "DARK" MONSTER WITH THE "LIGHT" ULTIMATE DRAGON, A DEADLY ORGAN REJECTION IS CAUSED.
THE BODY BECOMES UNSTABLE AND STARTS TO DECOMPOSE ...

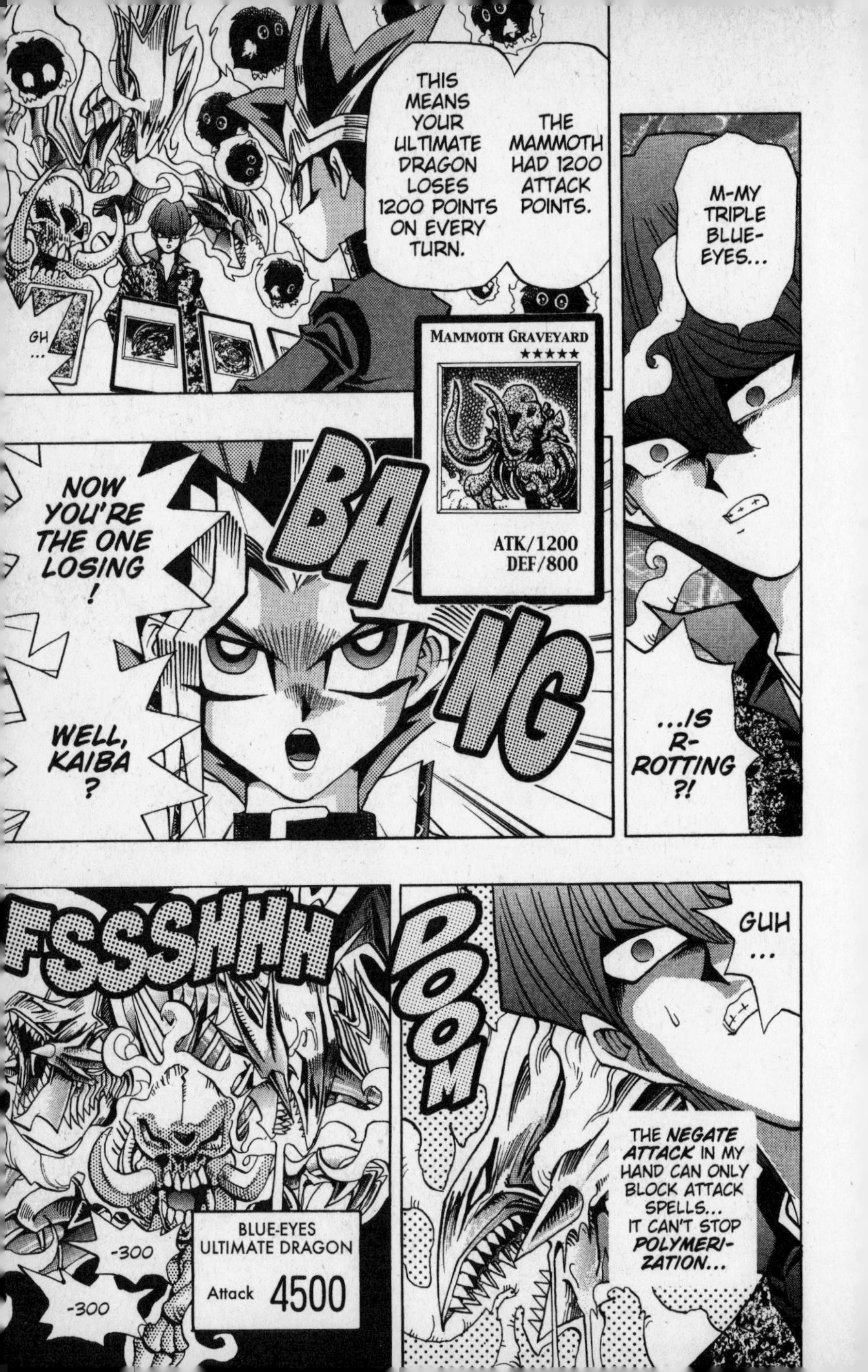
M-MY TRIPLE BLUE-EYES...
...IS R-ROTTING?!
THE MAMMOTH HAD 1200 ATTACK POINTS.
THIS MEANS YOUR ULTIMATE DRAGON LOSES 1200 POINTS ON EVERY TURN.
GH...
MAMMOTH GRAVEYARD
★★★★★
ATK/1200
DEF/800
BANG
NOW YOU'RE THE ONE LOSING!
WELL, KAIBA?
GUH...
DOOM
THE NEGATE ATTACK IN MY HAND CAN ONLY BLOCK ATTACK SPELLS... IT CAN'T STOP POLYMERIZATION...
FSSSHHH
BLUE-EYES ULTIMATE DRAGON
Attack 4500
-300
-300

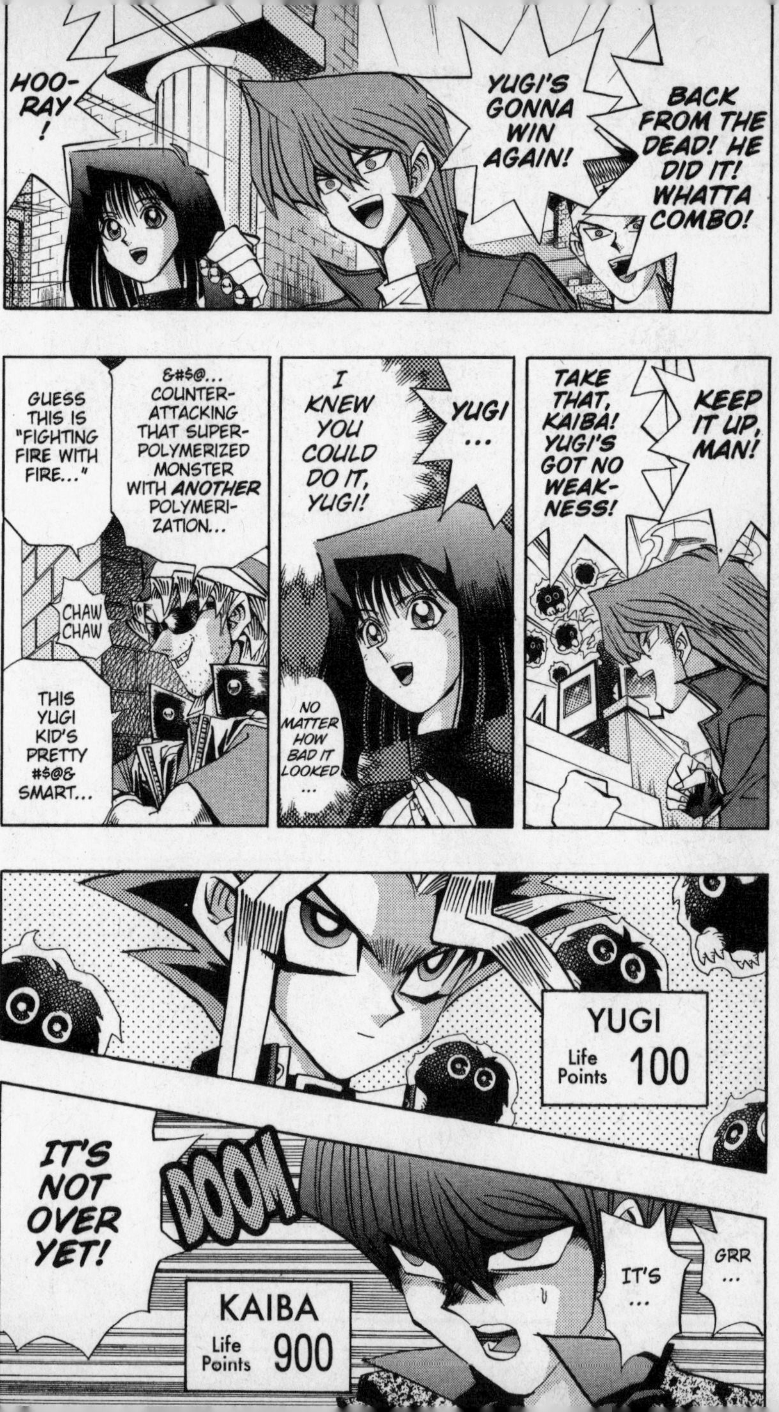
BACK FROM THE DEAD! HE DID IT! WHATTA COMBO!
YUGI'S GONNA WIN AGAIN!
HOORAY!
KEEP IT UP, MAN!
TAKE THAT, KAIBA! YUGI'S GOT NO WEAKNESS!
YUGI...
I KNEW YOU COULD DO IT, YUGI!
NO MATTER HOW BAD IT LOOKED...
&#$@... COUNTER-ATTACKING THAT SUPER-POLYMERIZED MONSTER WITH ANOTHER POLYMERIZATION...
GUESS THIS IS "FIGHTING FIRE WITH FIRE..."
CHAW CHAW
THIS YUGI KID'S PRETTY #$@& SMART...
YUGI Life Points 100
GRR...
IT'S...
DOOM
IT'S NOT OVER YET!
KAIBA Life Points 900

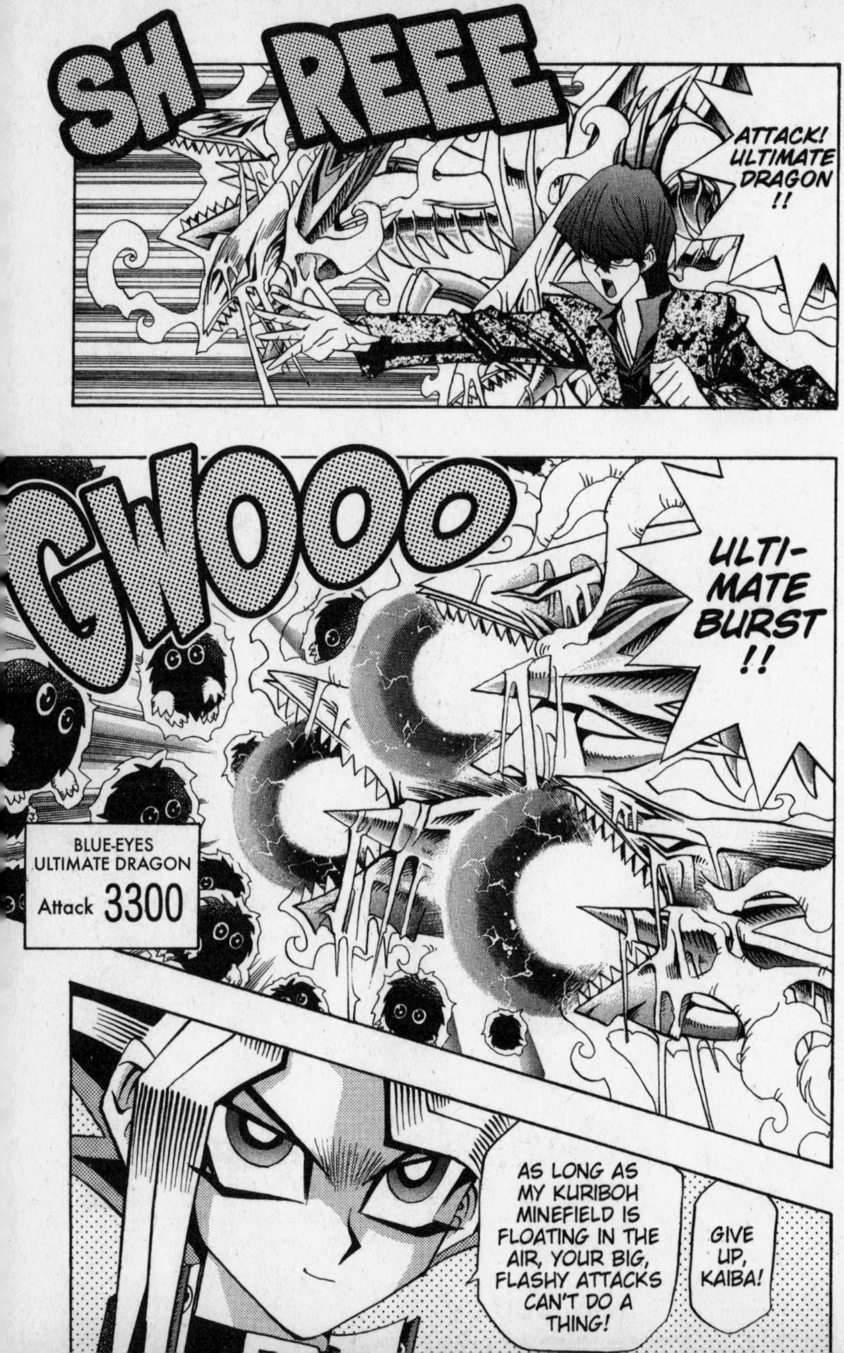
ATTACK! ULTIMATE DRAGON !!
SH REEE
ULTI-MATE BURST !!
GWOOO
BLUE-EYES ULTIMATE DRAGON
Attack 3300
GIVE UP, KAIBA!
AS LONG AS MY KURIBOH MINEFIELD IS FLOATING IN THE AIR, YOUR BIG, FLASHY ATTACKS CAN'T DO A THING!

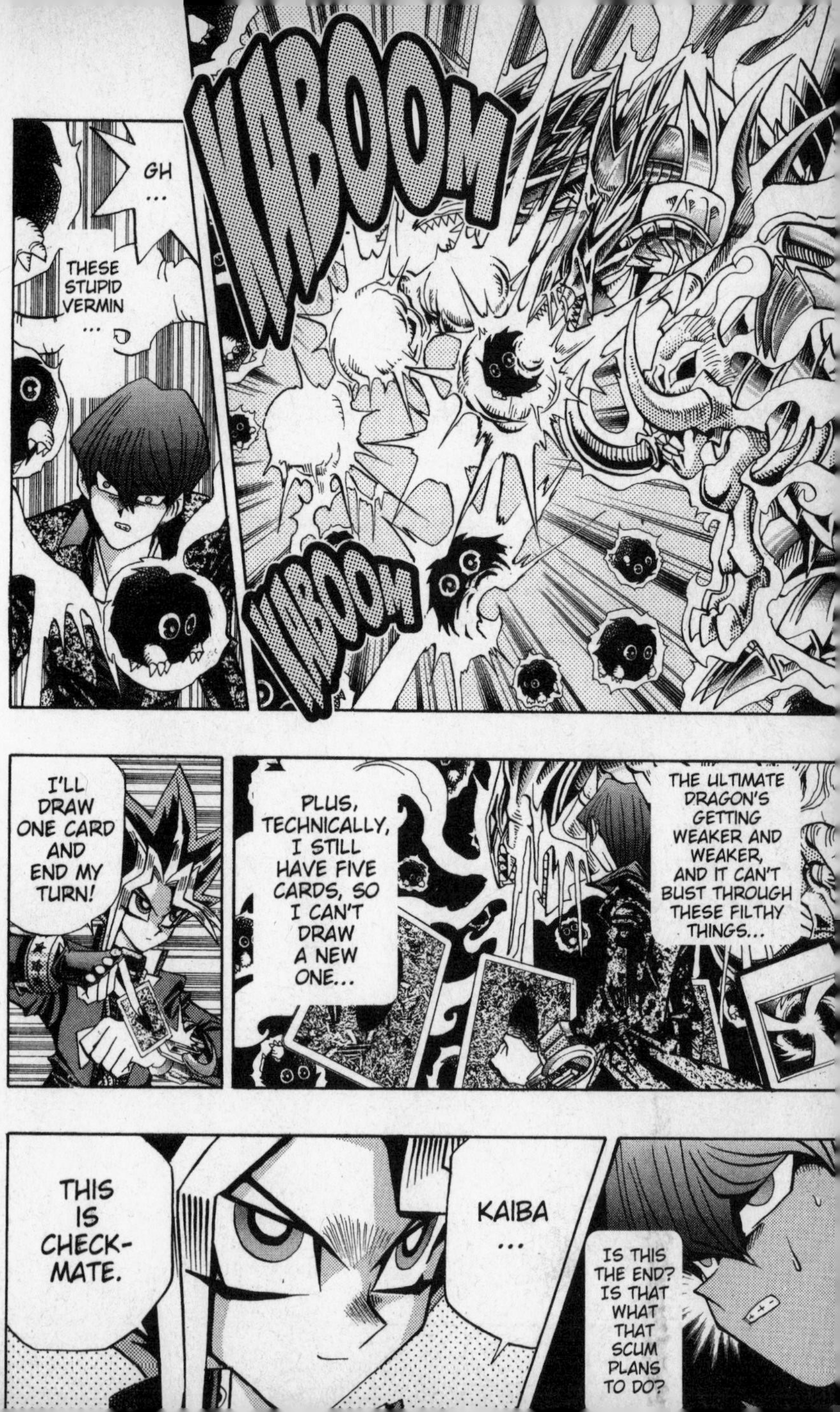
KABOOM
KABOOM
GH...
THESE STUPID VERMIN...
THE ULTIMATE DRAGON'S GETTING WEAKER AND WEAKER, AND IT CAN'T BUST THROUGH THESE FILTHY THINGS...
PLUS, TECHNICALLY, I STILL HAVE FIVE CARDS, SO I CAN'T DRAW A NEW ONE...
I'LL DRAW ONE CARD AND END MY TURN!
IS THIS THE END? IS THAT WHAT THAT SCUM PLANS TO DO?
KAIBA...
THIS IS CHECKMATE.

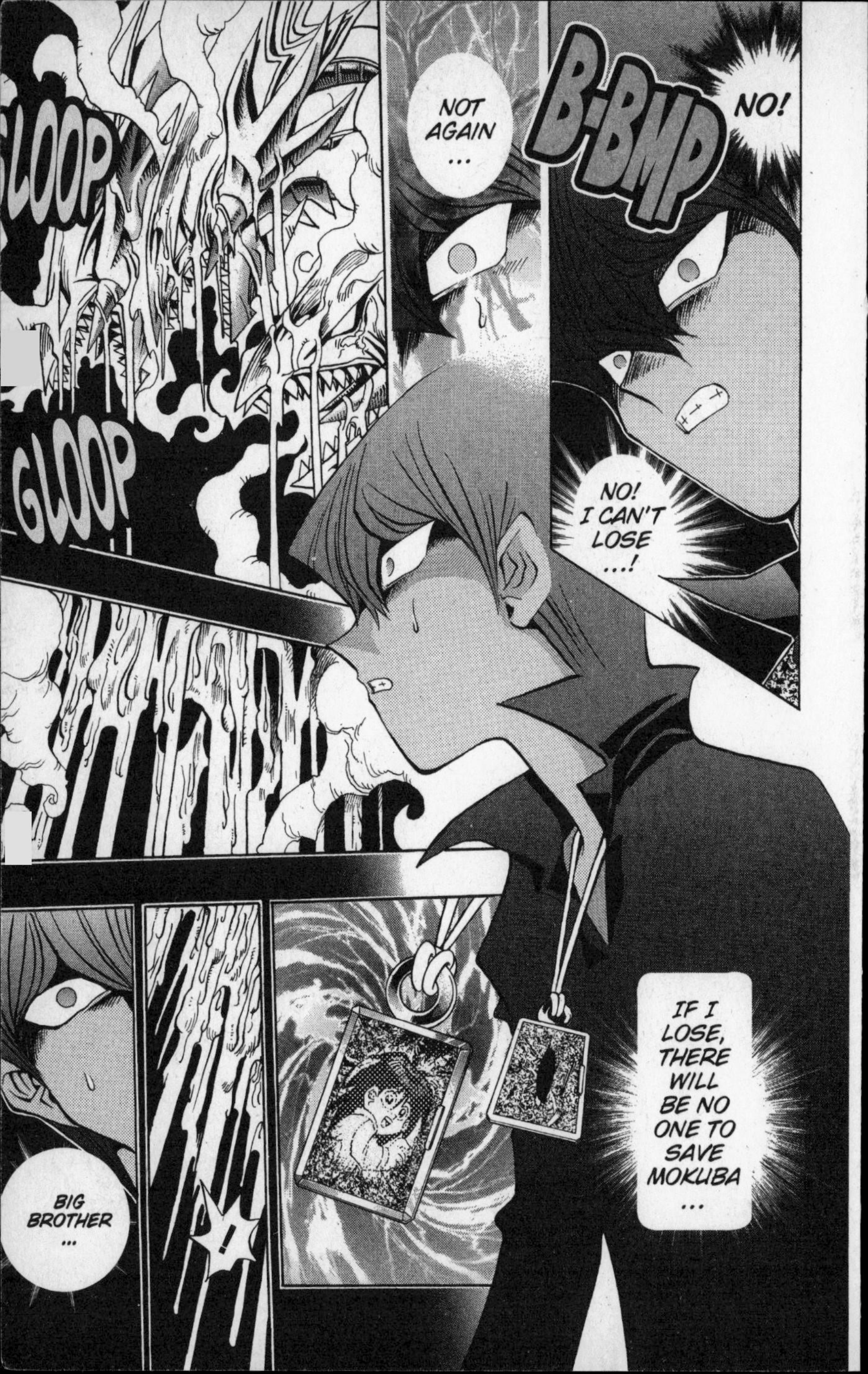
B-BMP
NO!
NOT AGAIN ...
NO! I CAN'T LOSE ...!
SLOOP
GLOOP
IF I LOSE, THERE WILL BE NO ONE TO SAVE MOKUBA ...
!
BIG BROTHER ...

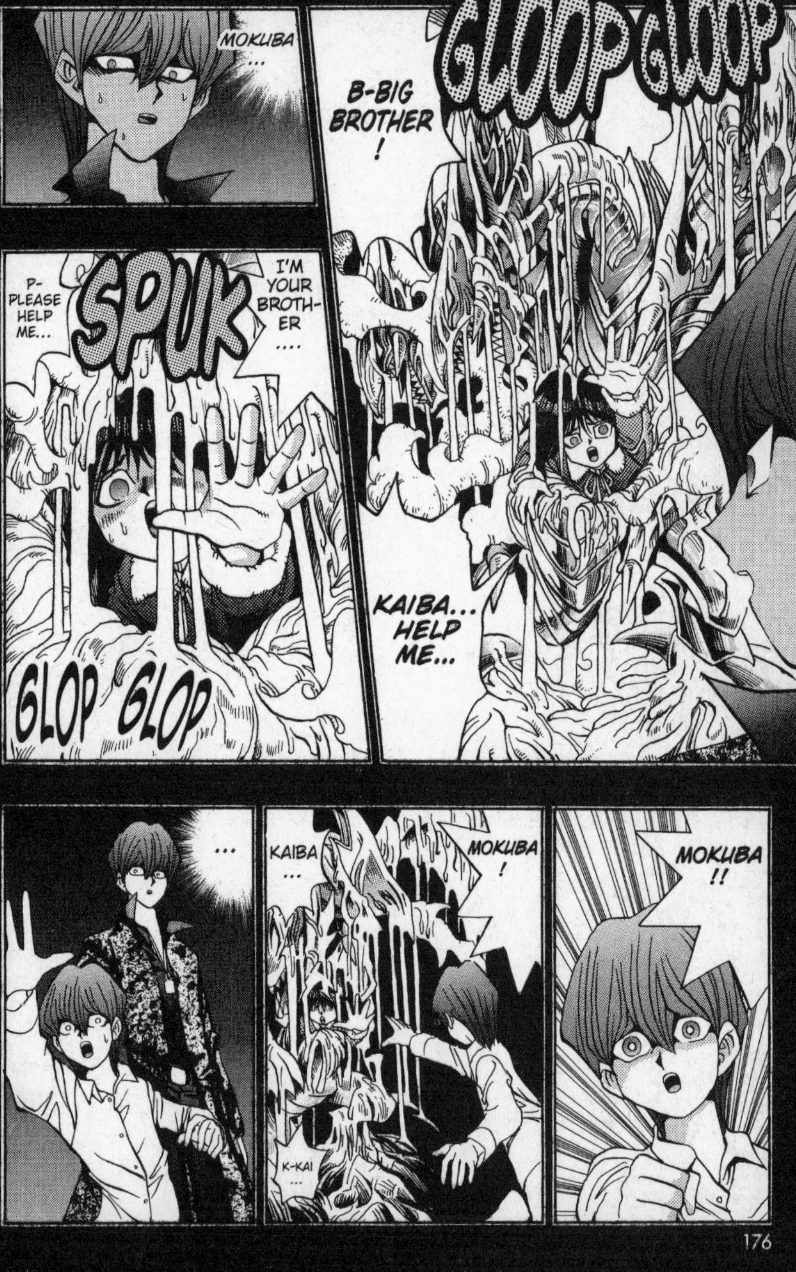
GLOOP GLOOP
B-BIG BROTHER !
KAIBA... HELP ME...
MOKUBA ...
I'M YOUR BROTH-ER ....
SPUK
P-PLEASE HELP ME...
GLOP GLOP
MOKUBA !!
MOKUBA !
KAIBA ...
K-KAI ...
...

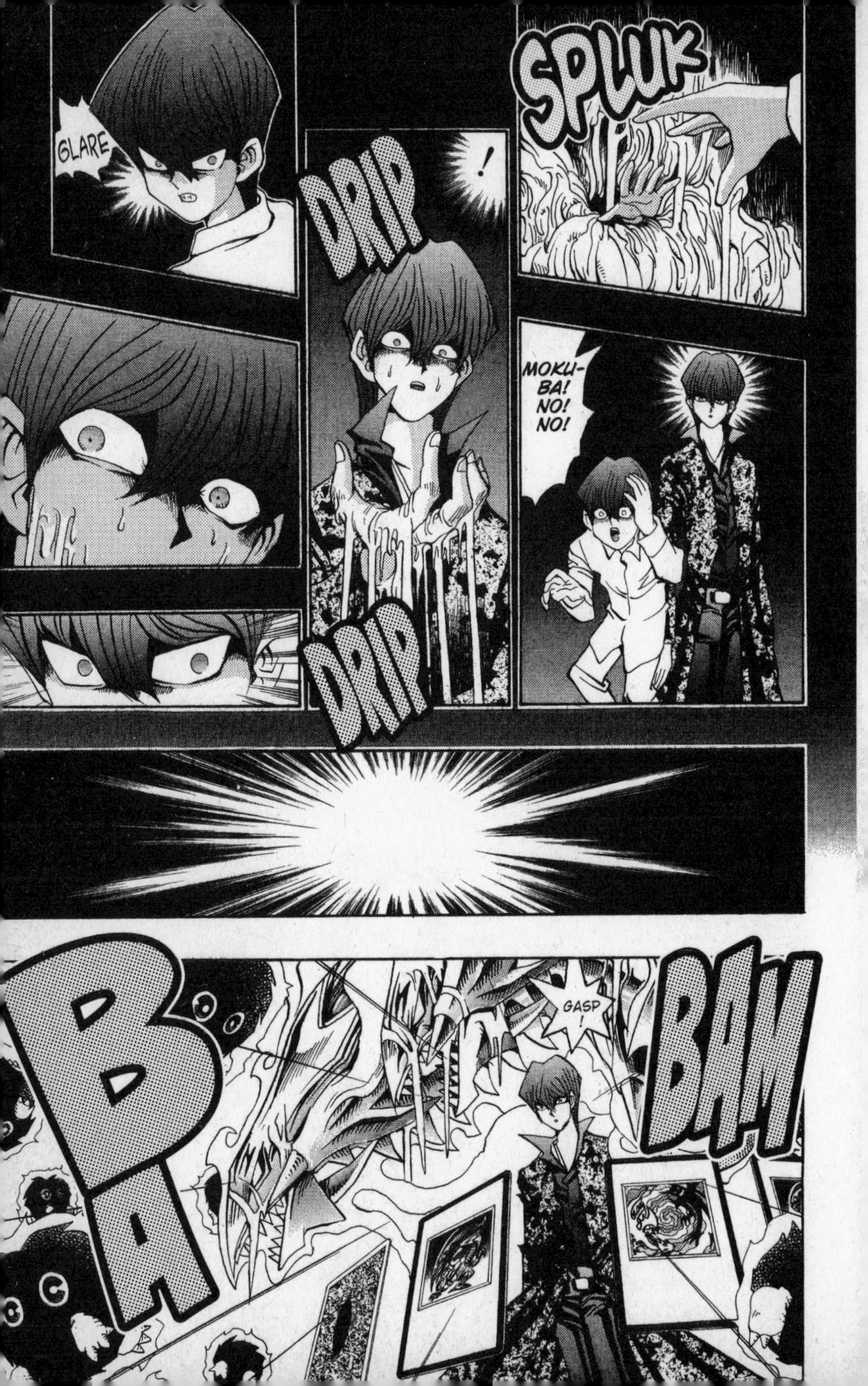
SPLUK
MOKU-BA! NO! NO!
!
DRIP
DRIP
GLARE
BAM
GASP!
BA

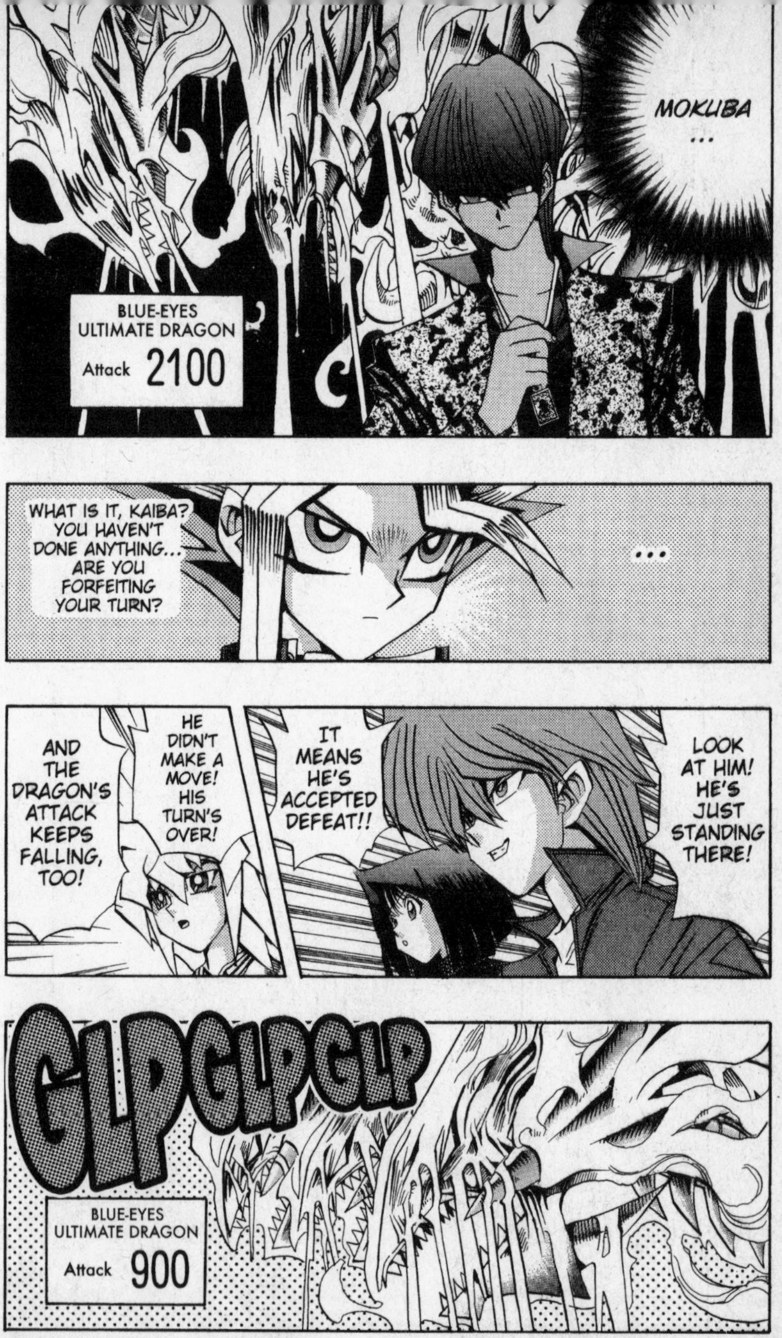
MOKUBA ...
BLUE-EYES ULTIMATE DRAGON Attack 2100
...
WHAT IS IT, KAIBA? YOU HAVEN'T DONE ANYTHING... ARE YOU FORFEITING YOUR TURN?
LOOK AT HIM! HE'S JUST STANDING THERE!
IT MEANS HE'S ACCEPTED DEFEAT!!
HE DIDN'T MAKE A MOVE! HIS TURN'S OVER!
AND THE DRAGON'S ATTACK KEEPS FALLING, TOO!
GLPGLPGLP
BLUE-EYES ULTIMATE DRAGON Attack 900

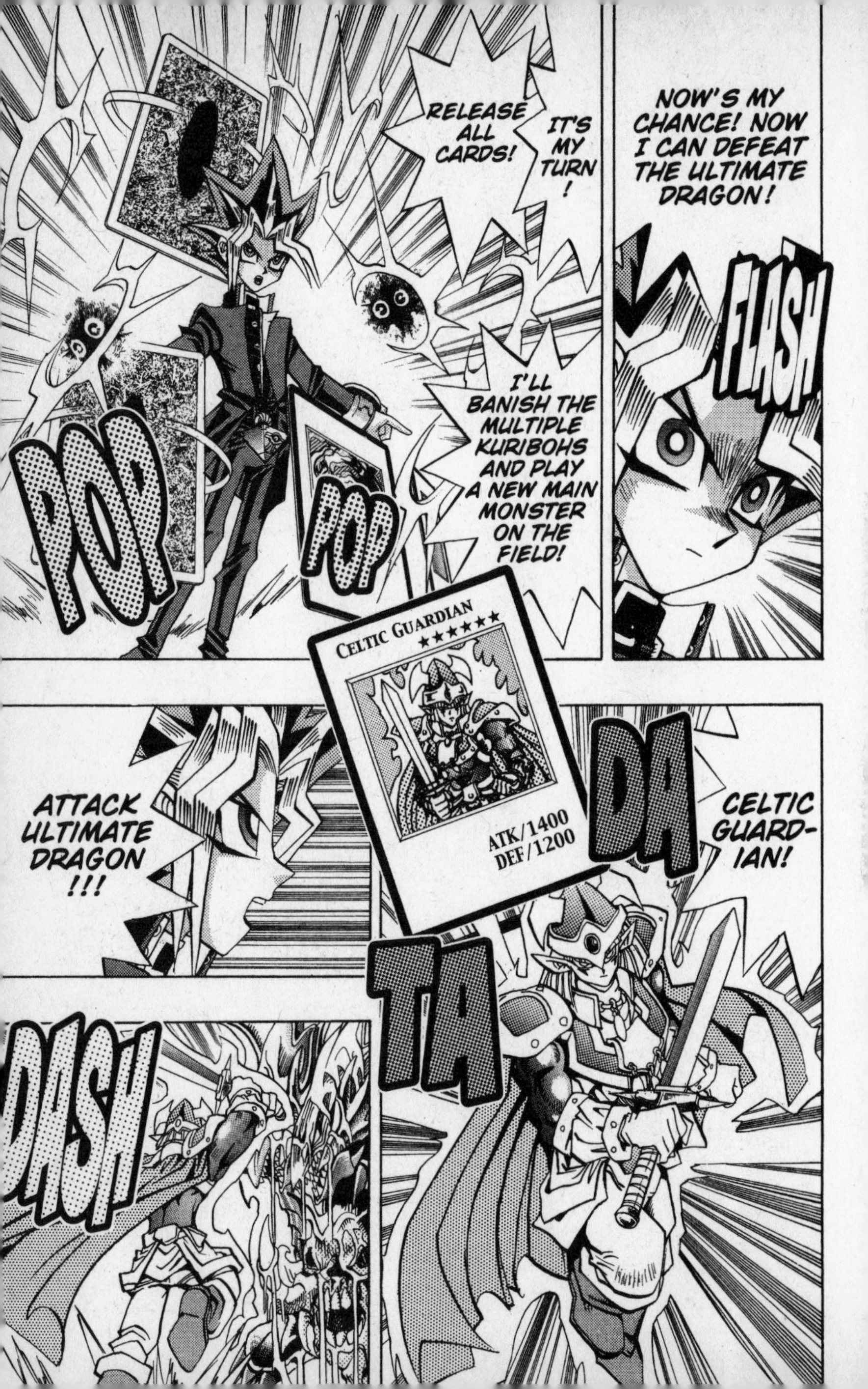
NOW'S MY CHANCE! NOW I CAN DEFEAT THE ULTIMATE DRAGON!
FLASH
IT'S MY TURN!
RELEASE ALL CARDS!
I'LL BANISH THE MULTIPLE KURIBOHS AND PLAY A NEW MAIN MONSTER ON THE FIELD!
POP
POP
CELTIC GUARDIAN!
DA
TA
CELTIC GUARDIAN
ATK/1400
DEF/1200
ATTACK ULTIMATE DRAGON!!!
DASH

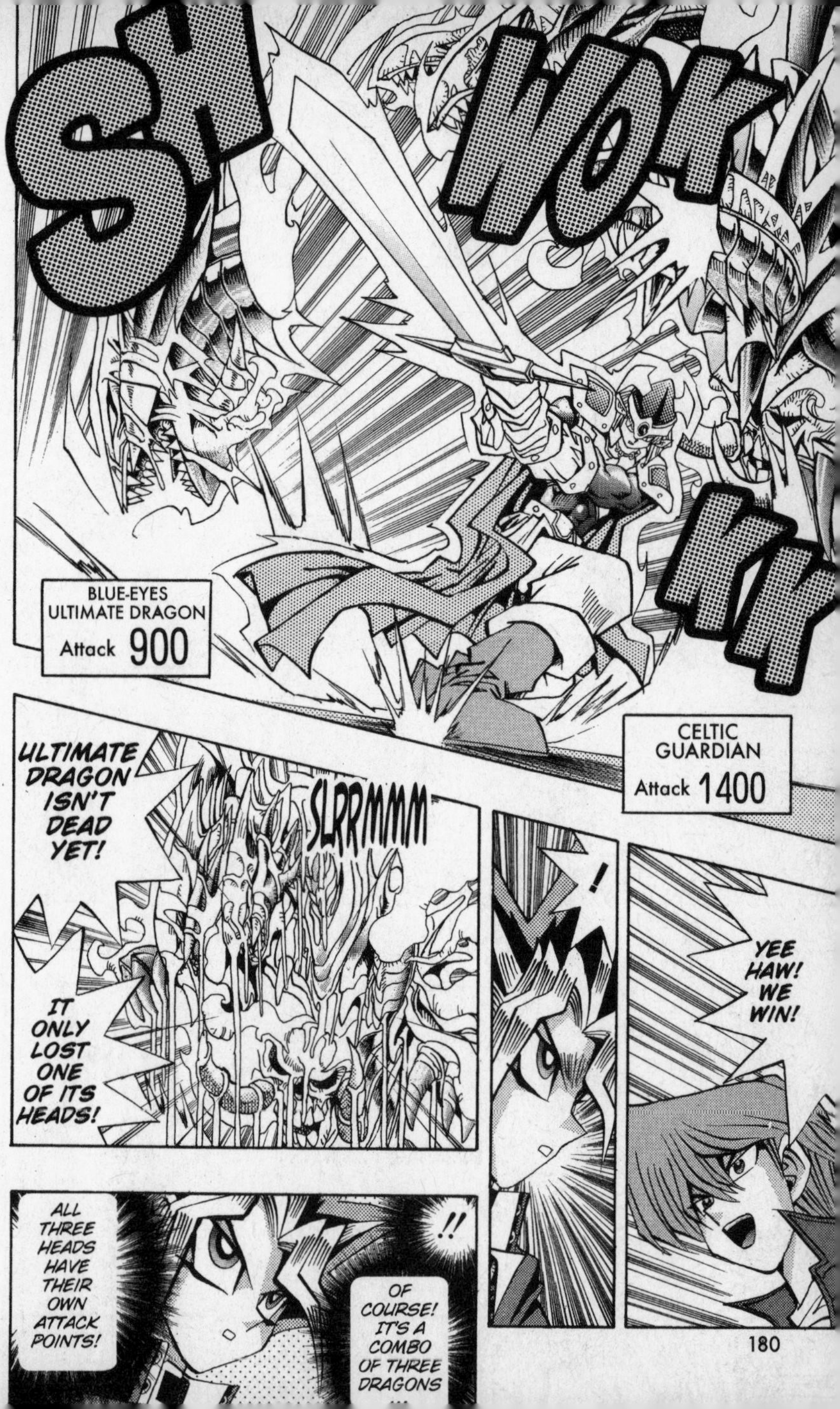
SHWOK
BLUE-EYES ULTIMATE DRAGON Attack 900
CELTIC GUARDIAN Attack 1400
YEE HAW! WE WIN!
!
ULTIMATE DRAGON ISN'T DEAD YET!
SLRRMMM
IT ONLY LOST ONE OF ITS HEADS!
!!
OF COURSE! IT'S A COMBO OF THREE DRAGONS
ALL THREE HEADS HAVE THEIR OWN ATTACK POINTS!

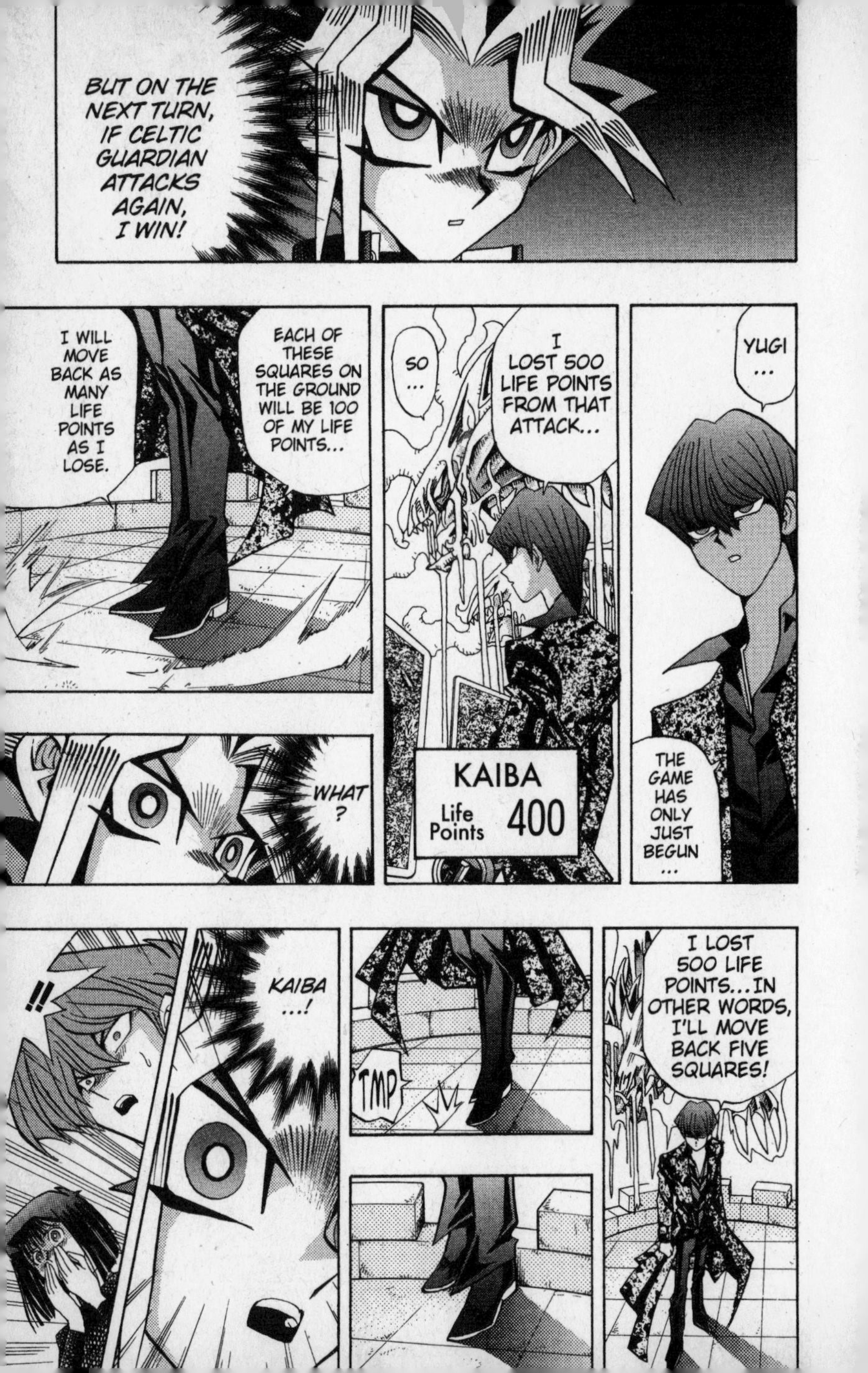

BUT ON THE NEXT TURN, IF CELTIC GUARDIAN ATTACKS AGAIN, I WIN!
YUGI ...
THE GAME HAS ONLY JUST BEGUN ...
I LOST 500 LIFE POINTS FROM THAT ATTACK...
SO ...
KAIBA Life Points 400
EACH OF THESE SQUARES ON THE GROUND WILL BE 100 OF MY LIFE POINTS...
I WILL MOVE BACK AS MANY LIFE POINTS AS I LOSE.
WHAT ?
I LOST 500 LIFE POINTS...IN OTHER WORDS, I'LL MOVE BACK FIVE SQUARES!
TMP
KAIBA ...!
!!

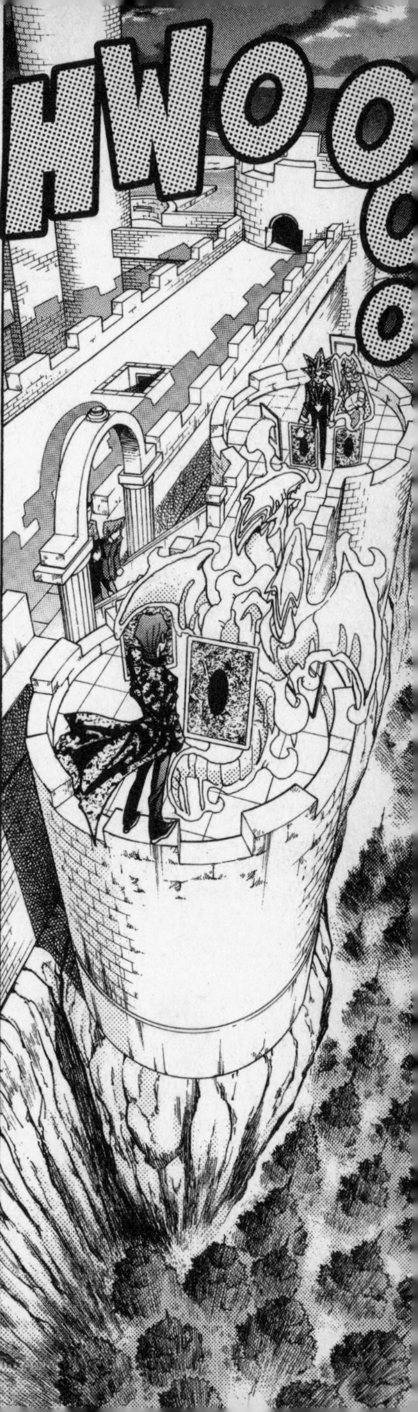
HWOOOO

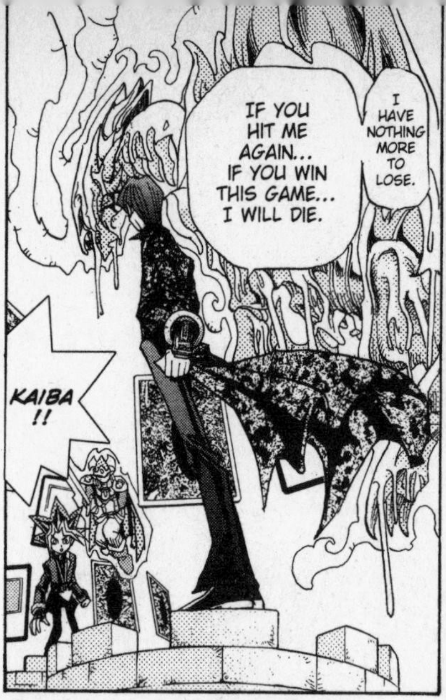
I HAVE NOTHING MORE TO LOSE.
IF YOU HIT ME AGAIN... IF YOU WIN THIS GAME... I WILL DIE.
KAIBA!!

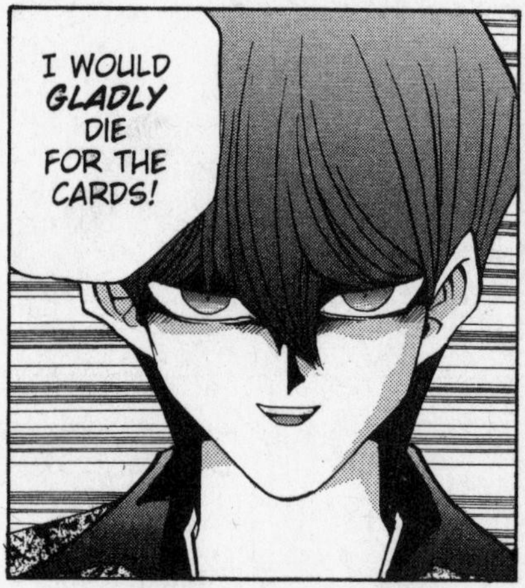
I WOULD **GLADLY** DIE FOR THE CARDS!

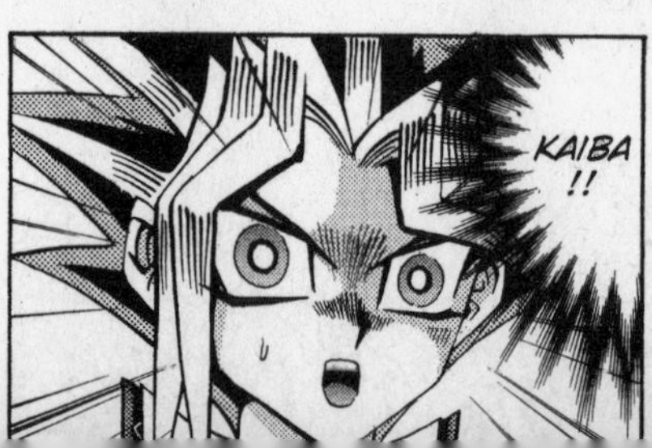
KAIBA!!

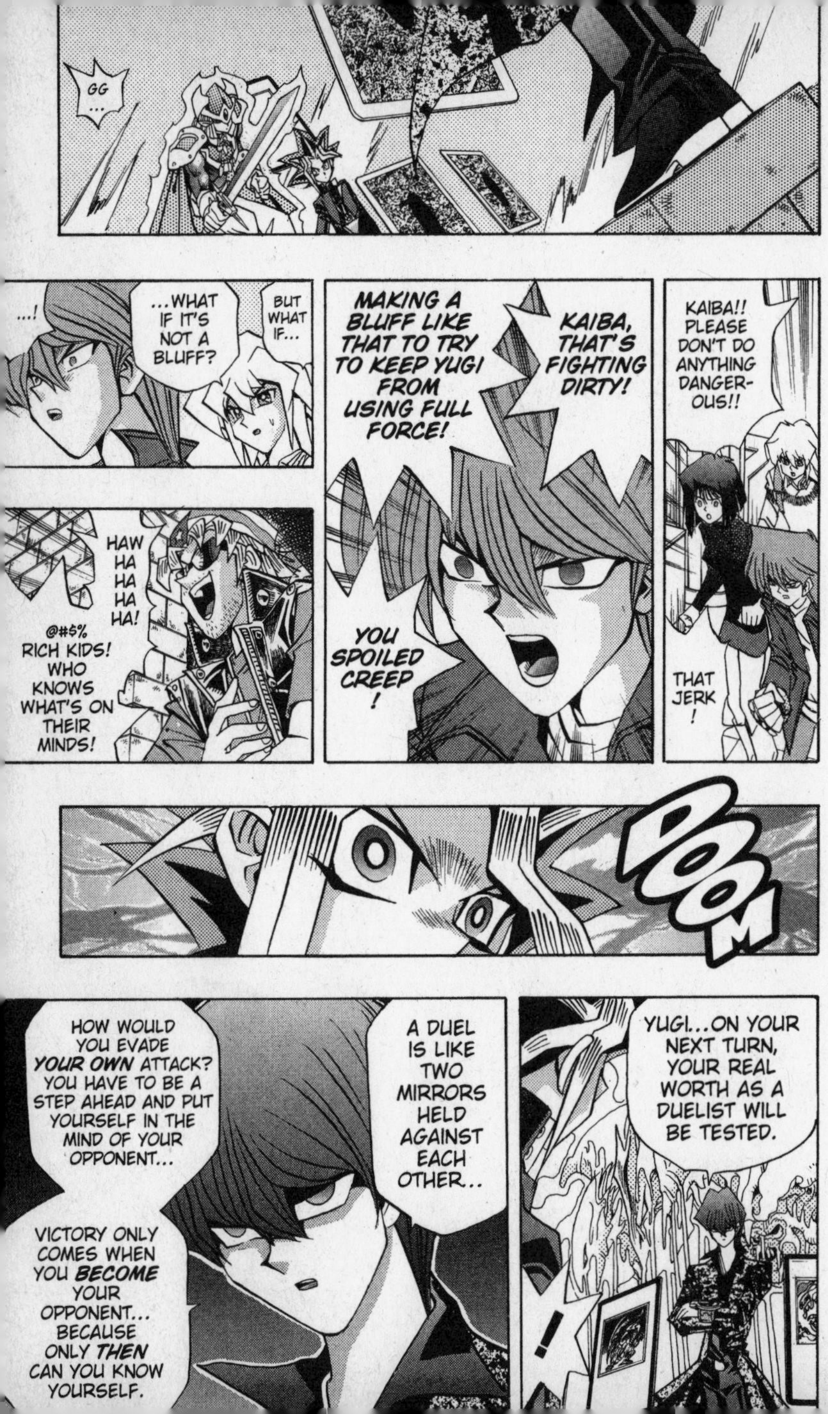
GG ...
KAIBA!! PLEASE DON'T DO ANYTHING DANGER-OUS!!
THAT JERK!
KAIBA, THAT'S FIGHTING DIRTY!
MAKING A BLUFF LIKE THAT TO TRY TO KEEP YUGI FROM USING FULL FORCE!
YOU SPOILED CREEP!
BUT WHAT IF...
...WHAT IF IT'S NOT A BLUFF?
...!
HAW HA HA HA HA!
@#$% RICH KIDS! WHO KNOWS WHAT'S ON THEIR MINDS!
DOOOM
YUGI...ON YOUR NEXT TURN, YOUR REAL WORTH AS A DUELIST WILL BE TESTED.
!
A DUEL IS LIKE TWO MIRRORS HELD AGAINST EACH OTHER...
HOW WOULD YOU EVADE YOUR OWN ATTACK? YOU HAVE TO BE A STEP AHEAD AND PUT YOURSELF IN THE MIND OF YOUR OPPONENT...
VICTORY ONLY COMES WHEN YOU BECOME YOUR OPPONENT... BECAUSE ONLY THEN CAN YOU KNOW YOURSELF.

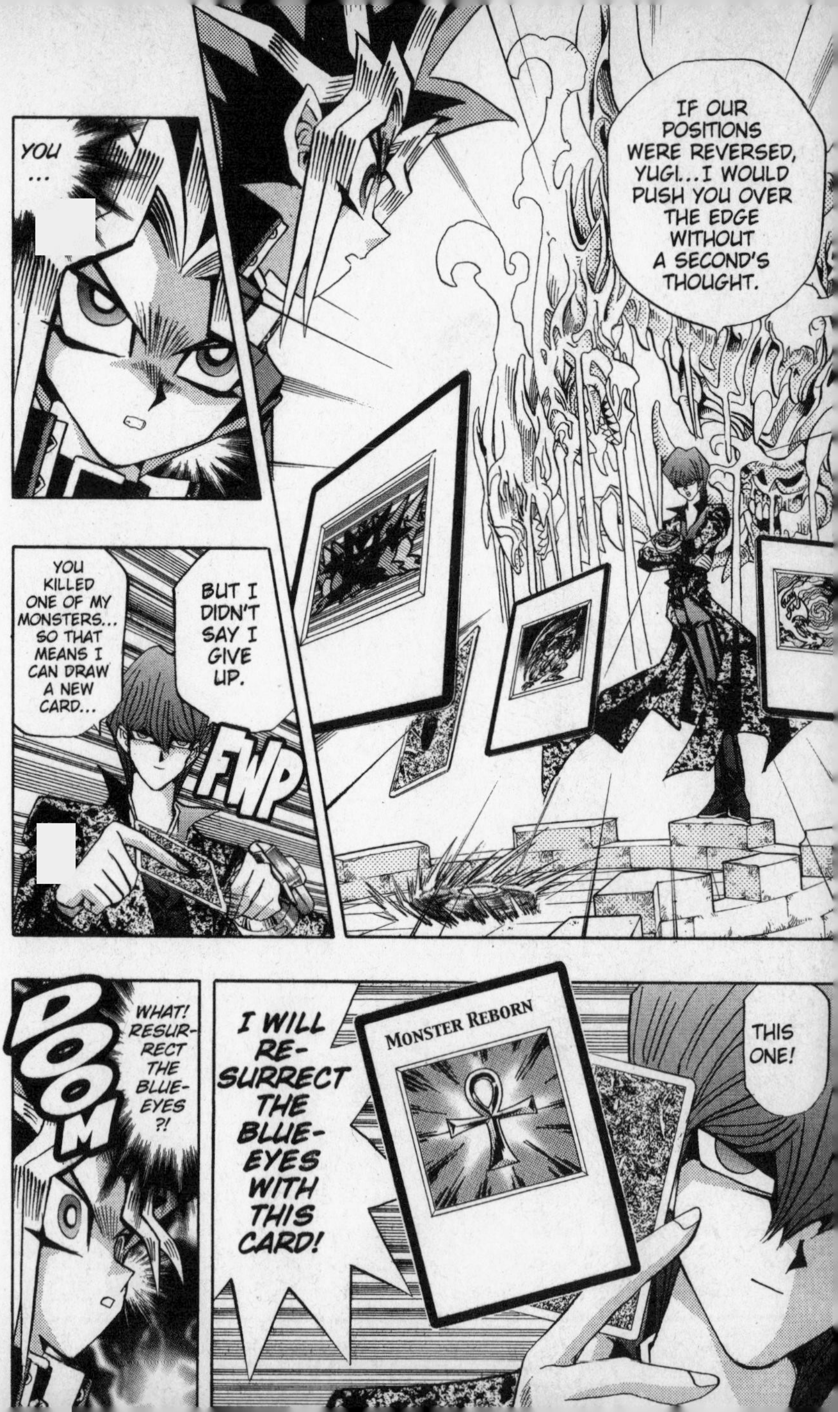
IF OUR POSITIONS WERE REVERSED, YUGI...I WOULD PUSH YOU OVER THE EDGE WITHOUT A SECOND'S THOUGHT.
YOU ...
BUT I DIDN'T SAY I GIVE UP.
YOU KILLED ONE OF MY MONSTERS... SO THAT MEANS I CAN DRAW A NEW CARD...
FWP
THIS ONE!
MONSTER REBORN
I WILL RE-SURRECT THE BLUE-EYES WITH THIS CARD!
WHAT! RESUR-RECT THE BLUE-EYES ?!
DOOOM

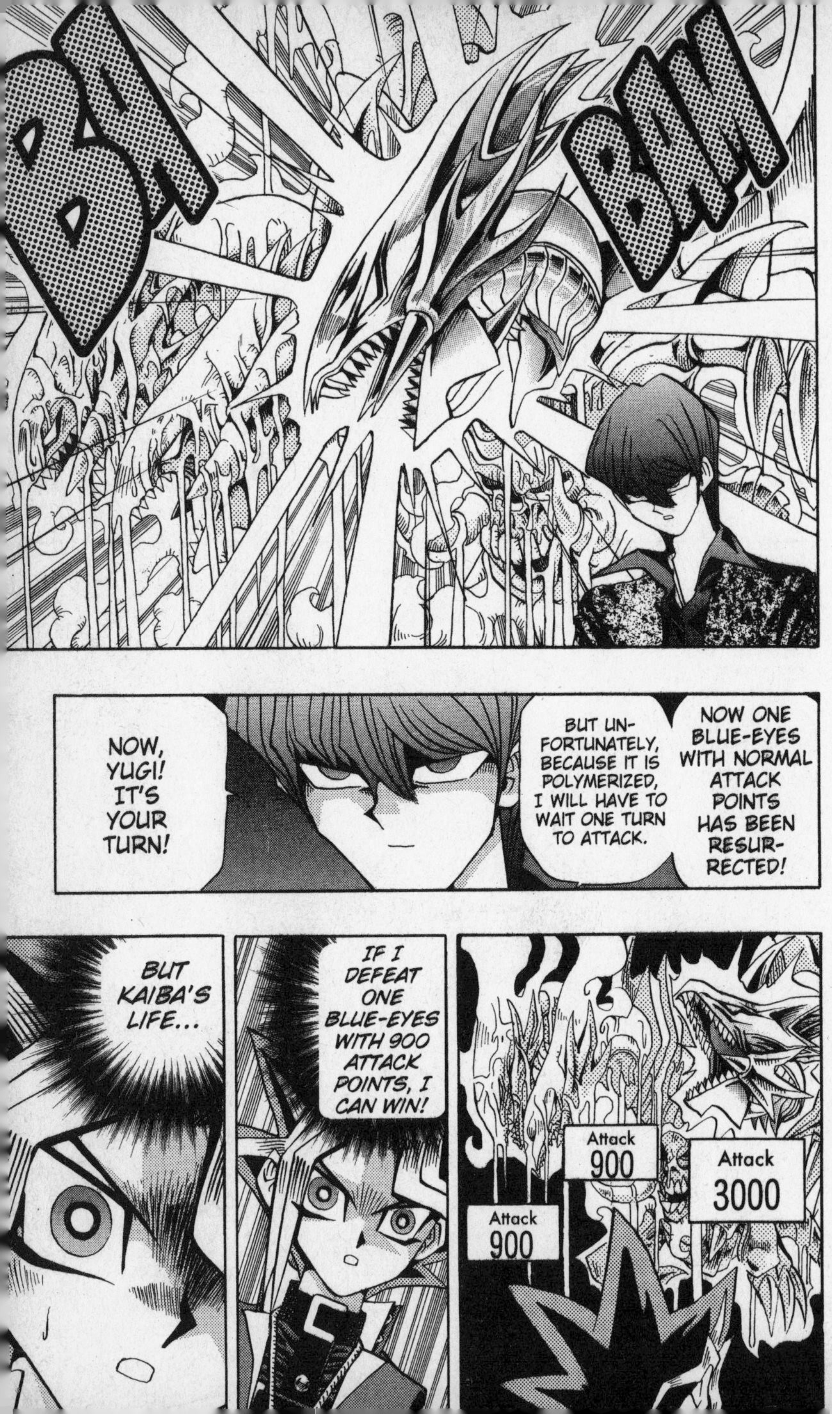

BA
BAM!
NOW ONE BLUE-EYES WITH NORMAL ATTACK POINTS HAS BEEN RESURRECTED!
BUT UNFORTUNATELY, BECAUSE IT IS POLYMERIZED, I WILL HAVE TO WAIT ONE TURN TO ATTACK.
NOW, YUGI! IT'S YOUR TURN!
Attack 3000
Attack 900
Attack 900
IF I DEFEAT ONE BLUE-EYES WITH 900 ATTACK POINTS, I CAN WIN!
BUT KAIBA'S LIFE...

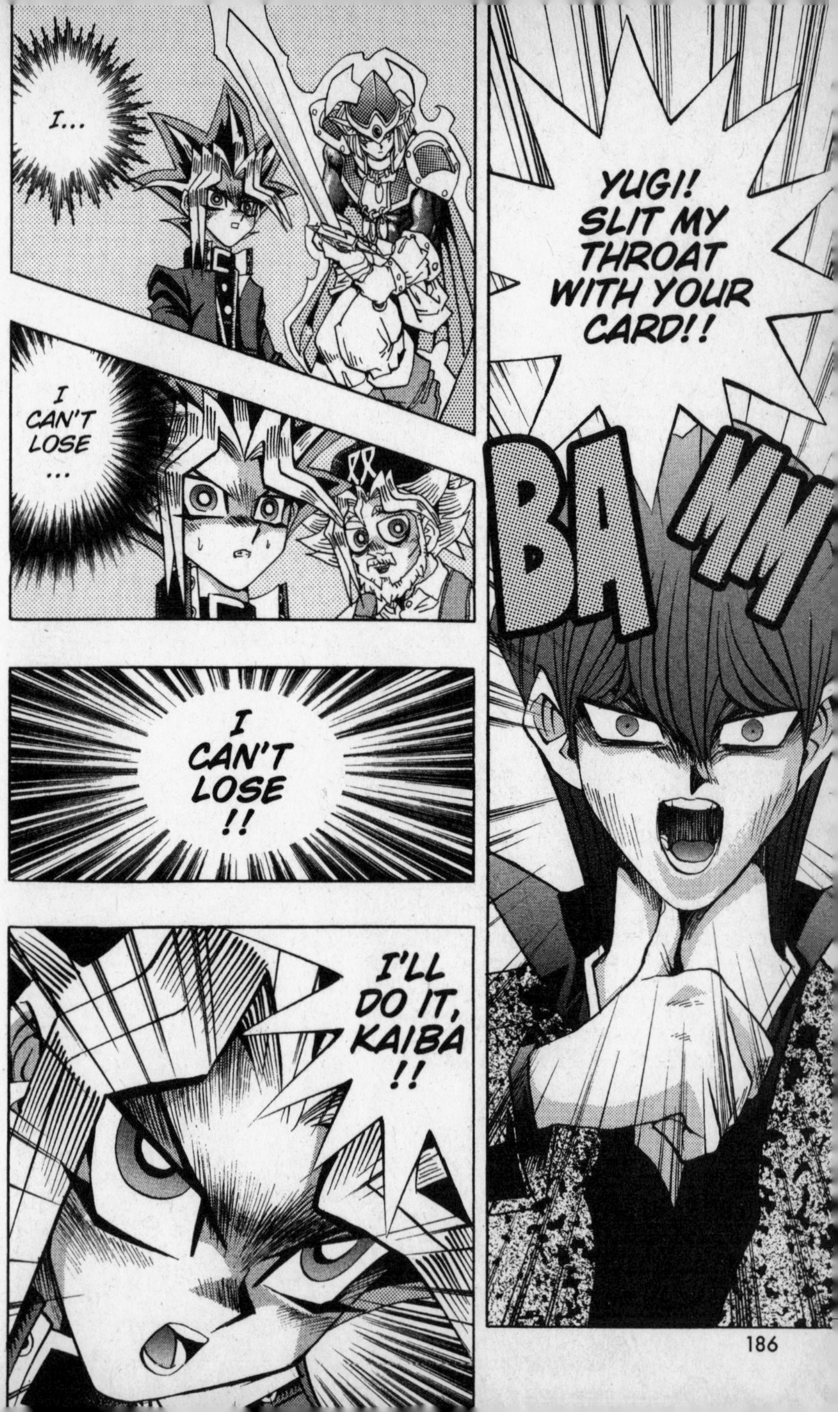
YUGI! SLIT MY THROAT WITH YOUR CARD!!
BAMM
I...
I CAN'T LOSE ...
I CAN'T LOSE !!
I'LL DO IT, KAIBA !!

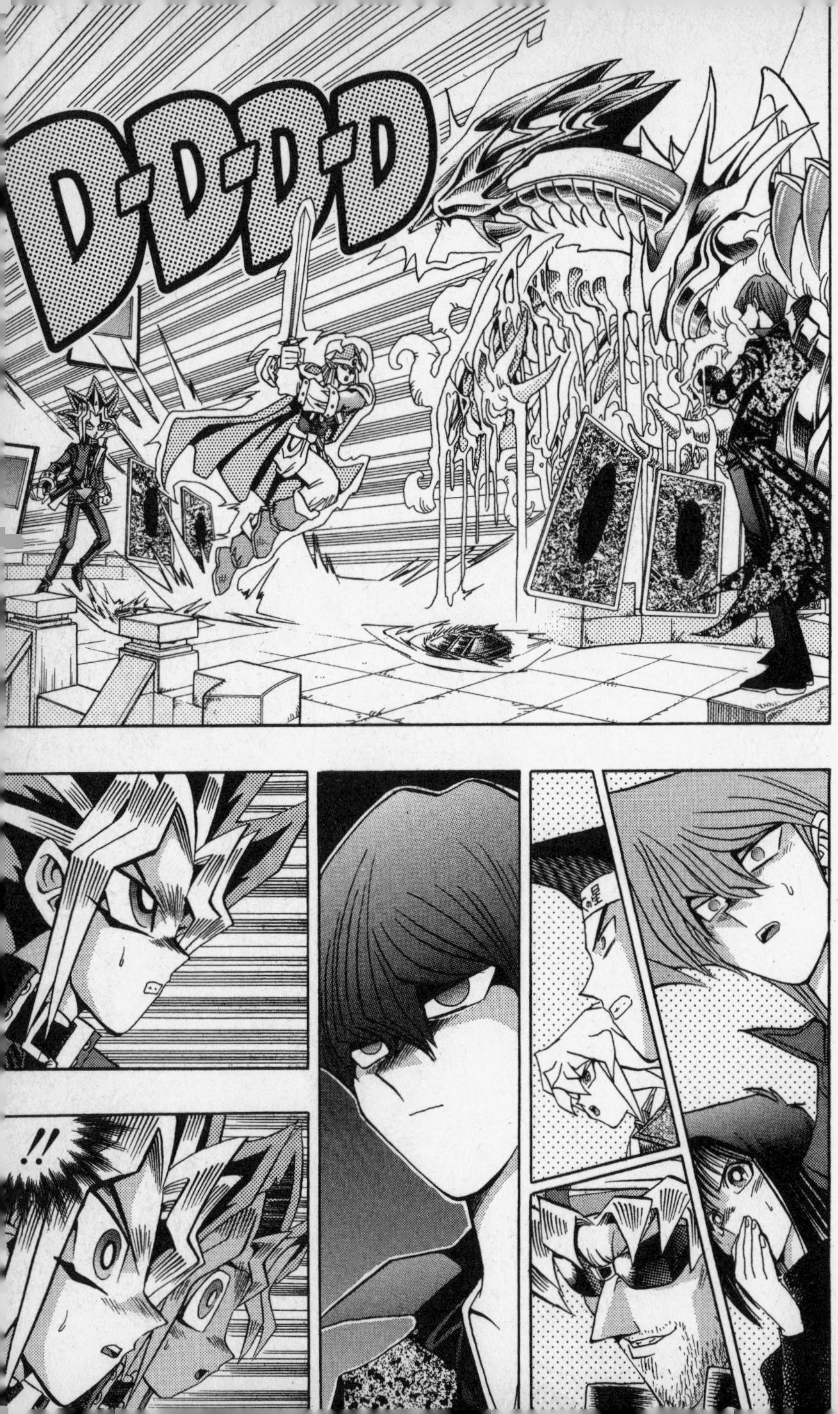
D-D-D-D
!!

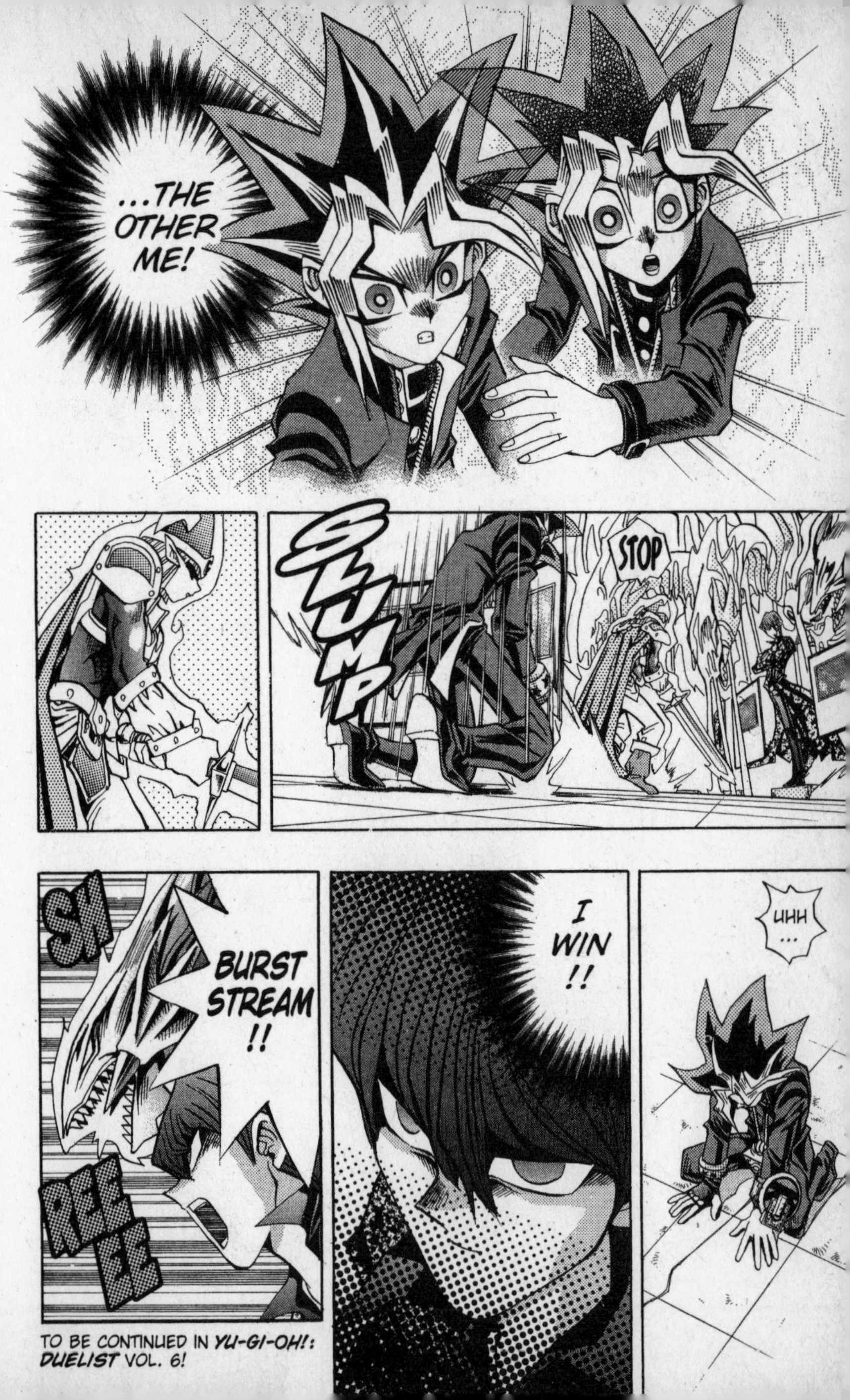
...THE OTHER ME!
STOP
SLUMP
UHH ...
I WIN !!
BURST STREAM !!
SHREEEE

TO BE CONTINUED IN ***YU-GI-OH!: DUELIST*** VOL. 6!

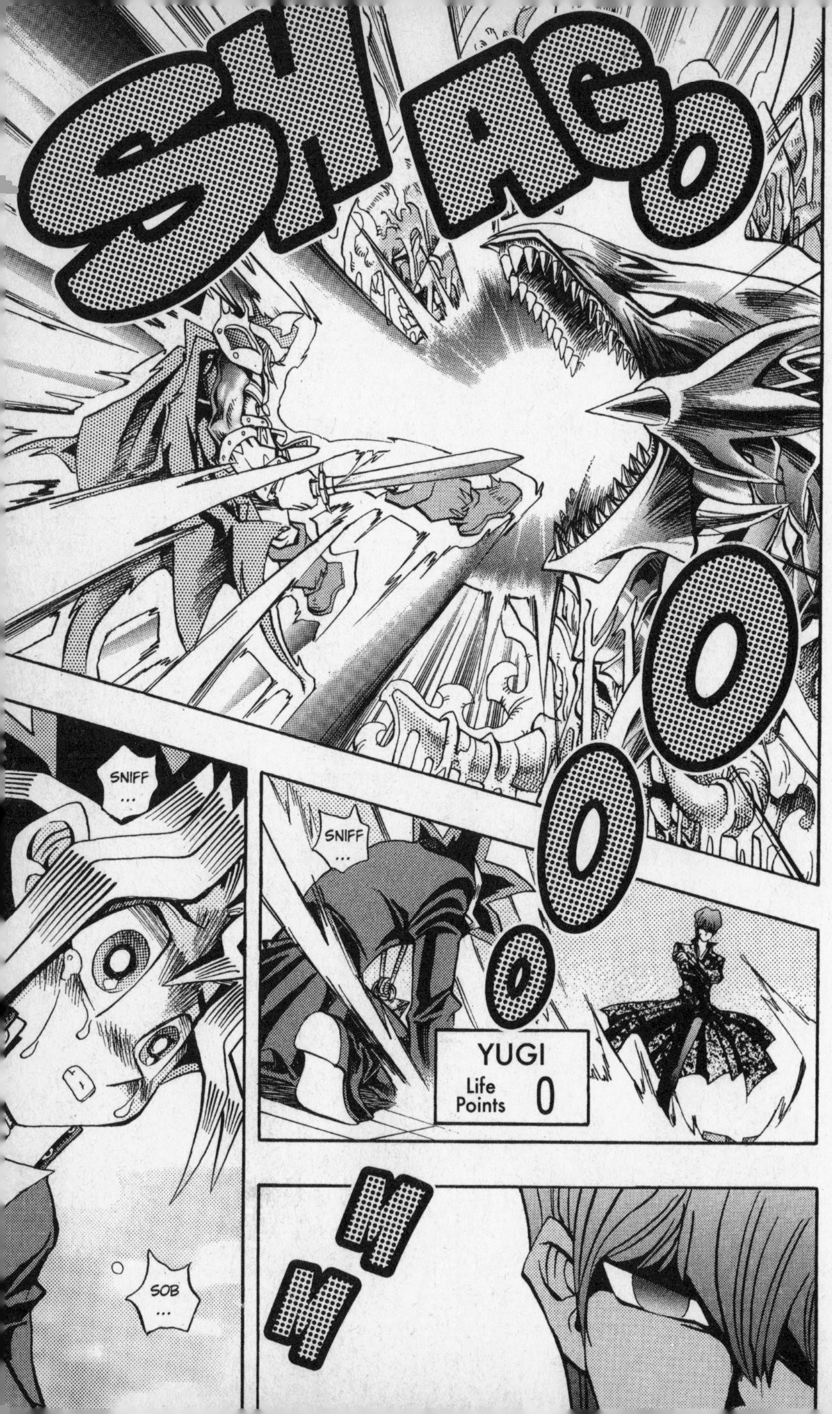
SHAGOOOO
SNIFF ...
YUGI
Life Points 0
SNIFF ...
SOB ...

MASTER OF THE CARDS

The "Duel Monsters" card game first appeared in volume two of the original **Yu-Gi-Oh!** graphic novel series, but it's in **Yu-Gi-Oh!: Duelist** (originally printed in Japan as volumes 8-31 of **Yu-Gi-Oh!**) that it gets really important. As many fans know, some of the card names are different between the English and Japanese versions. In case you play the game, or you're interested in playing, here's a rundown of the cards in this graphic novel. Some cards only appear in the **Yu-Gi-Oh!** video games, not in the actual collectible card game.

FIRST APPEARANCE IN THIS VOLUME	JAPANESE CARD NAME	ENGLISH CARD NAME
p.8	*Yûgô* (Fusion)	Polymerization
p.8	*Red-Eyes Black Dragon*	Red-Eyes Black Dragon
p.8	*Demon no Shôkan* (Demon Summoning)	Summoned Skull
p.8	*Black Demons Dragon*	Black Skull Dragon
p.12	*Force*	Ryoku (NOTE: "Ryoku" is Japanese for "strength")

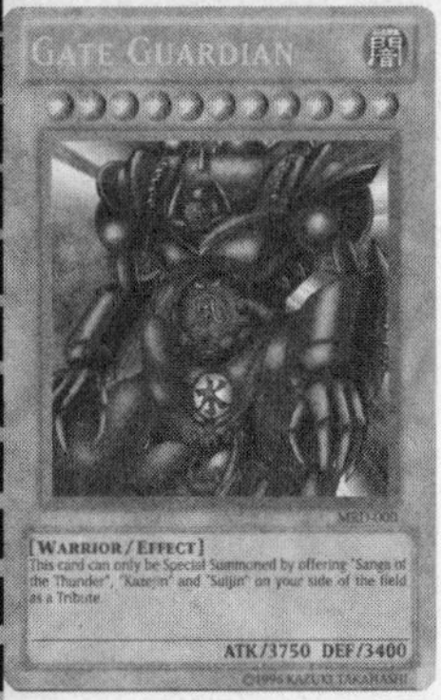
Gate Guardian
[Warrior / Effect]
This card can only be Special Summoned by offering "Sanga of the Thunder", "Kazejin" and "Suijin" on your side of the field as a Tribute.
ATK/3750 DEF/3400

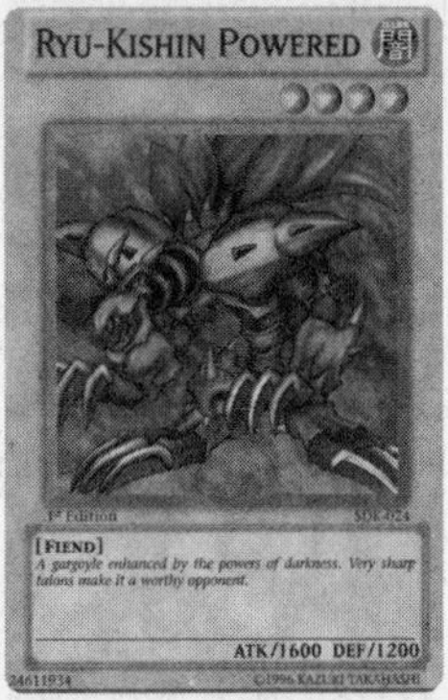
Ryu-Kishin Powered
1st Edition
SDK-024
[Fiend]
A gargoyle enhanced by the powers of darkness. Very sharp talons make it a worthy opponent.
ATK/1600 DEF/1200
24611934
©1996 KAZUKI TAKAHASHI

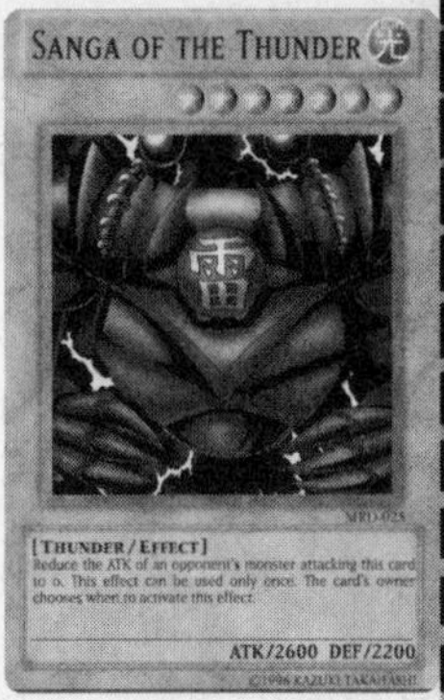
Sanga of the Thunder
[Thunder / Effect]
Reduce the ATK of an opponent's monster attacking this card to 0. This effect can be used only once. The card's owner chooses when to activate this effect.
ATK/2600 DEF/2200
©1996 KAZUKI TAKAHASHI

FIRST APPEARANCE IN THIS VOLUME	JAPANESE CARD NAME	ENGLISH CARD NAME
p.13	*Fûmashin Hyûga* (Wind Demon God Hyûga)	Kazejin (NOTE: "Kaze" is Japanese for "wind.")
p.13	*Raimashin Sanga* (Thunder Demon God Sanga)	Sanga of the Thunder
p.17	*Shisha Sosei* (Resurrection of the Dead)	Monster Reborn
p.18	*Suimashin Sûga* (Water Demon God Sûga)	Suijin (NOTE: "Sui" is Japanese for "Water.")
p.20	*Monomane Gensôshi* (Mimic Illusionist)	Copycat
p.22	*Shift Change*	Shift
p.79	*Gargoyle Powered*	Ryu-Kishin Powered (NOTE: "Ryu-Kishin" is Japanese for "Dragon Ogre/Fierce God.")
p.79	*Curse of Dragon*	Curse of Dragon

Kazejin
[Spellcaster/Effect]
Reduce the ATK of an opponent's monster attacking this card to 0. This effect can be used only once. The card's owner chooses when to activate this effect.
ATK/2400 DEF/2200

Suijin
[Aqua/Effect]
Reduce the ATK of an opponent's monster attacking this card to 0. This effect can be used only once. The card's owner chooses when to activate this effect.
ATK/2500 DEF/2400

Swordstalker
[Warrior]
A monster formed by the vengeful souls of those who passed away in battle.
ATK/2000 DEF/1600

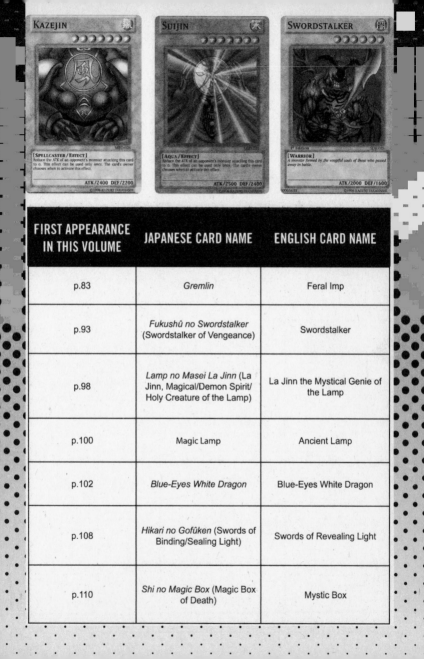

FIRST APPEARANCE IN THIS VOLUME	JAPANESE CARD NAME	ENGLISH CARD NAME
p.83	*Gremlin*	Feral Imp
p.93	*Fukushû no Swordstalker* (Swordstalker of Vengeance)	Swordstalker
p.98	*Lamp no Masei La Jinn* (La Jinn, Magical/Demon Spirit/ Holy Creature of the Lamp)	La Jinn the Mystical Genie of the Lamp
p.100	Magic Lamp	Ancient Lamp
p.102	*Blue-Eyes White Dragon*	Blue-Eyes White Dragon
p.108	*Hikari no Gofûken* (Swords of Binding/Sealing Light)	Swords of Revealing Light
p.110	*Shi no Magic Box* (Magic Box of Death)	Mystic Box

SAGGI THE DARK CLOWN 闇

[SPELLCASTER]
This clown appears from nowhere and executes very strange moves to avoid direct attacks.

ATK/ 600 DEF/1500

THE EYE OF TRUTH 罠

[TRAP CARD]

As long as this card remains face-up on the field, your opponent must show his/her hand. Your opponent increases his/her Life Points by 1000 points at each of his/her Standby Phases if he/she has a Spell Card in his/her hand.

GIANT SOLDIER OF STONE 地

[ROCK]
A giant warrior made of stone. A punch from this creature has earth-shaking results.

ATK/1300 DEF/2000

FIRST APPEARANCE IN THIS VOLUME	JAPANESE CARD NAME	ENGLISH CARD NAME
p.111	*Shinjitsu no Me* (Eye/Pupil of Truth)	The Eye of Truth
p.118	*Yami Dôkeshi no Saggi* (Saggi the Dark Clown)	Saggi the Dark Clown
p.118	*Shi no Deck Hakai* (Deck Destruction of Death) (NOTE: Symbol on card means "death")	Crush Card
p.120	*Ankoku Kishi Gaia* (Dark Knight Gaia)	Gaia the Fierce Knight
p.120	*Zôshoku* (Multiply)	Multiply
p.129	*Silver Fang*	Silver Fang

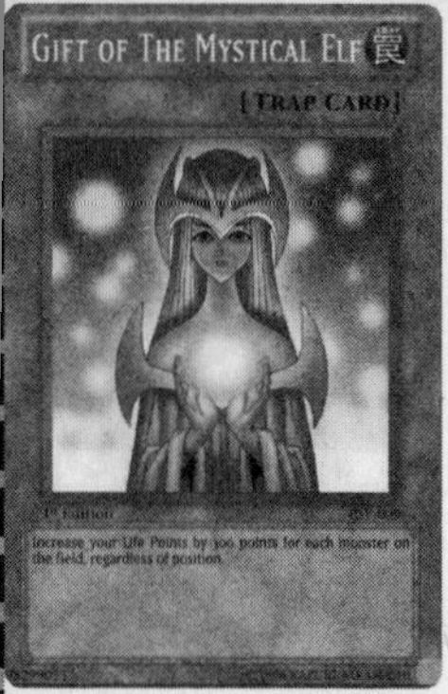
Gift of The Mystical Elf
[TRAP CARD]
Increase your Life Points by 300 points for each monster on the field, regardless of position.

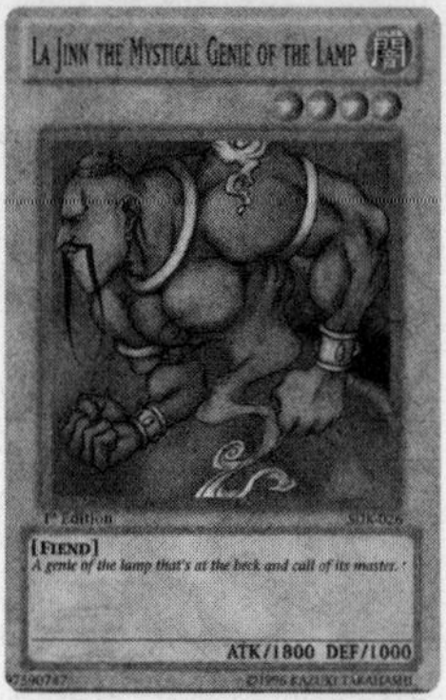
La Jinn the Mystical Genie of the Lamp
[FIEND]
A genie of the lamp that's at the beck and call of its master.
ATK/1800 DEF/1000

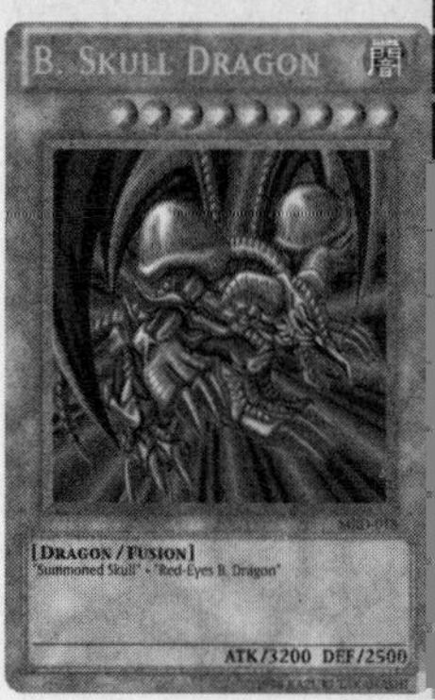
B. Skull Dragon
[DRAGON / FUSION]
"Summoned Skull" + "Red-Eyes B. Dragon"
ATK/3200 DEF/2500

FIRST APPEARANCE IN THIS VOLUME	JAPANESE CARD NAME	ENGLISH CARD NAME
p.130	*Holy Elf no Shukufuku* (Blessing of the Holy Elf)	Gift of the Mystical Elf
p.131	*Minotaurus*	Battle Ox
p.133	*Kôgeki no Muryokuka* (Nullificiation of Attack)	Negate Attack
p.133	*Ikkakujû no Horn* (Unicorn's Horn)	Horn of the Unicorn
p.133	*Monster Kaishû* (Monster Withdrawal)	Monster Recovery
p.134	*Guriforu*	Griffor (NOTE: Not a real game card. Called "Griffore" in the video games.)

MAMMOTH GRAVEYARD	KURIBOH	CELTIC GUARDIAN

[DINOSAUR]
A monument that protects the graves of its pack and is absolutely merciless when facing grave-robbers.
ATK/1200 DEF/800

[FIEND/EFFECT]
Discard this card from your hand to the Graveyard to make the damage inflicted to your Life Points by 1 opponent's monster 0. This effect must be activated during your opponent's Battle Phase.
ATK/300 DEF/200

[WARRIOR]
An elf who turned to wield a sword. Its battles are won with lightning-swift attacks.
ATK/1400 DEF/1200

FIRST APPEARANCE IN THIS VOLUME	JAPANESE CARD NAME	ENGLISH CARD NAME
p.134	*Mammoth no Hakaba* (Mammoth's Graveyard)	Mammoth Graveyard
p.142	*Ganseki no Kyohei* (Giant Soldier of Stone)	Giant Soldier of Stone
p.146	*Blue-Eyes Ultimate Dragon*	Blue-Eyes Ultimate Dragon
p.156	*Mahô Kôka no Ya* (Arrow of Magic Effects)	Living Arrow (NOTE: Not a real game card.)
p.160	*Kuribo*	Kuriboh
p.179	*Elf no Kenshi* (Elf Swordsman)	Celtic Guardian

IN THE NEXT VOLUME...

The impossible has happened—Yugi has LOST! Is this the end for our heroes? Meanwhile, Kaiba advances to the final round against Pegasus, fighting to rescue his brother. But are Kaiba's dragons stronger than Pegasus's rubbery, slapstick, fearsome toons? And what about Bandit Keith? All this in the most shocking volume of Yu-Gi-Oh! yet!

COMING JULY 2005!

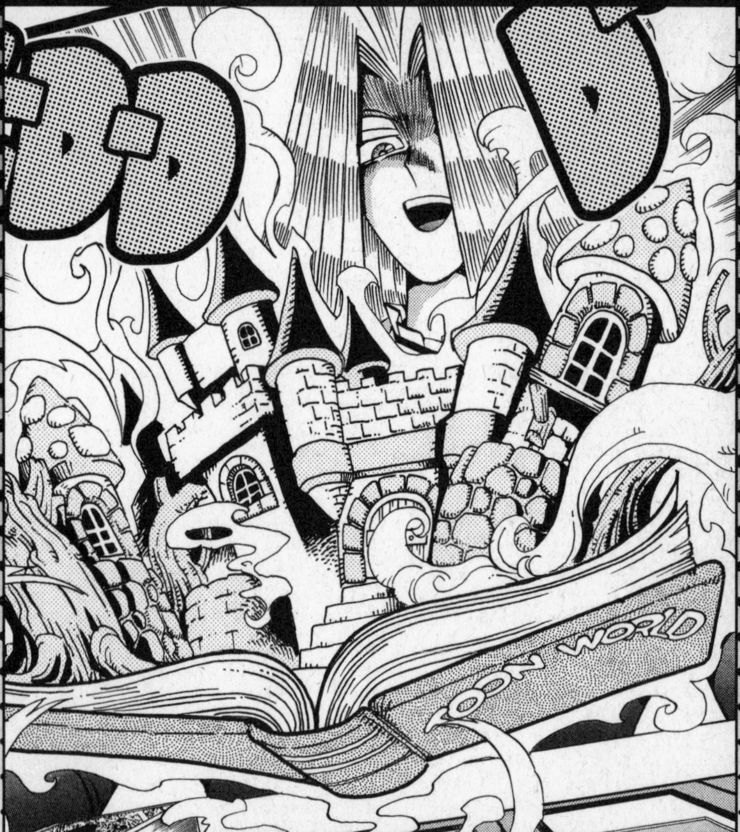
TOON WORLD

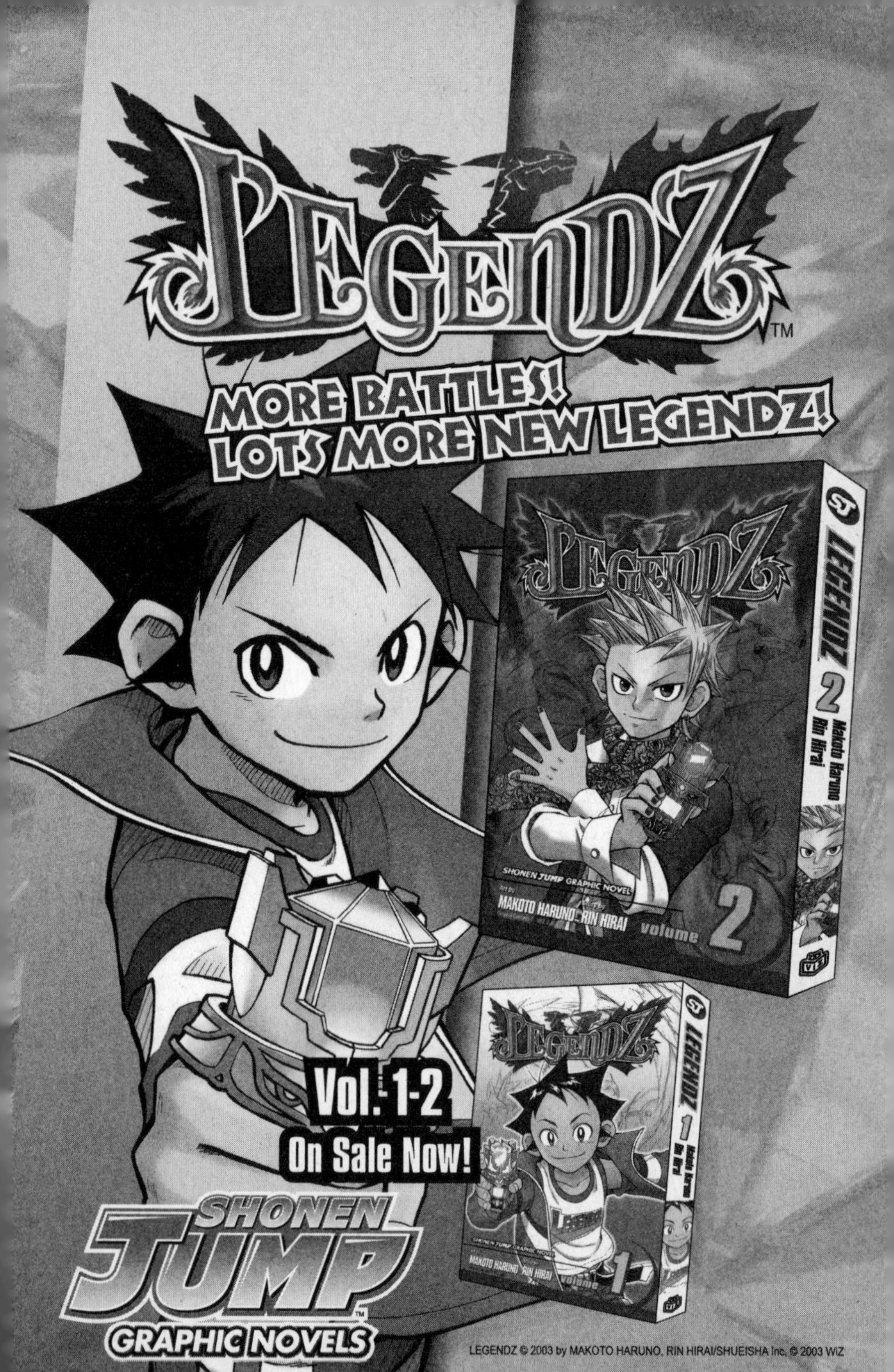

LEGENDZ™
MORE BATTLES!
LOTS MORE NEW LEGENDZ!
Vol. 1-2
On Sale Now!
SHONEN JUMP GRAPHIC NOVELS

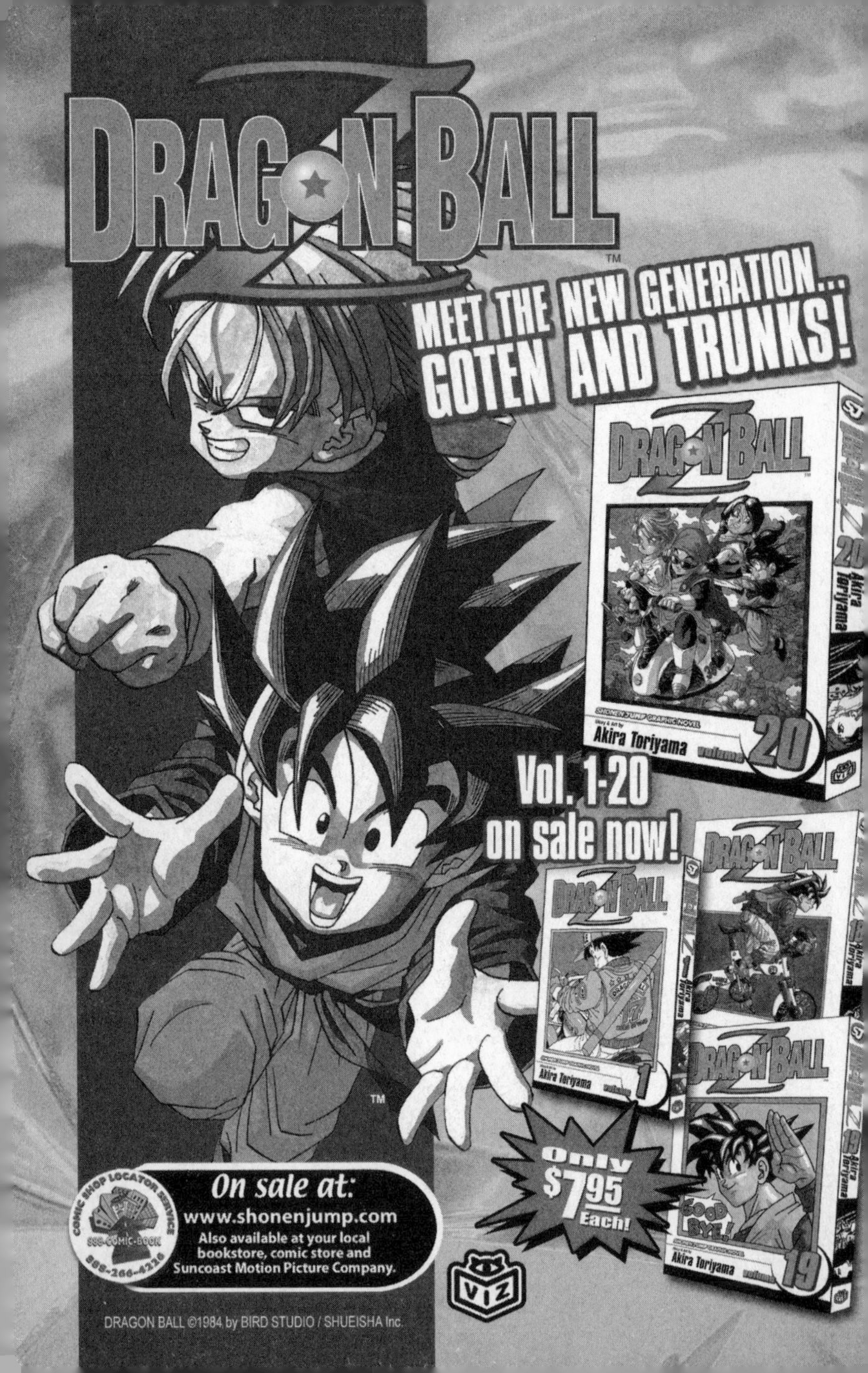

DRAGON BALL Z™
MEET THE NEW GENERATION...
GOTEN AND TRUNKS!
Vol. 1-20
on sale now!
Only
$7.95
Each!
On sale at:
www.shonenjump.com
Also available at your local bookstore, comic store and Suncoast Motion Picture Company.
COMIC SHOP LOCATOR SERVICE
888-COMIC-BOOK
888-266-4226
VIZ
DRAGON BALL ©1984 by BIRD STUDIO / SHUEISHA Inc.

SHONEN JUMP
THE WORLD'S MOST POPULAR MANGA

COMPLETE OUR SURVEY AND LET US KNOW WHAT YOU THINK!

☐ Please do NOT send me information about VIZ and SHONEN JUMP products, news and events, special offers, or other information.

☐ Please do NOT send me information from VIZ's trusted business partners.

Name: ______________________________

Address: ______________________________

City: ______________ **State:** ________ **Zip:** ______________

E-mail: ______________________________

☐ **Male** ☐ **Female** **Date of Birth** (mm/dd/yyyy): ____/____/______ (**Under 13? Parental consent required**)

1 Do you purchase SHONEN JUMP Magazine?

☐ Yes ☐ No **(if no, skip the next two questions)**

If **YES**, do you subscribe?

☐ Yes ☐ No

If **NO**, how often do you purchase SHONEN JUMP Magazine?

☐ 1-3 issues a year

☐ 4-6 issues a year

☐ more than 7 issues a year

2 Which SHONEN JUMP Graphic Novel did you purchase? **(please check one)**

☐ Beet the Vandel Buster ☐ Bleach ☐ Dragon Ball

☐ Dragon Ball Z ☐ Dr. Slump ☐ Eyeshield 21

☐ Hikaru no Go ☐ Hunter x Hunter ☐ I"s

☐ Knights of the Zodiac ☐ Legendz ☐ Naruto

☐ One Piece ☐ Rurouni Kenshin ☐ Shaman King

☐ The Prince of Tennis ☐ Ultimate Muscle ☐ Whistle!

☐ Yu-Gi-Oh! ☐ Yu-Gi-Oh!: Duelist ☐ YuYu Hakusho

☐ Other ______________________________

Will you purchase subsequent volumes?

☐ Yes ☐ No

3 How did you learn about this title? **(check all that apply)**

☐ Favorite title ☐ Advertisement ☐ Article

☐ Gift ☐ Read excerpt in SHONEN JUMP Magazine

☐ Recommendation ☐ Special offer ☐ Through TV animation

☐ Website ☐ Other ______________________________